ASIAN DEVELOPMENT OUTLOOK 2016 UPDATE

MEETING THE LOW-CARBON GROWTH CHALLENGE

50 YEARS

ADB

ASIAN DEVELOPMENT BANK

© 2016 Asian Development Bank
6 ADB Avenue, Mandaluyong City, 1550 Metro Manila, Philippines
Tel +63 2 632 4444; Fax +63 2 636 2444
www.adb.org

Some rights reserved. Published in 2016.
Printed in the Philippines.

ISBN 978-92-9257-603-5 (Print), 978-92-9257-604-2 (e-ISBN)
ISSN 1655-4809
Publication Stock No. FLS168438-3

Cataloging-In-Publication Data

Asian Development Bank.
        Asian development outlook 2016 update. Meeting the low-carbon growth challenge.
Mandaluyong City, Philippines: Asian Development Bank, 2016.

1. Economics.   2. Finance.   3. Asia.   I. Asian Development Bank.

Notes:
In this publication, "$" refers to US dollars.
ADB recognizes "China" by the name People's Republic of China.
Corrigenda to ADB publications may be found at http://www.adb.org/publications/corrigenda

Contents

Foreword

Steady growth endures in developing Asia despite persistent weakness in the external environment. Strong domestic consumption and investment, and economic resilience in the People's Republic of China (PRC) and India, compensate for the delayed pickup in growth in the major industrial economies of the United States (US), the euro area, and Japan. This *Update* to the *Asian Development Outlook 2016* published in March retains the earlier forecast for regional expansion at 5.7% in both 2016 and 2017.

The growth forecast for East Asia in 2016 is upgraded slightly following first-half results in the PRC that outperformed expectations. Strong fiscal and monetary stimulus boosted domestic demand, lifting growth expectations there to 6.6% in 2016 and 6.4% in 2017, a tad higher than anticipated in March. In South Asia, the forecasts are unchanged at 6.9% for 2016 and 7.3% for 2017, supported by steady improvement in an Indian economy buoyed by reform to the banking sector, the enactment of value-added tax legislation, and a favorable monsoon.

On the back of strong infrastructure investment in Indonesia, the Philippines, and Thailand, Southeast Asia's growth forecast is affirmed at 4.5% this year. In 2017, the subregion is expected to grow by 4.6% as external demand improves. Growth forecasts for Central Asia are cut, however, in response to persistently low global commodity prices and continued weakness in the Russian Federation. The Pacific has been buffeted by fiscal difficulties and extreme weather, similarly undermining its growth prospects.

Global commodity prices are projected to recover this year and next. Average inflation in developing Asia is thus seen to accelerate gradually to 2.6% in 2016 and 2.9% in 2017. By subregion, prices will edge up somewhat in East Asia on higher food prices but escalate more substantially in Central Asia following currency depreciation. In contrast, inflation will be curbed in Southeast Asia as increases in commodity prices remain modest and gradual.

The region as a whole faces many challenges that could frustrate growth. The external environment is uncertain, as changes to monetary policy in the advanced economies, especially the US, could disrupt capital flows in developing Asia. Political pressures to turn back the clock on open trade pose a threat to the region's exports, a particular concern after years of weakening external demand. This *Update* notes that, while debt in Asia is still manageable because decades of growth and prudent fiscal policy have kept public debt in check in most countries, private sector debt has risen rapidly. It could end up straining public sector guarantors of last resort and national budgets.

Climate change threatens to undermine the region's hard-won socioeconomic gains. Developing Asia has joined the global effort to contain this global threat, with 90% of regional economies embracing the 2015 Paris Agreement and submitting their mitigation pledges as intended nationally determined contributions. This is a good start, but all regions need to do more to achieve the Paris objective of limiting global mean temperature rise to no more than 2 degrees Celsius (2°C).

The energy sector presents the best opportunity for Asia to transition into low-carbon growth. This can be achieved with economic adjustment, substantial new investment to improve energy efficiency, and a shift to low-carbon energy sources. The region already possesses much of the technology to do this, but for all economies to enjoy the environmental and other benefits of low-carbon growth, the transition must be coordinated and timely.

The 2°C goal is achievable with a four-pronged approach that puts a price on carbon emissions, institutes appropriate regulations, supports investment in clean and efficient energy, and fosters international cooperation. Toward meeting this challenge, the Asian Development Bank stands ready with knowledge and finance to support national efforts.

TAKEHIKO NAKAO
President
Asian Development Bank

Acknowledgments

Asian Development Outlook 2016 Update was prepared by staff
of the Asian Development Bank (ADB) in the Central and West Asia
Department, East Asia Department, Pacific Department, South Asia
Department, Southeast Asia Department, and Economic Research and
Regional Cooperation Department, as well as in ADB resident missions.
Representatives of these departments constituted the Regional Economic
Outlook Task Force, which met regularly to coordinate and develop
consistent forecasts for the region.

The authors who contributed the sections are bylined in each chapter.
The subregional coordinators were Dominik Peschel for Central Asia,
Jurgen Conrad for East Asia, Masato Nakane for South Asia, Jin Cyhn
and Dulce Zara for Southeast Asia, and Christopher Edmonds and
Rommel Rabanal for the Pacific.

A team of economists in the Economic Research and Regional
Cooperation Department, led by Joseph E. Zveglich, Jr., director of the
Macroeconomics Research Division, coordinated the production of the
publication, assisted by Edith Laviña. Technical and research support
was provided by Shiela Camingue-Romance, Cindy Castillejos-Petalcorin,
Gemma Esther Estrada, Marthe Hinojales, Nedelyn Magtibay-Ramos,
Pilipinas Quising, Aleli Rosario, Dennis Sorino, Lea Sumulong, and
Mai Lin Villaruel. Additional research support was provided by
Emmanuel Alano, Zemma Ardaniel, Ruben Carlo Asuncion, Madeline
Dumaua-Cabauatan, and Raymond Gaspar. The economic editorial
advisors Robert Boumphrey, Joshua Greene, Richard Niebuhr, Anthony
Patrick, and Reza Vaez-Zadeh made substantive contributions to the
country chapters and regional outlook. Josef Yap provided editorial
advice on the theme chapter and the regional outlook.

The theme chapter benefited from the comments of Matthew E. Kahn,
Anbumozhi Venkatachalam, and Leena Srivastava. Internal reviewers
Preety Bhandari, Michael Rattinger, Daniele Ponzi, Bruce Dunn, and
Yongping Zhai provided insights throughout the process. The support
and guidance of the ADB Sustainable Development and Climate Change
Department is gratefully acknowledged.

Peter Fredenburg advised on ADB style and English usage.
Alvin Tubio handled typesetting and graphics generation, in which he
was assisted by Elenita Pura. Art direction for the cover design was by
Anthony Victoria, with artwork from Design Muscle. Critical support
for the printing and publishing of the report was provided by the
Printing Services Unit of the ADB Office of Administrative Services and
by the Publishing and Dissemination Unit of the ADB Department of
External Relations. Heili Ann Bravo, Fermirelyn Cruz, Rhia Bautista-
Piamonte, and Azaleah Tiongson provided administrative and
secretarial support.

The Department of External Relations, led by Satinder Bindra,
Omana Nair, and Erik Churchill, planned and coordinated the
dissemination of *Asian Development Outlook 2016 Update*.

Definitions

The economies discussed in *Asian Development Outlook 2016 Update* are classified by major analytic or geographic group. For the purposes of this publication, the following apply:

- **Association of Southeast Asian Nations (ASEAN)** comprises Brunei Darussalam, Cambodia, Indonesia, the Lao People's Democratic Republic, Malaysia, Myanmar, the Philippines, Singapore, Thailand, and Viet Nam.
- **Developing Asia** comprises the 45 members of the Asian Development Bank listed below.
- **Central Asia** comprises Armenia, Azerbaijan, Georgia, Kazakhstan, the Kyrgyz Republic, Tajikistan, Turkmenistan, and Uzbekistan.
- **East Asia** comprises the People's Republic of China; Hong Kong, China; the Republic of Korea; Mongolia; and Taipei,China.
- **South Asia** comprises Afghanistan, Bangladesh, Bhutan, India, the Maldives, Nepal, Pakistan, and Sri Lanka.
- **Southeast Asia** comprises Brunei Darussalam, Cambodia, Indonesia, the Lao People's Democratic Republic, Malaysia, Myanmar, the Philippines, Singapore, Thailand, and Viet Nam.
- **The Pacific** comprises the Cook Islands, Fiji, Kiribati, the Marshall Islands, the Federated States of Micronesia, Nauru, Papua New Guinea, Palau, Samoa, Solomon Islands, Timor-Leste, Tonga, Tuvalu, and Vanuatu.

Unless otherwise specified, the symbol "$" and the word "dollar" refer to US dollars. *ADO 2016 Update* is generally based on data available up to **2 September 2016**.

Abbreviations

°C	degree Celsius
ADB	Asian Development Bank
ADO	Asian Development Outlook
ASEAN	Association of Southeast Asian Nations
BAU	business as usual
CCA	contingent claims analysis
CCS	carbon capture and storage
CO_2e	carbon dioxide equivalent
EU	European Union
FDI	foreign direct investment
FIT	feed-in tariff
FY	fiscal year
GDP	gross domestic product
GHG	greenhouse gas
GII	green innovation index
GST	goods and services tax
$GtCO_2e$	gigaton (billion tons) of carbon dioxide equivalent
GVC	global value chain
IMF	International Monetary Fund
INDC	intended nationally determined contribution
IPCC	Intergovernmental Panel on Climate Change
$KgCO_2e$	kilogram of carbon dioxide equivalent
Lao PDR	Lao People's Democratic Republic
LULUCF	land use, land-use change, and forestry
M1	money that includes cash and checking accounts
M2	broad money that adds highly liquid accounts to M1
M3	broad money that adds time accounts to M2
mbd	million barrels per day
MEPS	minimum energy performance standard
$MtCO_2e$	metric ton of carbon dioxide equivalent
MWh	megawatt-hour
NDC	nationally determined contribution
NPL	nonperforming loan
OECD	Organisation for Economic Co-operation and Development
OPEC	Organization of the Petroleum Exporting Countries

PNG	Papua New Guinea
PPP	purchasing power parity
PRC	People's Republic of China
RCA	revealed comparative advantage
RERF	Revenue Equalization Reserve Fund of Kiribati
saar	seasonally adjusted annualized rate
SMEs	small and medium-sized enterprises
SOE	state-owned enterprise
toe	ton of oil equivalent
TPES	total primary energy supply
UK	United Kingdom
US	United States of America
VAT	value-added tax
WITCH	World Induced Technical Change Hybrid

ADO 2016 Update—Highlights

Growth has held up in developing Asia despite a difficult external environment. The region is expected to grow steadily at 5.7% in 2016 and 2017, the forecasts in this *Update* unchanged from *Asian Development Outlook 2016*.

While global commodity prices have begun to rebound, inflation remains largely subdued. Consumer prices will likely rise by 2.6% in 2016 and 2.9% in 2017.

Continued slow recovery in the United States, the euro area, and Japan presents a clear downside risk to the outlook. Uncertainty about the path of monetary policy in these economies, and the implications this has for capital flows, complicates macroeconomic management in developing Asia. Policy makers globally need to resist moves toward protectionism that would only undermine the recovery.

By transitioning to low-carbon growth, developing Asia is poised to reap outsized rewards as an essential player in the global effort to contain climate change.

Juzhong Zhuang
Deputy Chief Economist
Asian Development Bank

Developing Asia—staying the course

Steady growth in uncertain times

■ **Growth holds up in developing Asia despite stubborn global headwinds.** This *Update* retains the projections previously published in *Asian Development Outlook 2016 (ADO 2016)* in March. Gross domestic product (GDP) in the region is expected to grow at 5.7% in 2016 and 2017, slightly down from 5.9% in 2015. Stymied recovery in the major industrial economies, and drag from slower growth in the United States (US) in particular, has been counteracted by policy-supported domestic demand so far this year in some large economies in the region. Developing Asia is expected to maintain its growth pace into 2017, buoyed by an improving external environment and resilience in the region's two largest economies, the People's Republic of China (PRC) and India.

» **Recovery in the major industrial economies is delayed.** The preservation of growth envisioned in *ADO 2016* did not materialize in the major industrial economies: the US, the euro area, and Japan. This *Update* pares down its forecast for aggregate growth in 2016 to 1.4%, or 0.4 percentage points lower than the *ADO 2016* projection, before seeing it pick up in 2017 to 1.8%. This dour result will continue to hold back global economic activity to the forecast horizon. US growth in the first 2 quarters was softer, with low investment and frail trade. Growth in Japan started well in 2016, but prospects are subdued for the rest of the year as currency appreciation weighs heavily on Japan's exports. While growth in the euro area is maintained this year, heightened downside risks arising from political uncertainty will impinge on growth next year.

» **Policy tempers moderation in PRC growth as reform grounds its sustainability.** First-half GDP growth slowed to 6.7% in the PRC as structural reform continued, but it surpassed the March forecast for the year. Private consumption and services generated most of the growth in line with government objectives favoring sustainable growth supported by solid wage growth and urban job creation. While growth is still expected to be lower than in 2015, this *Update* slightly upgrades the March forecasts by 0.1 percentage points, to 6.6% in 2016 and 6.4% in 2017, in view of strong fiscal and monetary stimulus to boost domestic demand while external demand remains tepid.

» **Steady progress in reform helps India realize its growth targets.** Despite growth moderation in the first quarter of FY2016 (ending 31 March 2017), the *ADO 2016* forecast for growth at 7.4% in 2016 is retained on the strength of improved private consumption after recently approved increases in wages and pensions, and from expectations of a healthy monsoon lifting rural incomes. Recovery in private investment, as corporations successfully deleverage and bank reform boosts lending, will help drive growth to 7.8% in 2017. Legislation to create a national value-added tax should lift investor confidence, as this accomplished a key step toward a much more integrated, productive economy.

» **Southeast Asia largely met growth expectations in the first half.** Growth in the five large economies in the Association of Southeast Asian Nations (ASEAN) is expected to hit 4.8% in 2016, as projected in *ADO 2016*. Strong first-half performance in the Philippines and Thailand is offset by downgrades in the forecasts for Indonesia, Malaysia, and Viet Nam. Government investment in infrastructure has played an important role in supporting growth this year, particularly in Indonesia, the Philippines, and Thailand. This countered sluggish export demand and drought that caused agriculture to contract in all these economies except Indonesia in the first half of 2016. Growth is forecast to accelerate to 5.0% in 2017 on expectations of firmer demand from the major industrial economies, higher prices for export commodities, and rising investment in infrastructure.

» **Low oil prices impede Central Asia, as storms and fiscal woes buffet the Pacific.** This *Update* reduces the growth forecast for Central Asia this year and next. For the top energy exporters, the persistence of low global commodity prices continues to put fiscal spending under pressure that constrains growth. Recession in the Russian Federation exacerbates slowing growth in remittance-dependent economies. In the Pacific, cyclone damage in Fiji in February and fiscal difficulties in Papua New Guinea undercut forecasts for the larger Pacific economies this year. South Pacific economies enjoy upgraded output projections as unexpectedly strong tourism helped pushed growth higher, but not enough to sustain subregional growth prospects this year.

■ **Inflation will revive marginally in developing Asia with rising oil prices.** This *Update* revises the forecast for average inflation in the region slightly upward, from 2.5% to 2.6% in 2016 and from 2.7% to 2.9% in 2017. Global oil prices show an uptick since March this year but remain subdued, and food prices will increase marginally despite strong supply. However, variation by subregion is apparent. On the upside, a sharp rise for some foods in East Asia is pushing up otherwise muted inflation, and double-digit inflation is expected in Central Asia this year with sharp currency depreciation. Inflation is lower than earlier projected in almost all of ASEAN, suppressed by soft global food and fuel prices even as drought earlier this year disrupted domestic food supplies in some areas.

■ **Investment-related imports rein in the region's current account surplus.** The surplus is expected to narrow from the equivalent of 3.1% of GDP in 2015 to 2.4% in 2016, or 0.2 percentage points lower than forecast in *ADO 2016*. It is expected to drop further to 2.0% in 2017, which recalls its size in 2013 before the sharp drop in energy prices. While tempered energy prices continue to keep import bills low, demand for imports of capital goods and construction materials has surged in some countries. As weak global trade suppresses exports, there is no sign of reversion to the global imbalances that prevailed before the global financial crisis of 2008–2009.

■ **Risks to the region's outlook remain clearly tilted toward the downside.** The external environment remains fragile with slow recovery in the US, the euro area, and Japan. Interest rate hikes by the US Federal Reserve, though so far elusive, could disrupt capital flows and complicate macroeconomic management. Rhetoric against trade openness could jeopardize the progress made toward free trade and regional integration. Private debt is on the rise in many Asian economies, which could become unsustainable if economies struggle or interest rates rise sharply. Natural disasters are inherently unpredictable but clearly a mounting risk to the region in view of global climate change.

Responding to the trade slowdown

■ **Developing Asia's export growth has slowed since the global financial crisis.**
Expansion in the region's export volumes slowed to 4.7% per year in 2011–2015 from an annual average of 11.2% in 2000–2010. In the PRC, which accounts for roughly 40% of regional exports, growth in export volumes slowed from a pre-crisis pace of 18.3% per year to 6.4% in 2011–2015. Yet, even excluding the PRC, export growth has decelerated markedly. The slowdown is more pronounced than the moderation in regional GDP growth. While export growth was 1.5 times the rate of GDP growth before the global crisis, it was only 0.7 times GDP growth in 2011–2015.

■ **The export growth slowdown sums a mix of cyclical and structural factors.**
Weak post-crisis demand from the advanced economies for imports of Asian goods is a key cyclical factor that should reverse as the major industrial economies recover. Primary among the structural factors is growth moderation in the PRC. Structural adjustments under way there to lessen reliance on exports and investment have weakened demand in the PRC for imports from regional trading partners. The slowing of trade through global value chains as the PRC moves to production with higher value added is affecting trade in intermediate goods. Further, lower commodity prices have reduced real incomes in commodity exporters, crimping their imports as well. In this difficult environment since the global financial crisis, creeping protectionism has become a worrying trend that acts as a further brake on export growth.

■ **Despite the slowdown, undue pessimism about trade is unwarranted.** Cyclical factors are gradually lifting with some pickup in real terms of US imports from developing Asia. PRC rebalancing will open up new trading opportunities such as the development of more technologically sophisticated regional value chains in East Asia as the PRC moves up the value chain. Moreover, some regional economies, notably Bangladesh and Viet Nam, are well positioned to take over the labor-intensive segments of cross-border supply chains vacated by the PRC. Trade in services is growing and has potential for further expansion. Fostering new sources of export growth depends critically on implementing structural reform, investing in trade-related infrastructure, and removing barriers that hinder the involvement of small and medium-sized enterprises in global value chains. To turn back incipient protectionism, further work is needed to liberalize trade barriers, improve surveillance on nontariff measures, and conclude global and regional trade agreements.

Debt sustainability in Asia

■ **Most public debt ratios in developing Asia are sustainable.** Steady GDP growth and generally prudent fiscal policies combined to keep ratios of debt to GDP under control. Debt ratios have increased mostly where governments borrowed to finance large infrastructure or extractive investment projects. Assuming diligent debt management and the absence of major shocks, even these countries will see debt ratios stabilize and fall back in the future to the extent that their investment projects reach completion and finally boost output, exports, and fiscal revenues.

■ **Macroeconomic volatility worsens the risk of debt distress.** With amplified macroeconomic fluctuations, medium-term baseline projections of public and external debt ratios have become less reliable forecasters of debt sustainability. Probabilistic debt projections for Asian countries with volatile exchange rates and capital flows show that such volatility may translate into significantly higher debt ratios. This is a time for governments to strengthen their medium-term debt management strategies to support investor confidence and mitigate market instability.

■ **The deep slump in oil prices has pushed debt ratios higher for oil exporters.** Economies in Central Asia in particular have experienced slowing GDP growth and sharp currency depreciation under stubbornly low oil prices. Countries with large oil funds can use them as financial buffers to support debt sustainability and market confidence, drawing them down to uphold ongoing efforts toward socioeconomic reform and diversification. In Azerbaijan, for example, the local currency depreciated by half against the US dollar from 2014 to 2015, but the country has an oil fund worth nearly $37 billion, equal to 49% of GDP. It can provide a strong buffer to substitute for debt financing and keep the public debt ratio from rising above 40%, even if oil prices are slow to recover.

■ **Burgeoning private debt may end up weighing on national budgets and public debt.** Borrowing by households and nonfinancial corporations are major drivers of the region's total debt. From 2008 to the first quarter of 2016, the average ratio of household debt to GDP in Asia increased by 15 percentage points, while the ratio for nonfinancial corporations rose by 24 points. Corporate sectors in many economies in developing Asia carry considerable domestic debt. Nonfinancial corporate leverage reached 174% of GDP in the PRC in March 2016. Borrowing in domestic currency considerably mutes exposure to sudden capital reversals but not exposure to the risks associated with asset bubbles and rising nonperforming loan ratios. Household debt requires careful monitoring in Malaysia and Thailand, where it exceeds 70% of GDP. Excessive household leverage is not likely to set off a severe crisis in Asia as long as interest and unemployment rates are low.

Outlook by subregion

■ **Stable regional growth masks differing subregional fortunes.** Growth projections for this year are unchanged from *ADO 2016* for South and Southeast Asia but revised up for East Asia, which counterbalances downward revisions for Central Asia and the Pacific. Growth projections for 2017 are unchanged for East and South Asia and for the region as a whole.

■ **East Asia's outlook is boosted by strong growth in the PRC.** The largest subregion is expected to record mild growth moderation from 6.1% in 2015 to 5.8% in 2016—a slight upgrade from the *ADO 2016* forecast—and further to 5.6% in 2017. Surprisingly fast growth in the first half of this year in the PRC offset sluggishness in the rest of East Asia. Strong fiscal and monetary stimulus helped ease growth moderation in the PRC such that this *Update* raises growth forecasts for both years by 0.1 percentage points, to 6.6% in 2016 and 6.4% in 2017. Faltering domestic demand will deepen growth moderation in Hong Kong, China, while tepid domestic demand and persistent export weakness weigh on prospects for Taipei,China. The forecast for a sharp slowdown in Mongolia is revised up somewhat as mining fared better than previously expected. Inflation in the region is anticipated to exceed *ADO 2016* forecasts with newly deregulated administered prices and rising prices for services bumping up consumer prices in the PRC. Inflation in East Asia is projected to reach 1.9% in 2016 and 2.2% in 2017.

■ **South Asia manages to sustain its rapid growth.** This dynamic subregion is expected to realize the *ADO 2016* growth forecasts of 6.9% in 2016 increasing to 7.3% in 2017. India's growth forecast for 2016, maintained at 7.4%, will find support in strong private consumption stemming from double-digit increases in government wages and pensions. Major progress in restructuring bank balance sheets and reducing excessive leverage at large corporations has set the stage for an expected revival in investment that will drive growth higher to 7.8% in 2017. While Bangladesh and Pakistan now see slightly faster expansion in 2016 than anticipated, growth prospects for Sri Lanka edge lower on weak industrial performance and fiscal consolidation. Modest growth prevails in Afghanistan, the Maldives, and Nepal this year but is seen improving in 2017. The *Update* maintains inflation projections of 5.2% in 2016 rising to 5.7% in 2017, with low oil prices and effective macroeconomic management keeping consumer price pressures in check.

■ **Southeast Asia is on track to achieve higher growth this year.** Subregional growth is forecast to edge up from 4.4% in 2015 to 4.5% this year, as projected in *ADO 2016*. Strong performance in the Philippines and Thailand is offset by downgrades to forecasts for Indonesia, Malaysia, Singapore, and Viet Nam. Government infrastructure investment is a key contributor to growth in Indonesia, the Philippines, Singapore, and Thailand. For Indonesia, the biggest economy in Southeast Asia, growth is now seen at 5.0% in 2016, improving on 2015 but 0.2 percentage points below the earlier projection because investment is rising at a more moderate pace than anticipated. In 2017, growth in the subregion is still seen trending higher, though the forecast is trimmed by 0.2 percentage points to 4.6%. Inflation is lower than earlier projected, suppressed by soft global food and fuel prices. It is now seen slowing to 2.0% in 2016 before quickening to 2.9% in 2017 on higher global commodity prices and domestic demand.

■ **Central Asia stalls as low energy prices stymie growth.** This *Update* cuts the 2016 growth forecast for Central Asia from 2.1% in *ADO 2016* to 1.5%, reflecting more pessimistic projections for energy exporters Azerbaijan, Kazakhstan, and Turkmenistan. Depressed oil and gas prices and low external demand have weakened these economies, as have lower remittances in others, requiring cuts in public investment while limiting increases in social transfers. The 2017 growth forecast is revised down by 0.2 percentage points to 2.6%, with slower growth now projected for Turkmenistan. Severe currency depreciation in Kazakhstan after it moved to a floating exchange rate in August 2015 exacerbated inflation, which averaged 16.4% in January–August 2016. Inflation forecasts for Central Asia are raised from 10.8% to 11.5% in 2016 and from 5.9% to 6.4% in 2017, despite moderating consumer price pressures in Armenia, Georgia, the Kyrgyz Republic, and Turkmenistan.

■ **Pacific growth slows more than expected.** Several of the smaller economies in the Pacific are performing better than expected thanks to strong tourism. However, growth in the subregion as a whole is projected to be lower, largely because of fiscal contraction in Papua New Guinea, the predominant economy. Weather also played a role as cyclones damaged Fiji and as the North Pacific suffered drought earlier this year. Aggregate growth is now forecast at 2.7% in 2016—well off the 3.8% forecast in *ADO 2016*—but recovering to 3.5% in 2017. Rising oil prices and currency depreciation in Papua New Guinea have stirred consumer price pressures. Inflation in the Pacific is now forecast to average 4.7% in 2016, marginally higher than the *ADO 2016* projection, and 5.5% in 2017.

Meeting the low-carbon growth challenge

Global call to fight climate change

■ **Climate-related risks to developing Asia are severe.** The current path of rising greenhouse gas emissions and temperatures undermines agriculture and food security in Asia with greater heat stress, shorter rainy seasons, more withering droughts, and worsened pest and disease outbreaks. Longer heat waves and the wider transmission of human diseases threaten the health and productivity of workers in the labor-intensive mining and construction sectors, as well as agriculture. Intense storms occurring with greater frequency can, along with rising sea levels, imperil infrastructure and other fixed assets. If uncontrolled, climate change may lead to economic loss equivalent to 10% of GDP in 2100, reversing many hard-won socioeconomic gains in the region.

■ **Asia has joined the global fight to contain climate change.** In the 2015 Paris Agreement, developed and developing countries alike committed to reduce emissions to limit the average rise in global mean surface temperature. The goal is well below 2 degrees Celsius (2°C) above pre-industrial levels. To meet this goal, global emissions of greenhouse gases, especially carbon dioxide, will have to peak by the early 2020s and decline thereafter. More than 90% of economies in developing Asia have submitted their mitigation objectives in their intended nationally determined contributions. The pledges clearly indicate country aspirations with regard to climate action but must be converted into investment plans if the objectives are to be met. Globally, intended contributions to date put the world on a path toward a temperature rise of at least 2.7°C by 2100, missing the goal by a wide margin. The optimal mitigation path toward the 2°C goal requires that current intended contributions to emissions reductions to 2030 be doubled.

■ **Paris Agreement success depends critically on developing Asia.** Emissions from the region have risen rapidly from 25% of the global total in 1990–1999 to 40% in 2012. Without strong climate policies, the region will generate nearly 50% of all greenhouse gas emissions by 2030, and these emissions will double in volume by 2050. According to the World Resources Institute, the three most populous Asian economies were among the top five greenhouse gas emitters in 2015 (in descending order): the PRC, the US, India, the Russian Federation, and Indonesia. Even in per capita terms, the PRC and Indonesia already exceed the global average. Creating a global low-carbon economy is impossible without Asian engagement.

Assessing Asia's low-carbon transition

■ **Asia can do more toward the 2°C global climate goal.** The progressive implementation of national emissions reduction pledges implies that emissions from developing Asia can be halved by 2050 relative to a business-as-usual scenario in which the current paths of energy systems, land-use patterns, and industrial development evolve without future mitigation efforts. However, achieving the goal of limiting warming to 2°C requires reduction by three-quarters. With fossil fuels contributing over two-thirds of developing Asia's emissions, the region's low-carbon transition must start with the energy sector.

■ **Rapid emissions reduction requires redirected investment.** Even under business as usual, the region is investing in clean energy. However, achieving the 2°C goal is estimated to require developing Asia to invest through 2050 an additional $300 billion per year on clean power-supply technology and infrastructure such as renewable power, carbon capture and storage, smart grids, and energy storage. Reduced investment in fossil fuel extraction can offset 20% of this cost. With timely investment redirection, the region can avoid locking itself into a high-carbon development path that would be costly to reverse.

■ **The cost of switching to low-carbon pathways can be modest.** A low-carbon transition requires economic adjustment and substantial new investment in energy-efficient infrastructure and low-carbon energy generation. Simulations show that the economic costs for developing Asia under a global scenario of carbon taxation toward achieving the 2°C goal equate to a reduction in its average annual GDP growth rate by 0.1 percentage points. By 2050, this would mean regional GDP that is 4% smaller than it would be under the business-as-usual scenario. However, this projection does not take into account any benefits from reduced climate change or the many co-benefits of climate action enumerated below.

■ **Emissions trade and coordinated mitigation can reduce economic costs.** If climate action is fragmented, economies that mitigate emissions may lose competitiveness relative to those that do not, and therefore face higher costs. The economic costs of reduced greenhouse gas emissions are lower for an individual region if emissions trading mechanisms allow for mitigation to take place where costs are lowest. Moreover, international emissions trading offers an important opportunity to lower economic costs, especially in regions such as developing Asia where abatement costs that are lower than the global average enable the export of emissions allowances. Emissions trading could halve the region's economic costs for the 2°C scenario relative to the taxation scenario with no trading.

■ **Reducing greenhouse gas emissions promises large co-benefits.** Low-carbon growth can deliver environmental benefits by reducing air pollution, making cities more livable, and protecting the natural environment and its ecosystems. Data from the World Health Organization show a number of Asian cities suffer from high concentrations of particulate matter, including Delhi and Beijing. Low-carbon growth can help minimize costly pollution prevention measures.

  » **Less carbon dependence can provide healthier air to breathe.** Outdoor air pollution in developing Asia caused nearly 3 million premature deaths per year in 2010, including nearly 1.4 million in the PRC alone. Without better protection, air pollution mortality in the region could double such deaths by 2050. Even compared with a scenario of improved air quality regulation, the 2°C scenario will still avoid nearly 600,000 deaths each year.

  » **It can also preserve environmental resilience.** Mitigation measures can expand forests and their environmental services, including soil erosion control, biodiversity preservation, and pollination for agriculture. Simulations show that limiting warming to 2°C would mean 45 million more hectares of forest in developing Asia than would business as usual, and this forest cover would help to avert those impacts still posed under mitigated climate change.

■ **The returns on sound climate policy far outweigh their costs.** Mitigation in the 2°C scenario can eliminate an estimated 2%-of-GDP loss from climate change by 2050 and an 8% loss by 2100. Taking into account significant co-benefits such as better health from improved air quality, each $1 spent toward the 2°C scenario can generate more than $2 in gains. Delaying ambitious mitigation by even 10 years slashes the gross benefit–cost ratio by more than 30%.

Asia's potential for a low-carbon future

■ **Low-carbon energy generation offers the most mitigation potential.** Nearly half of the region's 2050 mitigation in the 2°C scenario can come from making energy production less carbon intensive, notably by deploying such renewables as wind, solar, and biomass and through carbon capture and storage. An ambitious mitigation effort leaves little room for new coal capacity in Asia that does not include carbon capture and storage. Much of the potential for emissions reduction can be realized through renewables, and technological progress is expected to offer further cost reductions.

■ **Energy efficiency can reduce emissions and stimulate economic growth.** Developing Asia's energy intensity, the energy used per dollar of GDP, is similar to the global average. By 2050 under the 2°C scenario, the region will be nearly 35% less energy intensive than it would be under business as usual. Estimates indicate that a third of the region's emissions reductions by 2050 toward the global 2°C goal can come from better energy efficiency.

■ **Reducing land-use emissions is a low-cost opportunity for Asia.** Reducing emissions from forest destruction, land degradation, agriculture, and other non-energy activities can contribute nearly 20% of the mitigation in developing Asia's national emissions reduction pledges to 2030. Southeast Asia has a higher deforestation rate than any other major tropical region, and 5 of the world's 10 most endangered forests are in Asia and the Pacific. The region's extensive tropical peat soils offer further opportunities. Their conservation, restoration, and improved management can avoid wildfires—with the consequent haze and release of billions of tons of carbon—and preserve their rich production potential.

■ **Asia stands to benefit from new carbon market opportunities.** Economies in developing Asia are already advancing technologies to reduce greenhouse gas emissions, accounting for over 35% of world exports of clean technology and holding 22% of such patents. Whereas the PRC is a leading exporter of solar energy panels, the Republic of Korea leads in patents for energy storage technology, the Philippines exhibits a comparative advantage in efficient lighting, and India shows significant potential for incremental innovation by adapting existing technologies like wind power to local needs.

Unlocking the low-carbon transition

■ **Asia can help meet the Paris objectives with a four-pronged approach.** Key policies include putting a price on carbon emissions, instituting appropriate regulations, supporting investment in clean and efficient energy, and fostering international action.

■ **Pricing carbon achieves mitigation efficiently.** At the core of the climate change problem is a fundamental market failure to reflect the full social, economic, and environmental costs of greenhouse gas emissions. Land-use arrangements and fossil fuel prices routinely fail to reflect the cost of damage from resulting carbon emissions, which encourages emitters to ignore their carbon output. In some cases, government subsidies on fuel and land use exacerbate this problem.

» **Removing costly subsidies is a critical first step.** Many Asian economies subsidize fossil fuels, which encourages their use while undercutting returns on clean energy investments. Likewise, a lack of clearly defined property rights and indiscriminate distribution of rights to logging and other uses can create incentives for deforestation, which emits a lot of carbon. Eliminating these subsidies can set the right incentives for resource use while freeing up public funds to support the low-carbon transition.

» **Carbon taxes can force emitters to consider their environmental costs.** Governments can compel firms to pay the costs of their emissions through a carbon tax. This approach is relatively straightforward to implement and makes carbon prices predictable, offering a reliable signal to investors.

» **Emissions trading can establish a common carbon price.** Within set emissions caps, trading systems facilitate the buying and selling of emissions allowances, establishing a uniform carbon price that provides an incentive for mitigation. Although the initial allocation of emissions allowances may pose political and distributional challenges, mitigation will be done more efficiently as long as the trading rules are enforced.

■ **Regulations are critical to promote clean energy and efficiency.** Carbon pricing should be complemented by an effective set of regulatory standards, as standards can spur the adoption of clean technologies. Governments may mandate—among other initiatives to curtail emissions—the use of renewable energy sources, lower emissions from vehicles, and improved energy efficiency for consumer goods, buildings, and industry. Although developing Asia has made progress toward such regulations, substantial gaps remain in coverage and stringency.

■ **Reducing risk and facilitating finance can spur clean energy investment.** The public sector can help attract private investment in clean energy by reducing risk, in part with consistent policy, and by supporting pilots of new technologies. Toward generating clean power, governments may offer risk guarantees and take equity stakes. To improve energy efficiency, energy service companies may promote technology diffusion. To augment the limited public funds available for investment in climate-compatible investments that are particularly risky because they require outsized initial capital outlays with long payback periods, governments can offer private financiers incentives such as interest subsidies for green loans, public–private partnerships, and guarantees for green bonds.

■ **International action must be rapid to meet the global climate challenge.** Accelerated action is critical because the sooner ambitious mitigation begins, the lower its ultimate cost. Estimates show early action reducing 2050 economic costs for the 2°C scenario by more than a quarter. Cooperative technology transfer can substantially accelerate the deployment of low-carbon solutions. Key to reducing global mitigation costs and distributing them more equitably is proper compensation for poorer countries that take advantage of their low abatement costs to further reduce their emissions. Achieving the ambitious Paris objectives requires immediate, urgent action from the whole global community.

GDP growth and inflation, % per year

	Growth rate of GDP					Inflation				
	2015	2016		2017		2015	2016		2017	
		ADO 2016	Update	ADO 2016	Update		ADO 2016	Update	ADO 2016	Update
Central Asia	3.0	2.1	1.5	2.8	2.6	6.1	10.8	11.5	5.9	6.4
Armenia	3.0	2.0	2.0	2.3	2.3	3.7	3.8	1.5	4.0	4.0
Azerbaijan	1.1	–1.0	–2.5	1.0	1.0	4.0	12.0	12.0	5.2	5.2
Georgia	2.8	2.5	3.0	3.5	4.0	4.0	5.0	3.0	4.0	4.0
Kazakhstan	1.2	0.7	0.1	1.0	1.0	6.6	12.6	14.7	4.6	6.0
Kyrgyz Republic	3.5	1.0	1.0	2.0	2.0	6.5	10.0	5.0	8.0	8.0
Tajikistan	6.0	3.8	3.8	4.0	4.0	5.1	8.5	8.5	7.5	7.5
Turkmenistan	6.5	6.5	5.5	7.0	5.5	5.5	6.6	5.0	6.0	4.4
Uzbekistan	8.0	6.9	6.9	7.3	7.3	8.5	10.0	10.0	11.0	11.0
East Asia	6.1	5.7	5.8	5.6	5.6	1.3	1.6	1.9	2.0	2.2
China, People's Rep. of	6.9	6.5	6.6	6.3	6.4	1.4	1.7	2.0	2.0	2.2
Hong Kong, China	2.4	2.1	1.5	2.2	2.0	3.0	2.5	2.4	2.7	2.5
Korea, Rep. of	2.6	2.6	2.6	2.8	2.8	0.7	1.4	1.1	2.0	2.0
Mongolia	2.3	0.1	0.3	0.5	1.4	6.6	3.0	3.2	7.0	5.4
Taipei,China	0.6	1.6	0.9	1.8	1.5	–0.3	0.7	1.3	1.2	1.5
South Asia	7.0	6.9	6.9	7.3	7.3	4.9	5.2	5.2	5.7	5.7
Afghanistan	0.8	2.0	2.0	3.0	3.0	–1.5	3.0	4.5	3.5	6.0
Bangladesh	6.6	6.7	7.1	6.9	6.9	6.4	6.2	5.9	6.5	6.1
Bhutan	5.9	6.4	6.4	6.1	6.1	6.6	4.0	3.3	5.0	4.6
India	7.6	7.4	7.4	7.8	7.8	4.9	5.4	5.4	5.8	5.8
Maldives	2.1	3.5	3.5	3.9	3.9	1.0	1.2	1.2	1.4	1.4
Nepal	2.3	1.5	0.8	4.8	4.8	7.2	10.5	9.9	8.2	8.5
Pakistan	4.0	4.5	4.7	4.8	5.2	4.5	3.2	2.9	4.5	4.7
Sri Lanka	4.8	5.3	5.0	5.8	5.5	3.8	4.5	4.5	5.0	5.0
Southeast Asia	4.4	4.5	4.5	4.8	4.6	2.7	2.6	2.0	2.9	2.9
Brunei Darussalam	–0.6	1.0	1.0	2.5	2.5	–0.4	0.2	–0.6	0.4	0.4
Cambodia	7.0	7.0	7.0	7.1	7.1	1.2	2.5	2.8	3.0	3.4
Indonesia	4.8	5.2	5.0	5.5	5.1	6.4	4.5	3.5	4.2	4.0
Lao People's Dem. Rep.	6.7	6.8	6.8	7.0	7.0	1.3	1.8	1.6	2.5	2.3
Malaysia	5.0	4.2	4.1	4.4	4.4	2.1	2.7	2.1	2.5	2.5
Myanmar	7.2	8.4	8.4	8.3	8.3	11.0	9.5	9.5	8.5	8.5
Philippines	5.9	6.0	6.4	6.1	6.2	1.4	2.3	1.8	2.7	2.8
Singapore	2.0	2.0	1.8	2.2	2.0	–0.5	–0.6	–0.8	0.4	0.8
Thailand	2.8	3.0	3.2	3.5	3.5	–0.9	0.6	0.4	2.0	2.0
Viet Nam	6.7	6.7	6.0	6.5	6.3	0.6	3.0	2.5	4.0	4.5
The Pacific	7.2	3.8	2.7	3.1	3.5	3.9	4.5	4.7	4.7	5.5
Cook Islands	4.8	0.0	4.2	0.2	4.0	3.0	1.8	0.7	2.0	2.0
Fiji	4.0	2.7	2.4	4.5	4.5	1.4	3.0	3.5	3.0	3.0
Kiribati	3.0	1.8	1.8	2.0	1.5	1.4	0.3	0.7	0.8	2.0
Marshall Islands	0.5	1.5	1.5	2.0	2.0	–2.2	2.0	–1.3	2.5	1.0
Micronesia, Fed. States of	1.4	2.5	2.0	3.5	2.5	–1.1	–0.3	–0.3	0.3	1.5
Nauru	–10.0	3.0	3.0	15.0	15.0	11.4	6.6	6.6	1.7	1.7
Palau	9.4	3.0	2.0	7.0	5.0	2.2	1.5	1.5	2.5	2.5
Papua New Guinea	9.9	4.3	2.2	2.4	3.0	6.0	6.0	6.5	6.0	7.5
Samoa	1.6	2.0	5.0	0.5	2.0	1.9	2.0	0.1	2.0	2.0
Solomon Islands	2.9	3.0	2.7	2.8	2.5	–0.3	4.4	3.3	5.7	4.5
Timor-Leste	4.1	4.5	5.0	5.5	5.5	0.6	2.0	1.2	3.0	3.0
Tonga	3.4	2.8	3.1	2.7	2.6	–0.7	–0.3	2.0	0.5	1.9
Tuvalu	3.5	3.5	3.0	3.0	3.0	3.5	3.5	2.0	2.0	2.0
Vanuatu	–1.0	2.5	3.5	3.8	3.8	2.5	1.9	1.9	2.4	2.4
Developing Asia	5.9	5.7	5.7	5.7	5.7	2.1	2.5	2.6	2.7	2.9

DEVELOPING ASIA— STAYING THE COURSE

1

Developing Asia—staying the course

Developing Asia is cautiously navigating steady growth despite delayed recovery in the advanced economies. The region is poised to achieve 5.7% growth in 2016 and 2017, as forecast in *Asian Development Outlook 2016* (*ADO 2016*) in March, only slightly lower than the 5.9% growth recorded in 2015. Collectively, regional economies are stable thanks to effective macroeconomic management. Many responded to the dour global environment with countercyclical measures that helped prop up domestic demand. Further, the implementation of long-waited structural reform in India brightened growth prospects. Managed growth deceleration in the People's Republic of China (PRC) reflects structural reform to reorient the economy to a more sustainable growth path (Figure 1.0.1).

Policy challenges are mounting, however, as the current weak external environment highlights the importance of adequate policy response even as policy makers need to rethink the growth model for the region. Ailing commodity prices strain in particular some natural resource exporters in the region, but no one is immune to global developments. Should external weakness drag on, policy stimulus will have difficulty sustaining domestic demand. The uncertain timing of recovery in the advanced economies means that developing Asia continues to be tested by disruptive capital flows that could complicate macroeconomic management. The need for structural reform to build resilience into economies is particularly pressing.

On top of economic and political risks are threats arising from climate change. Much of developing Asia is poorly equipped to cope with more frequent and catastrophic natural disasters, leaving some economies highly vulnerable to climate change. As disaster risk worsens, regional policy makers must think globally when considering local structural reform. It is vital to build economies and infrastructure for adaptation to climate change and recovery from its effects, but this is not enough. All countries, rich and poor, must mitigate climate change by reining in greenhouse gas emissions. Developing Asia's firm commitment to the global emissions target to mitigate climate change will bring benefits to all that far outweigh the costs.

1.0.1 GDP growth outlook for developing Asia and the industrial economies

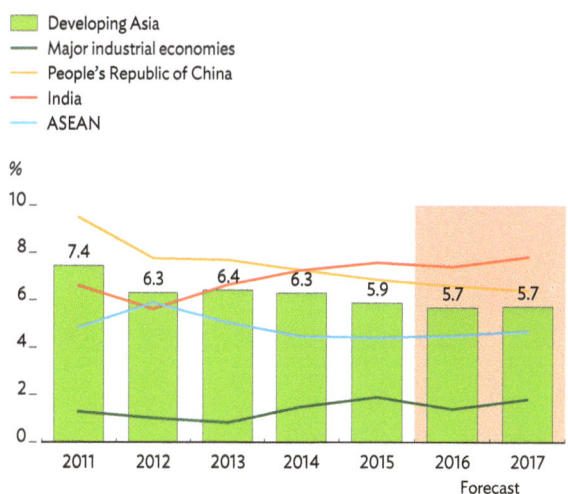

ASEAN = Association of Southeast Asian Nations.
Note: The industrial economies are the United States, the euro area, and Japan.
Sources: US Department of Commerce, Bureau of Economic Analysis, http://www.bea.gov; Eurostat, http://epp.eurostat.ec.europa.eu; Economic and Social Research Institute of Japan, http://www.esri.cao.go.jp; Haver Analytics; *Asian Development Outlook* database; ADB estimates.
Click here for figure data

This chapter was written by Akiko Terada-Hagiwara, Cindy Castillejos-Petalcorin, Ganeshan Wignaraja, Benno Ferrarini, Marthe Hinojales, Shiela Camingue-Romance, Nedelyn Magtibay-Ramos, Pilipinas Quising, Arief Ramayandi, and Dennis Sorino of the Economic Research and Regional Cooperation Department, ADB, Manila. Background materials from Donghyun Park and Shu Tian are gratefully acknowledged.

Steady growth in uncertain times

Developing Asia is expected to grow at 5.7% in 2016 and 2017, slightly down from the 5.9% recorded in 2015 (Figure 1.1.1). This *Update* retains the projections published in *ADO 2016* in March. Stubborn global headwinds have returned this year as weak economic growth in the advanced economies continues to stymie economic growth globally (Box 1.1.1). Yet, despite drag from the expected growth slowdown in the industrial economies this year and next, developing Asia remains resilient. The economies in the region have responded by implementing countercyclical policies that have succeeded to some extent in cushioning the impact from the international environment.

1.1.1 GDP growth forecasts for developing Asia, 2016 and 2017

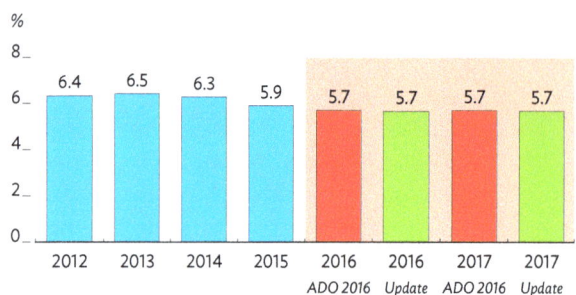

Source: Asian Development Outlook database.
Click here for figure data

Developing Asia's growth holds up

Growth in the PRC is still moderating much as expected, but the rest of the region stands to benefit from a 0.1 percentage point upgrade to the projection for PRC growth in 2016 and 2017. Further, better growth prospects for the larger Southeast Asian economies and solid growth in India also help the region as a whole overcome global drag. Despite continuing growth moderation in the PRC, the region will enjoy respectable growth again in 2017 that is solidly founded on growth in India and the PRC, its two largest economies.

The unchanged forecasts for Asia as a whole masks revisions for subregions and individual economies. While 6 of the 45 economies in the region retained their forecasts, 17 downward revisions balance 12 upward revisions of higher average magnitude (Figure 1.1.2). The significant revisions are for economies in Central Asia and the Pacific.

East Asia is the only subregion with upgraded aggregate growth forecasts, the increment being 0.1 percentage points in both 2016 and 2017, based on upgrades to the forecasts for the PRC and Mongolia. The trend is still for growth moderation in the next 2 years in view of planned structural reform in the PRC.

Growth forecasts for South and Southeast Asia in 2016 are retained. Southeast Asia is on track to reach growth at 4.5% this year as 6 of 10 economies are forecast to grow faster than in 2015. The forecast is retained despite downgrades for Indonesia, Malaysia, Singapore, and Viet Nam because of counterbalancing by unexpectedly strong performances in the Philippines and Thailand. While subregional growth in 2017 is expected to be higher at 4.6%, this is a slight downgrade from the 4.8% forecast in March. Prospects in Indonesia and Singapore are now seen to be softer

1.1.2 Frequency distribution of *Update* forecast changes versus *Asian Development Outlook 2016*

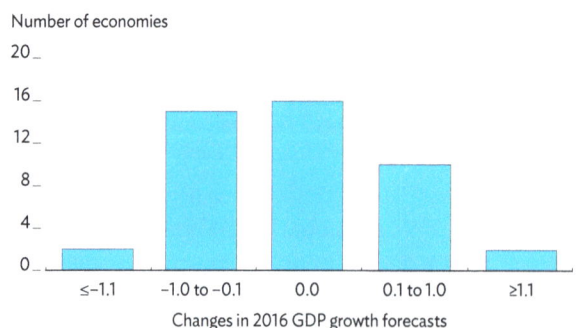

Source: Asian Development Outlook database.
Click here for figure data

1.1.1 Faltering growth in the major industrial economies

This *Update* revises down its aggregate growth projections for the advanced economies, from 1.8% to 1.4% in 2016 and from 1.9% to 1.8% in 2017 (box table). The preservation of growth envisioned in *ADO 2016* did not materialize in the advanced economies. Global economic growth is now expected to be lower to the forecast horizon. The downgrade for 2016 reflects a weaker performance in the US than expected, while Japan and the euro area are performing up to their relatively modest *ADO 2016* growth forecasts for 2016. For 2017, the growth forecast for Japan is somewhat upgraded while that for the euro area is downgraded. Inflation will remain subdued in 2016 but rise in tandem with an expected small increase in commodity prices in 2017.

GDP growth in the major industrial economies (%)

Area	2014 Actual	2015 Actual	2016 ADO 2016	2016 Update	2017 ADO 2016	2017 Update
Major industrial economies	1.5	1.9	1.8	1.4	1.9	1.8
United States	2.4	2.6	2.3	1.5	2.5	2.4
Euro area	0.9	1.6	1.5	1.5	1.6	1.4
Japan	–0.1	0.6	0.6	0.6	0.5	0.8

ADO = Asian Development Outlook.

Notes: Average growth rates are weighted by gross national income, Atlas method. More details in Table A1.1 on page 30.

Sources: US Department of Commerce, Bureau of Economic Analysis, http://www.bea.gov; Eurostat, http://ec.europa.eu/eurostat; Economic and Social Research Institute of Japan, http://www.esri.cao.go.jp; Consensus Forecasts; Bloomberg; CEIC Data Company; Haver; World Bank, Global Commodity Markets, http://www.worldbank.org; ADB estimates.

The US economy recorded a seasonally adjusted annualized rate (saar) of 1.2% in the second quarter, much slower than the 3.0% growth a year earlier. The latest release of GDP figures incorporated downward technical revisions to the fourth quarter of 2015 and the first quarter of 2016. Growth remains soft because of weak investment and limited public spending, but it found a lifeline in a strong rebound in private consumption supported by a healthy labor market. Weak trade growth reflected the sluggish world economy and a strong dollar that restrained US exports. However, the strong dollar also contributed to relatively low headline inflation averaging 1.0% in January–July. Meanwhile, the unemployment rate showed a slight uptick in August with increased labor participation. As inflation remains benign, the US Federal Reserve is likely to keep its benchmark interest rate unchanged until the end of the year while awaiting clearer signals of recovery. Slower growth in the first half prompts downward revisions to US GDP forecasts, to 1.5% from 2.3% in 2016 but only 0.1 percentage points lower to 2.4% in 2017.

The euro area started the year strongly with first quarter growth at 2.1% saar, supported by firm domestic demand,

but it appears to have since lost steam, despite a positive contribution from net exports, as growth slowed to 1.2% in the second quarter, dragged down by low investment. Growth across economies varied, with Spain and the Netherlands the leading performers as France and Italy stagnated. Germany slowed but still posted respectable growth at 1.7%, surpassing market expectations.

Various leading indicators registered mixed results, clouding future growth. Retail sales, economic sentiment, and consumer confidence weakened by midyear, which does not augur well for consumption in the coming quarters. Tepid growth in industrial production was consistent with the lower composite purchasing managers' index, suggesting continued weakness in investment. However, some bright spots were evident in early third quarter indicators of retail sales and in the resilience demonstrated by the purchasing managers' index even after the Brexit referendum.

The European Central Bank kept unchanged its interest rates and the size of its quantitative easing program, purchasing more than €1 trillion in September. The risk of deflation was staved off as inflation finally turned positive in June and edged up to 0.2% in July and August.

The growth outlook for the euro area in 2016 remains at the *ADO 2016* forecast of 1.5% in view of supportive fiscal and monetary policies. However, the pending separation of the United Kingdom from the European Union creates economic uncertainty for the region on top of the downside risks from a fragile global economy. This *Update* now sees euro area growth slowing in 2017 to 1.4%.

In line with expectations, Japan's economy grew by 0.8% saar in the first half of 2016. Robust growth in the first quarter was followed by near stagnation in the second. Total consumption and private investment were the main drivers of growth on the strength of higher demand for durable goods and of the leap year effect that comes with one additional day in February. The expansion in investment and consumption is expected to wane in the second half of the year in light of forward indicators on business conditions having deteriorated and consumer confidence having stagnated with dimming income prospects. Weak external demand, especially from Japan's main trading partner, the PRC, and sharp appreciation of the yen weighed on business sentiment.

Inflation remained muted in Japan, even turning slightly negative in the first half of the year. To revive growth and stimulate domestic demand, the government endorsed in August another round of stimulus measures worth ¥13.5 trillion, with a third of the budget allocated to additional government spending in FY2016 (ending 31 March 2017). Taking into account the delay of the expected surge in consumer spending along with the postponement of the value-added tax boost to October 2019, and the absence of any other strong catalyst, Japan will just maintain its 0.6% growth rate in 2016. The forecast is for rather stronger growth at 0.8% in 2017 on improving external demand and continuing fiscal stimulus.

as the fragile external environment continues to cloud the investment climate.

South Asia is now developing Asia's fastest growing subregion, driven by solid growth in India. Growth forecasts in *ADO 2016* are retained, with growth seen to slow slightly to 6.9% in 2016 before reaccelerating to 7.3% in 2017. The growth forecasts for India, the subregion's largest economy, are similarly unchanged for both years, providing the main resistance to global headwinds. Growth forecasts for 2016 are retained for Afghanistan, the Maldives, and Bhutan; revised up for Bangladesh and Pakistan; and lowered for Nepal and Sri Lanka. The growth projections for next year are retained for all economies except Pakistan, which is higher, and Sri Lanka, which is lower.

Growth forecasts for Central Asia and the Pacific are substantially downgraded as the larger economies in these two subregions suffered deep fiscal deficits that forced cutbacks in public investment and social transfers. Central Asian economies have been further hampered by lower oil and gas prices and persistent recession in the Russian Federation. The four oil-producing economies have been required to adjust to lower income from oil, while the four other economies have seen a sharp drop in the workers' remittances from Kazakhstan and the Russian Federation that traditionally provide a lot of income. These factors informed downward revisions to growth forecasts for Central Asia, by 0.6 percentage points to 1.5% in 2016 and by 0.2 percentage points to 2.6% in 2017.

In the Pacific, meanwhile, the growth forecast for 2016 is slashed from 3.8% to 2.7% as fiscal woes continue in Papua New Guinea, the largest economy in the subregion. This is despite some of the smaller economies—the Cook Islands, Samoa, and Tonga—performing above expectations on strong tourism, and Vanuatu and Timor-Leste lifting their economies with the implementation of reconstruction projects. Positive in-country trends in the Pacific economies are seen to persist into next year, bringing a rebound in subregional growth to 3.5%, higher than the 3.1% forecast in *ADO 2016*.

Domestic demand the backbone of growth

Among the 11 economies in the region with quarterly data, 5 of them—the PRC, the Republic of Korea, the Philippines, Singapore, and Thailand—posted expansion in the first half of 2016 that exceed the full-year forecast in *ADO 2016* (Figure 1.1.3). Last year, only 2 did.

For 6 of the 10 economies with demand-side disaggregation, the dominant source of growth was private consumer spending (Figure 1.1.4). This was boosted by generally low consumer prices and higher wages in the PRC, Indonesia, and India; tax cuts and government incentives for

1.1.3 2016 GDP forecasts in *Asian Development Outlook 2016* versus first half results

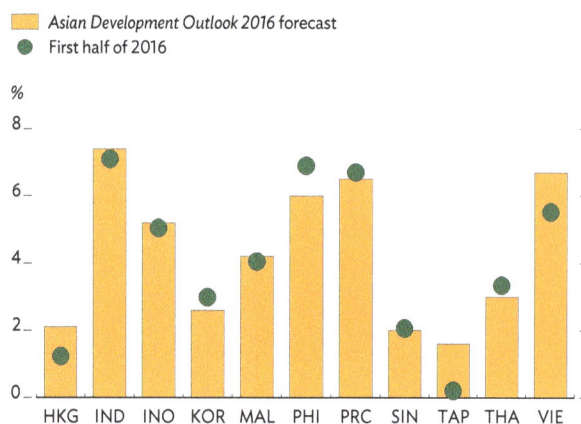

HKG = Hong Kong, China, IND = India, INO = Indonesia, KOR = Republic of Korea, MAL = Malaysia, PHI = Philippines, PRC = People's Republic of China, SIN = Singapore, TAP = Taipei,China, THA = Thailand, VIE = Viet Nam.
Note: For India, April–June 2016, which is the first quarter of FY2017.
Source: Haver Analytics (accessed 14 September 2016).
Click here for figure data

1.1.4 Demand-side contributions to growth, selected economies

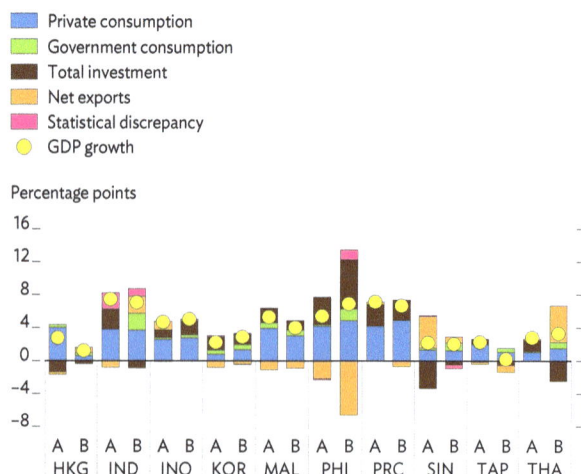

A = first half of 2015, B = first half of 2016, HKG = Hong Kong, China, IND = India, INO = Indonesia, KOR = Republic of Korea, MAL = Malaysia, PHI = Philippines, PRC = People's Republic of China, SIN = Singapore, TAP = Taipei,China, THA = Thailand.
Note: For the PRC, data on private consumption also cover government consumption.
Sources: Haver Analytics and CEIC Data Company (both accessed 8 September 2016).
Click here for figure data

spending in Indonesia, the Republic of Korea, and Thailand; and better employment conditions and election-related spending in the Philippines. On the other hand, a squeeze on consumption is evident in Singapore, Taipei,China, and Hong Kong, China as concerns linger over sluggish global demand and softer labor conditions.

Investment spending led by the public sector in 5 of the 10 economies also contributed significantly to growth. Notably, governments in the PRC, Indonesia, the Republic of Korea, the Philippines, and Thailand provided strong fiscal and monetary support to spur investment. Reflecting the poor health of the global economy, weaker net exports reduced growth in 5 economies in January–June 2016, notably the PRC, Malaysia, and the Philippines.

Buoyed by accommodative fiscal and monetary policies in the region, consumer confidence was generally stable in the first 8 months of 2016, supporting private consumption as the main driver of regional growth. In the Philippines, sentiment has consistently trended upward, albeit from negative territory (Figure 1.1.5). The Philippine consumer outlook posted in the third quarter of 2016 its first positive reading of the year, the result of high marks for economic growth and stronger peace and order.

Yet two economies continue to see softening consumer confidence and reduced private consumption contributions to growth. Reflecting lingering concerns over the economy, consumer sentiment in Taipei,China fell in June 2016 to its lowest in 30 months. Confidence continued to drop as the newly elected government failed to communicate effectively how it would improve the sagging economy. Similar sentiments were seen in Hong Kong, China, where consumers postponed major household purchases over uncertainty about economic prospects.

Retail sales show a similar trend, dipping early this year in some economies but beginning to recover by the start of the second quarter (Figure 1.1.6). Retail sales in the PRC remained strong and exceeded expectations in August 2016, averaging 10% increases year on year in the previous 8 months. The continued rise is attributed to sales of automobiles, appliances, and clothing. In the Republic of Korea, retail sales posted in June 2016 their largest gain since January 2011. This was a rebound from a low base in the same period last year when sales plummeted because of an outbreak of Middle East respiratory syndrome.

Despite sluggish consumer sentiment, government policy support helped retail sales in Taipei,China rise in July to their best rate since the start of 2016 as consumers bought automobiles, motorcycles, clothing, and footwear. This trend may not be sustained, however, in view of the dimming economic prospects for the rest of the year. Meanwhile, retail sales in Hong Kong, China have fallen in most categories for most of 2016 in line with the continued slowdown affecting inbound tourism and local consumption spending restrained by volatile asset

1.1.5 Consumer confidence and expectations, selected developing Asia

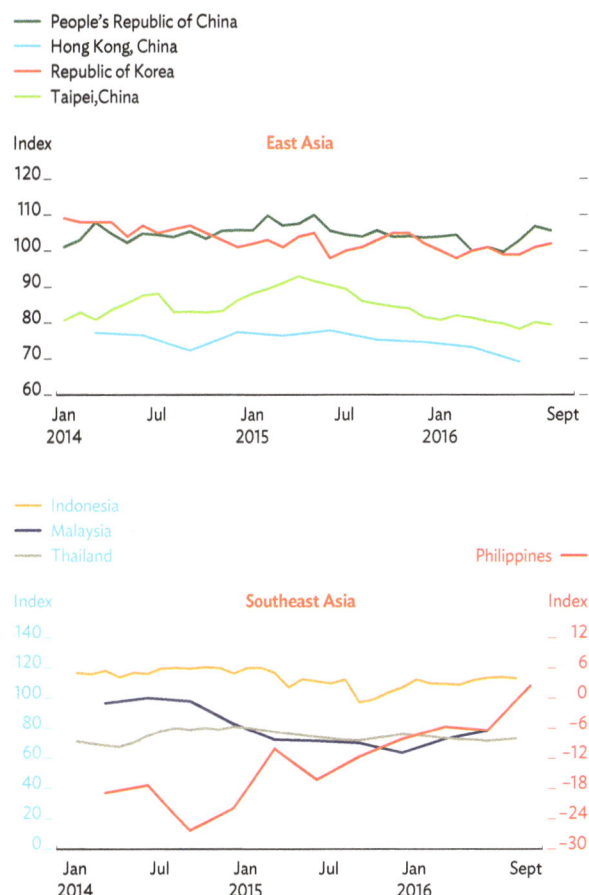

- People's Republic of China
- Hong Kong, China
- Republic of Korea
- Taipei,China

- Indonesia
- Malaysia
- Thailand
- Philippines

Notes: Data for Malaysia, the Philippines, and Hong Kong, China are quarterly. For the PRC, Indonesia, the Republic of Korea, Malaysia, Thailand, and Taipei,China, a rating above 100 indicates rising optimism and a score below 100 means deepening pessimism. Data for Hong Kong, China, use January 2000 as the base year. For the Philippines, the data record the percentage of households that answered in the affirmative less the percentage of households that answered in the negative, with zero dividing favorable from unfavorable views.

Source: CEIC Data Company (accessed 12 September 2016).

Click here for figure data

1.1.6 Retail sales, selected developing Asia

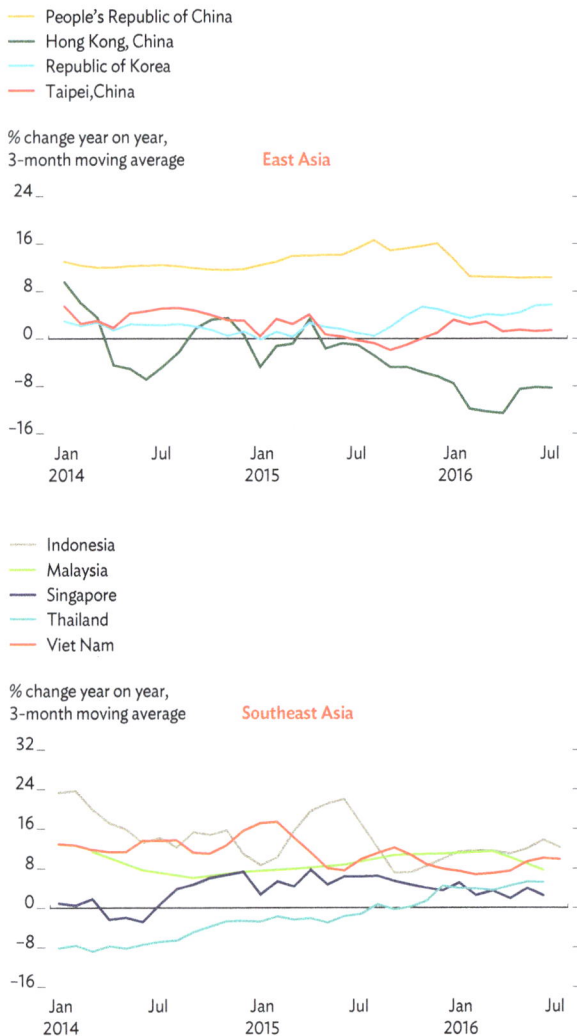

— People's Republic of China
— Hong Kong, China
— Republic of Korea
— Taipei,China

% change year on year,
3-month moving average   **East Asia**

1.1.7 Industrial production index

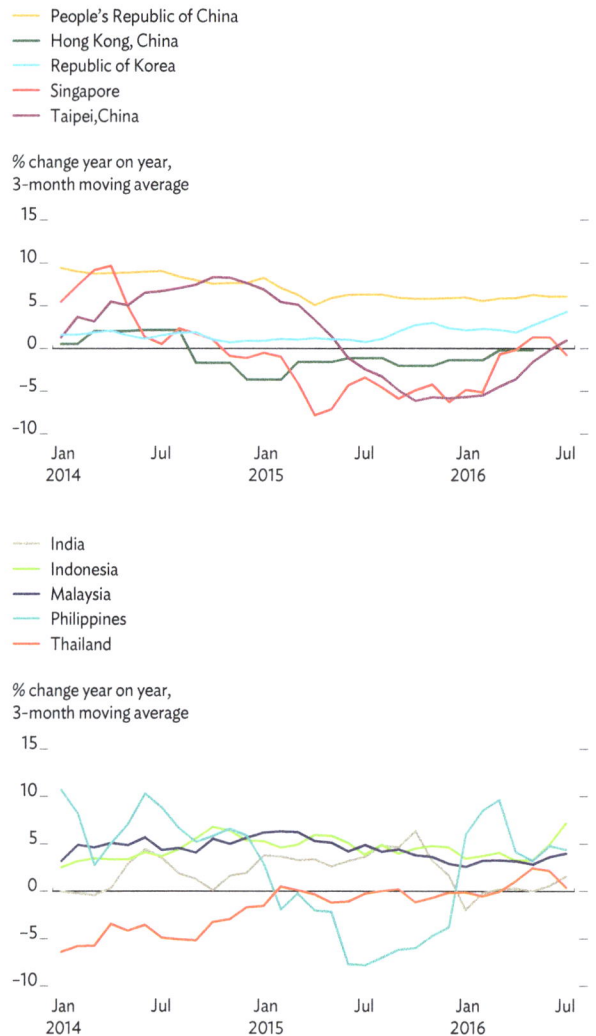

— People's Republic of China
— Hong Kong, China
— Republic of Korea
— Singapore
— Taipei,China

% change year on year,
3-month moving average

---- Indonesia
— Malaysia
— Singapore
— Thailand
— Viet Nam

% change year on year,
3-month moving average   **Southeast Asia**

Note: Data for Malaysia refer to year-on-year quarterly percentage change.
Source: Haver Analytics (accessed 12 September 2016).
Click here for figure data

---- India
— Indonesia
— Malaysia
— Philippines
— Thailand

% change year on year,
3-month moving average

Note: Data for Malaysia refer to year-on-year quarterly percentage change.
Source: Haver Analytics (accessed 12 September 2016).
Click here for figure data

markets. Retail sales in Thailand improved in the first 6 months of the year, benefitting from high tourist arrivals, and Viet Nam had a similar experience. In Indonesia, retail sales expansion was supported by higher incomes and lower inflation.

Signs of bottoming out appear in recent industrial production trends in East and Southeast Asia (Figure 1.1.7). Growth has been modest and trending generally upward since the second quarter of 2016, auguring well for growth stabilization in the region. There has been moderate expansion in export-oriented industries such as semiconductors and petrochemicals in Malaysia, automobiles in Indonesia and Thailand, and food and textiles in Indonesia and the Philippines.

A positive pattern is evident in the Nikkei purchasing managers' index for India and the PRC (Figure 1.1.8). The composite index for the PRC has been above the 50.0 threshold since March, reaching a 17-month high in August. The pattern has been in line with some strengthening of economic growth. The index for India showed strong expansion at 54.6 in August. The rise was attributed to improved demand from both domestic and external markets and brisk growth in new business orders. India recently adopted structural reform to attract more foreign direct investment and adopted legislation to allow a national value-added tax that will create a more integrated, productive economy.

Low oil prices subduing inflation

Regional inflation continues to sulk far below its 10-year average of about 4%. Global oil prices trended higher from a low in January 2016 but remained depressed. The average price of Brent crude oil in the year to date is below $50 per barrel, about half of the price at its last peak in June 2014. A limited recovery in demand seen in 2017 should see oil prices rise, albeit only moderately. Global food prices trended higher to midyear 2016 but averaged 2% lower than a year earlier. Many economies have nevertheless seen hikes in local food prices following weather disruptions. These factors and the impact of large currency devaluations in Central Asia prompt an upward revision in the regional inflation forecast to 2.6% in 2016, rising to 2.9% in 2017 but still lower than the 3.0% regional average in 2014 (Figure 1.1.9).

Among the 25 economies in developing Asia that publish monthly inflation data, about 60% had lower inflation in the year to date than forecast for the whole year in *ADO 2016* (Figure 1.1.10). Those economies that exceeded the *ADO 2016* forecast were beset by either currency depreciation, as was Kazakhstan, or food supply disruption, as was caused by flooding in Myanmar.

Variation distinguishes subregions. The inflation forecast for Central Asia in 2016 is revised up to 11.5% following sharp currency depreciation that fanned inflation in Kazakhstan and more than counterbalances lowered inflation forecasts for Armenia, Georgia, the Kyrgyz Republic, and Turkmenistan. Inflation in Central Asia is expected to slow to 6.4% next year as the pass-through of currency depreciation wanes.

The forecast for consumer prices in East Asia incorporates pressures in the PRC from higher agricultural prices. This pushes the forecast subregional average in 2016 up to 1.9%, with an additional slight rise in 2017 as administered prices are further deregulated and prices for services rise. Prices in the Republic of Korea will gradually accelerate over the forecast period as poor weather pushes up food prices. Depressed domestic demand will keep consumer prices in Hong Kong, China at bay, while uncharacteristically moderate inflation is seen in Mongolia this year, edging up next year with currency depreciation. Inflation is forecast to turn positive this year in Taipei,China at long last with higher prices for some food items caused by bad weather, and as the authorities' expansionary policies take effect.

1.1.8 Purchasing managers' index, PRC and India

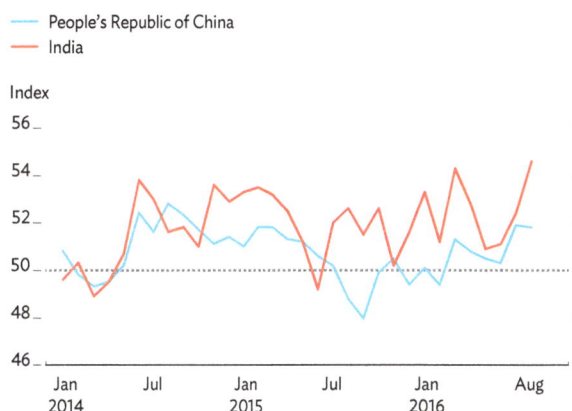

— People's Republic of China
— India

Note: A survey reading of over 50 shows expansion and below 50 contraction.
Source: Bloomberg (accessed 14 September 2016).
Click here for figure data

1.1.9 Subregional inflation, developing Asia

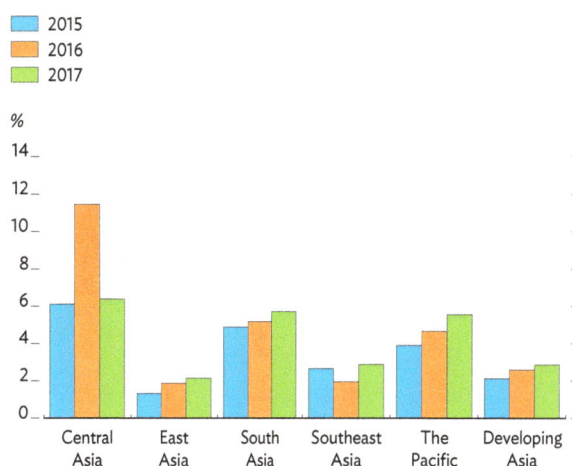

■ 2015
■ 2016
■ 2017

Source: Asian Development Outlook database.
Click here for figure data

Southeast Asia is the only subregion in which inflation is milder than projected in March, with downward revisions to forecasts in 8 of the 10 economies. For Indonesia, the inflation forecast is lowered by 1.0 percentage point to 3.5%, mainly because the government decided in April to reduce fuel prices. Inflation in Indonesia next year is seen picking up to average 4.0%, this forecast also trimmed from March. For the Philippines, the inflation projection for 2016 is lowered to 1.8% from 2.3% as El Niño affected food prices less than anticipated. Consumer prices are declining again in Brunei Darussalam and Singapore but are expected to rise slightly in 2017. In Myanmar, on the other hand, the inflation forecast for 2016 remains near double-digits after floods badly damaged agriculture and pushed up food prices. Subregional inflation is seen quickening to 2.9% in 2017 on higher global prices for food and fuel and on firmer domestic demand in most of the economies.

Inflation forecasts for South Asia are unchanged at 5.2% in 2016 and 5.7% in 2017. Estimates and forecasts for India, the Maldives, and Sri Lanka are unchanged. Excepting Afghanistan, average inflation in 2016 in the rest of the subregion is now expected lower than forecast in *ADO 2016* as inflation is held down by lower commodity prices, unproblematic food supply, and stable currencies—augmented by stiffened demand-management policies. In the Pacific, the forecast for average inflation is revised up for both years because of currency depreciation in Papua New Guinea and supply disruptions caused by extreme weather.

Most governments in developing Asia have maintained policy interest rates consistent with the low-inflation environment. Where low inflation persists—in Armenia, the PRC, Indonesia, Kyrgyz Republic, the Republic of Korea, Malaysia, and Pakistan—policy rates were cut to help boost consumption and investment and thus stimulate the economy. Already low policy rates were retained in the Philippines, Thailand, and Viet Nam to continue supporting growth. Policy rates were increased, on the other hand, in Azerbaijan and Turkmenistan to rein in inflation.

Weak demand trimming surpluses

Merchandise exports fell in most economies in developing Asia in the first half of the year, continuing a trend from 2015 (Figure 1.1.11). Battling sluggish external demand in a depressed global environment, exports were further weakened by low global commodity prices that took especially high tolls on the region's top hydrocarbon and resource exporters, particularly in Central Asia. Languishing demand, especially from the PRC, dampened export growth in many regional economies. A few economies seem to have started to recover, notably Viet Nam on brisk exports of phones and other electronics, and Bangladesh on robust demand for its garment exports.

1.1.10 Year-to-date inflation, selected economies

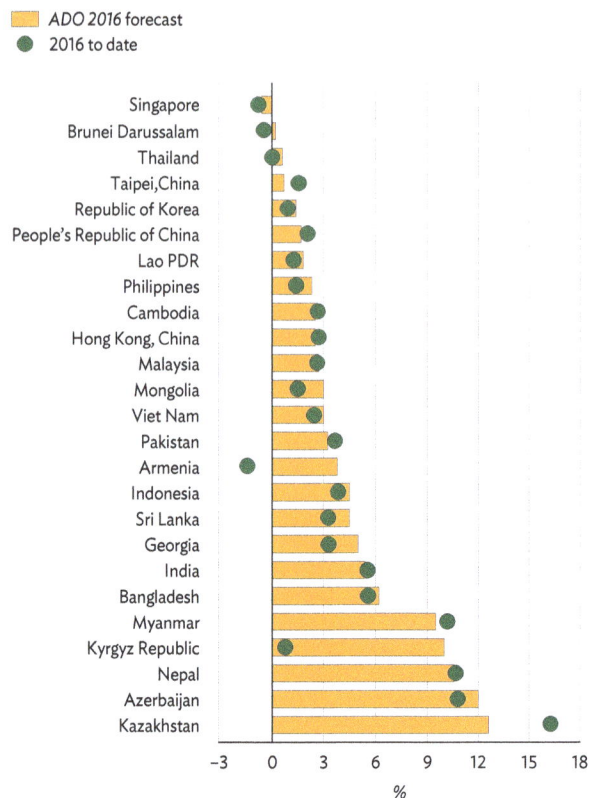

Lao PDR = Lao People's Democratic Republic.
Sources: CEIC Data Company and Haver Analytics (both accessed 14 September 2016).
Click here for figure data

1.1.11 Change in export and import value

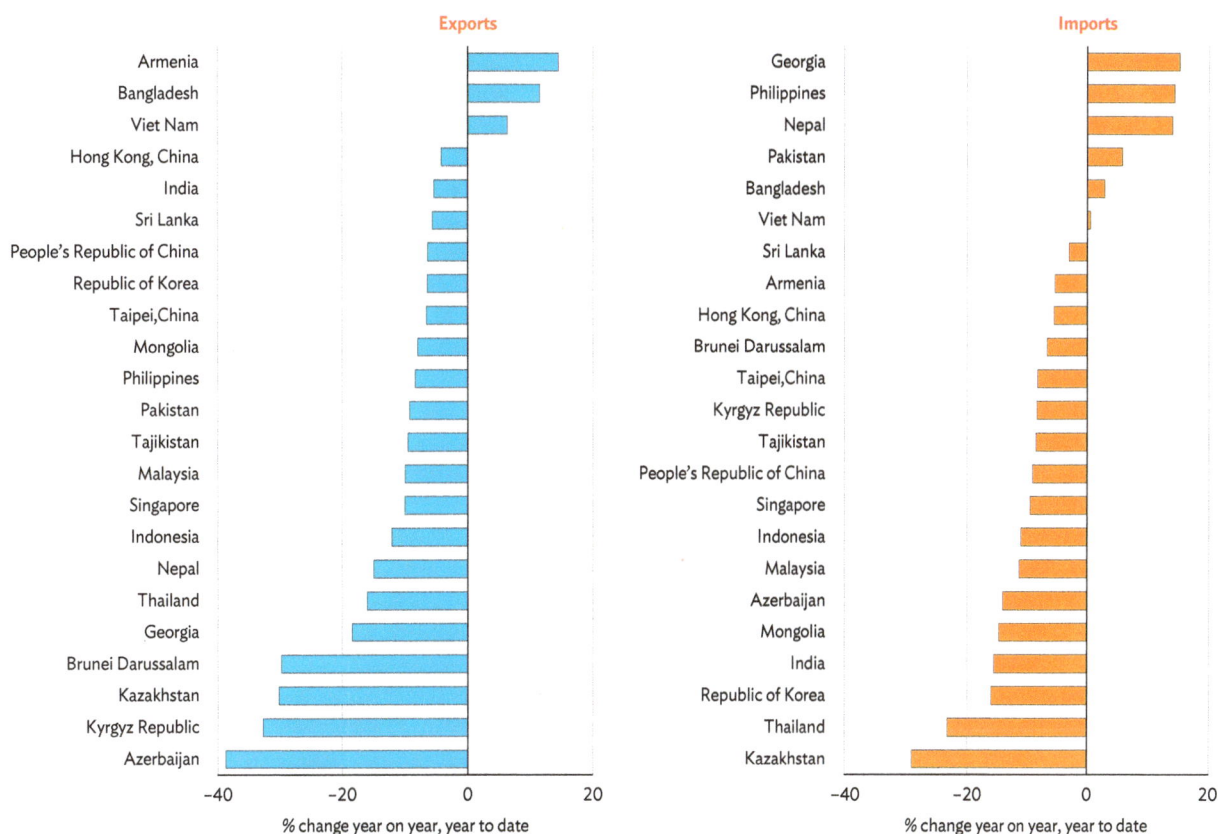

Exports

| Armenia |
| Bangladesh |
| Viet Nam |
| Hong Kong, China |
| India |
| Sri Lanka |
| People's Republic of China |
| Republic of Korea |
| Taipei,China |
| Mongolia |
| Philippines |
| Pakistan |
| Tajikistan |
| Malaysia |
| Singapore |
| Indonesia |
| Nepal |
| Thailand |
| Georgia |
| Brunei Darussalam |
| Kazakhstan |
| Kyrgyz Republic |
| Azerbaijan |

% change year on year, year to date

Imports

| Georgia |
| Philippines |
| Nepal |
| Pakistan |
| Bangladesh |
| Viet Nam |
| Sri Lanka |
| Armenia |
| Hong Kong, China |
| Brunei Darussalam |
| Taipei,China |
| Kyrgyz Republic |
| Tajikistan |
| People's Republic of China |
| Singapore |
| Indonesia |
| Malaysia |
| Azerbaijan |
| Mongolia |
| India |
| Republic of Korea |
| Thailand |
| Kazakhstan |

% change year on year, year to date

Note: Data are as of July 2016, except for the Kyrgyz Republic (May 2016); Azerbaijan, Bangladesh, Brunei Darussalam, and Kazakhstan (June 2016); and the People's Republic of China, Georgia, the Republic of Korea, Mongolia, Pakistan, Viet Nam, and Taipei,China (August 2016).
Sources: Haver Analytics and CEIC Data Company (both accessed 14 September 2016).
Click here for figure data

Falling merchandise imports mirrored the export performance, reflecting much lower prices for imported oil than a year earlier and moderating domestic demand that shelved planned investment and production expansion. East and Southeast Asian economies in particular have been hurt by declining demand from the PRC for intermediate manufactures, of which these subregions are the prime suppliers.

The weak trade performance is manifested in developing Asia's current account balances. The regional average current account balance is still expected to show surpluses in 2016 and 2017 but narrower than in the past and below the March forecasts. The revision of the combined current account forecast for 2016 is 0.2 percentage points lower at 2.4% of combined GDP because of low external demand for commodities and manufactured goods. The current account forecast for 2017 is revised down to 2.0% of GDP as the region will continue to face weak external demand. Current account deficits in Central and South Asia are still more than offset by surpluses in the rest of developing Asia (Figure 1.1.12).

1.1.12 Current account balance, developing Asia

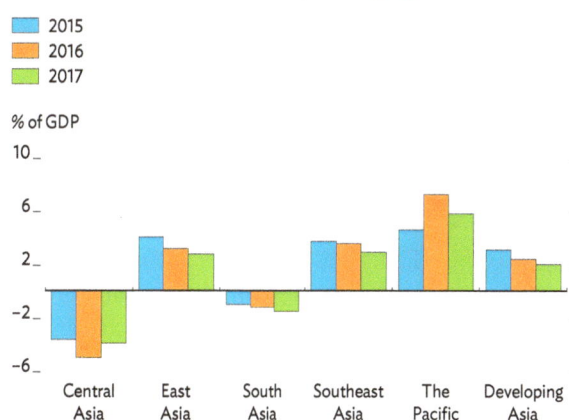

■ 2015
■ 2016
■ 2017

% of GDP

| Central Asia | East Asia | South Asia | Southeast Asia | The Pacific | Developing Asia |

Source: Asian Development Outlook database.
Click here for figure data

Current account deficits are expected in Central Asia and South Asia this year and next. The projected current account deficit for Central Asia in 2016 is now 5.0% of GDP, 1.1 percentage points higher than forecast in *ADO 2016*. The adjustment is mainly from a worsening current account deficit in Kazakhstan. Weak import demand is helping to contain Central Asia's widening current account deficit, but the projection for 2017 is nevertheless revised higher to 3.9% of GDP. South Asia's forecast current account deficit is revised lower to 1.1% of GDP in 2016 on an improved outlook for India, as well as a stronger outcome for Bangladesh, but still widens to 1.6% in 2017 as the region's demand for imports picks up.

Surpluses in East and Southeast Asia are on a narrowing trend. In East Asia, the combined current account surplus will taper from 3.1% of GDP in 2016 to 2.7% in 2017 because of weak exports and falling services trade. These figures are both revised down by about half a percentage point mainly because of growing services deficits in the PRC, which will pull down the projected surplus for the PRC from 2.0% of GDP in 2016 to 1.7% in 2017, both these numbers about three-quarters of a percentage point lower than forecast in *ADO 2016*. All other economies in East Asia except Mongolia will post surpluses. The deficit in Mongolia will be wider than earlier anticipated in both 2016 and 2017 because of lower ore quality in the main copper mine, as well as higher machinery and fuel imports for mine construction.

The projection for Southeast Asia's current account surplus in 2016 is revised up to 3.4% of GDP from 2.8% in *ADO 2016*, mainly on upward revisions for current account surpluses in Singapore, Thailand, and Viet Nam. Despite anticipated improvement in external demand from major trading partners next year, the subregional surplus will narrow to 2.7% in 2017, as forecast in March, with resumed imports of raw materials and capital goods for production in the larger economies in the subregion.

The Pacific has enjoyed current account surpluses in recent years, mainly from large royalties received by Timor-Leste from its large offshore petroleum sector and high revenues in several island states from fishing licenses. These factors, together with an improved trade balance outlook for Papua New Guinea, will see the subregional current account surplus expand to equal 7.2% of GDP in 2016 before it narrows to 5.8% in 2017. Both of these forecasts are higher than in *ADO 2016*.

Risks to the outlook

Developing Asia continues to grow at respectable rates even as the external environment remains clouded, oil prices start trending upward, and inevitable hikes in US interest rates continue to loom. Risks to the region's outlook tilt, however, to the downside.

The US Federal Reserve has been prudent in its monetary stance. A hasty rate hike could prompt rapid capital withdrawal from emerging markets that would destabilize some economies. Concerns about global financial stability in the wake of Brexit have no doubt influenced the Fed's decision to keep rates steady. But now that a measure of stability has returned to global markets, the Fed will be guided primarily by domestic factors, which points to a rate hike. Although a disappointing report on nonfarm job creation in September suggests that the rate hike may not come until the end of the year, the generally healthy state of the US economy warrants monetary tightening that starts this year before picking up in 2017. However, the abrupt capital flows experienced in 2013 in connection with the so-called "taper tantrum" must be avoided.

More generally, low interest rates in the advanced economies continue to pose risks to financial stability in emerging markets. Given persistently weak domestic activity, monetary authorities in the region will face a challenging situation for macroeconomic management. While the world is currently fixated on the Fed's intentions regarding US interest rates, the exceptionally loose monetary policies pursued by central banks in the advanced economies since the global financial crisis have encouraged potentially destabilizing capital flows into emerging markets. Going beyond interest rates that are merely low, some central banks, including those of the euro area and Japan, have set rates below zero. While banks have fared well so far, negative interest rates could, if maintained too long, impair their profitability and the soundness of the banking sector as a whole. Low interest rates could encourage risk-taking in banks and, over time, tighten their lending channels given their uncertain deposit bases. Large capital flows and associated currency fluctuations have been observed since the 2008 global financial crisis (Box 1.1.2).

Political risks associated with anti-globalization sentiment are intensifying and may bring protectionism. The Brexit vote, which has worsened uncertainty about the near-term outlook for the United Kingdom and the European Union, is a particularly high-profile instance of a backlash against globalization and greater integration. The upcoming US presidential election features strident rhetoric against free trade and immigration. Rising popular support for political parties that oppose free trade and immigration reflects deep-seated disillusion about globalization among voters who have not benefited from it.

Other risks within the region threaten regional integration. Contention over the South China Sea may reduce flows of goods and services between the parties involved. Separately, as domestic industry develops in the PRC, the vertical production chains that the region has developed over recent decades may wither, thereby weakening the case for greater integration.

Fossil energy prices are showing signs of life, but volatility remains. Whether or not the upward trend is sustainable is still questionable, but many economies in the region are net energy importers, so sharp rises in energy prices could dampen economic growth. On the other hand, energy-exporters still suffer under relatively low prices and trade volumes, crimping fiscal revenues and economic activity, particularly new investment in the energy sector. While many energy exporters have sovereign wealth funds to allow early windfalls to be applied to later contingencies, prolonged low energy prices will require reviews on how the funds should be managed and used. In connection with recession and currency depreciation in the Russian Federation, rising public debt helps to explain why fiscal crises are chief among the concerns of some governments in Central Asia.

1.1.2 How very low interest rates in the industrial economies affect Asia

Sweden initiated the first experimental negative interest rate policy in July 2009. Since then, others that have followed suit include Denmark, Hungary, Switzerland, and—most significantly—the euro area and Japan. Negative rates aim to achieve price stability mainly by preventing rapid currency appreciation. They can supplement quantitative easing. Negative interest rates have succeeded in easing bank lending behavior and evidently have expanded credit modestly in some economies. Inflation, meanwhile, has not picked up under very low interest rates as much as had been feared because demand has remained anemic and growth slow.

Beyond the direct effects that negative rates have on the banking system of the implementing economy, they have indirect effects on emerging markets in Asia. In most economies that have adopted negative rates, banks have stable lending margins (box figure 1). The trend is actually slightly upward for most euro area economies and for the United Kingdom, Sweden, and Switzerland. Where lending margins are compressed because it is hard to lower deposit rates without driving away depositors, banks offset declining interest revenues by turning more to fee-based services and by increasing lending volumes. This is reflected in their stable operating income (box figure 2). Thus, evidence is limited so far of negative interest rates damaging bank profitability.

Negative interest rates motivate banks in the advanced economies to seek opportunities elsewhere. In light of uncertain growth prospects at home in the advanced economies, global investors are attracted to faster-growing emerging markets with solid fundamentals. Interest rate spreads are wider in emerging markets, raising yield differentials on assets. In the years immediately following the global financial crisis, capital flooded into emerging Asia, especially as portfolio and other investment. Flows started to reverse in mid-2014 as the prospects improved for higher rates in the US. So far, capital flows prompted by interest rate gaps appear to have responded more to the US than to economies that have adopted negative interest rates.

Meanwhile, negative interest rates and, more generally, low interest rates in the advanced economies give emerging Asian economies greater scope to cut their own interest rates against the backdrop of slowing growth and muted inflation. This is what happened in the first half of 2016, when many emerging Asian economies sequentially reduced their interest rates to spur growth and fend off deflationary pressures.

The risk is renewed volatile capital flows in search of higher short-term returns, especially if the US recovery and monetary tightening do not materialize as expected. A climate of low global interest rates and volatile capital flows stokes asset price volatility and the creation of economic bubbles. In fact, global real estate and commodity markets rose in the first half of the 2016. Higher valuations and the prospect of capital gains also attract more investment into stock markets. Stock markets in major emerging Asian economies surged in the first half of 2016. As asset price volatility can complicate macroeconomic management and hamper growth prospects in the region, it would be prudent for regional authorities to keep a close eye on how the advanced economies' low and negative interest rates affect capital flows into the region.

1 Net interest margins for banks, selected advanced economies

- United Kingdom
- Germany
- Italy
- Sweden
- Switzerland
- Spain
- Japan

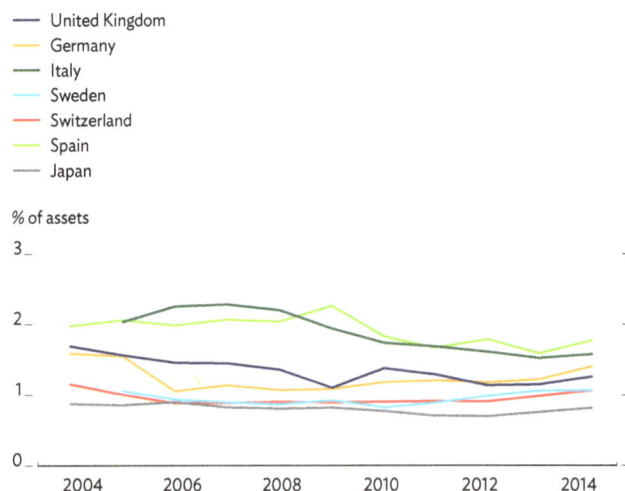

Note: This ratio is the net interest income expressed as a percentage of total earning assets. The higher this figure the cheaper the funding or the higher the margin the bank is commanding. Banks in the top 80% are ranked by total assets at the end of 2014. The numbers are unweighted averages.

Source: Bankscope (accessed 19 September 2016).

Click here for figure data

2 Other bank operating income, selected advanced economies

- Germany
- Japan
- Spain
- Sweden
- Switzerland
- Italy
- United Kingdom

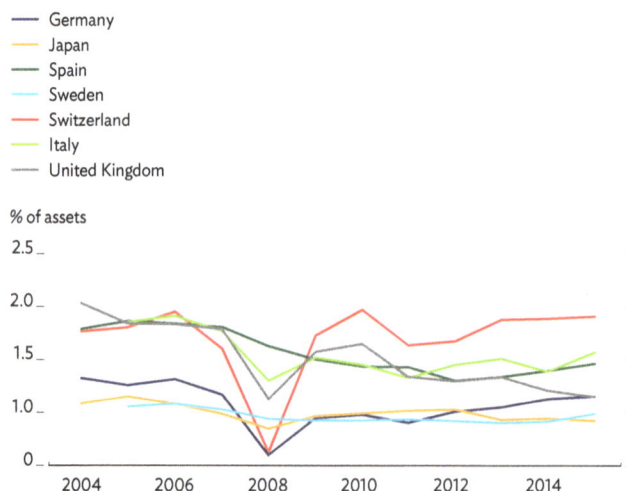

Note: This ratio indicates the extent to which fees and other income represent a greater percentage of bank earnings. Banks in the top 80% are ranked by total assets at the end of 2014. The numbers are unweighted averages.

Source: Bankscope (accessed 19 September 2016).

Click here for figure data

1.1.13 Recent significant disasters and estimated damage in developing Asia

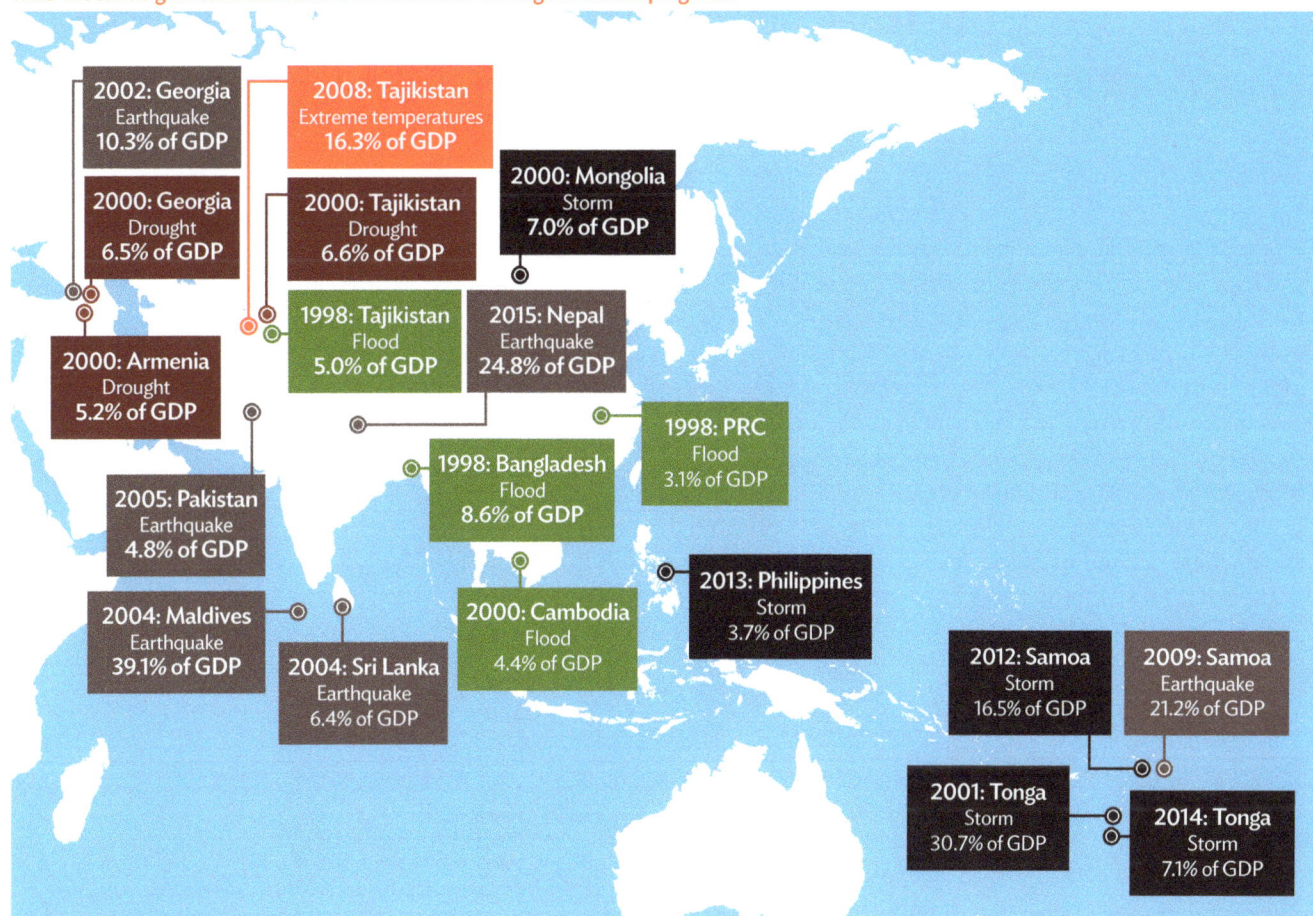

2002: Georgia Earthquake 10.3% of GDP	**2008: Tajikistan** Extreme temperatures 16.3% of GDP
2000: Georgia Drought 6.5% of GDP	**2000: Tajikistan** Drought 6.6% of GDP
2000: Mongolia Storm 7.0% of GDP	
2000: Armenia Drought 5.2% of GDP	**1998: Tajikistan** Flood 5.0% of GDP
2015: Nepal Earthquake 24.8% of GDP	**1998: PRC** Flood 3.1% of GDP
2005: Pakistan Earthquake 4.8% of GDP	**1998: Bangladesh** Flood 8.6% of GDP
2004: Maldives Earthquake 39.1% of GDP	**2000: Cambodia** Flood 4.4% of GDP
2004: Sri Lanka Earthquake 6.4% of GDP	**2013: Philippines** Storm 3.7% of GDP
2012: Samoa Storm 16.5% of GDP	**2009: Samoa** Earthquake 21.2% of GDP
2001: Tonga Storm 30.7% of GDP	**2014: Tonga** Storm 7.1% of GDP

PRC = People's Republic of China.
Source: ADB estimates using data from International Disaster Database (http://www.emdat.be).

Finally, natural catastrophes have severely affected some economies in the region in recent years (Figure 1.1.13). Damage has generally been greater than what they can reasonably prepare to handle. Recent disasters such as in Nepal, the Philippines, and Tonga highlight the extent of the problem. About 50 natural disasters hit developing Asia yearly, with extreme weather accounting for most. The damage has been particularly bad in small island economies such as the Maldives, Samoa, and Tonga, where coping capacity is limited.

Research confirms a link between the changes in the global climate so far experienced and the rise in the number and severity of weather-related natural disasters such as typhoons and droughts. As such, developing Asia has a strong stake in the global fight against climate change. This is the topic of this *Update's* theme chapter.

Responding to the trade slowdown

Export-led growth has powered developing Asia's rise and prosperity in the past several decades. Global trade grew twice as fast as global GDP until the global financial crisis of 2008–2009, after which trade growth slowed such that it currently just keeps pace with growth in global output (IMF 2016a). The underlying causes of the global trade slowdown have attracted increasing attention, and there is an ongoing debate on the relative contributions of cyclical and structural factors (e.g., Hoekman 2015, Freund 2016).

Regional exports have slowed in line with the global trend. Policy makers need to ask what explains the export slowdown in developing Asia, whether it is likely to become a new normal for the region, and what policies could foster new sources of export growth.

Mapping the export slowdown

Developing Asia's exports grew rapidly in real terms at an annual rate of 11.2% in 2000–2010 (Figure 1.2.1). Excepting a brief rebound in 2010, the region's export volume growth has slowed since the crisis, recording annual growth of 4.7% in 2011–2015. A major concern is that developing Asia's exports actually declined by 0.8% in 2015, which was a particularly bad year for world trade. Regional trends follow the lead of export growth in the PRC, which contributes about 40% of developing Asia's export value. PRC export growth slowed from an annual average of 18.3% in 2001–2010 to 6.4% in 2011–2015, falling into a 2.1% decline in 2015. The slowdown in developing Asia excluding the PRC was less pronounced as growth halved from 8.0% in 2001–2010 to 4.1% in 2011–2015, still growing marginally in 2015 at 0.8%.

The export slowdown in developing Asia is also visible in relation to GDP growth (Figure 1.2.2). The ratio of export growth to GDP growth in real terms halved from 1.5 in 2001–2010 to 0.7 in 2011–2015. An even starker picture appears in the figure on the right, which compares a shorter period before the crisis with the past few years. It shows the ratio of export growth to GDP growth plunging twice as quickly, from 2.1 in 2003–2006 to 0.5 in 2012–2015.

The slowdown has meant that developing Asia's export growth in 2011–2015 was, at 4.1%, similar to the 4.3% averaged by other developing economies and not much higher than the 3.6% of the advanced economies—two groups that developing Asia has historically outperformed in export growth.

The export slowdown is pervasive across developing Asia. Of 36 developing economies in Asia for which data were available, 20 had

1.2.1 Volume growth of goods and services exports

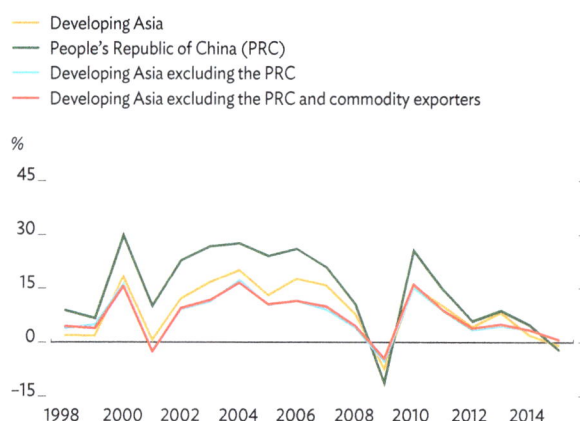

- Developing Asia
- People's Republic of China (PRC)
- Developing Asia excluding the PRC
- Developing Asia excluding the PRC and commodity exporters

Note: Developing Asia refers to the developing member countries of the Asian Development Bank. Commodity exporters are Azerbaijan, Brunei Darussalam, Kazakhstan, Malaysia, Papua New Guinea, Timor-Leste, Turkmenistan, and Uzbekistan.

Sources: ADB estimates based on data from International Monetary Fund. 2016. *World Economic Outlook* (April) and World Bank. World Development Indicators online database (accessed 11 August 2016).

Click here for figure data

1.2.2 Export and gross domestic product growth

- Export volume
- Gross domestic product

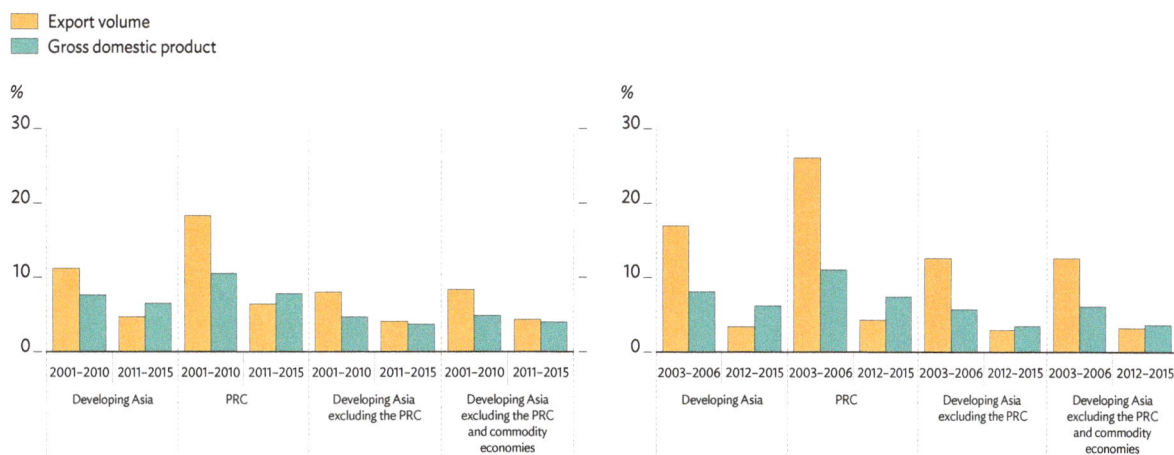

PRC = People's Republic of China.

Note: Developing Asia refers to the developing member countries of the Asian Development Bank. Commodity exporters are Azerbaijan, Brunei Darussalam, Kazakhstan, Malaysia, Papua New Guinea, Timor-Leste, Turkmenistan, and Uzbekistan.

Sources: ADB estimates based on data from the IMF Direction of Trade Statistics database, United States Department of Labor, Federal Reserve Bank of St. Louis, and Eurostat (accessed 16 August 2016).

Click here for figure data

slower export volume growth in 2011–2015 than in 2001–2010. This includes most of the region's largest traders: the PRC, Kazakhstan, the Republic of Korea, India, Malaysia, Pakistan, Singapore, Thailand, Taipei,China, and Hong Kong, China. Meanwhile, Cambodia, Indonesia, the Philippines, and Viet Nam showed stronger export growth.

Explaining the export slowdown

A prevalent explanation for the export slowdown in developing Asia is weak demand in the advanced economies for Asian goods because of cyclical factors or the lingering effects of macroeconomic shocks stemming from the crisis. Either effect is temporary and likely to be reversed as the advanced economies recover. Differences exist in demand for Asian imports among the advanced economies (Figure 1.2.3). Annual real growth in US imports from developing Asia picked up modestly from 5.1% in 2001–2010 to 5.8% in 2011–2015, indicating recovery in the US economy. Meanwhile, growth in Japan's imports from developing Asia slowed from 8.1% in the earlier period to 1.2% in the latter, and that of the European Union slowed from 7.2% in 2007–2010 (a shorter period for lack of import price indexes) to 0.7% in 2011–2015.

Cyclical factors clearly explain part of the export slowdown in developing Asia but are not the whole story. Several structural factors with a more permanent effect are notable, but so far it is difficult to disentangle the factors and weigh their individual influence on Asia's export slowdown.

First, slower growth in the PRC and the gradual shift away from manufacturing production and investment have weakened demand in the PRC for imports from developing Asia and globally.

1.2.3 Real growth in goods imports from developing Asia

- United States
- European Union
- Japan

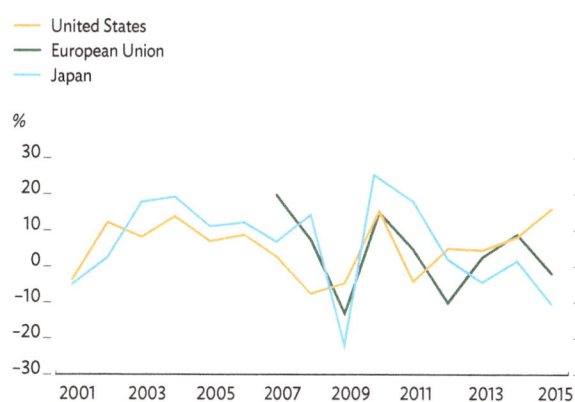

Note: Import growth was deflated using import price indexes for all commodities and/or total industries from national data sources in the European Union, Japan, and the United States.

Source: ADB estimates based on data from the International Monetary Fund database Direction of Trade Statistics, United States Department of Labor, Federal Reserve Bank of St. Louis, and Eurostat (accessed 23 August 2016).

Click here for figure data

PRC imports of commodities from developing Asia, in particular fuel and minerals, fell from $50.1 billion in 2012 to $34.1 billion in 2015 (Figure 1.2.4). Further, PRC imports of intermediate goods—which sustain industrial production in the global value chains (GVCs) that have distributed production stages across Asia and driven the region's ascent as the global factory—fell from $289.1 billion in 2014 to $266.6 billion in 2015.

Second, growth in GVCs is slowing, affecting trade in intermediate goods in the region. Developing Asia's ratio of intermediate goods to manufactured exports, a crude proxy for GVC trade, fell from 58.2 in 2001–2010 to 54.7 in 2011–2015 (Figure 1.2.5). This reflects a fall in the PRC ratio from 48.7 to 40.5 as the ratio for other regional economies rose from 65.0% to 70.5%.

Changes to GVCs and intermediate goods trade in developing Asia demand careful interpretation. Rising wages and other factor costs are encouraging a deepening of industrialization in the PRC, one aspect of which is GVCs growing more local roots. Structural shifts are visible in the composition of industrial output in the PRC since 2000 (Figure 1.2.6). More intermediate goods are being produced domestically, and more value added. This has been accompanied by a fall in imported intermediates. Another shift is that some GVC production stages, particularly labor-intensive ones, are beginning to migrate from the PRC to lower-cost locations, notably in Cambodia, Thailand, and Viet Nam (Coleman et al. 2014).

Third, lower commodity prices reduced real incomes in commodity producers in the region, crimping their imports. As a group, commodity producers' imports fell from $149.6 billion in 2013 to $134.4 billion in 2015 (Figure 1.2.7). While this largely reflects reduced imports to Malaysia, other commodity-producing economies also experienced declines in import values.

Fourth, creeping protectionism since the crisis may have also dragged on trade in developing Asia. Import tariffs have fallen both globally and in developing Asia. From 2000 to 2014, average import tariffs in developing Asia fell by nearly half, from 13.9% to 7.9%. However, opaque nontariff measures appear to have risen, particularly since the crisis. These include antidumping actions, quantitative restrictions, countervailing duties, sanitary and phytosanitary rules, and technical barriers to trade. The number of nontariff measures imposed on developing Asia by outsiders more than tripled from 2,263 in 2000 to 7,190 in 2015 (Figure 1.2.8). In the same period, the number imposed by developing Asia more than quadrupled from 534 to 2,217.

Fifth, the increasing role of exports of services (including digital service exports and services embodied in GVCs) may not be properly reflected in international trade statistics

1.2.4 PRC imports of goods from developing Asia

- Manufactures not elsewhere specified
- Assembly
- Intermediate goods
- Mining
- Fuels
- Agricultural products

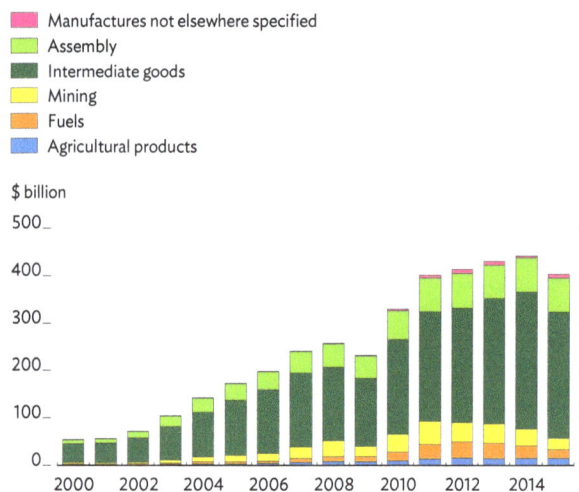

PRC = People's Republic of China.

Notes: Commodity classification is based on UN Comtrade's Broad Economic Categories (BEC). Agricultural products include primary and processed food and beverages (BEC 11 and 12). Fuels include primary and processed fuels and lubricants (BEC 31 and 32). Mining includes primary industrial supplies not elsewhere specified (BEC 21). Intermediate goods include processed industrial supplies not elsewhere specified (BEC 22), parts and accessories of capital goods except transport equipment (BEC 42), and parts and accessories of transport equipment (BEC 53). Assembly includes capital goods except transport equipment (BEC 41), passenger motor cars and other transport equipment (BEC 51 and 52), and all consumer goods not elsewhere specified, durable, semi-durable, and nondurable (BEC 61, 62, and 63). Manufactures include all goods not elsewhere specified (BEC 7).
Source: UN Comtrade database (accessed 24 August 2016).
Click here for figure data

1.2.5 Share of imported intermediate goods in manufacturing exports

- Developing Asia
- People's Republic of China
- Developing Asia excluding the PRC

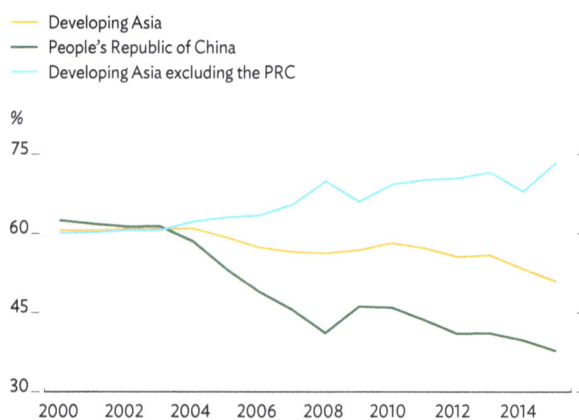

Notes: Classification of intermediate goods, referred to as parts and components, is based on the concept used by Constantinescu, Mattoo, and Ruta (2015). Intermediate goods is defined as the sum of the following three BEC categories: processed industrial supplies not elsewhere specified (BEC 22), parts and accessories of capital goods except transport equipment (BEC 42), and parts and accessories of transport equipment (BEC 53). Manufacturing products are defined as the sum of Standard International Trade Classification categories 5, 6, 7, and 8 (less 68).
Source: ADB estimates based on data from the UN Comtrade online database. http://comtrade.un.org/data (accessed 24 August 2016).
Click here for figure data

because they are difficult to measure. The same is true of smuggling and other unofficial trade. Statistics may overstate the slowdown in goods exports in regional trade, including within GVCs, and understate the growing importance to developing Asia of services exports. A further uncertainty in relation to GVCs is how much of services trade is embodied in value added in goods trading, for which there is a paucity of data.

Exploring implications

While developing Asia's exports have slowed, the mounting pessimism that has greeted this trend seems misplaced. A gradual recovery in the advanced economies can stimulate new sources of export growth in developing Asia. Likewise, rebalancing in the PRC will open up new trading opportunities for that economy and the region's other dynamic economies. Many developments can bring new sources of export growth.

The evidence that industrialization in the PRC is deepening comes from more domestic production of intermediate goods, higher value added, and signs of increased innovation capability (Figure 1.2.6). The deepening of industrialization now evident in the PRC and reflected in higher value added and the building of innovation capability was first seen in Asia in Japan and subsequently in the Republic of Korea. This implies the development of more technologically sophisticated regional value chains and related services in East Asia that can propel a new phase of regional and global trade growth. The spread of robotics, internet connectivity, advances in miniaturization, and process-centered research and development, and various organizational innovations are increasingly likely to feature in GVCs in this new phase of trade growth.

Some developing economies are well positioned to benefit from growth moderation and structural shifts in the PRC. Bangladesh, India, Viet Nam, and other members of the Association of Southeast Asian Nations (ASEAN) face the intriguing prospect of replacing the PRC in labor-intensive segments of GVCs as global demand rises for the range of products that the PRC currently produces, from clothing to consumer electronics (Abiad et al. 2016). These Asian economies are increasingly open to export-oriented foreign direct investment and offer relatively low wages with reasonably good labor productivity.

Services constitute the largest sector in most economies in developing Asia, but they are rarely traded because of trade restrictions, skills gaps, and problems with internet connectivity. Digital trade, professional services, financial services, and GVC-related services are areas with potential for trade growth. The PRC is likely to further expand its role as an exporter and importer of services (Constantinescu, Mattoo, and Ruta 2016).

1.2.6 Manufacturing output in the People's Republic of China

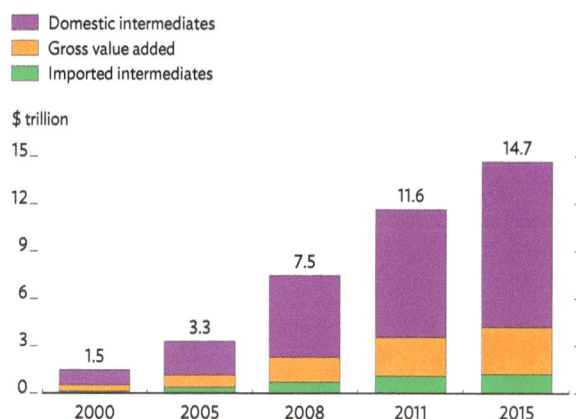

Source: ADB Multi-Regional Input Output Table database, 2016 (accessed 30 August 2016).
Click here for figure data

1.2.7 Commodity exporters' goods imports from developing Asia

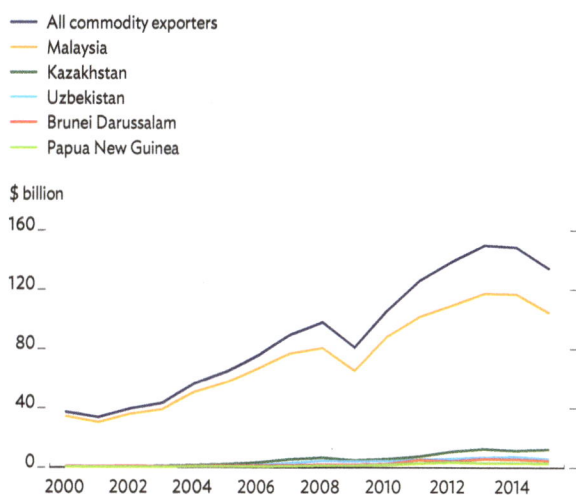

Note: Commodity exporters include Azerbaijan, Brunei Darussalam, Kazakhstan, Malaysia, Papua New Guinea, Turkmenistan, and Uzbekistan.
Source: International Monetary Fund. Direction of Trade Statistics online database (accessed 26 August 2016).
Click here for figure data

India is also likely to expand its trade in information technology services and witness the emergence of other commercial services exports. ASEAN and South Asian economies have opportunities to further develop tourism, including from markets in other regional economies, and other commercial services exports.

Small and medium-sized enterprises, which together are the largest generators of jobs in developing Asia, can play a greater role in the region's GVCs and services trade, either indirectly as suppliers to large firms or as direct exporters (Wignaraja 2015, Jinjarak and Wignaraja 2016). Such firms are typically hampered by lack of access to finance from commercial banks, gaps in technological capabilities, and cumbersome bureaucratic regulations relating to business startup and operation.

To realize these trading opportunities, it is important to continue to implement structural reform to upgrade skills, enhance finance for small and medium-sized enterprises, invest in seaports and other trade-related and digital infrastructure, and streamline behind-the-border barriers such as cumbersome local government regulations and labor laws. Policy makers should liberalize goods and services trade by reducing import tariffs where possible and instituting better surveillance of nontariff measures. The World Trade Organization's Trade Facilitation Agreement promises to reduce the region's trade costs, though only 19 economies in developing Asia have ratified it to date. Large trade agreements like the Regional Comprehensive Economic Partnership and the Trans-Pacific Partnership can help generate market access for services and spread good regulatory practices.

1.2.8 Nontariff measures in force

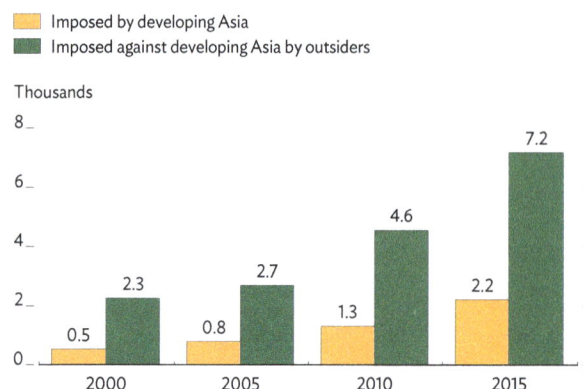

Notes: A stock approach is used wherein measures in force at the selected date are recorded. Measures in force are discounted from measures initiated, and measures withdrawn are discounted from measures in force. Nontariff measures include antidumping actions, countervailing duties, quantitative restrictions, safeguards, sanitary and phytosanitary rules both regular and emergency, special safeguards, regular technical barriers to trade, tariff-rate quotas, and export subsidies.

Source: World Trade Organization. Integrated Trade Intelligence Portal. www.wto.org (accessed 31 August 2016).

Click here for figure data

Debt sustainability in Asia

The surge in global liquidity in the aftermath of the global financial crisis of 2008–2009 has been reflected in a sharp rise in external liabilities taken on by many economies in developing Asia, which is often accompanied by rising commercial and household debt. A result is increased macroeconomic vulnerability in the region to the capital flow reversals and unpredictable financial markets that are features of a more volatile global environment. The US Federal Reserve's tightening cycle and geopolitical risk—to the extent that these variables exacerbate financial market jitters—contribute to fiscal risk in the region, demanding policy makers' careful vigilance.

Rising private debt adds to a broader range of pressures on fiscal positions in the region. While some countries have been suffering a slump in oil revenues, others have seen debt ratios spike as a result of state-backed borrowing for infrastructure investment in extractive or energy sectors. Most economies have seen heightened macroeconomic uncertainty translate into less stable projections of their medium-term public debt dynamics. Even though Asian debt appears to be manageable on the whole, policy makers should closely monitor fiscal risks and assure that it is duly reflected in their medium-term debt management strategies.

Trends in Asia's debt

Despite a volatile global economic environment, public debt ratios remain on a sustainable track in most of developing Asia (Ferrarini and Ramayandi 2015). Sustained economic growth, low interest rates, and prudent fiscal policy are responsible for this outcome. Most economies saw public debt ratios increase modestly or even decline from 2010 to 2015, but a few experienced substantial buildup of debt (Figure 1.3.1).

Increases were highest where governments borrowed to finance large infrastructure or extractive investment projects, such as hydropower plants in Bhutan, mines in Mongolia, natural gas projects in Papua New Guinea, or post-tsunami reconstruction and tourism infrastructure upgrade in the Maldives. For debt ratios to either stabilize or decline in the future, these projects will have to boost output, exports, and fiscal revenues. Fiscal management and debt sustainability in these countries would benefit from adherence to medium-term fiscal frameworks premised on realistic macroeconomic and fiscal assumptions.

Public debt ratios also increased sharply, albeit from a low base, in the hydrocarbon-exporting economies of

1.3.1 Public debt/GDP in developing Asia

%, 2015

AFG = Afghanistan, ARM = Armenia, AZE = Azerbaijan, BAN = Bangladesh, BHU = Bhutan, BRU = Brunei Darussalam, CAM = Cambodia, FIJ = Fiji, GEO = Georgia, HKG = Hong Kong, China, IND = India, INO = Indonesia, KAZ = Kazakhstan, KIR = Kiribati, KOR = Republic of Korea, KGZ = Kyrgyz Republic, LAO = Lao People's Democratic Republic, MAL = Malaysia, MLD = Maldives, MSI = Marshall Islands, FSM = Federated States of Micronesia, MON = Mongolia, MYA = Myanmar, NEP = Nepal, PAK = Pakistan, PNG = Papua New Guinea, PHI = Philippines, PRC = People's Republic of China, SAM = Samoa, SIN = Singapore, SOL = Solomon Islands, SRI = Sri Lanka, TAP = Taipei,China, TAJ = Tajikistan, THA = Thailand, TUR = Turkmenistan, TUV = Tuvalu, UZB = Uzbekistan, VAN = Vanuatu, VIE = Viet Nam.

Source: International Monetary Fund. 2016. *World Economic Outlook*, April; various Article IV reports.

Click here for figure data

Central Asia following the collapse of commodity prices in late 2014. Pressure on these economies' debt ratios will persist for as long as commodity prices remain depressed, and consensus forecasts suggest that the downswing in oil prices will be prolonged. However, the sizeable funds accumulated when export prices were high provide resources to get through the current slump.

Prudent debt management is required also in India, Pakistan, and Sri Lanka, where general government debt ratios have long been high by regional standards. Fortunately, these ratios are trending downward because the rate of economic growth has since the early 2000s outpaced interest paid on debt outstanding. However, these economies remain susceptible to a trend reversal that may be caused by a slowdown in economic growth or a significant rise in the effective interest rate. For Sri Lanka, where a significant share of debt is external, additional pressure is likely to come from the interest rate cycle of the US Federal Reserve. Interest rates pose less risk to India and Pakistan, where public debt is held mostly by domestic investors. However, where a significant share of such debt is short term, as in Pakistan, rollover risks are high and debt dynamics remain vulnerable to shocks. For all these economies, staying on course with fiscal consolidation through sound debt management and the progressive expansion of the tax base will help provide the fiscal resources and resilience needed to cope with future domestic or external shocks.

Uncertain debt projections

The hesitant pace of recovery in the global economy and the threat of sudden capital flow reversals heighten macroeconomic vulnerability in the region. As a result, medium-term baseline projections of public debt ratios have become less reliable for forecasting future debt ratios. Debt sustainability analysis should be upgraded to allow for a broad spectrum of possible outcomes and macroeconomic situations, and to reflect more fully market perceptions of risk.

Indonesia, for example, has experienced in recent years high exchange rate volatility associated with unstable cross-border capital flows in response to expected and actual changes in US monetary policy. The volatility and uncertainty of the current economic environment is reflected in a comparison of the forecast of likely paths of the debt ratio in 2011 and 2015 using fan chart analysis (Figure 1.3.2). The projections reflect the co-movement of key macroeconomic variables driving Indonesia's debt dynamics. In 2015, a public debt ratio above 60% of GDP within a 5-year horizon could not be ruled out, as the orange cone shows. This forecast contrasted sharply with the 2011 projection in green mainly because it was much wider, extending three times higher than the baseline and well above the comfort zone of an emerging economy.

1.3.2 Public debt projections for Indonesia, 2011 versus 2015

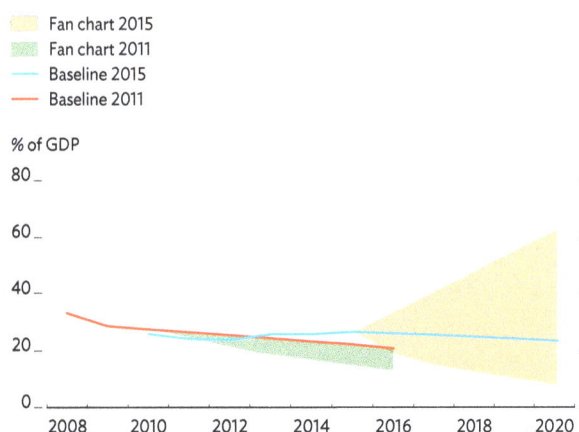

Note: Fans define the 5th and 95th percentile of the probability distribution.
Source: Ferrarini and Ramayandi 2015.
Click here for figure data

1.3.3 Public debt projections for Georgia, 2011 versus 2015

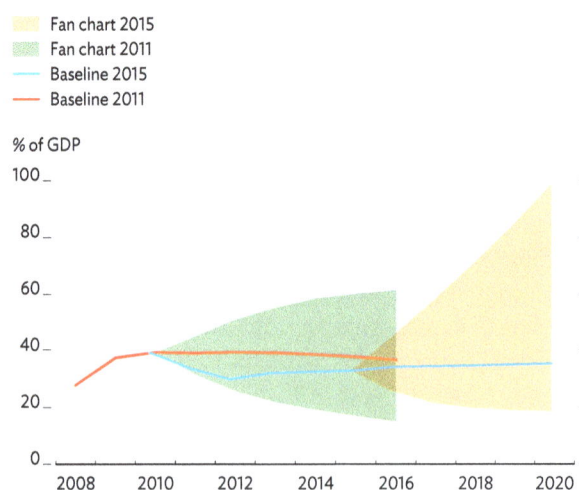

Note: Fans define the 5th and 95th percentile of the probability distribution.
Source: Ferrarini and Ramayandi 2015.
Click here for figure data

For Georgia, baseline projections that have hardly changed since 2011 indicate a stable debt ratio equal to about 40% of GDP (Figure 1.3.3). However, the uncertainty surrounding these projections had broadened considerably by 2015. Georgia had been buffeted by a combination of external shocks, including recession in the Russian Federation, lower remittances, and sharp currency devaluation in neighboring countries. Uncertainty about Georgia's macroeconomy and debt ratio heightened in the short term and spiked in the medium term. While the debt ratio will not necessarily reach the possible extreme, the forecast signals policy makers to be alert and closely monitor the country's debt dynamics and currency risks in particular.

Heightened uncertainty and volatile market perceptions of sovereign fiscal risk in Asia have been highlighted by a recent study applying contingent claims analysis (CCA) to five Asian economies: Indonesia, the Republic of Korea, Malaysia, the Philippines, and Thailand (Briere, Ferrarini, and Ramayandi 2016). The CCA approach consolidates government and central bank balance sheets and then infers the value and volatility of sovereign assets, which are usually not directly observable, from the value and volatility of sovereign liabilities, which usually are (Gray et al. 2008). CCA then derives indicators of sovereign risk such as the distance to distress. A risk-based measure of debt sustainability, distance to distress gauges the likelihood that a sovereign's total asset value will fall below its repayment obligations. It falls to zero when a country's assets are valued at less than its repayment obligations, requiring the government to renegotiate or default on its debt.

None of the countries analyzed came close to risking default based on data from the recent past. That said, the distance to distress metric can also capture increased volatility and some episodes of heightened risk. For example, the so-called "taper tantrum" in May 2013, prompted by speculation about US interest rates, caused massive capital outflows from Indonesia, worsening market perceptions and sovereign asset values and thereby causing the distance to distress to shrink markedly (Figure 1.3.4). Similarly for Malaysia, CCA picks up highly volatile market perceptions that stem from Malaysia's grappling with unstable capital flows and sharp declines in commodity prices since late 2014. The Malaysian ringgit depreciated steeply against the US dollar, but economic growth remained resilient. Indeed, CCA suggests that Malaysia remains at a safe distance from the distress line while navigating its economy through the uncertain global economic environment.

Oil funds as a buffer

Major oil exporters in Central Asia such as Kazakhstan and Azerbaijan have been hit by the slump in oil prices since 2014. The damage done to fiscal and financial health has been exacerbated by lower trade with and remittances from the Russian Federation as it copes with its own economic recession, and also by a slowdown in the PRC, tepid domestic

1.3.4 Distance to distress in Indonesia and Malaysia

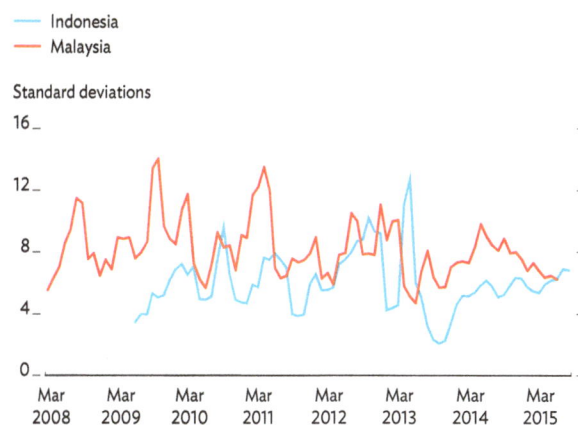

Note: Distance to distress is measured as the number of standard deviations of the sovereign assets value from total repayment obligations or liabilities.
Source: Briere, Ferrarini, and Ramayandi 2016.
Click here for figure data

economic growth, and currency depreciation (Figure 1.3.5). In Azerbaijan, for example, the manat depreciated by half from 2014 to 2015, which accounted for 10.2 percentage points of the 17.2 point rise in public debt in 2015 (Ferrarini, Greene, and Hinojales, forthcoming). Debt financing and public debt ratios are also being driven by the need to sustain structural adjustment spending.

International development lenders have been called upon to offer countercyclical lending to some governments. Such loans provide liquidity on terms more favorable than can bond placements on international markets, but they fall short of filling the financing gap. To maintain fiscal spending and ongoing socioeconomic reform, the major hydrocarbon exporters in the region can rely on their vast oil funds. For example, during the upswing in oil prices, the State Oil Fund of Azerbaijan accumulated nearly $37 billion, equal to 49% of GDP, even as it provided an average of 41% of consolidated government revenues from 2010 to 2015.

A recent study assesses the scope for drawing down oil funds to provide buffers that prevent debt ratios from rising excessively in a scenario with persistently low oil prices (Ferrarini, Greene, and Hinojales, forthcoming). For example, simulations of a hypothetical Central Asian economy similar to Azerbaijan assume a pessimistic scenario that caps future oil prices at $40 per barrel. They show that oil fund asset sales of $0.8 billion–$2.6 billion annually to 2021 would adequately substitute for debt financing and keep the public debt ratio from rising above 40% (Figure 1.3.6). The oil fund would, of course, shrink faster than in a scenario with no such buffering, but it would be restored when the oil price turned up again.

Now two caveats: A price slump could be long or deep enough to deplete any financial buffer. Moreover, oil funds are typically invested in a broad range of assets of varying liquidity that could limit the amount and speed of disinvestment. But a knee-jerk imperative to preserve oil fund assets can go too far. A temporary drawdown to finance a structural and economic transformation vital to securing future generations' welfare and potential would support, rather than undermine, intergenerational equity.

Vulnerability from private sector debt

While public debt ratios in developing Asia are generally contained and fairly stable, the same cannot be said for private debt, which has been rising faster in Asia than in other emerging regions. Private debt in the region is reflected in external debt. Past experience suggests that this is a concern, as privately leveraged boom cycles may burst and end up weighing on national budgets and public debt.

Rapid economic growth and high rates of savings since the Asian financial crisis of 1997–1998 provide regional firms with ample pools

1.3.5 Public debt/GDP in Azerbaijan and Kazakhstan

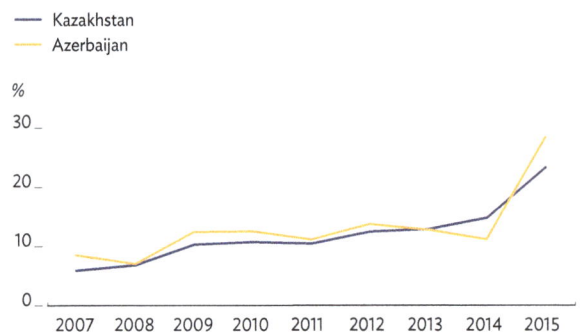

Sources: Fiscal Monitor database April 2016, IMF; national sources.
Click here for figure data

1.3.6 Hypothetical Azerbaijan public debt/GDP and oil fund assets, with and without debt stabilization

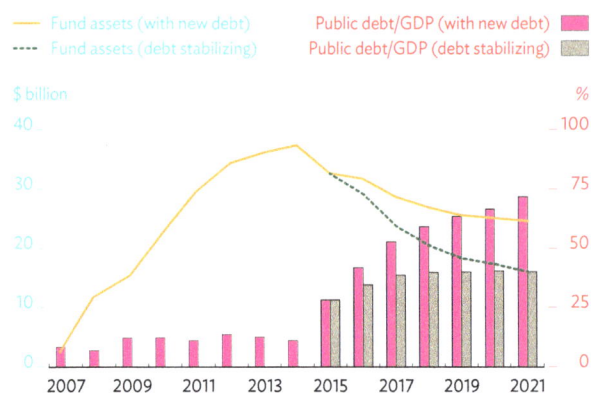

Note: The simulations assume a pessimistic scenario in which the oil price rises from the current $25/barrel to a cap of $40/barrel in 2020.
Source: Adapted from Ferrarini, Greene, and Hinojales, forthcoming.
Click here for figure data

of domestic financing. However, firms have ramped up borrowing from overseas as well through bank loans and offshore bonds issued by their foreign subsidiaries, partly absorbing the flood of money that authorities in the advanced economies have pumped into circulation since the global financial crisis to buoy their own anemic economies, driving interest rates close to zero and even beyond. From 2010 to the first quarter of 2016, the external debt ratio of regional economies (or of those that disclose the data) increased by more than 10 percentage points, placing developing Asia second among emerging markets after only Eastern Europe (Figure 1.3.7).

This increase is mainly private debt incurred through either direct borrowing or intercompany lending. The latter is particularly true of economies with significant extractive industries such as Georgia, the Kyrgyz Republic, Mongolia, and Papua New Guinea (Figure 1.3.8). Banks' external borrowings play lesser roles, and public external debt has actually shrunk slightly, as is consistent with the ample liquidity generally present within the economies.

Alongside borrowing by Asian companies, growing household debt is a major driver of the region's debt accumulation. From 2008 to the first quarter of 2016, the average ratio of household debt to GDP in Asia increased by 15 percentage points, while the ratio for nonfinancial corporations rose by 24 points, most notably in the PRC and Hong Kong, China (Figures 1.3.9 and 1.3.10). By contrast, government debt increased by 7.8 points and financial sector debt declined by 1.5 points (IIF 2016). It is not surprising that nonfinancial corporate debt scaled by GDP is highest in economies with internationally integrated capital markets, such as the Republic of Korea, Singapore, and Hong Kong, China. At 174% of GDP, nonfinancial corporate leverage is high in the PRC as well but mostly on account of domestic, not external, borrowing in real estate and by state-owned enterprises (SOEs).

1.3.7 External debt/GDP in emerging markets

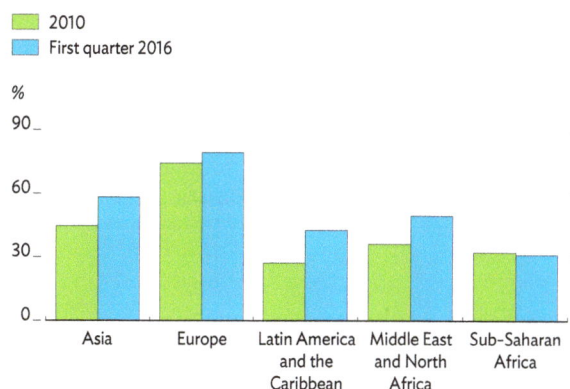

Note: Data are until the first quarter of 2016 except for Bangladesh, Burkina Faso, Cambodia, Costa Rica, Cote d'Ivoire, Dominica, Dominican Republic, Ecuador, Egypt, El Salvador, Madagascar, Mongolia, Nepal, Nicaragua, Solomon Islands, Suriname, Tunisia, and Uganda, whose data end in 2015.
Sources: International Monetary Fund and World Bank; Quarterly External Debt Statistics database; World Bank. World Development Indicators.
Click here for figure data

1.3.8 Change in external debt/GDP in developing Asia, 2010 to the first quarter of 2016

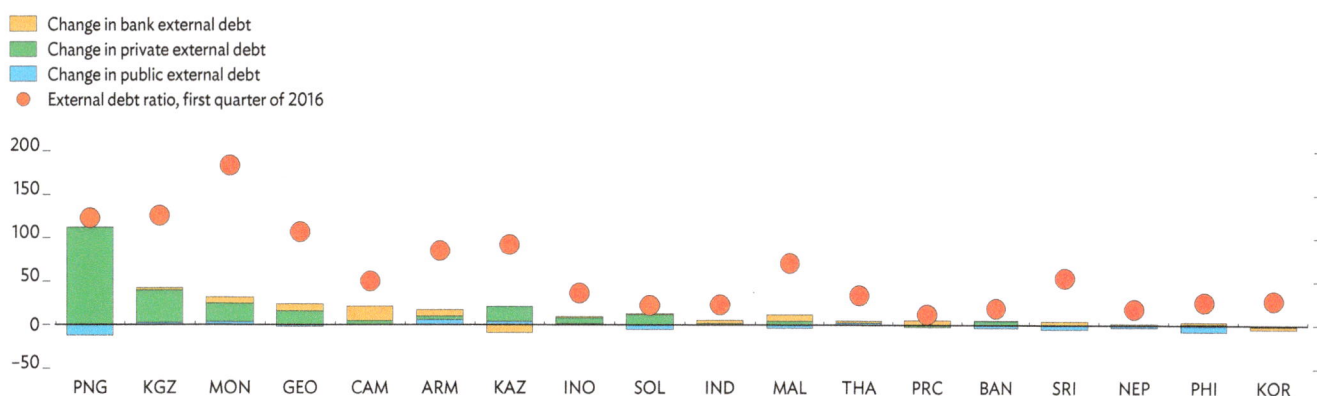

ARM = Armenia, BAN = Bangladesh, CAM = Cambodia, GEO = Georgia, IND = India, INO = Indonesia, KAZ = Kazakhstan, KGZ = Kyrgyz Republic, KOR = Republic of Korea, MAL = Malaysia, MON = Mongolia, NEP = Nepal, PHI = Philippines, PNG = Papua New Guinea, PRC = People's Republic of China, SOL = Solomon Islands, SRI = Sri Lanka, THA = Thailand.
Notes: Bars represent change from 2010 to the first quarter of 2016, except for Cambodia (change from 2010 to 2015), Bangladesh and Solomon Islands (change from 2011 to 2015), Papua New Guinea (change from 2011 to 2014), Nepal and Sri Lanka (change from 2012 to 2015), Malaysia (change from 2012 to the first quarter of 2016), and Mongolia (change from 2013 to 2015). The same end years apply to these economies' external debt ratios.
Source: International Monetary Fund and World Bank. *Quarterly External Debt Statistics* database; World Bank. *World Development Indicators* online database.
Click here for figure data

1.3.1 Public and corporate debt in the PRC

General government debt in the PRC was stable at less than 40% of GDP in 2015, not particularly large compared with other economies in the region (Figure 1.3.1 on page 21) (IMF 2016c). However, this headline ratio misses a far more complex picture of public debt in the PRC if general government debt is considered together with off-budget liabilities, both explicit and contingent, incurred by local governments through their financing platforms. The International Monetary Fund expects that this so-called augmented public debt ratio will rise to nearly 74% of GDP in 2021 from 56% in 2015. Projections further suggest that this ratio could breach 100% of GDP if a contingent liability shock forced the government to bail out banks to the tune of 10% of their assets.

Rising private debt in the PRC adds to total debt stock, which now stands at 280% of GDP. The liabilities of SOEs, equal to 115% of GDP, impose an immense contingent burden, explicit or implicit, on the general government budget and debt (Moody's 2016a, b). PRC corporate fundamentals have weakened under excess capacity compounded by moderating domestic and external demand. Profits have fallen sharply, particularly for SOEs, and a rising share of debt is held by firms with weak capacity to pay interest expenses on outstanding debt. Nonperforming loans are proliferating, and in 2015 more than 14% of all corporate loans in the PRC were at risk, up from less than 2% in 2009 (box figure). This excludes bad debt in the country's shadow banking system, the share of which is estimated by Deutsche Bank to have grown more than threefold from the end of 2012 to the first quarter of 2016, to equal about 10% of bank assets (S&P Global Ratings 2016).

An opaque and complex network of banks and nonbank institutions has been behind this credit surge, which is mounting at twice the pace of nominal GDP growth. Corporate debt is being pushed higher as SOE and private sector profitability diminishes and economic growth becomes increasingly credit-intensive. Further, credit growth has fed asset bubbles in the property, equity, and bond markets, fueling concerns about the growing risks of a disruptive adjustment or hard landing.

No doubt, any financial bailout in the PRC has the potential to weigh on the government budget and raise the public debt ratio significantly. A clean-up would prove more difficult than back in 1999, when the government established asset management companies to absorb bad loans from four major state banks with a book value equal to almost 20% of GDP. Double-digit growth in the decade

that followed shrank the relative value of those toxic assets and government-backed bonds to less than 5% of GDP (Mitchell 2016). Today, not only has growth in the PRC slowed by half, sharply curtailing its capacity to deflate toxic assets, but the authorities would face a much more complex task trying to sort the good from the bad in the heavy entanglements of the financial sector (Mitchell 2016).

However, the risk of a full-blown financial crisis in the PRC remains remote. Debt is mostly domestically funded (Figure 1.3.10 on page 27) and funneled through a financial system that is largely backed and tightly controlled by the government. Also, the PRC has ample room for policy maneuver both fiscal and monetary, and its capital account is closed. This mitigates the risk of domestic difficulties spilling over but cannot entirely insulate the country's external position. Indeed, the economy recorded substantial capital outflows and saw its foreign exchange reserves shrink in 2015 and again earlier this year.

Even if a hard landing is averted, the growing debt overhang in the PRC imposes significant costs on the economy from widespread misallocation, slower economic transformation, and consequently diminished growth prospects. Unless rebalancing efforts eventually succeed in taming credit growth and tackling the corporate debt problem, the costs of flushing toxic debt from the system are bound to increase and ultimately bear more heavily on the PRC.

Corporate debt at risk

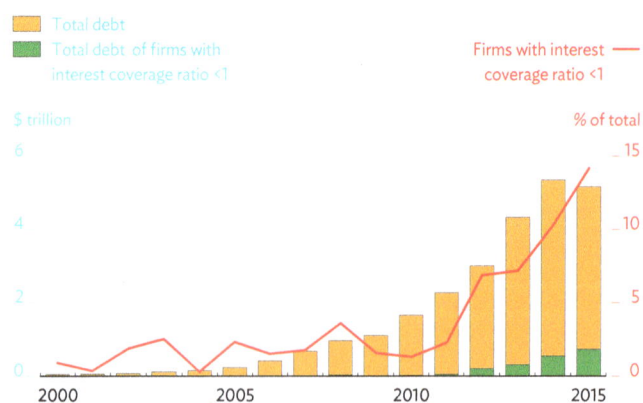

Note: Interest coverage ratio is calculated as earnings before interest, taxes, depreciation, and amortization divided by the interest expense of the firm.

Source: ADB estimates using S&P Capital IQ database. Methodology adapted from International Monetary Fund. 2016. *Global Financial Stability Report—Potent Policies for Successful Normalization.* April.
Click here for figure data

A risk for emerging markets whose corporate sectors are leveraged internationally is sharp reversal of capital flows, which may confront them with an unfavorable combination of interest rate, rollover, and currency risks. Most of the heavy corporate leveraging in regional economies is domestic, however, which considerably mutes exposure to external shocks (Figure 1.3.10). Nevertheless, domestic factors can also heighten risk in these economies. As discussed in Box 1.3.1, any severe disruption to economic growth and earnings in the PRC, for example, could see the nonperforming loan ratio surge, asset prices collapse, and the government stuck with the toxic assets of unsustainable local investment platforms, SOEs, and failing corporations (Chivakul and Lam 2015).

Highly leveraged households constitute a further risk in economies where debt has risen rapidly. Ratios of household debt to GDP in Malaysia and Thailand exceeded 70% in the first quarter of this year, and the ratio in the PRC has more than doubled since 2008 to 40% (IIF 2016). When measured against personal disposable income, household debt in a number of regional economies was in 2014 already at least as high as it was in the US in 2007 when the subprime mortgage crisis hit (Deloitte 2015). Still, elevated household debt is not likely to set off a severe crisis in Asia as long as interest and unemployment rates are low. Such is the case of the Republic of Korea, whose households have long been the most leveraged in the region. Moreover, the country's banking sector is resilient, profitable, and well capitalized, as are those of the other economies in the region where household debt has been on the rise.

Monitoring and reporting fiscal risk

Even though Asian debt appears to be manageable on the whole, there is little room for complacency. Policy makers should closely monitor fiscal risks, and the more vulnerable economies in the region would do well to follow advice from the International Monetary Fund that the time is ripe to ensure that their medium-term debt management strategies are effective and transparent enough to reassure investors and mitigate market instability (IMF 2016b). Moreover, further scope exists in most countries to improve reporting on the state of public finances to facilitate effective and timely risk analysis. Such improvements range from explicit budgeting of local government financing vehicles to quantifying the risk of natural disasters and contingent liabilities in countries' fiscal risk statements. In this regard, the International Monetary Fund emphasizes following up on risk analyses with mitigation policies such as curbing exposure to SOE liability or strengthening firewalls to limit spillover across economic sectors.

1.3.9 Household debt/GDP, selected Asian economies

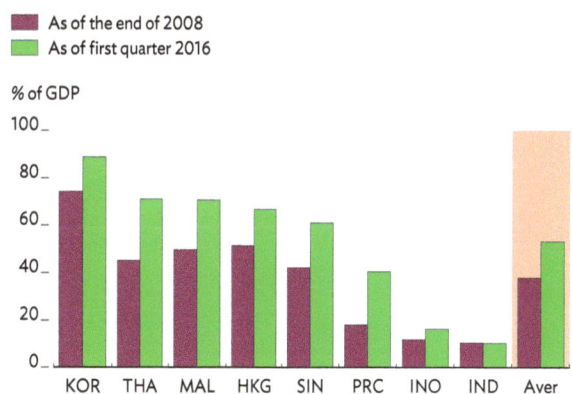

As of the end of 2008
As of first quarter 2016

Aver = simple average of the Asia sample, HKG = Hong Kong, China, IND = India, INO = Indonesia, KOR = Republic of Korea, MAL = Malaysia, PRC = People's Republic of China, SIN = Singapore, THA = Thailand.
Source: IIF 2016.
Click here for figure data

1.3.10 Nonfinancial corporate debt/GDP, selected Asian economies

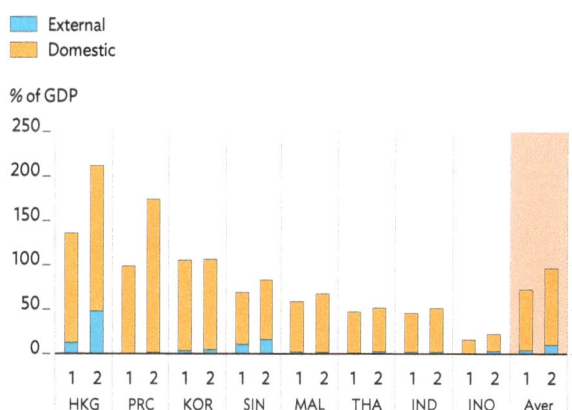

External
Domestic

1 = 2008, 2 = First quarter of 2016.

Aver = simple average of the Asia sample, HKG = Hong Kong, China, IND = India, INO = Indonesia, KOR = Republic of Korea, MAL = Malaysia, PRC = People's Republic of China, SIN = Singapore, THA = Thailand.
Sources: IIF 2016; Locational Banking Statistics database and Debt Securities database, Bank for International Settlements; ADB estimates.
Click here for figure data

References

Abiad, A., M. Lee, M. Pundit, and A. Ramayandi. 2016. Moderating Growth and Structural Change in the People's Republic of China: Implications for Developing Asia and Beyond. *ADB Briefs* No. 53. Asian Development Bank.

Briere, M., B. Ferrarini, and A. Ramayandi. 2016. Contingent Claims Analysis of Sovereign Debt Sustainability in Asian Emerging Markets. *ADB Economics Working Paper Series* No. 486. Asian Development Bank.

Chivakul, M. and W. R. Lam. 2015. Assessing China's Corporate Sector Vulnerabilities. *IMF Working Paper* 15/72. International Monetary Fund.

Coleman, G., I. Kalish, D. Konigsburg, and S. Xu. 2014. *Competitiveness: Catching the Next Wave China*. Deloitte Touche Tohmatsu. September.

Constantinescu, C., A. Mattoo, and M. Ruta. 2015. The Global Trade Slowdown: Cyclical or Structural? *IMF Working Paper* No. 15/6. International Monetary Fund.

_____. 2016. *Global Trade Watch: Trade Developments in 2015*. World Bank.

Deloitte. 2015. Prudent No More. *Asia Pacific Economic Outlook Q3 2015*. http://dupress.com/articles/asia-household-debt-levels/

Ferrarini, B. and A. Ramayandi. 2015. Public Debt Sustainability in Developing Asia: An Update. *ADB Economics Working Paper Series* No. 468. Asian Development Bank.

Ferrarini, B., J. Greene, and M. Hinojales. Forthcoming. Debt Sustainability Analysis for Oil Exporters with Sovereign Wealth Funds—A Case Study of Azerbaijan. *ADB Working Paper Series*. Asian Development Bank.

Freund, C. 2016. The Global Trade Slowdown and Secular Stagnation. *Trade and Investment Policy Watch* 20 April. Peterson Institute for International Economics. https://piie.com/blogs/trade-investment-policy-watch/global-trade-slowdown-and-secular-stagnation

Gray, D., C. H. Lim, E. Loukoianova, and S. Malone. 2008. A Risk-Based Debt Sustainability Framework: Incorporating Balance Sheets and Uncertainty. *IMF Working Paper* WP/08/40. International Monetary Fund.

Hoekman, B. 2015. *The Global Trade Slowdown: A New Normal?* Center for Economic Policy Research.

IIF. 2016. *EM Debt Monitor*. Institute of International Finance. March.

IMF. 2016a. *World Economic Outlook*. International Monetary Fund.

_____. 2016b. *Fiscal Monitor—Acting Now, Acting Together*. International Monetary Fund. April.

_____. 2016c. People's Republic of China: 2016 Article IV Consultation Staff Report. *International Monetary Fund Country Report* No. 16/270. International Monetary Fund.

Jinjarak, Y. and G. Wignaraja. 2016. An Empirical Assessment of the Export-Financial Constraint Relationship: How Different are Small and Medium Enterprises? *World Development* (79).

Mitchell, T. 2016. China's Debt Shrinking Machine Loses its Magical Power. *The Financial Times* (online). 26 April.

Moody's Investors Service. 2016a. Government of China: Sovereign Exposed to Sizeable, Rising Contingent Liabilities. *Inside China.* 25 July.

_____. 2016b. China Credit: Authorities Have Tools to Avert Financial Crisis, but Erosion of Credit Quality Likely. *Inside China.* 25 July.

S&P Global Ratings. 2016. China Bad Debt Data May Understate Banking Risk. *Finance Asia.* 28 July.

Wignaraja, G. 2015. Factors Affecting Entry into Supply Chain Trade: An Analysis of Firms in Southeast Asia. *Asia and the Pacific Policy Studies* 2(3).

Annex: Global growth falters

Growth in the major industrial economies fell short of expectations. Together, the United States (US), the euro area, and Japan are forecast to expand by 1.4% in 2016, down from the 1.9% recorded in 2015 and 0.4 percentage points lower than the *ADO 2016* projection (Table A1.1). Revised GDP series for the US show a weak start in the first half of the year. Although the euro area has so far shrugged off the blow from the United Kingdom (UK) referendum to leave the European Union, the result of the vote has heightened uncertainty about that region's prospects. Japan continues its modest expansion, but the slow pace has led the government to alter its plans for medium-term fiscal consolidation. The forecast growth pickup in the advanced economies in 2017 is also downgraded by 0.1 percentage points to 1.8% as more rapid recovery remains elusive.

Oil and food prices have picked up faster than expected in *ADO 2016*. Yet even as commodity prices bounce back, inflation in the advanced economies remains subdued, allowing accommodative monetary stances to continue. The US Federal reserve has delayed further interest rate increases to no earlier than the end of 2016. Meanwhile, monetary authorities in the euro area and Japan may well extend and expand their quantitative easing programs.

A1.1 Baseline assumptions on the international economy

	2014	2015	2016		2017	
	Actual		*ADO 2016*	*Update*	*ADO 2016*	*Update*
GDP growth (%)						
Major industrial economies[a]	1.5	1.9	1.8	1.4	1.9	1.8
United States	2.4	2.6	2.3	1.5	2.5	2.4
Euro area	0.9	1.6	1.5	1.5	1.7	1.4
Japan	−0.1	0.6	0.6	0.6	0.3	0.8
Prices and inflation						
Brent crude spot prices (average, $ per barrel)	98.9	52.4	38.0	43.0	45.0	50.0
Food index (2010 = 100, % change)	−7.2	−15.4	−1.0	2.0	1.0	2.0
Consumer price index inflation (major industrial economies' average, %)	1.3	0.2	1.1	0.8	2.0	1.7
Interest rates						
United States federal funds rate (average, %)	0.1	0.1	0.6	0.4	1.4	1.0
European Central Bank refinancing rate (average, %)	0.2	0.1	0.0	0.0	0.0	0.0
Bank of Japan overnight call rate (average, %)	0.1	0.1	0.0	0.0	0.0	0.0
$ Libor[b] (%)	0.2	0.2	0.6	0.4	1.4	1.0

ADO = *Asian Development Outlook*, GDP = gross domestic product.

[a] Average growth rates are weighted by gross national income, Atlas method.

[b] Average London interbank offered rate quotations on 1-month loans.

Sources: US Department of Commerce, Bureau of Economic Analysis, http://www.bea.gov; Eurostat, http://ec.europa.eu/eurostat; Economic and Social Research Institute of Japan, http://www.esri.cao.go.jp; Consensus Forecasts; Bloomberg; CEIC Data Company; Haver Analytics; and the World Bank, Global Commodity Markets, http://www.worldbank.org; ADB estimates.

Recent developments in the major industrial economies

United States

US economic activity was off to a weak start in the first half of 2016. Growth remained soft in the second quarter, recording a seasonally adjusted annualized rate (saar) of 1.1% as private investment and government spending fell (Figure A1.1). Growth in the second quarter came mainly from private consumption, which contributed 3.0 percentage points to growth, up by 2.0 percentage points from the first quarter. This increase outweighed a 1.7 percentage point fall in private investment. Trade remained weakened by the unfavorable implications of a strong dollar and feeble global growth. A slight positive contribution from net exports to growth compensated for the 0.3 percentage point subtraction by government spending.

As the main pillar of growth, private consumption grew at a solid 4.4% saar, despite some weakening of consumer confidence from the first quarter to the second. The April–June average of the consumer confidence index (2007 = 100) was 91.8, versus a 92.8 average in the first quarter. The index started to rebound toward the end of the second quarter, however, and has continued to strengthen since then, returning to an 11-month high of 97.8 in August. This suggests a trend toward higher consumer confidence that will support even stronger consumption growth in the third quarter.

Investment continued to decline in the first half of 2016, with contraction averaging 6.5% saar in contrast with 5.4% expansion in the same period of 2015. Industrial production and purchasing managers' indexes tended to be weaker than the 2015 average, but their readings still suggest that production is expanding, albeit only moderately (Figure A1.2). The trends in these indexes suggest that US economic recovery will continue to be gradual.

Employment growth recovered in June to August. After a rise of 24,000 nonfarm jobs reported in May, the weakest gain in more than 5 years, more than 270,000 were added in both June and July, then 151,000 in August. The low May figure now appears to have been a deviation reflecting a strike at Verizon telecom. Despite the rebound in employment, the unemployment rate nudged back up to 4.9% after reaching a low of 4.7% in May. This is not worrying, however, as it mainly reflects increased participation in the labor force. The average length of unemployment in the first 8 months of 2016 shortened to 28.0 weeks from 29.9 weeks in the same period last year, and average earnings continue to rise gradually as slack in the labor market is slowly taken up.

The strong US dollar helped keep headline inflation low at 1.0% in June and 0.8% in July. However, core inflation has been rising faster, hovering above 2.0% in the first half of 2016

A1.1 Demand-side contributions to growth, United States

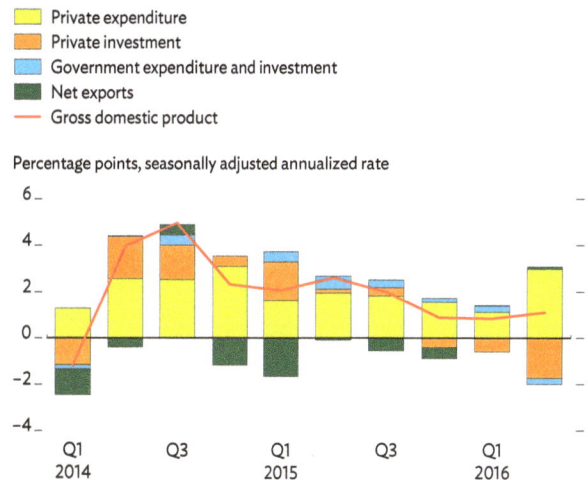

- ▮ Private expenditure
- ▮ Private investment
- ▮ Government expenditure and investment
- ▮ Net exports
- — Gross domestic product

Percentage points, seasonally adjusted annualized rate

Q = quarter.
Sources: US Department of Commerce. Bureau of Economic Analysis. http://www.bea.gov; Haver Analytics (both accessed 2 September 2016).
Click here for figure data

A1.2 Business activity and consumer confidence indicators, United States

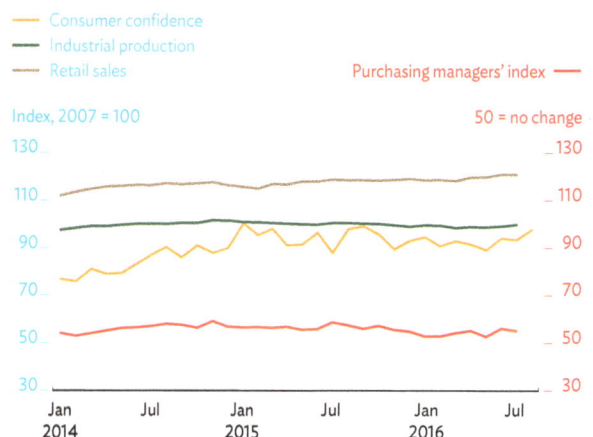

- — Consumer confidence
- — Industrial production
- — Retail sales
- — Purchasing managers' index

Index, 2007 = 100   50 = no change

Note: For the purchasing managers' index, a reading below 50 signals deterioration of activity, above 50 improvement. The index is compiled by the Institute for Supply Management.
Source: Haver Analytics (accessed 2 September 2016).
Click here for figure data

(Figure A1.3). Together with the slow expansion in the first half, low headline inflation may cause the US Federal Reserve to remain cautious about timing its tightening of monetary policy. The Fed is keeping the interest rate unchanged at the end of the third quarter but noting a strengthening case for gradual future rate hikes. As a result, the continuing low-interest environment should keep supporting credit expansion that should in turn promote growth.

Earlier in the year, the authorities announced that GDP expanded by 1.1% saar in the first quarter. However, technical revisions to the GDP series in July reset growth in the fourth quarter of 2015 from 1.4% to 0.9% and in the first quarter of 2016 from 1.1% to 0.8%, leaving the economy growing at a 1.0% saar in the first half of 2016. Strength in the recent labor report suggests a growth rebound in the second half of 2016. Nevertheless, slow growth in the first half of the year suggests a downward revision for the US growth projection in 2016 to 1.5% from 2.3% in ADO 2016. The 2017 growth rate is projected to be slightly lower than forecast, at 2.4%.

Euro area

The euro area started the year with GDP growing in the first quarter at a strong 2.1% saar, reflecting firm domestic demand. However, the weaker 1.2% expansion in the second quarter suggests that the region is still struggling to establish its recovery (Figure A1.4). While softer in the second quarter, domestic demand continued to benefit from low oil prices, accommodative monetary policy, and rising employment. The external sector provided much-needed support to growth, as drag in total investment more than offset positive contributions from private and government consumption. Exports grew faster than since the second quarter of 2015, and, with imports limited by weak domestic demand, net exports contributed 1.5 percentage points to growth. Performance varied across the major economies. In the second quarter, growth was highest in Spain at 3.3%, followed by the Netherlands at 2.5%, with both improving on their first quarter growth. Germany weakened but still beat market expectations with growth at 1.7%, mainly because of higher net exports. Greece managed to reverse its contraction in the first quarter, though expansion was only by 0.7%. Italy stagnated, however, and France contracted by 0.2% as domestic demand stalled across the board.

Retail sales contracted in June after recovering somewhat in April and May, suggesting that consumer confidence was still subdued (Figure A1.5). Industrial production rebounded in June but not enough to offset contraction in May. The average composite purchasing managers' index for the second quarter was 53.1, slightly below the previous quarter's average, suggesting that investment remains weak. And while market confidence was generally optimistic entering the second quarter,

A1.3 Inflation, United States

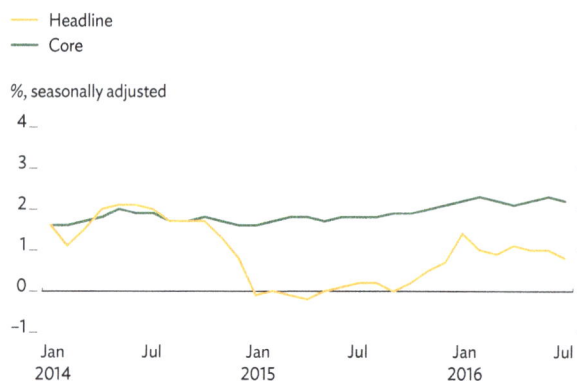

— Headline
— Core

%, seasonally adjusted

Source: Haver Analytics (accessed 2 September 2016).
Click here for figure data

A1.4 Demand-side contributions to growth, euro area

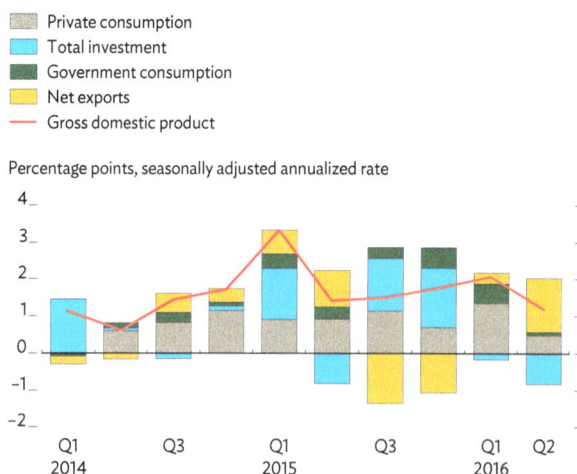

▦ Private consumption
▦ Total investment
▦ Government consumption
▦ Net exports
— Gross domestic product

Percentage points, seasonally adjusted annualized rate

Q = quarter.
Source: Haver Analytics (accessed 2 September 2016).
Click here for figure data

indicators of economic sentiment and consumer confidence both deteriorated in June, most likely because of heightened uncertainty approaching the 23 June Brexit referendum in the UK.

The European Central Bank decided to leave interest rates unchanged at its August meeting. The current size of its quantitative easing program also remained unchanged, including its scheduled run to the end of March 2017. In September, central bank bond purchases under the program exceeded €1 trillion. Inflation came in at an encouraging 0.1% in June, the first positive reading since January. It rose to 0.2% in July and August as energy price deflation continued to ease. However, market inflation expectations remain well below the central bank target of 2% amid persistent downward pressures on inflation, including muted producer prices. Some base effects could come into play later this year, nudging prices higher.

The composite purchasing managers' index continued to improve from June despite the surprise referendum result for Brexit, providing a positive sign for expansion in the third quarter notwithstanding a worsening in economic sentiment in August (Figure A1.6). The seasonally adjusted unemployment rate in July— stable at 10.1% since April—was also the lowest since 2011. This bodes well for consumption, and retail sales recovered strongly in July. However, the boost to growth from low oil prices and the weak euro experienced early in the year is fading. Moreover, the uncertainty introduced by the Brexit vote heightens downside risks.

Weighing the various developments, the *ADO 2016* forecast for GDP growth this year is maintained at 1.5%, with growth expected to be steady in the second half in view of supportive fiscal and monetary policies. However, a slight slowing in growth is likely in 2017 as the impact of the pending UK exit from the European Union (EU) will be felt more fully across the EU, through both direct trade channels and indirect financial channels. Domestic demand is likely to suffer in a prolonged period of separation negotiations and heightened political and economic uncertainty across the euro area, which will come on top of a fragile global economy and jittery financial markets. Altogether, these headwinds should limit GDP growth to 1.4% in 2017.

Risks to the forecast now tilt further to the downside. Uncertainty about the modality and timing of the UK separation from the EU adds to other risks already weighing on economic sentiment, such as the unresolved migration and Greek crises. Any protracted slowdown in the UK economy would weaken the euro area's export performance. In addition, firms may take a wait-and-see approach, delaying new investment or hiring decisions. Finally, any major setback during UK–EU negotiations could unsettle financial markets and possibly weaken asset prices, which could lead in turn to lower capital spending, fewer job prospects, and weaker growth.

A1.5 Selected economic indicators, euro area

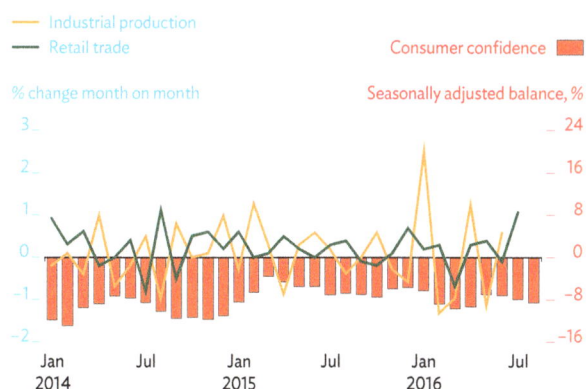

Source: Haver Analytics (accessed 2 September 2016).
Click here for figure data

A1.6 Economic sentiment and purchasing managers' indexes, euro area

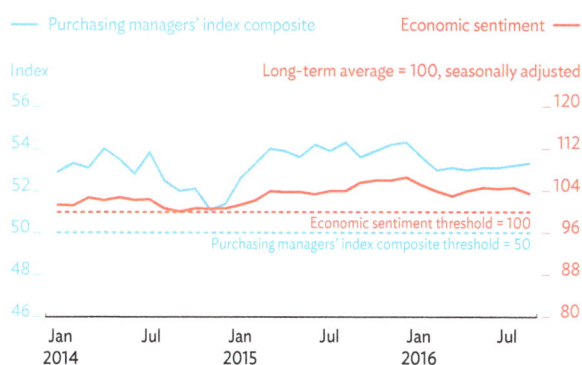

Sources: Bloomberg and Haver Analytics (both accessed 2 September 2016).
Click here for figure data

Japan

Japan's economy grew by 0.8% saar in the first half of 2016, in line with expectations. Domestic consumption and investment were the main growth drivers (Figure A1.7). Private consumption contributed 0.4 percentage points to expansion, supported by higher demand for durable goods and the leap year effect that comes with an additional day in February. Home investments contributed 0.1 percentage points as new residential buildings were built in anticipation of purchases to beat the hike in the value-added tax (VAT) originally scheduled for 2017. With the fast pace of expansion in the implementation of supplemental budgets of 2015, public consumption added 0.5 percentage points to growth in the first half of 2016. The drivers of growth during the first half of 2016 now appear temporary, especially as the VAT hike has been rescheduled to October 2019, and are less likely to continue into the second half of 2016.

Meanwhile, contraction in private nonresidential investment dragged on growth in the first half of the year. Weakness in the global economy, particularly in Japan's main trading partner, the People's Republic of China, helps explain caution in business investment, as does the sharp appreciation of the Japanese yen, which slashed the corporate revenues of exporters. Both exports and imports shrank in the first half of 2016 in real terms, with net exports shaving growth in the first half of the year (Figure A1.8). As external demand remains weak, these trends are expected to continue.

Forward-looking indicators suggest that the real sector will remain weak in the near term. The purchasing managers' index fell below 50 in March, indicating contraction, and the Tankan survey of business conditions has continued to slow since the fourth quarter of 2015. Consumer confidence has not shown a clear downward trend, but it stagnated at a low 41.0 in the second quarter of 2016 because of dim income prospects. Consumer confidence in the employment situation has also fallen since the second quarter of last year.

After the effects of the April 2014 VAT hike dissipated last year, headline consumer price inflation turned negative in the first half of this year, falling just below zero because of weak underlying domestic demand (Figure A1.9). The Bank of Japan, the central bank, estimates that energy prices subtracted 0.6 percentage points from core consumer inflation. Headline inflation is projected to remain just above zero in FY2016 (ending 31 March 2017). This trend is expected to dissipate in 2017, and inflation should return as global oil prices gradually recover. The GDP deflator has also been trending down, but it remained positive, averaging 2.0% in 2015, and it is expected to average about 1.0% in 2016.

The central bank continued to respond with measures to offset prevailing weakness in the economy. Its already accommodative policy, including purchases of Japanese government bonds, was augmented with negative interest

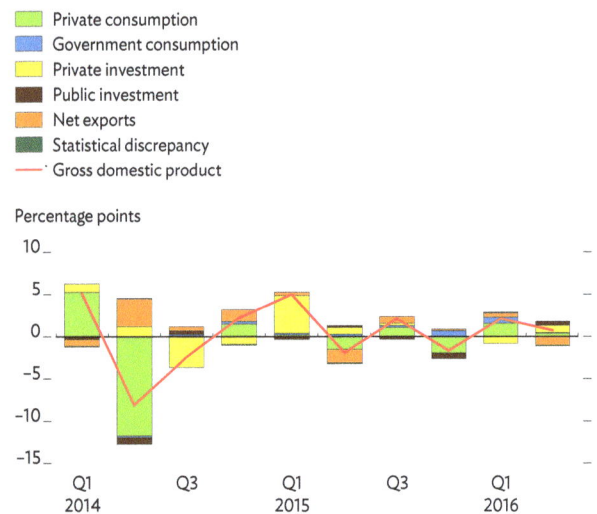

A1.7 Demand-side contributions to growth, Japan

- Private consumption
- Government consumption
- Private investment
- Public investment
- Net exports
- Statistical discrepancy
- Gross domestic product

Percentage points

Q = quarter.
Source: Haver Analytics (accessed 8 September 2016).
Click here for figure data

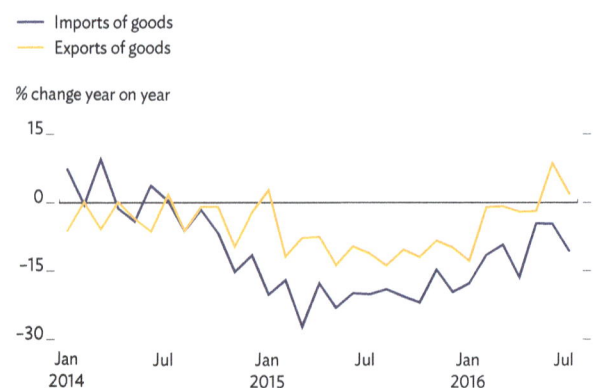

A1.8 Merchandise exports and imports, Japan

- Imports of goods
- Exports of goods

% change year on year

Source: Haver Analytics (accessed 8 September 2016).
Click here for figure data

rates introduced in January 2016 and higher purchases of exchange-traded funds in July. As worsening uncertainty and volatility have dampened investment confidence, the government approved in August a fiscal stimulus package worth ¥13.5 trillion, of which ¥4.6 trillion, roughly 1% of GDP, is additional government spending for FY2016.

With the VAT hike previously scheduled for 2017 now postponed to October 2019, accelerated purchases of durable goods and housing are no longer expected in the second half of 2016. The higher yen is another heavy burden on Japan's prospects, clouding business sentiment through reduced corporate profits for exporters. The recently approved fiscal stimulus is expected to boost domestic demand to a degree later this year and in 2017, while external demand is expected to improve in 2017 but only gradually.

As private consumption and external demand remain modest, the economy continues to operate below potential output, with the cabinet office estimating the shortfall equal to 1.1% of GDP at the end of the first quarter of 2016. Taking the various factors into account, Japan's growth outlook for 2016 is maintained at the 0.6% projected in March but for 2017 is revised up to 0.8% from the previously forecast 0.3%, as no VAT increase will dampen private consumption.

Australia and New Zealand

The Australian economy is expected to grow moderately in 2016 and 2017. In the second quarter of 2016, the economy expanded by 2.1% saar, slower than the 4.3% recorded in the previous quarter (Figure A1.10). Consumption is the main driver of growth, contributing 2.2 percentage points as net exports subtracted 0.9 percentage points and fixed capital formation contributed almost nothing. Seasonally adjusted retail sales were stagnant in July 2016, falling to virtually zero growth from 0.1% growth in June. Consumer sentiment returned to positive territory in August 2016, rising to 101.0 points from 99.1 in July. The seasonally adjusted unemployment rate declined marginally to 5.7% in July from 5.8% in the previous month. The Australian Industry Group's performance of manufacturing index, for which 50 is the threshold for growth, decreased to 46.9 in August from 56.4 in July, lower than the 53.7 average in the first 7 months of 2016 and indicating contraction in manufacturing. Inflation was a seasonally adjusted 1.0% in the second quarter of 2016, below the previous quarter's 1.3% and less than the target of 2.0%–3.0% set by the Reserve Bank of Australia, the central bank. At its 2 August 2016 meeting, the central bank cut its policy rate from 1.75% to an all-time low of 1.50%.

With risks to the outlook from falling investment and inadequate improvement in the labor market, panelists for the FocusEconomics Consensus Forecast predict GDP to grow by 2.8% in both 2016 and 2017, above the estimated 2.5% in 2015.

A1.9 Inflation, GDP deflator, and real effective exchange rate, Japan

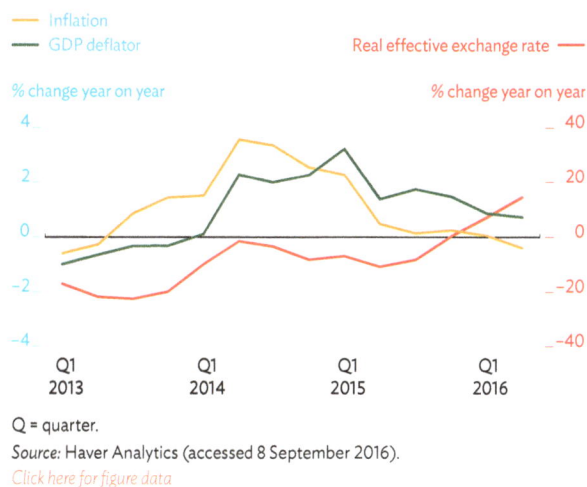

Q = quarter.
Source: Haver Analytics (accessed 8 September 2016).
Click here for figure data

A1.10 Demand-side contributions to growth, Australia

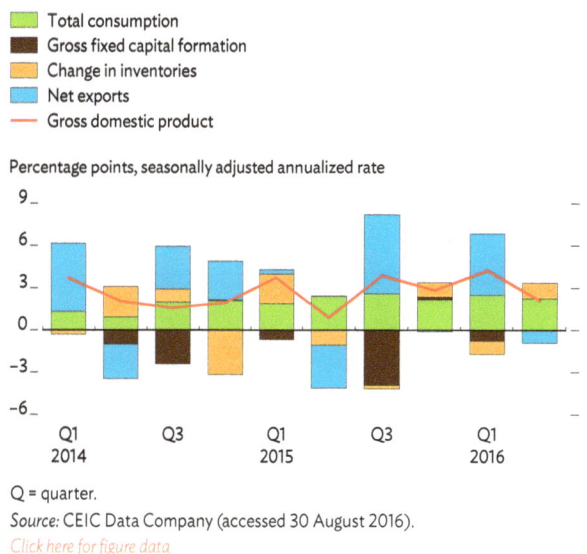

Q = quarter.
Source: CEIC Data Company (accessed 30 August 2016).
Click here for figure data

New Zealand's growth slowed from 3.1% saar in the fourth quarter of 2015 to 1.9% in the first quarter of 2016, with net exports reducing growth by 1.5 percentage points and change in inventories by 1.3 points (Figure A1.11). Consumption bolstered growth, adding 1.4 percentage points, as did fixed capital, adding 2.3 points. In the second quarter, retail sales rose by 5.5%, better than the previous quarter's 4.8%. The index of manufacturing performance dropped to 55.8 in July from 57.6 in June, remaining above the threshold at 50 that indicates expansion. The business confidence index fell to 15.5 in August from 16.0 in July—still better than the 3.2 in March that was the lowest so far in 2016. Consumer confidence stayed above 100, though it declined by 3.6 points to 106.0 in the second quarter. Inflation stayed far below the target range of 1.0%–3.0% set by the Reserve Bank of New Zealand, the central bank, stabilizing at 0.4% in the first and second quarters of 2016, up from 0.1% in the last quarter of 2015. The seasonally adjusted unemployment rate declined marginally to 5.1% in the second quarter from 5.2% of the previous quarter.

FocusEconomics Consensus Forecast panelists project GDP growth in 2016 and 2017 to increase slightly to 2.6% from 2.5% in 2015. Downside risks to the outlook are weakness in key sectors and threats to the country's financial system.

Commodity prices

Commodity prices are showing an uptick this year but remain subdued. Developments in the global economic and political arena, as well as supply disruptions, caused wide fluctuations in oil prices, but they remain low because of high oil inventories. Food prices reversed their more than 3-year slide in the second quarter of 2016, but favorable supply conditions and low oil prices are tempering inflationary pressures.

Oil price movements and prospects

The price of Brent crude reached a multiyear low in late January of this year before breaking out of its long-term trend to exceed $50/barrel in the first week of June, finally averaging $48/barrel that month (Figure A1.12). The climb in the monthly average price of Brent crude continued for 5 straight months, the longest such stretch since June 2014.

Several factors exerted upward pressure on crude oil prices: improving economic data and related indicators showing growth in global oil demand accelerating, the onset of the summer driving season in North America, ongoing declines in rig count and crude oil production in the US, and worsening oil supply outages. At the same time, the strengthening of the dollar and the failure again of the Organization of the Petroleum Exporting Countries (OPEC) to agree on a production ceiling in June hampered further price increases. After easing in July, oil markets rallied more than

A1.11 Demand-side contributions to growth, New Zealand

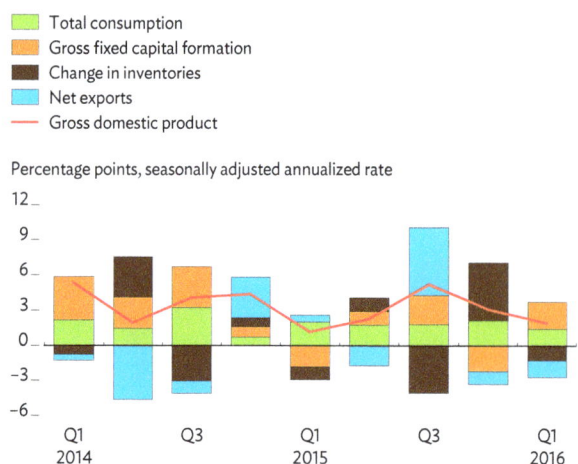

Q = quarter.
Source: CEIC Data Company (accessed 30 August 2016).
Click here for figure data

A1.12 Price of Brent crude

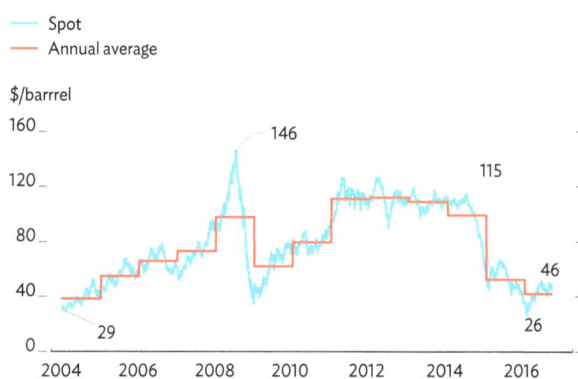

Sources: Bloomberg; World Bank. Commodity Price Data (Pink Sheet). http://www.worldbank.org (both accessed 15 September 2016).
Click here for figure data

20% in August on news that major oil producers had formed a consensus to cut production, though no formal agreement was reached. Oil prices ended August at $46/barrel, little changed from a year earlier.

In its August 2016 report, the International Energy Agency reported global oil demand to have risen by 1.5 million barrels per day (mbd) in the first half of 2016 over the same period of 2015 in response to low oil prices and improving economic conditions. The agency forecasts that global oil demand will increase by 1.4 mbd in 2016 and 1.2 mbd in 2017, mostly outside the Organisation for Economic Co-operation and Development (OECD). Oil consumption outside of the OECD grew by 1.2 mbd in 2015 and is projected to rise by almost as much in 2016 and in 2017. India and the PRC are expected to be the largest contributors to oil demand growth outside of the OECD, accounting for more than 40% of the forecast increase in 2016 and 2017.

Global oil supplies were 0.4 mbd higher in the first half of 2016 than a year earlier, with OPEC growth at 1.1 mbd as Saudi Arabia and others continued to ramp up production that more than offset a 0.7 mbd decline in other production. OPEC crude production held steady in July to average an all-time high of 33.4 mbd. Iraq, though still beset by internal conflicts, achieved production highs of 4.3 mbd. Iranian production has been constant since May at about 3.6 mbd, now appearing to be back at capacity following the lifting of sanctions in January. However, total non-OPEC production was down from the previous year as production declined year on year in Canada, the PRC, Mexico, and the US. The International Energy Agency forecasts non-OPEC supply to decline by 0.9 mbd in 2016 (with US oil production expected to fall the most) before recovering by 0.3 mbd in 2017.

Oil prices will remain volatile ahead of the informal OPEC meeting in Algeria in late September. Recent supply disruptions in Canada, Libya, and Nigeria—and lingering expectations that demand is catching up with supply—are exerting upward pressure on prices. However, a huge global oil inventory buildup is constraining them. Futures prices suggest Brent crude will trade within the narrow range of $45–$47/barrel for the remainder of 2016 (Figure A1.13), up from an average price to 15 September of $41.90/barrel. Moving into 2017, the oil market faces several uncertainties including the possibility of a joint oil production freeze. Barring additional major supply disruptions, the price of Brent crude is forecast to average $43/barrel in 2016 before recovering to $50/barrel in 2017.

A1.13 Brent crude futures and spot price

— Average spot price
--- 2 September 2015
--- 4 March 2016
--- 2 September 2016

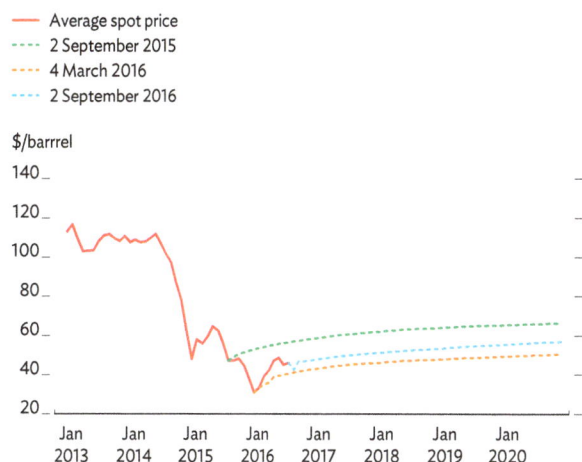

$/barrrel

Source: Bloomberg (accessed 5 September 2016).
Click here for figure data

Food price movements and prospects

The food price index has continued to climb, rising by 7.8% in August from a year earlier (Figure A1.14). This is the fourth consecutive month that the food price index recorded positive growth year on year. Indexes for edible oils and other food were both higher than a year earlier. The edible oils index rose by 14.6% in August, mainly on price rallies for palm oil and soybeans. A palm oil shortage in Asia because of El Niño weather issues raised demand for soybean oil and meal.

The "other food" index rose by 10.8% year on year as banana, orange, and sugar prices strengthened. El Niño has cut production and raised prices for bananas and oranges, while sugar prices have been on the rise since March 2016. Apart from these commodities, favorable supply conditions have pushed most grain prices down, with the largest declines for barley at 31.9%, wheat at 16.7%, and maize at 7.4%. By contrast, benchmark rice prices rose by 11.3% year on year on dwindling supply.

The US Department of Agriculture maintained its positive world agricultural outlook and raised its forecast for global grain production during the 2016/17 crop year by 30 million tons in its August assessment from its July assessment of 2.52 billion tons. Global wheat production is expected to reach record highs because of excellent conditions in Australia, Canada, Kazakhstan, the Russian Federation, and Ukraine. Higher production is also expected for maize because of high planted area and yields in Argentina, India, Mexico, and the US, which will more than offset reductions in Canada and the EU. Forecast rice production, though slightly lower than in the July assessment, is still anticipated to be higher than in the previous year, at 481.1 million tons. Because of projected increases in production and high stock carryover, the stock-to-use ratio will rise slightly despite a projected increase in global grain consumption.

Prospects for edible oil and oilseeds are positive, as soybeans and palm oil production are forecast to recover from last season's decline under El Niño. Soybean production is projected to rise by 5.7%, with increases in Brazil and the US offsetting reductions in India and Ukraine. Palm oil production is also up on high yields in Indonesia and Malaysia. Production forecasts for red meat and poultry in 2017 have been raised on lower projections for feed prices. However, world consumption of sugar will continue to exceed production, reducing stocks to their lowest since 2010/11 and exerting upward pressure on sugar prices.

Although El Niño ended last May, some of its effects are still manifested in somewhat higher commodity prices. Most climate models predict that any effects from La Niña later this year will be weak. In view of well-supplied markets for most grains, oilseeds, edible oils, and other food commodities, as well as continued low oil prices, food prices are expected to increase by only 2% in 2016 and a further 2% in 2017.

External environment in sum

As growth in the major industrial economies falters, developing Asia can anticipate continued weak demand for its exports. However, no return to recession is expected in the advanced economies. The pickup in commodities prices should provide some relief for commodity exporters. Moreover, the moderate rate of price recovery for these goods is unlikely to excite the low inflation prevailing in the region. Taking this with the accommodative monetary policies pursued by monetary authorities in the US, the euro area, and Japan, central bankers in most developing Asian economies will feel little pressure to tighten their monetary policies.

A1.14 Food commodity price indexes

— Food
— Edible oils
— Grains
— Other food

2010 = 100

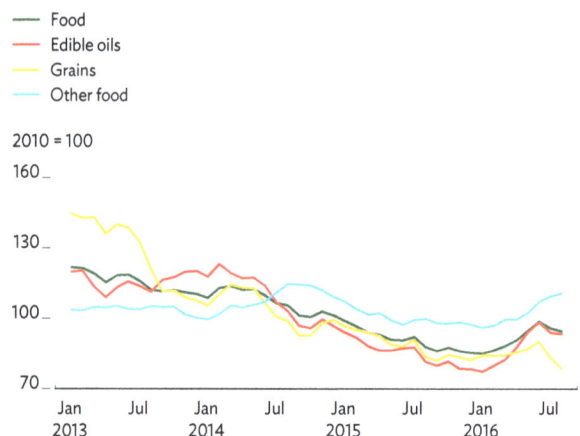

Source: World Bank. Commodity Price Data (Pink Sheet). http://www.worldbank.org (accessed 5 September 2016).
Click here for figure data

2

MEETING THE LOW-CARBON GROWTH CHALLENGE

Meeting the low-carbon growth challenge

Developing Asia has a critical role to play ushering in a new era of sustainable development. The region is both highly exposed to the risks of climate change and able to contribute to mitigating them. With its greenhouse gas (GHG) emissions, especially carbon dioxide, growing more rapidly than in any other region, developing Asia has a stake in the global climate change agenda that has never been larger or more significant (Figure 2.1.1). Climate-related natural disasters are expected to proliferate as the earth gets warmer. Rising risk and vulnerability will dampen economic growth in the region with significant impact on water resources, agriculture, fisheries, health, and tourism, threatening to exacerbate inequality and roll back years of development gains.

To date, 41 governments in developing Asia have submitted intended emissions reductions to the 2015 Paris Agreement on climate change, the first climate treaty that brings together emissions-reduction goals from developed and developing countries alike. The goal of the Paris Agreement is to limit the rise in global mean surface temperature to less than 2 degrees Celsius (°C) above pre-industrial levels (if possible, to less than 1.5°C higher). The treaty has wide-ranging consequences for development policy worldwide and will shape growth and investment decisions over the next 20 years. If implemented as planned, the agreement will put the global economy on course toward more sustainable growth and reduce the impacts of climate change on the poorest and most vulnerable populations.

Developing Asia is at a crossroads. By choosing to pursue low-carbon growth now, governments in the region can avoid getting locked into carbon-intensive infrastructure that will be costlier to change later. They will also bring forward the benefits of climate action in terms of reducing the human and ecological costs of growth dependent on fossil fuels. In light of the risks posed by uncontrolled climate change, developing Asia has much to gain from leading the transition to low-carbon development.

2.1.1 Average annual growth rate of greenhouse gas emissions, 1990–2012

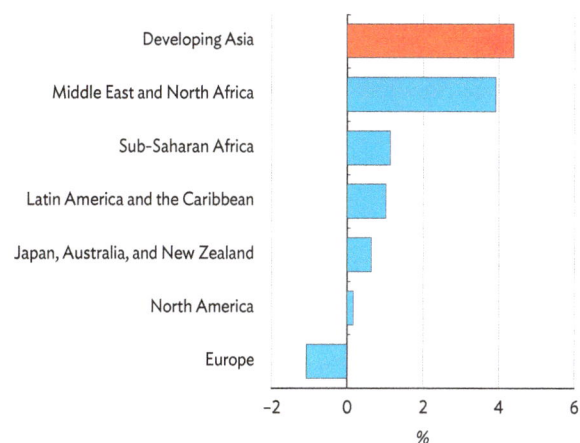

Source: CAIT Climate Data Explorer. 2015. World Resources Institute. http://cait.wri.org (accessed 3 August 2016).
Click here for figure data

This chapter was written by Shikha Jha, Minsoo Lee, and David Anthony Raitzer of the Economic Research and Regional Cooperation Department, ADB, Manila, and Samuel Fankhauser, Alex Kazaglis, and Sugandha Srivastav of Vivid Economics, London, England. It draws on the background papers listed at the end of the chapter. Background materials from Aaron Batten, James Roop, Patrick Safran, Sonia Chand Sandhu, and Ramola Singru are gratefully acknowledged.

Global call to fight climate change

Climate change is unlike most other environmental problems. Its impacts are global in scale, affecting all nations and people with potentially devastating consequences. Unmitigated GHG emissions could in the long term bring about climate regimes absent for millions of years, since a time long before humans arrived and the planet was a very different place. Without urgent action, global mean temperatures could rise by about 4°C by 2100. The last time global average temperatures were that high, 3 million years ago, average sea levels were 20 meters higher (IPCC 2013, Fankhauser and Stern 2016). The recurrence of planetary changes on this scale is uncertain but not impossible.

Some changes can already be observed: Oceans have warmed, polar ice caps have diminished, and sea levels have risen. The world is fast approaching 1.5°C mean warming. Every month of 2016 has been hotter than previously in global terms, beating the record set in 2015. Temperatures in the first 6 months of 2016 were 1.3°C above pre-industrial levels (World Meteorological Organization 2016).

Scientists agree that the long-term risks posed by these trends are unprecedented. As temperatures rise, the risk increases of breaching potentially hazardous environmental tipping points. Most of these abrupt shifts, such as the permanent melting of ice sheets or the thawing of permafrost, are expected only with larger temperature increases and will occur, if ever, only in the future. However, some effects, like the bleaching of coral reefs, could occur with as little temperature rise as 1.5°C–2.0°C (Drijfhout et al. 2015).

In Asia, it is expected that breaching the 2°C threshold will cause more frequent and severe coastal inundation and erosion, wildfires, heavy precipitation, and drought (IPCC 2014). The attribution of individual climate events to man-made emissions is difficult, but scientists are increasingly certain that human-induced climate change has already worsened the risk of weather extremes like floods, storms, and droughts, as well as such upshots as wildfires.

Low-carbon development is the only way forward if the world is serious about achieving growth that is sustainable over the long term. To avert dangerous climate change, global emissions will have to peak within the coming decades.

Asia's severe climate risks

Developing Asia's physical features and socioeconomic conditions leave the region particularly exposed to climate risks. Geographic location and features render some of its societies vulnerable to natural disasters. Populations living in low-lying areas, especially along coasts, will suffer the most. Flooding and cyclones in the Indian Ocean already pose threats to low-lying countries like Bangladesh. Archipelagic countries like the Philippines and others in the Pacific are also vulnerable (Alano and Lee 2016).

The 2016 Global Climate Risk Index ranked 6 developing economies in Asia among the top 10 countries most affected by climate risk from 1995 to 2014 based on frequency, death tolls, and economic losses. In order they are Myanmar, the Philippines, Bangladesh, Viet Nam, Pakistan, and Thailand (Figure 2.1.2). Meanwhile, 8 of the top 10 countries in the 2016 World Risk Index are in the region (ranked in order): Vanuatu, Tonga, the Philippines, Bangladesh, Solomon Islands, Brunei Darussalam, Cambodia, and Papua New Guinea. In the latest United Nations Economic Vulnerability Index, 9 of the 20 most economically vulnerable countries in 2015 were Pacific island states.

The Intergovernmental Panel on Climate Change (IPCC) has predicted a higher incidence of extreme events such as heat waves and more intense tropical cyclones as the global mean temperature rises (IPCC 2014). Extreme weather threatens infrastructure and critical services such as electricity and water supply, overwhelming emergency services and health care facilities.

From 2000 to 2015, disasters such as floods and storms caused losses from damage to property, crops, and livestock totaling $6 billion in Bangladesh and $21 billion in Pakistan (Eskander, Fankhauser, and Jha 2016). Weather-related disasters account for 90% of annual damage from all natural disasters in the Philippines, making it one of the countries most exposed to climate change risks. Annually, an average of 19 typhoons pass close enough to affect the archipelago, the centers of 9 or 10 of which make landfall (Cinco et al. 2016, Anttila-Hughes and Hsiang 2013). Typhoon Haiyan was the strongest typhoon ever to hit the country. Even for a country that is used to being battered by typhoons every year, the devastation was staggering, causing damage and losses estimated to equal 0.9% of GDP (NEDA 2013).

Climate vulnerability is exacerbated by low incomes and insufficient adaptive capacity. Poor infrastructure in the region will leave countries at the mercy of an escalating number of natural disasters brought by climate change. The region's growing population and migration to coastal areas to participate in industrialization and trade will increase the number of people at risk. Countries with low- or lower-middle incomes struggle to meet the daily needs of their growing populations, and low-income households spend a high portion of their incomes on food. They are therefore the most sensitive to weather-related shocks that can make daily staples unaffordable (Hallegatte et al. 2016). Additional adverse consequences are expected where scarcity limits access to such resources as water, energy, and appropriate infrastructure.

Biophysical risk

Climate change threatens freshwater supplies, particularly in large river basins, adding water insecurity to the energy and food insecurity many residents already endure. The IPCC predicts that warmer temperatures, evaporation, and glacial melt will put the region's drylands under

2.1.2 Global Climate Risk Index 2016 list of the 10 most affected countries, 1995–2014

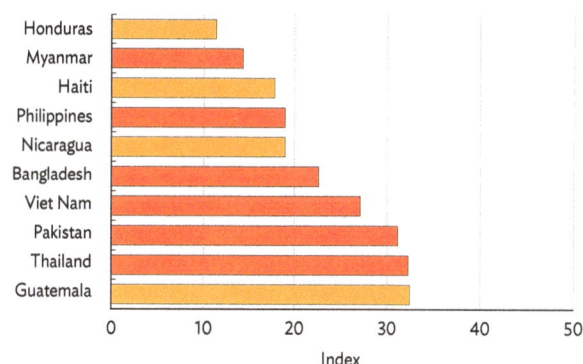

Note: This index is based on the impacts of extreme weather events such as storms, floods, and heat waves over a 20-year period in terms of deaths and GDP losses. A low score indicates high vulnerability and susceptibility but limited coping and adaptive capacity.
Source: Germanwatch. 2016. The Global Climate Risk Index 2016. https://germanwatch.org/fr/download/13503.pdf
Click here for figure data

worsening stress, such that by 2040 or 2050 the water resources available will have decreased by 10%–30% (IPCC 2014).

Submergence, coastal flooding, and coastal erosion are other risks associated with climate change as glaciers melt and sea levels rise. The impact of sea level rise will be devastating for the low-lying islands of the Pacific and densely populated coastal regions of highly vulnerable economies in developing Asia such as Bangladesh, the People's Republic of China (PRC), India, the Maldives, and Viet Nam. Rates of sea level rise in Solomon Islands, for example, over the past 20 years are among the highest globally, averaging 7–10 millimeters per year. The country consists of 1,000 mostly volcanic islands, but that number is shrinking. Rising seas and coast erosion had by 2014 completely submerged 5 of its 20 vegetated reef islands and reduced the land area of another 6 such islands by more than 20% from their 1947 measurements (Albert et al. 2016).

Other natural resources will be similarly affected. Ocean acidification and coral bleaching may cause fish stocks to crash, severely reducing fish catches. Forests will suffer intrusion by exotic species, many of which are pests and disease agents poised to spread into areas where native species have little or no resistance. Meanwhile, fire risks will increase as rainy periods shorten. Ecosystem services essential to crop pollination, water regulation, and maintaining biodiversity balance may fail.

Climate change aggravates health risks from heat waves, vector-borne diseases, and water shortages and contamination. Heat-related mortality will increase, as will the risk of morbidity from diarrhea, dengue fever, and malaria as changes in temperature and rainfall alter the distribution of waterborne illnesses and their vectors. Meanwhile, lower food production will exacerbate undernutrition and its associated health risks, especially in poor areas.

Economic risk

The region depends heavily on climate-sensitive agriculture and land use for livelihoods. In particular, Central Asia relies on scarce water resources that are under threat from climate change. This is critical as the IPCC has predicted that the region will likely go through a cycle of water boom and bust to end up with considerably less seasonal rainfall and more frequent droughts (IPCC 2014). Evidence already shows extreme heat disrupting the growing season in Bangladesh, India, and Pakistan.

Climate change disrupts livelihoods that depend on natural resources, particularly for the poor in highly vulnerable areas (Hijoka et al. 2014). Reduced marine biodiversity poses a challenge to fisheries and their downstream industries. Health risks from climate change will disrupt work and production, placing at risk agricultural productivity in particular. Excessive heat, reduced precipitation, and higher evapotranspiration will desiccate soils, diminishing crop yields and threatening food security. More frequent droughts and floods will cause production losses in cropping systems and livestock rearing, and reduced surface water availability will constrain irrigation coverage. Heat during crop flowering periods may cause sterility and reduced yields. New pest and disease epidemics will arise as climate zones shift.

Sea level rise and the resulting salinity intrusion will degrade land in the highly productive rice deltas of developing Asia. When agriculture is adversely affected and food prices rise, the poor and food insecure suffer most.

Many other sectors are equally dependent on maintaining current climatic conditions. In many Asian economies, tourism is a key driver of economic growth. The sector depends on good weather at often exposed and vulnerable geographical locations and will likely be severely affected by climate change through sea level rise, water stress, and storm surges. The Maldives, for example, relies on marine life and beaches to sustain a tourism industry that contributes over 30% of GDP. A sea level rise of 1 meter would, without further coastal protection, render the island nation nearly completely inundated by about 2085 (Anthoff, Nicholls, and Tol 2010). When Fiji took a direct hit from Cyclone Winston in February 2016, the strongest storm ever to hit the country, tourist cancellations were as high as 25% in the immediate aftermath (ADB 2016).

Social risk

Continual exposure to highly intense climatic events may disrupt social protection programs, hamper capital accumulation, and impede economic growth. These costs will affect long-term development plans unless measures are taken to effectively deal with impacts, both short term and long. As the region grows, the cost of climate-related disasters will increase further as more high-value assets are exposed to risk (World Bank 2013). Slower economic growth arising from climate change will frustrate poverty reduction.

Climate change creates pressures for large-scale migration and displacement of people. Migration is likely to result directly from climate change in two dominant forms: migration associated with real or perceived direct environmental hazards, and migration associated with real or perceived reduction in access to natural resources and their effective use (ADB 2012).

Rising sea levels are expected to bring about significant changes in migration patterns throughout the developing world. The typical migration patterns of communities and entire countries will be altered (Asuncion and Lee 2016). For example, Kiribati has been drawing up plans for the migration of its residents to safer ground. It bought nearly 25 square kilometers in Fiji, an island nation about 2,000 kilometers away, as a potential resettlement area. However, Fiji itself is vulnerable to powerful cyclones.

The economy-wide costs of climate change

Vulnerable economies in developing Asia can expect growth to be dampened by significant impacts from climate change on sectors that depend on natural resources. Economic losses may exacerbate inequality and roll back years of development gains. Damage to particular sectors can be understood and measured on the bases of existing circumstances, but forecasting economy-wide effects is more challenging as they depend on a wide array of interactions.

The relationship between temperature and aggregate economic activity has traditionally been quantified by examining the historical relationship between fluctuations in a country's temperature and variations in its economic performance. A panel regression model for the nonlinear response effects of economic growth to historic temperature shows that agricultural output growth can be badly affected by climate change (Box 2.1.1). Longer hot periods will take a mounting toll on those who work outdoors in economic areas beyond agriculture, such as in construction or mining, threatening to set up additional channels by which higher temperatures significantly affect economic productivity overall. Economic productivity starts to decline when temperatures climb above an optimal average annual temperature of 14.2°C (Lee, Villaruel, and Gaspar 2016). Of the 31 economies in developing Asia included in this study, two-thirds are already beyond this critical temperature threshold, which illustrates how broadly vulnerable the region is to temperature variation (Figure 2.1.3).

The current path of rising temperatures and emissions could leave GDP across the region 10% lower in 2100 than under a scenario with no climate change (Lee, Villaruel, and Gaspar 2016). The impacts of temperature change on aggregate GDP have been previously forecasted by subregion using other approaches: For Southeast Asia the economic impact has been found to be on the order 11% of GDP by 2100 (Raitzer et al. 2015), for South Asia 9% (Ahmed and Suphachalasai 2014), and for East Asia 5% (Westphal, Hughes, and Brömmelhörster 2013).

Adaptation no substitute for mitigation

Climate change will worsen poverty because the poor are disproportionately exposed and vulnerable to climate shocks (Hallegatte et al. 2016). The challenge is how to protect poor and rural households from climate change, as they rely heavily on climate-sensitive resources (Hunter 2007). Numerous adaptation options have been identified to cope with climate change. Specific examples include improving livestock and fishery breeding systems, changing cropping patterns, altering the application of fertilizers and pesticides, introducing higher-yielding crop varieties and early maturing varieties to improve avoidance of climatic shocks, and improving irrigation systems and their efficiency. However, farm households will still be at risk if income derives from only a single source. Baez, Kronick, and Mason (2013) suggests diversifying household income along with resources, both within agriculture and toward off-farm enterprises. Farmers must be adept at responding to climate signals by changing their planting strategies, adjusting herd sizes, and diversifying their income sources (Eskander, Fankhauser, and Jha 2016).

2.1.3 Developing Asia's temperature threshold

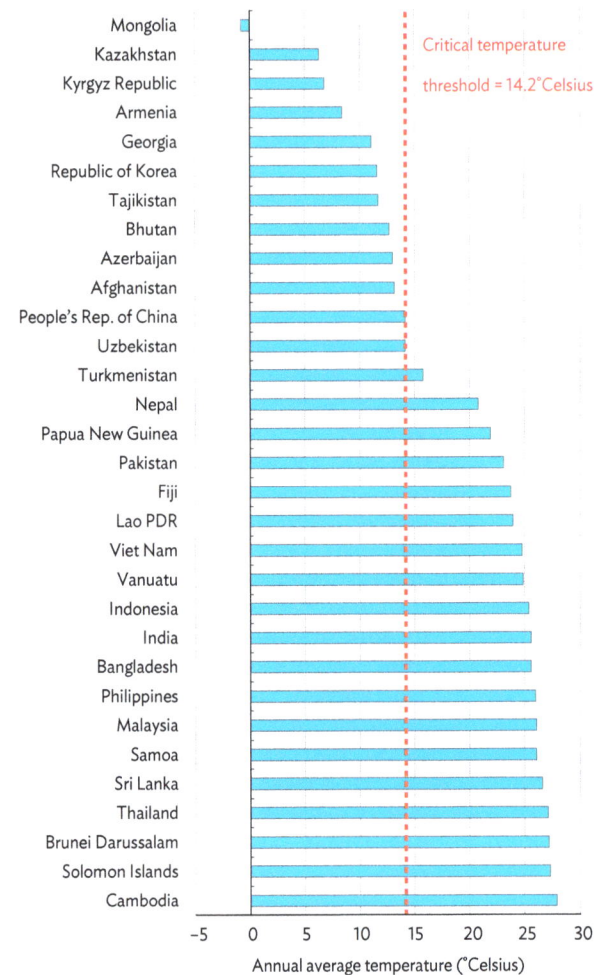

Lao PDR = Lao People's Democratic Republic.
Source: Lee, Villaruel, and Gaspar 2016.
Click here for figure data

2.1.1 Methodology for estimating a critical temperature threshold value using a nonlinear panel model

General framework

The global nonlinear response function of economic production on temperature is expressed in [Eq. 1] following the Burke, Hsiang, and Miguel (2015) framework.

$$Y(\overline{T}) = \Sigma_i Y_i(\overline{T}) = \Sigma_i \int_{-\infty}^{\infty} f_i(T) \cdot g_i(T - \overline{T}) dT \qquad \text{[Eq. 1]}$$

It predicts a smooth concave function reflecting gradual but increasing losses in total economic output $Y(\overline{T})$ as average temperature $\overline{T}$ rises and a country warms on average. This framework enables macro-level data to mimic the response on temperature observed from high-frequency micro-level data such as crop yields, among others.

The empirical approach is designed as follows:

$$\Delta Y_{it} = h(T_{it}) + \lambda_1 P_{it} + \lambda_2 P_{it}^2 + \mu_i + \nu_t + \theta_i t + \theta_{i2} t^2 + \varepsilon_{it},$$

where $h(T_{it}) = \beta_1 T + \beta_2 T^2$ \qquad [Eq. 2]

ΔY_{it} refers to the change in the natural log of GDP per capita of country i at time t. T_{it} is the annual average temperature expressed in degree Celsius of country i at time t. P_{it} is the annual total precipitation expressed in thousand millimeters in country i at time t. Time-invariant factors (e.g., history, culture, or topography), year fixed effects such as abrupt global events, and the quadratic country-specific time trends are incorporated in the model to produce more robust results.

The critical temperature threshold at which economic productivity starts to decline can be derived by getting the partial derivative of [Eq. 2] output with respect to T and equate to zero.

$$\frac{\partial(\Delta Y)}{\partial T} = \frac{\partial[h(T)]}{\partial T} = \beta_1 + 2\beta_2 T$$

Impact estimates

$$GDP\ per\ capita_{it}^{scenario} = GDP\ per\ capita_{it-1}^{scenario} * (1 + \eta_{it} + \delta_{it}) \quad \text{[Eq. 3]}$$

η_{it} refers to the growth rate from business as usual scenario (Box 2.2.1 on page 54). δ_{it} refers to the predicted growth loss or gain resulting from higher temperature in year t. It is derived from the following equation applying the pooled historical response function $h(T)$:

$$\delta_{it} = h(T_{it}^+) - h(\overline{T}_i), \qquad \text{[Eq. 4]}$$

where T_{it}^+ is the projected temperature for the years 2015 up to 2100 under different scenarios (Table 2.2.2 on page 55).

To estimate the impact, [Eq. 5] computes the difference of per capita GDP under different scenarios relative to per capita GDP under the business as usual scenario.

$$Loss_{it}^{scenario} = \left[\left(\frac{GDP\ per\ capita_{it}^{scenario}}{GDP\ per\ capita_{it}^{business\ as\ usual}} \right) - 1 \right] * 100 \quad \text{[Eq. 5]}$$

Source: Lee, Villaruel, and Gaspar 2016.

However, adaptation raises a large set of policy challenges of its own. Policy makers have to become much more aware of the consequences their development choices have on climate vulnerability. These consequences can be considerable. Asia's future vulnerability to climate change is shaped to a large extent by development decisions made today. The large-scale urbanization of coastlines, for example, has been shown to amplify the risks of coastal flooding (Hanson et al. 2011). Choi (2016) showed that urbanization contributed to higher damage from disasters in advanced countries from 1990 to 2010. It therefore makes sense to tackle climate risks in tandem with development planning and investment decisions as they are made.

Putting a proactive adaptation plan into action is not easy. Effective adaptation requires information, capital, and forethought. In many parts of developing Asia, the capacity necessary for effective adaptation response is limited. This is particularly true in low-income countries, as strong evidence exists that adaptation capacity correlates with income (Fankhauser and McDermott 2014). Failing adaptation, recovery is still possible, even from devastating events, but with a sometimes immense toll in human hardship.

While adaptation can help to manage some challenges posed by climate change, many of the most profound challenges can be only partly offset at best. For example, the degree to which damage from cyclones can be averted is limited, and agricultural mitigation strategies, such as the planting of crop varieties that tolerate such abiotic stresses as submersion, salinity, and drought, can avert only some losses. In other words, there are limits to adaptation.

Mitigation is needed to restrict climate change to risks that can be managed. Developing Asia has some of the world's poorest and most vulnerable populations, whose livelihoods are fundamentally tied to natural resources. Unmitigated climate change could reverse decades of progress in poverty alleviation and jeopardize Asia's ambitions to pursue development that is economically, socially, and environmentally sustainable. The region has much to gain from the success of the global effort against climate change, perhaps more than most others. To secure the region's future, ambitious mitigation is in Asia's interests.

Global consensus to combat climate change

The 2015 Paris Agreement on climate change is a milestone in global climate diplomacy. It marks a broad new consensus that all countries can and should contribute in the effort to reduce GHG emissions in the context of their national circumstances. It strengthens and respects the pledges already made by many nations. A total of 187 members of the United Nations Framework Convention on Climate Change, including nearly all developing countries in Asia, are signatories. The emissions reduction pledges and climate action plans submitted in the context of the international climate change negotiations are in many ways only the beginning. The process of formulation and implementation of the initial and subsequent pledges provides opportunities for all countries to consider national climate change actions in conjunction with broader national development objectives.

Global consensus

The gathering of world leaders in Paris showed global commitment to the urgent acceleration of efforts to tackle climate change, one of the most profound and complex transnational problems of our era. Under the Paris Agreement, each country has made pledges, known as intended nationally determined contributions (INDCs), to reduce its emissions. The INDCs inform the international community of national climate change efforts. Once the Paris Agreement is ratified, the INDCs will become nationally determined contributions (NDCs) that will provide the basis for a pledge and review system to be launched in 2023. Every 5 years, countries will update their NDCs, and a collective review of the targets, a "global stock take," will be conducted. A key feature of these stock takes is that NDCs must be more ambitious than previous pledges. It is hoped that this will force global emissions onto a trajectory that is consistent with holding warming to well below 2°C (Jotzo and Kemp 2016).

The Paris Agreement includes important measures to help developing countries implement their NDCs, including financing systems, technology transfer, and capacity building.

Assistance is further provided to help developing countries adapt to those impacts of climate change that can no longer be avoided.

Achieving the objectives of the Paris Agreement will be difficult and require immediate, urgent action from all countries. To have a reasonable chance of keeping global warming well below 2°C, global emissions will have to peak by the early 2030s. As the emissions trajectory moves from meeting current INDC goals in 2030 to emissions reduction that has a reasonably good chance of achieving the 2°C goal, global emissions will have to fall precipitously.

The sharp fall required after 2030 is a consequence of a relatively lenient emissions regime before then. Each global temperature target reflects a budget, as it were, of remaining GHG emissions that may still be released into the atmosphere without forfeiting the 2°C goal. The less rising emissions are checked early on, the faster they will have to fall later to remain within budget. The IPCC has calculated that, for a reasonable chance of staying below 2°C, the remaining "carbon space" for the main long-lived GHG, carbon dioxide (CO_2), is 600–1,000 billion tons of CO_2 (IPCC 2013). This takes into account the likely contribution from all other GHGs, which will also have to be controlled. This leaves less than 25 years of emissions at current levels. This basic carbon arithmetic explains why it is important to bring the peaking of global emissions forward.

Asia's contributions to the Paris Agreement

Asian countries began to take action on climate change long before the Paris Agreement was negotiated in 2015. They were motivated by a growing recognition of climate risks and their crucial role in mitigating them but also by local environmental factors. They identified strong synergies between climate policy and action to improve air quality and began to recognize the damaging effects of current land-use practices on local environments. The Republic of Korea was among the first to adopt a national strategy of green growth with its 2009 Framework Act on Low Carbon Green Growth, and it has pursued innovation in key technologies to mitigate climate change. Similarly, the PRC has made the promotion of green economy sectors a strategic objective of its 5-year plans (Townshend et al. 2013). As a result, the Government of the PRC has slowed the construction of new coal-fired power plants, and coal consumption has levelled off. This change has helped slow emissions growth in the PRC.

As of 12 September 2016, over 90% of developing economies in Asia had submitted their INDCs for reducing GHG emissions and communicating other relevant climate policy actions. Their targets differ greatly in terms of their ambition and in the way that they are expressed. Some INDCs contain absolute targets, either for total emissions or for the year in which emissions will peak. Many are expressed as a decrease in emissions against a business as usual baseline, which may or may not be specified. Yet other pledges take the form of a target for emissions intensity, or emissions per unit of GDP. Some pledges are unconditional, while others are conditional or contingent on financial and technical support from the international community. For example, Thailand has an unconditional pledge of 20% below business as usual by 2030, and a conditional target of 25%. The Annex on pages 86–89 summarizes the intended contributions made in Asian INDCs toward both mitigation and adaptation.

The primary target of the PRC INDC is a 60%–65% unconditional reduction in emissions intensity below the 2005 level by 2030, accompanied by a pledge to peak CO_2 emissions by 2030 at the latest. The PRC will pilot provincial emissions trading systems and provide a sectoral breakdown of a wide array of mitigation actions. The centerpiece of the Indian INDC is a conditional target to reduce emissions intensity by 33%–35% from the 2005 level by 2030, which is contingent on receiving adequate financial, technological, and capacity-building support from developed countries. India aims to achieve 40% cumulative electrical power installed capacity from sources other than fossil fuels by 2030. It also seeks to increase forest cover to sequester the equivalent of 2.5–3.0 billion tons of CO_2 by 2030. Indonesia has an unconditional target to reduce emissions by 29% from trends under business as usual by 2030. This will be increased to a 41% reduction if there is a global agreement and both bilateral and multilateral provision of finance, capacity building, and technology under technical cooperation. Its economy-wide target is supplemented by a renewable energy target to derive 23% of energy use from new and renewable energy sources by 2025.

Alongside the economy-wide reduction targets are sector-specific climate actions and priorities. The most prevalent sector targets are on renewable energy. These generally require that a certain percentage of electricity generation or consumption be derived from renewable energy sources in the future. Nine economies in developing Asia—Bhutan, Brunei Darussalam, Cambodia, the PRC, India, the Lao People's Democratic Republic, Myanmar, Nepal, and Viet Nam—have forestry targets toward maintaining or increasing their percentage of land area that is forested. Brunei Darussalam, Fiji, Palau, Tonga, and Vanuatu propose energy efficiency targets.

While these targets mark a significant improvement from the scenario without strong climate policy, they are insufficient to limit global warming to well below 2°C. The world is at a turning point, and developing Asia has a critical role to play in the success of the Paris Agreement on climate change.

Paris Agreement dependent on Asia

The global pledges under the Paris Agreement, and Asia's contribution to them, are important first steps. However, more is needed to meet the Paris objectives. The combined effect of the pledges is to put the world on a path toward a temperature rise of at least 2.7°C by 2100 (and 2.9°C according to the model presented subsequently), missing the Paris goal by a wide margin (Gütschow et. al 2015). The optimal mitigation path toward the 2°C goal requires double the emissions reduction by 2030 believed to come from current INDCs.

2.1.4 Developing Asia's share of CO_2 equivalent emissions since 1990

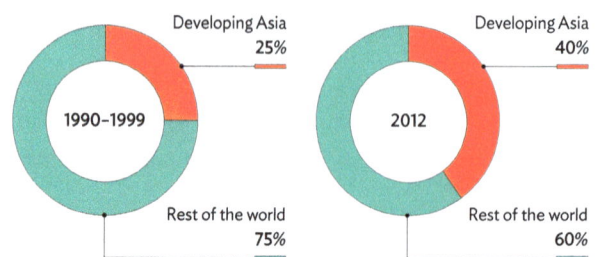

1990–1999
Developing Asia 25%
Rest of the world 75%

2012
Developing Asia 40%
Rest of the world 60%

CO_2 = carbon dioxide.
Source: CAIT Climate Data Explorer. 2015. World Resources Institute. http://cait.wri.org (accessed 3 August 2016).
Click here for figure data

Historically, Asia's GHG emissions have been relatively low, but following a period of rapid economic development, the region has become a substantial source of emissions. From 1990 to 1999, developing Asia contributed about 25% to global emissions. Following its rapid GDP growth at the beginning of the new millennium, developing Asia in 2012 accounted for almost 40% of global GHG emissions, largely from the PRC (Figure 2.1.4). The three most populous Asian economies were among the top five greenhouse gas emitters: the PRC, the US, India, the Russian Federation, and Indonesia (Figure 2.1.5). In per capita terms, two of them, Indonesia and the PRC, have emissions exceeding the global average (Figure 2.1.6). India's per capita emissions are still relatively low but growing.

From 2000 to 2012, absolute emissions grew at an annual rate of 8% in the PRC and 5% in India, substantially higher than the global average of 2%. In the first decade of the new millennium, the PRC emitted more GHGs than in the whole of 1800s (Boden, Marland, and Andres 2015). Other economies in developing Asia, including Indonesia, have seen emissions increase in line with the global average. However, some countries in Central Asia have had lower growth in emissions because of structural change from high emissions under the planned economy of the former Soviet Union.

In 2012, Asia was the world's largest source of GHG emissions in terms of both total volume, at 19 billion tons of CO_2 equivalent per annum, and emissions growth rate. Without strong climate policies, those emissions will double in volume by 2050, and the region will be responsible for nearly half of all GHG emissions by 2030. Asia's share in current and expected future emissions is so large relative to the emission cuts required that stabilizing climate change is no longer possible without Asia's help. At the same time, developing Asia has substantial opportunities to cut emissions at low cost and make a significant contribution to the global emissions-reduction effort. Creating a global low-carbon economy requires Asia's engagement.

Bringing global emissions within the 2°C limit requires urgent action. Otherwise, developing Asia will lock itself into a high-carbon future that would be costly to reverse.

2.1.5 Top 10 greenhouse gas emitters, 2012

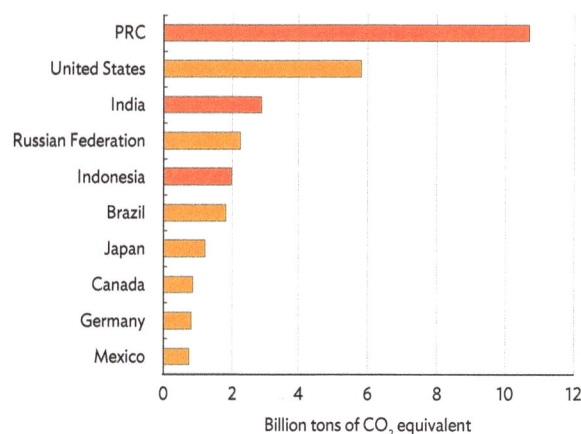

CO_2 = carbon dioxide, PRC = People's Republic of China.
Source: CAIT Climate Data Explorer. 2015. World Resources Institute. http://cait.wri.org (accessed 3 August 2016).
Click here for figure data

2.1.6 Greenhouse emissions per capita in selected countries, 2012

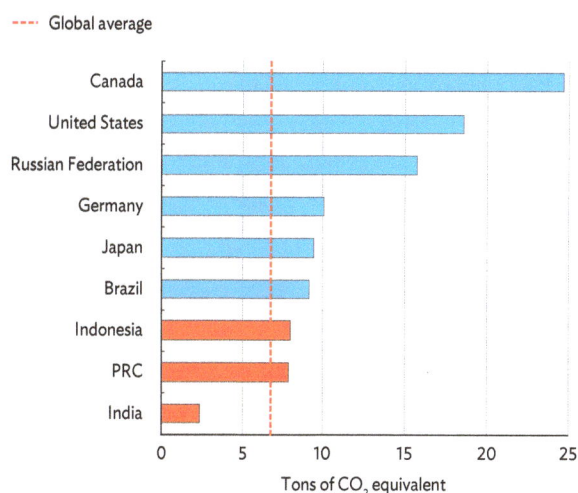

CO_2 = carbon dioxide, PRC = People's Republic of China.
Source: CAIT Climate Data Explorer. 2015. World Resources Institute. http://cait.wri.org (accessed 3 August 2016).
Click here for figure data

Assessing Asia's low-carbon transition

A substantial global effort is required to meet the 2°C warming limit under the Paris Agreement, within which Asia has a critical role to play. Asia is developing rapidly. Whether and how it embarks upon a low-carbon trajectory will depend on crucial energy, infrastructure, and urban planning choices now being made in the public and private spheres for the short to medium term. Achieving the goal of the Paris Agreement permits only a very narrow window for adding new high-carbon infrastructure such as power plants that use fossil fuels and urban assets such as buildings that are not designed to be climate compatible. As fossil fuels contribute as much as 70% of emissions from developing Asia, the region's low-carbon transition must focus on the energy sector, which has substantial potential to reduce emissions.

Current situation

The largest sources of developing Asia's GHG emissions in 2012 were electricity generation, manufacturing, and land use, which collectively account for more than 80% (Figure 2.2.1). Electricity generation was the fastest-growing source of emissions from 1990 to 2012, in both relative and absolute terms. Transportation is growing rapidly in relative terms but from a lower base.

The sources of emissions vary within Asia. For example, in Indonesia and Papua New Guinea, land use emits more than any other source, principally because of deforestation. Many of these emissions in Indonesia result from the deforestation of peat swamps containing thousands of tons of carbon per hectare. Electricity generation and manufacturing are much more dominant in the rest of developing Asia, accounting for most regional GHG emissions.

Energy emissions are increasing rapidly in part because of Asia's growing reliance on fossil fuels for energy (Figure 2.2.2). In 1990, fossil fuels provided 70% of developing Asia's primary energy. By 2014, this proportion had grown to 85%. The starkest feature of this shift is the rise of coal to occupy a dominant share in the energy mix. Modern renewable power contributes very little energy regionally. In combination with rapidly rising energy consumption, this means that the region is on a carbon-intensive development trajectory.

Most of developing Asia has made progress in reducing the energy intensity and carbon intensity of economic output,

2.2.1 Greenhouse gas emissions by sector, 1990–2012

- Others
- Transportation
- Manufacturing industry and construction
- Electricity generation
- Agriculture and other land uses

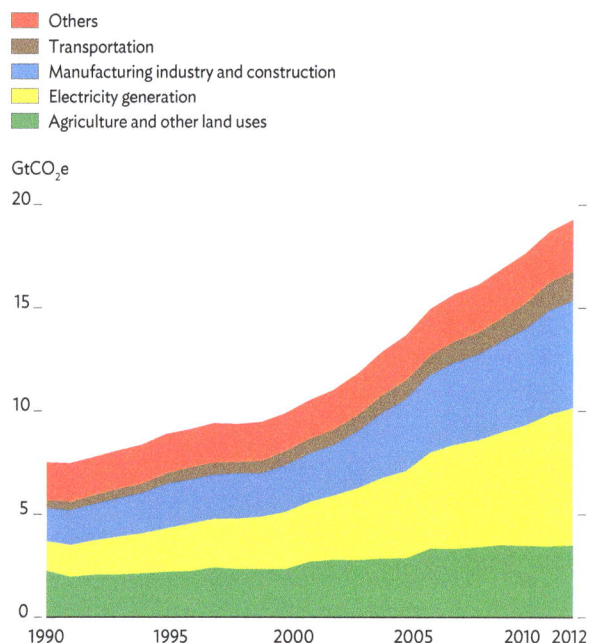

$GtCO_2e$ = billion tons of carbon dioxide equivalent.
Notes: Manufacturing industry and construction includes industrial processes. Others includes waste, fugitive emissions, and other fuel combustion.
Sources: FAO. 2014. FAOSTAT Emission Database; OECD/IEA. 2014. Climate Data Explorer, World Resources Institute. http://cait.wri.org/historical (accessed 3 August 2016).
Click here for figure data

2.2.2 Composition of primary energy supply in developing Asia, 1990–2014

- Renewables and biomass
- Nuclear
- Gas
- Oil
- Coal

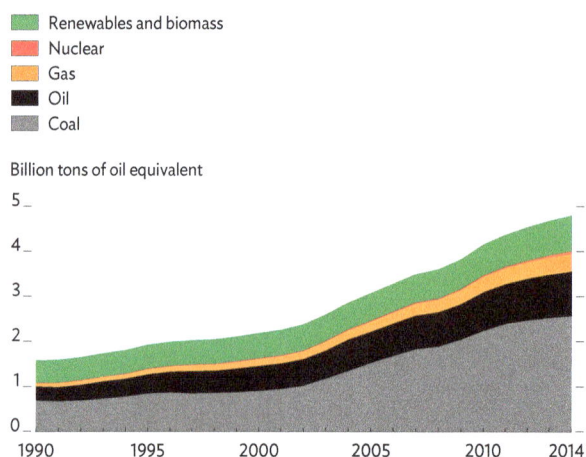

Source: International Energy Agency. Country profile database. http://www.iea.org/statistics/statisticssearch (accessed 3 August 2016).
Click here for figure data

2.2.1 Energy sector performance in developing Asia

	TPES/population (toe/capita)		TPES/GDP at PPP (toe/real 2010 $1,000)		Electricity use per capita (MWh/capita)		Energy CO$_2$ per capita (tCO$_2$/capita)		Energy CO$_2$/GDP at PPP (kgCO$_2$/real 2010 $)	
	1990	2013	1990	2013	1990	2013	1990	2013	1990	2013
Developing Asia	0.6	1.3	0.3	0.2	0.5	2.1	1.4	3.6	0.7	0.4
OECD	4.2	4.2	0.2	0.1	6.6	8.1	10.3	9.6	0.4	0.3
World	1.7	1.9	0.2	0.2	2.1	3.0	3.9	4.5	0.5	0.4

CO$_2$ = carbon dioxide, GDP at PPP = gross domestic product at purchasing power parity, kgCO$_2$ = kilogram of carbon dioxide, MWh = megawatt-hour, OECD = Organisation for Economic Co-operation and Development, tCO$_2$ = ton of carbon dioxide, toe = ton of oil equivalent, TPES = total primary energy supply.

Source: International Energy Agency. Country profile database. http://www.iea.org/statistics/statisticssearch (accessed 3 August 2016).

largely through structural transformation toward services. However, the region's performance in ensuring equitable energy supply and access still trails the developed world. The regional average electricity use per capita is a fraction of the Organisation for Economic Co-operation and Development (OECD) average of 8 megawatt-hours (Table 2.2.1). Similarly, primary energy supply per capita is only one-third of the OECD average of 4 tons of oil equivalent per capita, but it is rapidly rising in tandem with economic growth and improved electricity access. In combination with rising energy use, a growing share of primary energy from fossil fuels has driven the rapid emissions growth experienced to date. Building a low-carbon economy for developing Asia and stabilizing global climate change depend on changing this pattern.

Modeling Asia's carbon future

Asia must change course over the coming decades if global climate change is to be contained. Using a detailed model can reveal the potential that exists to change emissions trends, the mechanisms to do so, and the costs entailed. Simulations were run for this report using a global computable general equilibrium dynamic optimization model that includes a detailed representation of the energy sector (Box 2.2.1).

Four main emissions scenarios were modeled to show alternative courses that Asia could follow to ascertain the consequences of climate policy choices. The first scenario, business as usual, assumes no efforts specifically for climate change mitigation beyond actions already taken up to 2015. This is the base case to which all other scenarios are compared. The second scenario, INDC, assumes the implementation of the current INDCs up to 2030 and mitigation strengthening at a constant rate thereafter. Note that climate change exceeds the 2°C goal in this scenario. The third scenario, INDC to 2°C, strengthens the assumed post-2030 mitigation to ensure the Paris goal is met, with warming limited to 2°C up to 2100. The fourth emissions scenario, Optimal 2°C, takes the lowest-cost long-term mitigation trajectory and assumes upfront mitigation action beyond the INDCs. All scenarios are global and apply the same framework of mitigation assumptions to all world regions.

The four emissions scenarios are intersected with international cooperation in the form of emissions trade among countries to give a total

2.2.1 The World Induced Technical Change Hybrid model

The World Induced Technical Change Hybrid (WITCH) model is a dynamic optimization model of the world economy designed to assess climate change mitigation policies in the 14 large regions represented. It features an aggregated economic optimal growth model hard linked to bottom-up representation of the energy sector with highly detailed representation of energy generation technologies and a rich array of fuel types.

The model endogenously represents technical change through research, spillover, and learning by doing, and this technical change affects energy efficiency, costs, and the deployment of advanced energy technologies. To determine investment in research and capital stocks, the model maximizes intertemporal social welfare simultaneously across regions such that each region has the best strategy, taking the strategies of other regions as fixed.

The model is linked to the Global Biosphere Management Model of the International Institute for Applied System Analysis to include abatement through changes in agriculture, forestry, and other land uses, as well as to incorporate trade-offs between that abatement and biofuel production. It is augmented to reflect emissions from peat soil in Indonesia. WITCH is coupled with an air pollution model that simulates pollution distribution from the energy sector, and changes in ambient pollutant concentrations are applied in crop and epidemiological models to quantify effects on crops and human health.

WITCH generates optimal mitigation pathways and actions given a particular climate objective. It identifies changes to innovation, energy and land-use systems, investment requirements, macroeconomic effects, and co-benefits of actions. While the version of the model created for this report is new, previous versions have been part of many model comparisons and were widely cited in the *Fifth Assessment Report* of the United Nations Intergovernmental Panel on Climate Change (IPCC 2014).

The World Induced Technical Change Hybrid model structure

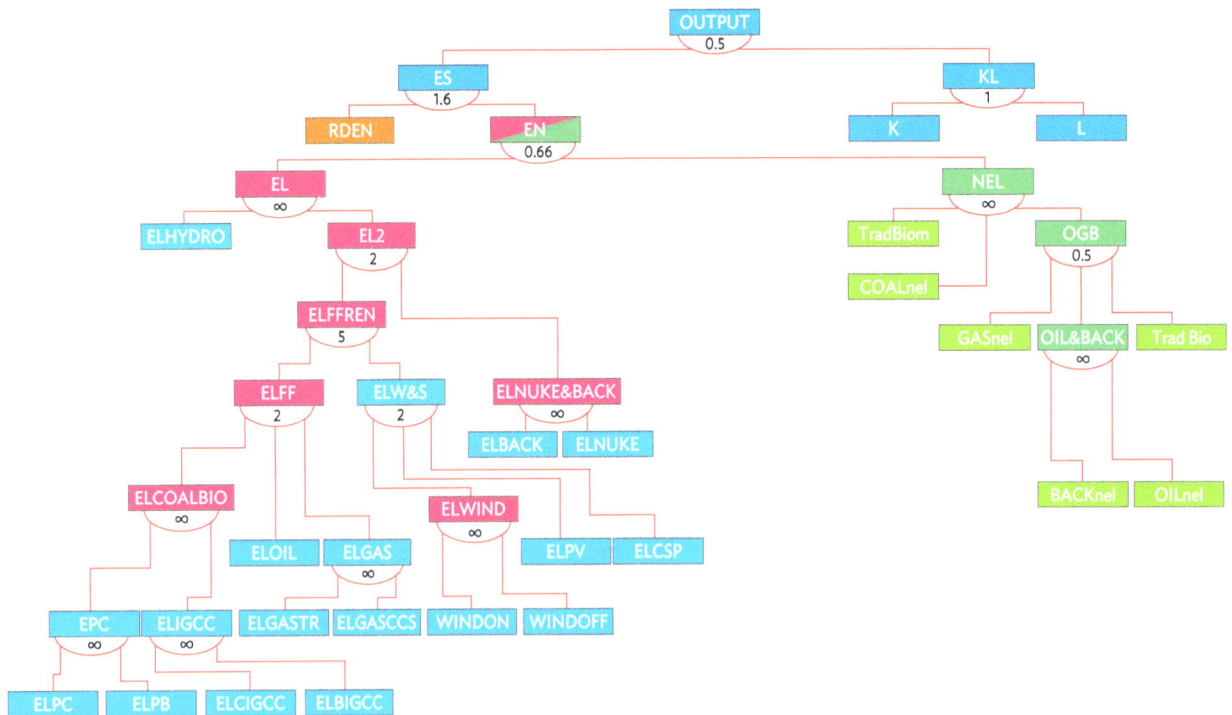

BACKnel = advanced biofuels (backstop for nonelectric energy), CCS = carbon capture and storage, COALnel = coal for nonelectric energy, EL = electric energy, EL2 = electricity generation without hydro, ELBACK = electricity generated with backstop, ELBIGCC = electricity generated with biomass with CCS, ELCOALBIO = electricity generated with coal and biomass, ELCSP = electricity generated with concentrated solar power, ELFF = fossil fuel electricity, ELFFREN = electricity generated with fossil fuels and renewables, ELGAS = lectricity generated with gas, ELGASCCS = electricity generated with gas with CCS, ELGASTR = electricity generated with gas turbines, ELHYDRO = electricity generated with hydroelectric power, ELIGCC = sum of electricity generated through integrated gasification combined cycle (IGCC) with CCS based on coal and biomass, ELCIGCC = electricity generated with coal IGCC plus CCS, ELNUKE = electricity generated with nuclear, ELNUKE&BACK = electricity generated with nuclear and backstop, ELOIL = electricity generated with oil, ELPB = electricity generated with biomass, ELPC = electricity generated with pulverised coal, ELPV = electricity generated with photovoltaics, ELW&S = electricity generated with wind and solar, ELWIND = electricity generated with wind energy, EN = Energy, EPC = electricity generated with coal and biomass without CCS, ES = energy services, GASnel = gas for nonelectric energy, K = capital invested in the production of final good, KL = capital–labor aggregate, L = labor, NEL = nonelectric labor, OGB = oil, backstop, gas, and biofuel, OIL&BACK = oil and backstop for nonelectric energy, OILnel = oil for nonelectric energy without transportation (industrial and residential), OUTPUT = gross domestic product, RDEN = energy research and development capital, Trad Bio = traditional (1st generation) biofuels, TradBiom = traditional biomass, WINDOFF = electricity generated with offshore wind, WINDON = electricity generated with onshore wind.

Source: Emmerling et al. 2016.

2.2.2 Scenario matrix assessed

	No trade in emissions	Global trade in emissions
Business as usual	Reference scenario following the Shared Socioeconomic Pathway 2, the scenario in which current trends continue, which the Integrated Assessment Modeling Consortium has agreed (Moss et al. 2010)	
INDC	Regions meet their emission targets until 2030, including the Cancùn 2020 pledges and the INDCs 2030; post-2030 carbon prices extrapolated increasing at an annual 3% rate	The same no-trade emission profile is reached, but regions are allowed to trade emission permits immediately.
INDC to 2°C	Global tax from 2030 leading to a global average temperature increase at the end of the century of 2°C	The no-trade emission profile is reached, but regions are allowed to trade emission permits after 2030. Permits are allocated based on contraction and convergence.[a]
Optimal 2°C		Global cap and trade leading to global average temperature by the end of the century. Permits are allocated based on contraction and convergence.

°C = degree Celsius, INDC = intended nationally determined contribution.

[a] Contraction and convergence see the allocation of emissions allowances gradually progress over a span of 30 years from shares based on historical emissions to national allocations that are equal per capita (Meyer 2000).

Source: Reis et al. 2016.

of six policy scenarios. In the INDC and the INDC to 2°C emissions scenarios, there are scenario variants, one with only domestic actions and no international carbon trade, and the other with carbon trade (termed "with trade"). Optimal 2°C is implemented assuming carbon trade (Table 2.2.2).

Under business as usual, developing Asia's emissions will rise rapidly from 18 billion tons of CO_2 equivalent in 2010 to 40 billion tons in 2050. This brings the region's share of global emissions from nearly 40% in 2010 to nearly 50% in 2030. A large portion of these emissions are from the PRC, as shown in Figure 2.2.3. Emissions from developing Asia at 40 billion tons in 2050 would exceed the allowance of less than 30 billion tons from the entire globe if the world adhered to the Paris Agreement objective of limiting warming to 2°C. Clearly, stabilizing climate change would be impossible without the region's active participation.

Asia's INDCs are a substantial indication of potential commitment from the region to curtail GHG emissions. However, like the INDCs of other regions, they are insufficient to put the world on a pathway to a maximum of 2°C warming or to ensure that Asian emissions peak in the 2020s as the 2°C path demands. INDCs, even if strengthened at a constant rate, yield emissions mitigation of less than half by 2050, which falls short of the 70% reduction or more that is necessary under the scenarios to limit temperature rise to 2°C (Figure 2.2.4). An economically optimal pathway to keep warming below 2°C would start action more quickly than the INDCs, as mitigation in 2030 needs to be more than double what the INDCs specify.

INDCs are heterogeneous mitigation targets that feature different ambitions, baseline emissions per capita, and baseline assumptions about emissions growth. Using a harmonized set of business-as-usual projections across regions, Figure 2.2.5 shows that the INDC scenario

2.2.3 Greenhouse gas emissions from Asia and rest of the world under business as usual

- Rest of the world
- South Asia
- Indonesia
- India
- East and Southeast Asia and the Pacific
- People's Republic of China

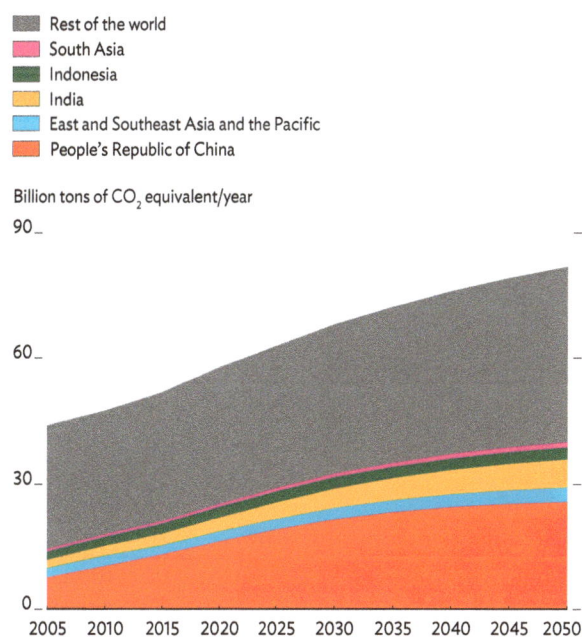

Billion tons of CO_2 equivalent/year

CO_2 = carbon dioxide.

Notes: East and Southeast Asia and the Pacific includes American Samoa, Brunei, Cambodia, Fiji, French Polynesia, Guam, Kiribati, the Lao People's Democratic Republic, Malaysia, the Marshall Islands, the Federated States of Micronesia, Mongolia, Myanmar, New Caledonia, the Northern Mariana Islands, Palau, Papua New Guinea, the Philippines, Samoa, Singapore, Solomon Islands, Thailand, Timor-Leste, Tonga, Vanuatu, Viet Nam, Taipei,China, and Hong Kong, China. South Asia includes Afghanistan, Bangladesh, Bhutan, the Maldives, Nepal, Pakistan, and Sri Lanka.

Source: Reis et al. 2016.

Click here for figure data

reflects cuts in emissions to 2050 by half from the PRC and by nearly 40% from Indonesia. India has a 20% reduction, while the remaining regions have lower targets. The variability in reductions suggests that certain countries may have scope for larger ambitions, especially if their emissions per capita are at or above the global average.

Unless today's investment and development decisions already consider climate change, developing Asia may find itself on a high-emissions trail of no return.

Investing to reduce emissions

Given the large share of energy-related emissions in GHG output, moving from high-carbon fuels to low-carbon energy sources is critical for climate-compatible growth. Taking carbon out of the energy system requires a fundamental shift in the energy mix through large-scale investment in low-carbon energy technologies such as wind, solar, sustainable biomass, and carbon capture and storage (CCS). It also depends on investment in energy efficiency.

Such a dramatic transition for Asia's energy system requires considerable investment in energy supply. Model simulations show new energy supply investments from 2015 to 2050 rising from just over $23 trillion under business as usual to nearly $34 trillion in aggregate for the INDC to 2°C and Optimal 2°C scenarios (Figure 2.2.6). Additional investment in energy production using CCS and renewables, the energy grid, and energy storage comes to $17 trillion under the 2°C scenarios, but about $7 trillion of this is offset by reduced investment in fossil fuels, leaving a net increase of $10 trillion, or $300 billion per year.

Increased investment is evenly split between renewables and the grid, including energy storage needed to facilitate the increased use of renewables. CCS investment needs are nearly $5 trillion under the 2°C scenarios but are similar to declines in energy generation using fossil fuels. Investment in energy research increases from $100 billion under business as usual to around $250 billion. The additional investment required under the INDC scenario is a bit over half of that of the INDC to 2°C scenario, with most of the additional investment in renewables and the grid.

Asia risks locking itself into a high-carbon development path that will be costly to reverse unless today's investment and development decisions take climate change into account. Additional energy investments for mitigation pose both costs in terms of increased capital requirements and benefits through lower variable energy costs and greater efficiency, with knock-on effects that run through the economy. Meanwhile, investments in fossil fuels totaling trillions of dollars will become unnecessary under mitigation.

2.2.4 Developing Asia emissions by scenario

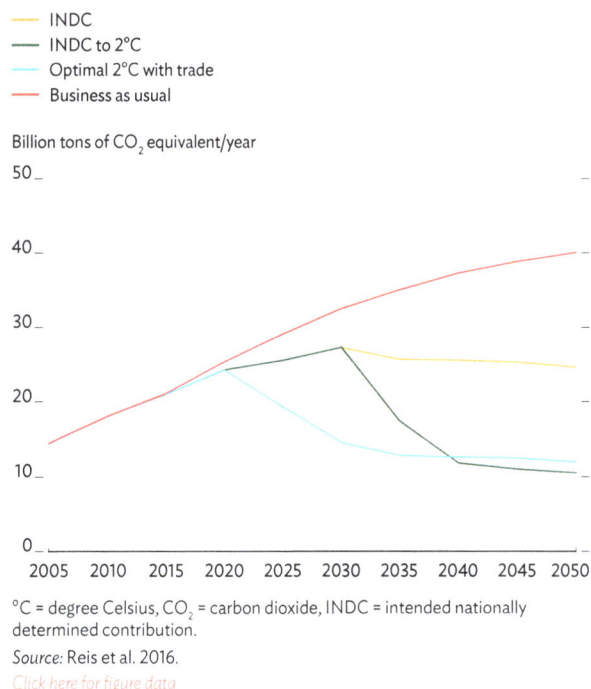

°C = degree Celsius, CO$_2$ = carbon dioxide, INDC = intended nationally determined contribution.
Source: Reis et al. 2016.
Click here for figure data

2.2.5 Emissions reductions under the INDC and INDC to 2°C scenarios by 2050

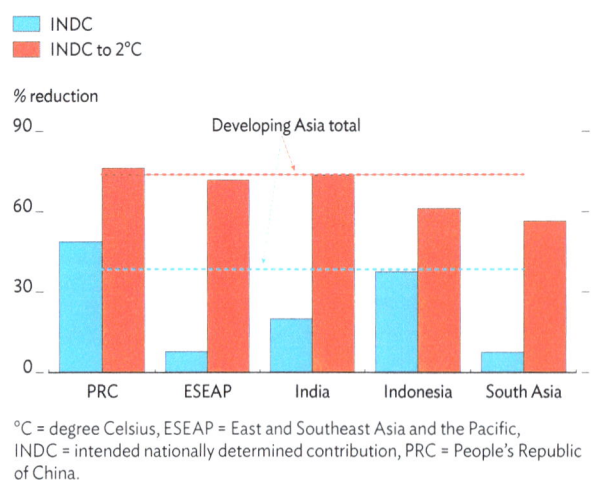

°C = degree Celsius, ESEAP = East and Southeast Asia and the Pacific, INDC = intended nationally determined contribution, PRC = People's Republic of China.

Notes: East and Southeast Asia and the Pacific includes American Samoa, Brunei, Cambodia, Fiji, French Polynesia, Guam, Kiribati, the Lao People's Democratic Republic, Malaysia, the Marshall Islands, the Federated States of Micronesia, Mongolia, Myanmar, New Caledonia, the Northern Mariana Islands, Palau, Papua New Guinea, the Philippines, Samoa, Singapore, Solomon Islands, Thailand, Timor-Leste, Tonga, Vanuatu, Viet Nam, Taipei,China, and Hong Kong, China. South Asia includes Afghanistan, Bangladesh, Bhutan, the Maldives, Nepal, Pakistan, and Sri Lanka.

Source: Reis et al. 2016.
Click here for figure data

Costing the low-carbon transition

Ambitious mitigation means that additional investment into energy is needed alongside economic adjustment as economies transition to a new energy system. All this entails costs but also benefits as the new energy system will be more efficient and have lower fuel costs. As a result, the economy-wide costs of ambitious mitigation in terms of lost GDP are relatively modest. Even in the highest economic cost scenario, the effect on annual GDP growth is a loss of 0.1 percentage points, or 4% of GDP by 2050 compared with business as usual (Figure 2.2.7). International carbon-offset trade, or the sale and purchase of emissions allowances among countries, cuts these costs by nearly half for developing Asia.

The main INDC scenario has the lowest economy-wide costs among all emissions scenarios. The peak cost without trade is 1.1% of GDP in 2030, after which costs fall to well below 1% of GDP by 2050. If trade in carbon allowances among countries can be used to achieve INDCs, costs in 2030 are nearly halved.

The Optimal 2°C scenario frontloads mitigation efforts in the 2020s and 2030s, doubling them in the period over the INDC scenario. However, after 2040, it has lower costs than the INDC to 2°C scenario, and by 2050, the economic costs are lower by more than 25%. This illustrates how early action on mitigation can reap long-term rewards.

As described below, an additional comparator scenario, INDC to 2°C low-cost CCS, considers substantially lower capital costs for CCS over time. This can be compared with the INDC to 2°C with trade scenario to determine whether results are sensitive to assumptions about this important but unproven technology. The simulation results show that economic costs are only mildly sensitive to assumptions about CCS, as the 2050 cost difference between the low-capital-cost CCS variation of the INDC to 2°C scenario and in the main INDC to 2°C scenario is less than 15%.

Breaking down Asia into subregions shows wider variation (Figure 2.2.8). In 2050, economic costs under the INDC scenario remain small in all regions. However, variation across regions increases under the more ambitious scenarios. India and the rest of South Asia benefit from ambitious mitigation using allowance trade, as the subregion's low emissions per capita allow it to export excess, unneeded emissions allowances for profit. Indonesia and the PRC face higher relative economic costs because of their higher emissions per capita, which means they need to undertake greater emissions reduction. In Indonesia, this cost is higher as well because of that country's relatively limited potential to deploy lower-cost wind and solar power, and its greater reliance instead on switching from fossil fuels to biomass in the energy system. In all regions, the Optimal 2°C scenario has lower 2050 costs than the INDC to 2°C scenario. This confirms that early action is in the interest of all countries in the region.

2.2.6 Investment in energy supply in developing Asia, 2015–2050

- Research
- Renewables
- Nuclear
- Grid and storage
- Fossil fuels with CCS
- Fossil fuels
- Oil extraction

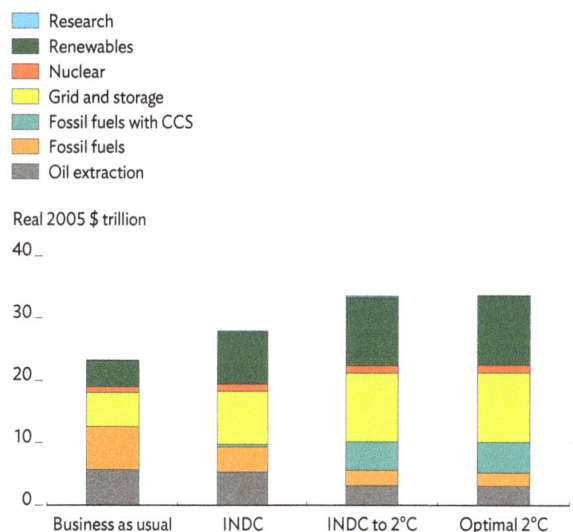

°C = degree Celsius, CCS = carbon capture and storage, INDC = intended nationally determined contribution.
Source: Reis et al. 2016.
Click here for figure data

2.2.7 Economic cost of emissions reduction as a percentage of GDP in developing Asia

- INDC
- INDC with trade
- INDC to 2°C under low-cost CCS with trade
- INDC to 2°C with trade
- INDC to 2°C
- Optimal 2°C with trade

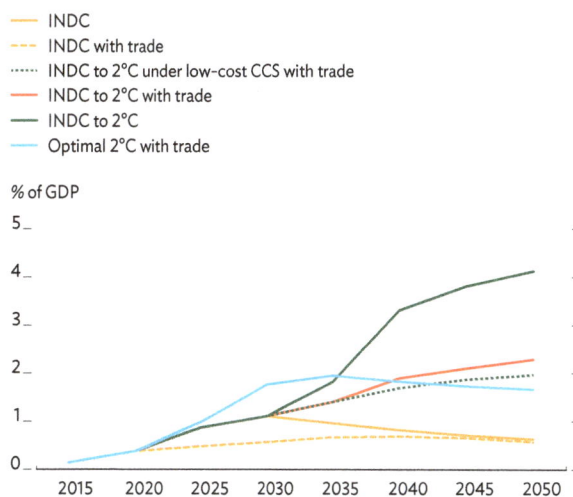

°C = degree Celsius, CCS = carbon capture and storage, INDC = intended nationally determined contribution.
Source: Reis et al. 2016.
Click here for figure data

2.2.8 Economic cost as percentage of GDP

- INDC
- INDC to 2°C with trade
- INDC to 2°C
- Optimal 2°C with trade

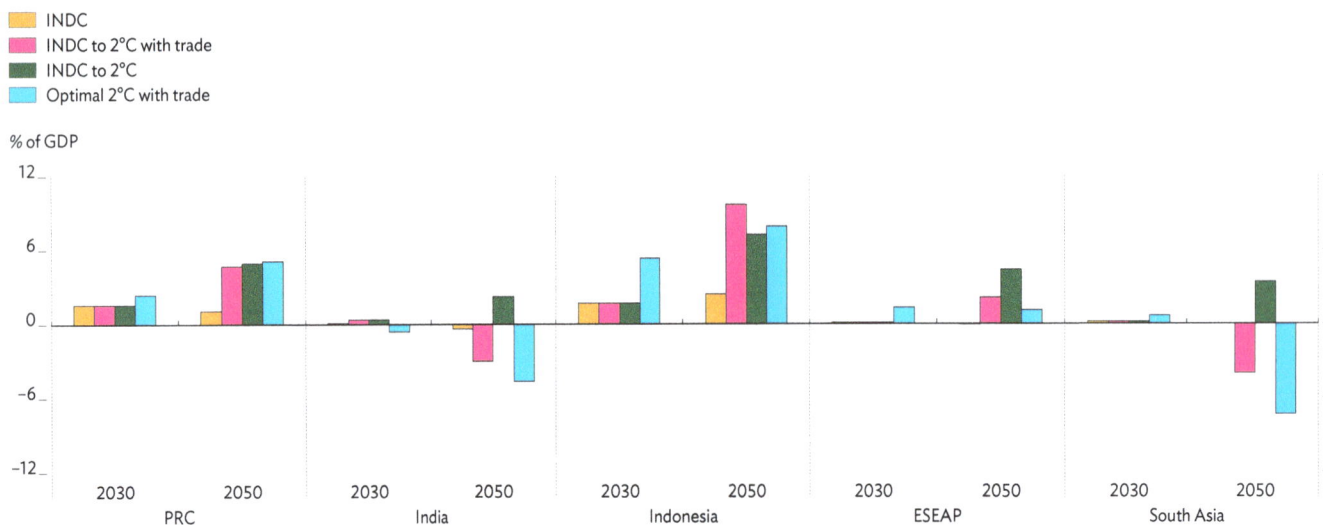

°C = degree Celsius, ESEAP = East and Southeast Asia and the Pacific, INDC = intended nationally determined contribution, PRC = People's Republic of China.

Notes: East and Southeast Asia and the Pacific includes American Samoa, Brunei, Cambodia, Fiji, French Polynesia, Guam, Kiribati, the Lao People's Democratic Republic, Malaysia, the Marshall Islands, the Federated States of Micronesia, Mongolia, Myanmar, New Caledonia, the Northern Mariana Islands, Palau, Papua New Guinea, the Philippines, Samoa, Singapore, Solomon Islands, Thailand, Timor-Leste, Tonga, Vanuatu, Viet Nam, Taipei,China, and Hong Kong, China. South Asia includes Afghanistan, Bangladesh, Bhutan, the Maldives, Nepal, Pakistan, and Sri Lanka.

Source: Reis et al. 2016.

Click here for figure data

Under the INDC scenario, the discounted value of 2050 carbon prices (at 5%, which is comparable to the rate of economic growth) is under $10/ton of CO2 equivalent in all regions (Figure 2.2.9). The INDC to 2°C scenario equalizes carbon prices by 2050 at $33/ton. This further underscores the importance of engaging in early action and global cooperation.

Global cooperation and trade will reduce costs and help developing Asia meet the increased investment needs of a 2°C trajectory. International trade in emissions allowances improves economic efficiency because it harmonizes carbon prices across regions. In the absence of trade, some regions face very high mitigation costs while others face very low costs. Costs can be reduced overall if more mitigation occurs in lower-cost areas than in higher-cost areas. This is illustrated for the INDC scenario in Figure 2.2.10, where carbon prices vary by region from almost nothing to $160/ton of CO_2 equivalent in 2050. The PRC, Europe, Indonesia, and the US all have much higher costs than the global price established by trade markets and thus become buyers of carbon permits when trade is included. The other areas in developing Asia have lower prices and become sellers. This income directly benefits sellers in India and rest of South Asia (Figure 2.2.10).

In essence, this is a win-win situation since high emitters per capita get access to lower-cost mitigation opportunities and low emitters per capita make a net gain by selling carbon credits and improving local environmental outcomes.

2.2.9 2050 marginal abatement costs discounted at 5%

- INDC
- INDC to 2°C

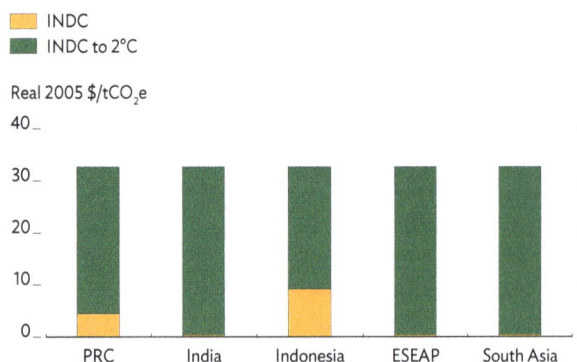

°C = degree Celsius, tCO$_2$e = ton of carbon dioxide equivalent, ESEAP = East and Southeast Asia and the Pacific, INDC = intended nationally determined contribution, PRC = People's Republic of China.

Notes: East and Southeast Asia and the Pacific includes American Samoa, Brunei, Cambodia, Fiji, French Polynesia, Guam, Kiribati, the Lao People's Democratic Republic, Malaysia, the Marshall Islands, the Federated States of Micronesia, Mongolia, Myanmar, New Caledonia, the Northern Mariana Islands, Palau, Papua New Guinea, the Philippines, Samoa, Singapore, Solomon Islands, Thailand, Timor-Leste, Tonga, Vanuatu, Viet Nam, Taipei,China, and Hong Kong, China. South Asia includes Afghanistan, Bangladesh, Bhutan, the Maldives, Nepal, Pakistan, and Sri Lanka.

Source: Reis et al. 2016.

Click here for figure data

Co-benefits from reduced emissions

Low-carbon growth offers immense benefits through effects other than reduced climate change. Against economic costs in the short term, action on climate change can bring substantial environmental co-benefits for Asia across several dimensions, including the environment, health, and safety. The main such co-benefits are better air quality, less traffic congestion, a healthier environment, diversified and enhanced energy security, and a safer future for generations to come (Sovacool 2016).

Reduced air pollution

Reduced air pollution has emerged as perhaps the most important and tangible potential co-benefit of climate action. Poor air quality in urban areas in particular is a substantial economic and social cost in developing Asia, which has the world's most polluted cities, including Delhi, Beijing, and many other cities in the PRC (Figure 2.2.11). Outdoor air pollution is implicated in nearly 3 million premature deaths per year in developing Asia, nearly 1.4 million of them in the PRC. The number of deaths in the region may double by 2050 without concerted pollution control (Figure 2.2.12).

The sources of GHG emissions and air pollution in the most polluted areas are largely the same: fossil fuels burned to power industry and transport and to generate electricity. In transport, diesel emissions are a cause of worsening air pollution in many cities.

However, technologies to abate local air pollution problems, caused principally by particulate matter and its precursors, do not directly control GHG emissions, which pose global problems. End-of-pipe technologies such as catalytic converters for vehicles and flue gas desulfurization for coal-fired power plants have been used successfully to reduce local air pollution in developed countries but do not provide concomitant reductions in GHG emissions. As air pollution is a localized problem that can be addressed at somewhat lower cost than climate change, national and local political leaders may feel more compelled to reduce air pollution than to reduce GHG emissions.

While modeling for this study shows that end-of-pipe technologies have potential to cut pollution substantially, it also illustrates that low-carbon growth can further reduce pollution and associated mortality. So, while technologies that control air pollution may reduce 2050 mortality by 1.7 million premature deaths annually in developing Asia, the INDC to 2°C scenario averts an additional 600,000 deaths on top of this (Figure 2.2.13).

This is a very large co-benefit. Valuing mortality in a manner consistent with the US Environmental Protection Agency (EPA 2016) but adjusted for per capita GDP in each region and time, the difference

2.2.10 Marginal abatement costs in the INDC scenario

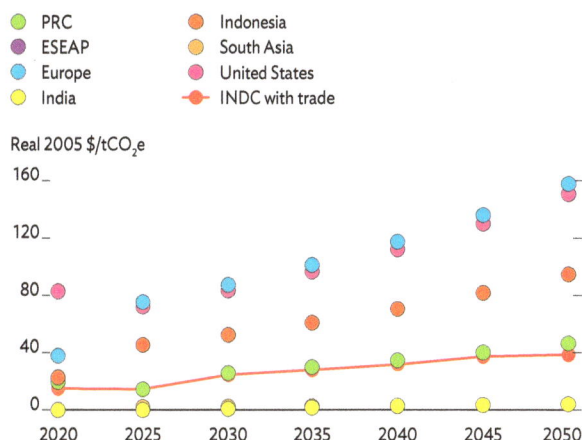

Legend: PRC, ESEAP, Europe, India, Indonesia, South Asia, United States, INDC with trade

Real 2005 $/tCO$_2$e

°C = degree Celsius, tCO$_2$e = ton of carbon dioxide equivalent, ESEAP = East and Southeast Asia and the Pacific, INDC = intended nationally determined contribution, PRC = People's Republic of China.

Notes: East and Southeast Asia and the Pacific includes American Samoa, Brunei, Cambodia, Fiji, French Polynesia, Guam, Kiribati, the Lao People's Democratic Republic, Malaysia, the Marshall Islands, the Federated States of Micronesia, Mongolia, Myanmar, New Caledonia, the Northern Mariana Islands, Palau, Papua New Guinea, the Philippines, Samoa, Singapore, Solomon Islands, Thailand, Timor-Leste, Tonga, Vanuatu, Viet Nam, Taipei,China, and Hong Kong, China. South Asia includes Afghanistan, Bangladesh, Bhutan, the Maldives, Nepal, Pakistan, and Sri Lanka.

Source: Reis et al. 2016.

Click here for figure data

2.2.11 Highest particulate matter 2.5 µg/m^3 air pollution by city, 2013–2014

Annual mean µg/m^3

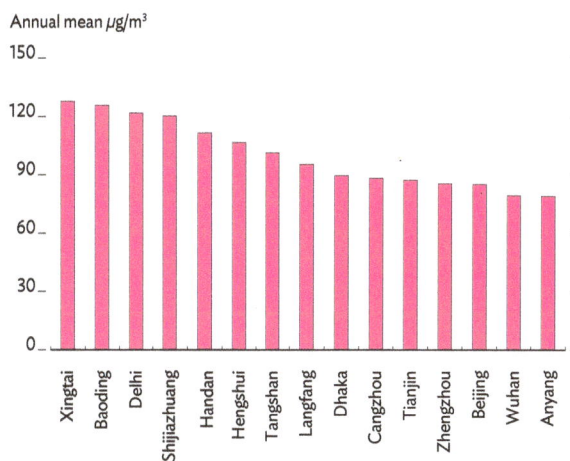

Cities: Xingtai, Baoding, Delhi, Shijiazhuang, Handan, Hengshui, Tangshan, Langfang, Dhaka, Cangzhou, Tianjin, Zhengzhou, Beijing, Wuhan, Anyang

µg/m^3 = micrograms per cubic meter.

Note: Includes only cities that directly measure at three or more stations particulate matter 2.5 µg/m^3, a leading cause of respiratory illness.

Source: World Health Organization.

Click here for figure data

between the scenario without improving pollution control and the INDC to 2°C or Optimal 2°C scenario equals 10% of GDP in 2050. Relative to a scenario of improving pollution control over time, these two 2°C scenarios provide additional co-benefits that equate to about 2.5% of GDP. This offsets more than 65% of economic costs to the region without trade and all economic costs with trade. It should be noted that the discussion is restricted to mortality, and that reduced morbidity from pollution will improve labor productivity and create additional benefits.

Rising carbon emissions and falling air quality affect a country's natural assets beyond its human capital. The benefits of reduced air pollution go beyond human health. For example, reduced air pollution also benefits agriculture because pollutants can adversely affect crop yields.

Crop model simulations show that, without pollution control, 45 million tons of rice, 44 million tons of wheat, 13 million tons of maize, and 2 million tons of soybeans may be lost in Asia annually by 2050 to the effects of pollution, even without counting the effects of climate change. This damage in Asia alone may equate to a loss of 5% of global production of rice and wheat in 2050.

Air pollution control can eliminate about 75% of these losses, but mitigation under the INDC or INDC to 2°C scenarios saves even more agricultural production. Relative to a scenario of improved end-of-pipe technologies, the 2°C scenario saves each year an additional 4 million tons of rice, 3 million tons of wheat, and 1 million tons of maize valued at over $2 billion (Figure 2.2.14). Retaining this production becomes essential because, even without climate change, food supply will be challenged to keep up with demand. Moreover, because food is an absolute necessity, small dips in production can cause huge increases in prices for consumers. As it is the poor who spend the greatest share of their income on food, such spikes would worsen poverty.

Preserve natural resources

The 45 million hectares of additional forest under the 2°C mitigation scenario will provide substantial environmental benefits in terms of recreational values, watershed services, biodiversity, pollination services, and non-timber forest products. Moreover, these services will help to improve adaptive capacity to counter the effects of climate change that remain after mitigation, especially in sectors dependent on natural resources such as agriculture. Reduced air pollution will help to avoid damage to these ecosystems beyond the effects of climate change. This will improve the quality of natural resources as well as their quantity.

2.2.12 Premature deaths from air pollution under a scenario without improving pollution control

- India
- Indonesia
- East and Southeast Asia and the Pacific
- People's Republic of China
- South Asia

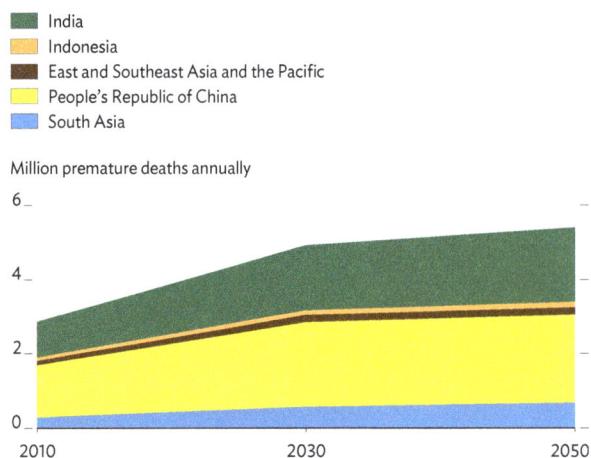

Million premature deaths annually

Notes: Air pollution covers ozone and particulate matter pollution only. East and Southeast Asia and the Pacific includes American Samoa, Brunei, Cambodia, Fiji, French Polynesia, Guam, Kiribati, the Lao People's Democratic Republic, Malaysia, the Marshall Islands, the Federated States of Micronesia, Mongolia, Myanmar, New Caledonia, the Northern Mariana Islands, Palau, Papua New Guinea, the Philippines, Samoa, Singapore, Solomon Islands, Thailand, Timor-Leste, Tonga, Vanuatu, Viet Nam, Taipei,China, and Hong Kong, China. South Asia includes Afghanistan, Bangladesh, Bhutan, the Maldives, Nepal, Pakistan, and Sri Lanka.
Source: Reis et al. 2016.
Click here for figure data

2.2.13 Lives saved annually from premature death in 2050 from air pollution, relative to a scenario without new pollution control

- South Asia
- Indonesia
- India
- East and Southeast Asia and the Pacific
- People's Republic of China

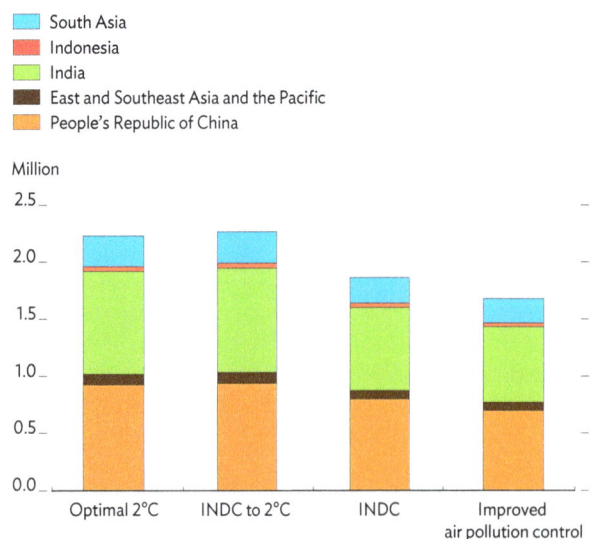

Million

°C = degree Celsius, INDC = intended nationally determined contribution.
Notes: Air pollution covers ozone and particulate matter pollution only. East and Southeast Asia and the Pacific includes American Samoa, Brunei, Cambodia, Fiji, French Polynesia, Guam, Kiribati, the Lao People's Democratic Republic, Malaysia, the Marshall Islands, the Federated States of Micronesia, Mongolia, Myanmar, New Caledonia, the Northern Mariana Islands, Palau, Papua New Guinea, the Philippines, Samoa, Singapore, Solomon Islands, Thailand, Timor-Leste, Tonga, Vanuatu, Viet Nam, Taipei,China, and Hong Kong, China. South Asia includes Afghanistan, Bangladesh, Bhutan, the Maldives, Nepal, Pakistan, and Sri Lanka.
Source: Reis et al. 2016.
Click here for figure data

Reduced transportation congestion

Mitigation in the transportation sector will often involve modal shifts from private vehicles to buses and other public transport, and from road freight to rail and waterways. The benefits from these shifts are beyond the scope of the modeling conducted here, but reducing the number of private vehicles will ease traffic congestion, shorten travel times, and avoid accidents (Shaw et al. 2014). Reduced travel times and labor losses from injury will contribute to better labor productivity. Shifts in spatial configurations to improve transport efficiency will often make cities more livable, curtailing sprawl and making them more friendly to pedestrians.

Energy system predictability and resilience

A more diversified energy mix, as is found in the following section on mitigation scenarios, may create additional benefits not captured in the modeling in this chapter. A diverse portfolio of technologies helps to ensure that factor price volatility for fossil fuels such as oil does not substantially affect the economics of energy systems or fuel consumption (Sovacool 2016). Less reliance on fossil fuels lessens vulnerability to supply disruptions that could be caused by economic shocks, geopolitical developments, or natural disasters. This is especially important for those Asian economies that rely heavily on energy imports.

This is just a subset of the actual co-benefits of mitigation. Low-carbon growth has innumerable other benefits, including heightened competitiveness, green jobs, and spillover effects to the broader economy from greater innovation.

Climate policies can reap large economic returns

Developing Asia has much to gain from climate action, as climate change poses substantial risks to regional economies. Figure 2.2.15 presents the effects of climate change on GDP under the modeled scenarios, drawing on the econometric model of Lee, Villaruel, and Gaspar 2016 (Box 2.1.1 on page 47). The business as usual scenario shows 4°C mean global warming by 2100, which causes losses equal to 3.3% of GDP by 2050 and more than 10% of GDP by 2100. In contrast, the 2°C scenarios limit losses to 1.4%–1.8% of GDP by 2050 and to around 2% by 2100. The INDC scenario has losses about halfway between business as usual and the 2°C scenario. This means that the gains derived from having a climate policy reach 4% of GDP in the INDC scenario and 8% in the 2°C scenarios by 2100.

2.2.14 Reduction in 2050 crop losses from ozone pollution in developing Asia by modeled scenario

- INDC to 2°C
- INDC
- Air pollution control

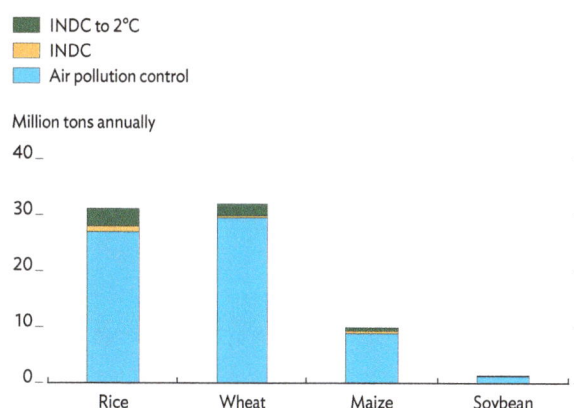

°C = degree Celsius, INDC = intended nationally determined contribution.
Source: Reis et al. 2016.
Click here for figure data

2.2.15 Effects of climate change on developing Asia's GDP under modeled scenarios

- INDC to 2°C
- Business as usual
- INDC
- Optimal 2°C

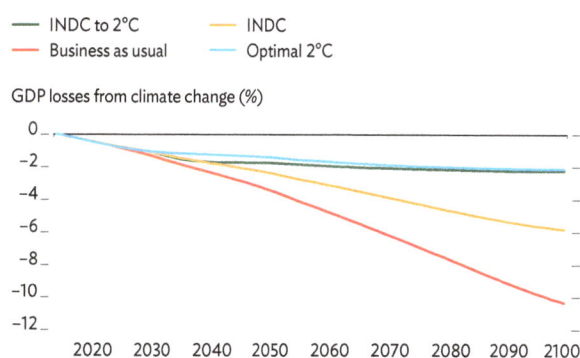

°C = degree Celsius, INDC = intended nationally determined contribution.
Source: Lee, Villaruel, and Gaspar 2016.
Click here for figure data

2.2.16 Economic benefits from avoided climate change in 2050 under modeled scenarios by region

- Gains under INDC
- Additional gains under Optimal 2°C

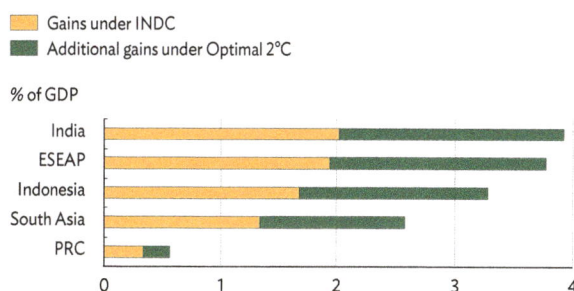

°C = degree Celsius, ESEAP = East and Southeast Asia and the Pacific, INDC = intended nationally determined contribution, PRC = People's Republic of China.

Notes: East and Southeast Asia and the Pacific includes American Samoa, Brunei, Cambodia, Fiji, French Polynesia, Guam, Kiribati, the Lao People's Democratic Republic, Malaysia, the Marshall Islands, the Federated States of Micronesia, Mongolia, Myanmar, New Caledonia, the Northern Mariana Islands, Palau, Papua New Guinea, the Philippines, Samoa, Singapore, Solomon Islands, Thailand, Timor-Leste, Tonga, Vanuatu, Viet Nam, Taipei,China, and Hong Kong, China. South Asia includes Afghanistan, Bangladesh, Bhutan, the Maldives, Nepal, Pakistan, and Sri Lanka.
Source: Lee, Villaruel, and Gaspar 2016.
Click here for figure data

The gains from reduced climate change are greatest in India, Indonesia, and the rest of East and Southeast Asia, and slightly less in the rest of South Asia (Figure 2.2.16). However, these expected gains are not matched by INDC ambition, in that India, the rest of South Asia, and Southeast Asia have only modest goals despite standing to benefit the most from the 2°C scenarios. This suggests that it may be in the economic interests of many Asian countries to do more to lead the way to greater global emissions reduction.

Estimates of economic costs, economic benefits from less climate change, and co-benefits (notably mortality reductions presented here relative to a scenario with improved end-of-pipe pollution control) can be combined to illustrate indicatively how the low-carbon transition affects the region on balance. The left panel of Figure 2.2.17 illustrates that the net cost rarely reaches 1% of GDP, even in the most ambitious scenarios, and that benefits exceed costs most quickly in the Optimal 2°C scenario. In the other scenarios, benefits exceed costs by the mid-2030s to 2040s. By 2050, the net effect on GDP is a 2%–3% gain for the 2°C scenarios with trade, with the highest gain in the optimal scenario of early action. INDC mitigation has about half of these gains. The lowest gain is in the INDC 2°C scenario without trade.

The effects in dollar terms are more pronounced as GDP grows over time. In all scenarios, the flow of benefits vastly exceeds costs over the 21st century. The Optimal 2°C scenario has high payoff, in which each $1.0 of economic cost generates $2.2 of benefits in present value terms (discounted at 5%), and benefits exceed costs within a decade of action. Initially, co-benefits generate the most gains, while benefits from avoided climate change catch up later and eventually dominate benefits after 2050.

Delaying the onset of ambitious mitigation by about a decade in the INDC to 2°C scenario with trade reduces the payoff from mitigation. In this scenario, each $1.0 of economic cost creates $1.5 of present value benefits, which is 30% lower. Removing trade further lowers this to just over $1 of benefits per $1 of cost because the economic costs of mitigation rise further. The INDC scenario, because of lower costs under declining marginal benefits from mitigation, initially has a higher $2.6 of benefits per $1.0 of economic cost but ultimately generates less than half of the benefits of the 2°C scenarios.

Calculating an internal rate of return (IRR) on the flows of net costs and benefits reveals the effect of the differences in overall benefits that accrue. The Optimal 2°C scenario has an impressive 22% IRR. The INDC to 2°C scenario with trade has an IRR of 11%, as does the INDC scenario. The INDC to 2°C scenario without trade has an IRR of 7%, or far less than what can be achieved with trade and/or earlier action. Coordinated, early, and ambitious action has the potential to more than double the returns to the region from adopting a climate policy. Asia's low-carbon transition has to start now to capture the full benefits of investment in mitigation.

2.2.17 Net annual costs and benefits of modeled mitigation scenarios for developing Asia, as percentage of GDP (top) and in absolute amounts under the Optimal 2°C scenario (bottom)

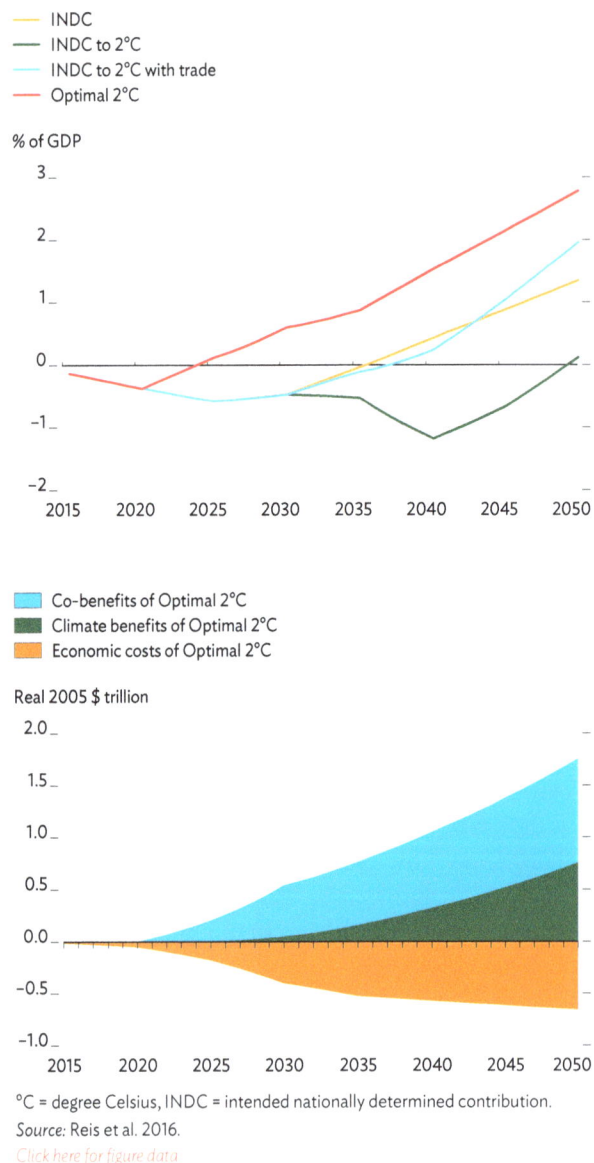

— INDC
— INDC to 2°C
— INDC to 2°C with trade
— Optimal 2°C

% of GDP

Co-benefits of Optimal 2°C
Climate benefits of Optimal 2°C
Economic costs of Optimal 2°C

Real 2005 $ trillion

°C = degree Celsius, INDC = intended nationally determined contribution.
Source: Reis et al. 2016.
Click here for figure data

Asia's potential for a low-carbon future

Substantial effort is required from developing Asia toward meeting the internationally agreed climate objective. However, feasible pathways are available to decarbonize developing Asia's economies at manageable cost. These pathways are underpinned by three principle mitigation mechanisms: reducing the carbon intensity of energy sources, improving energy efficiency, and reducing emissions from land use. In transitioning to a low-carbon future, decision makers making energy and infrastructure choices in the short term can play a vital role. Many opportunities exist in the transition to a low-carbon future as new markets develop for low-carbon goods and services.

The INDC to 2°C scenario envisions national mitigation pledges continuing to 2030, at which point countries switch to more ambitious mitigation on a path to limiting warming to 2°C by 2100. Under this scenario, nearly half of mitigation achieved in developing Asia in 2050 will come from replacing carbon-intensive energy with low-carbon energy sources (Figure 2.3.1). The second largest source of mitigation, at one-third, is through improving energy efficiency. Finally, most of the balance of mitigation will be achieved through changes in land use and other low-cost abatement options.

2.3.1 Decomposition of mitigation sources in the INDC scenario versus the INDC to 2°C scenarios

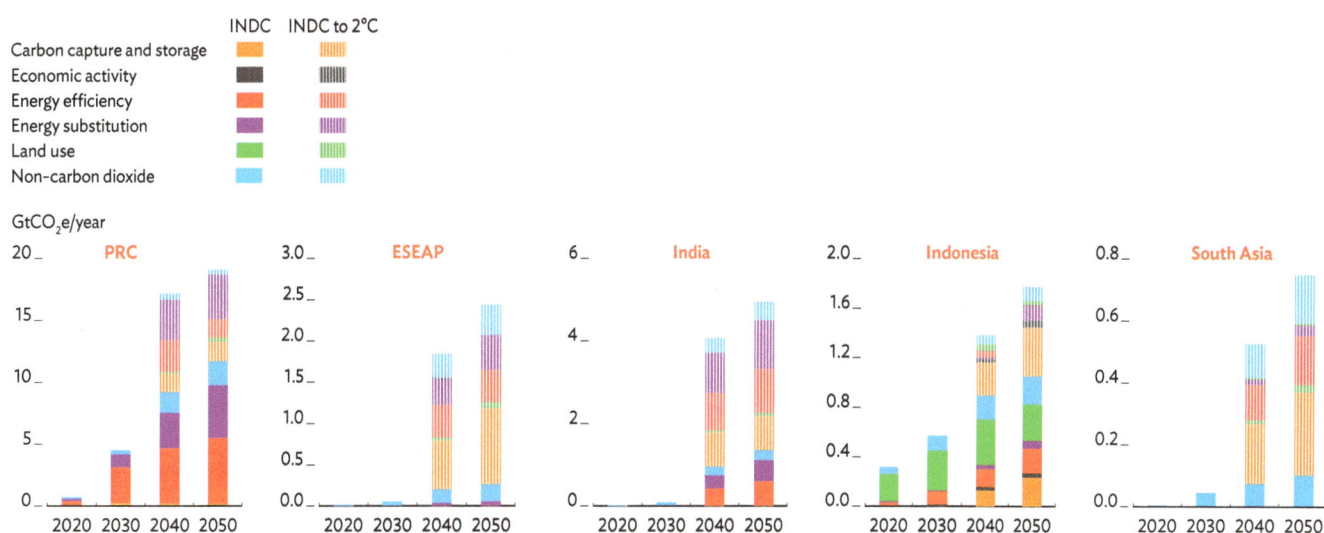

°C = degree Celsius, ESEAP = East and Southeast Asia and the Pacific, GtCO$_2$e = billion tons of carbon dioxide equivalent, INDC = intended nationally determined contribution, PRC = People's Republic of China.

Notes: INDC to 2°C values are additional to those of INDC, such that they sum to total INDC to 2°C mitigation when considered together. East and Southeast Asia and the Pacific includes American Samoa, Brunei, Cambodia, Fiji, French Polynesia, Guam, Kiribati, the Lao People's Democratic Republic, Malaysia, the Marshall Islands, the Federated States of Micronesia, Mongolia, Myanmar, New Caledonia, the Northern Mariana Islands, Palau, Papua New Guinea, the Philippines, Samoa, Singapore, Solomon Islands, Thailand, Timor-Leste, Tonga, Vanuatu, Viet Nam, Taipei,China, and Hong Kong, China. South Asia includes Afghanistan, Bangladesh, Bhutan, the Maldives, Nepal, Pakistan, and Sri Lanka.

Source: Reis et al. 2016.

Click here for figure data

Under the INDC scenario, mitigation relies more on improving energy efficiency and abating emissions from land use, as well as emissions other than carbon dioxide. Outside of the PRC and India, changing the energy mix makes a smaller contribution. As the INDC scenario contains variable goals for different countries, countries with less ambitious contributions achieve less abatement.

With more stringent mitigation in the INDC to 2°C scenario, the sources of mitigation shift. Low-carbon energy and CCS together become dominant, and CCS is deployed to some degree in all areas from 2040. Mitigation begins to converge more across areas, with all them improving energy efficiency and shifting energy types to reduce emissions.

At the same time, there is considerable variation in these patterns by area. In Indonesia, for example, land use is the largest source of mitigation to 2030 and still a primary source to 2050. Energy efficiency is particularly important to mitigation in the PRC. Those areas that need to catch up because they had less ambitious INDCs will need to employ more CCS to enable the transition toward the 2°C pathway.

Mitigation from low-carbon energy generation

Emissions will be reduced mainly by transforming Asia's energy system. Under business as usual, energy from coal more than doubles from 2010 to 2050 (Figure 2.3.2). The INDC scenario has coal energy peaking by 2030, but under more stringent mitigation under the INDC to 2°C scenario and the Optimal 2°C scenario, it peaks even earlier, by 2020. More broadly, in the 2°C scenarios, fossil fuel energy peaks by 2030 or earlier. The one fossil fuel less dramatically reduced is oil because it is difficult to substitute in transportation quickly. Later in the century, emissions will need to shift away from oil toward such clean alternatives as electric vehicles, though these options are expected to achieve dominant market positions only after 2050.

In contrast with fossil fuels, low-carbon energy rises rapidly. By the 2030s, the 2°C scenarios show more energy from non-biomass renewables than from coal, and by the 2050s nearly half of energy is from such renewables and biomass. Wind shows the greatest expansion potential, followed by biomass.

The required energy transitions have substantial implications for subregions with vast fossil fuel reserves such as Central Asia. To meet climate change targets, some of these reserves will have to stay in the ground.

Electricity generation is at the center of many of the transformations depicted. In the 2°C scenarios, conventional coal and gas disappear from the energy mix by the late 2030s,

2.3.2 Primary energy composition in developing Asia under modeled scenarios

Legend:
- Hydro
- Gas
- Coal
- Biomass
- Wind
- Solar
- Oil
- Nuclear

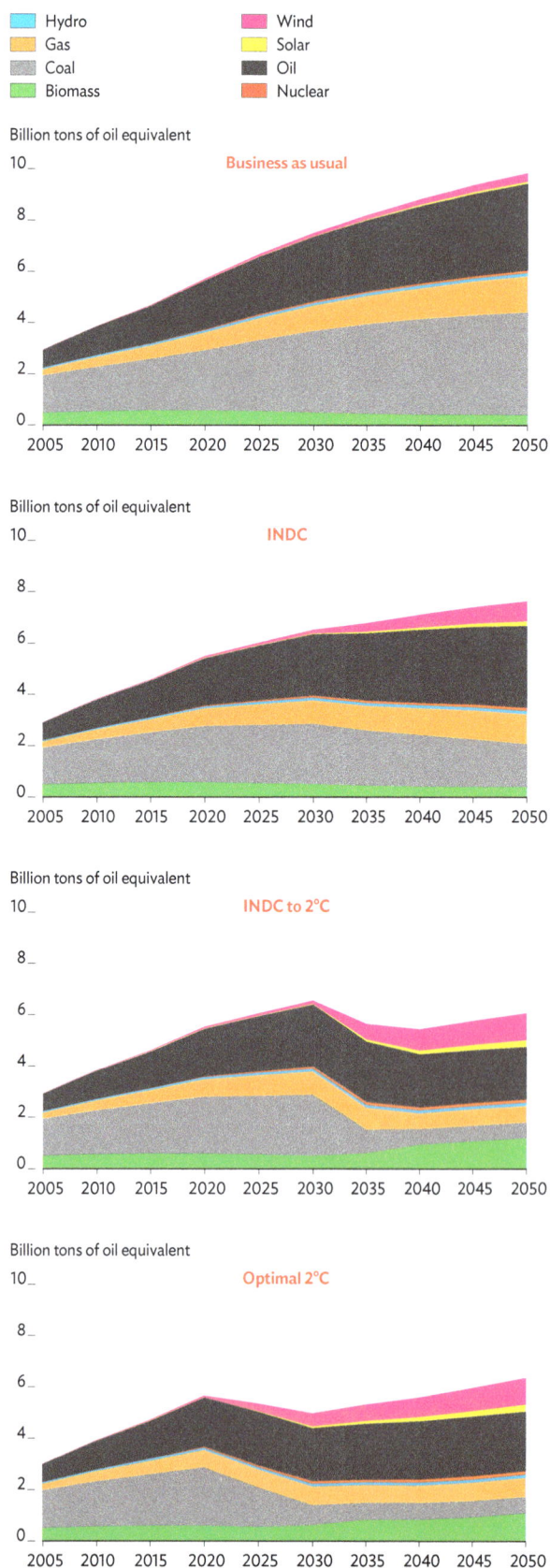

°C = degree Celsius, INDC = intended nationally determined contribution.
Source: Reis et al. 2016.
Click here for figure data

2.3.3 Electricity generation in developing Asia under modeled scenarios

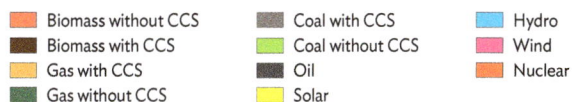

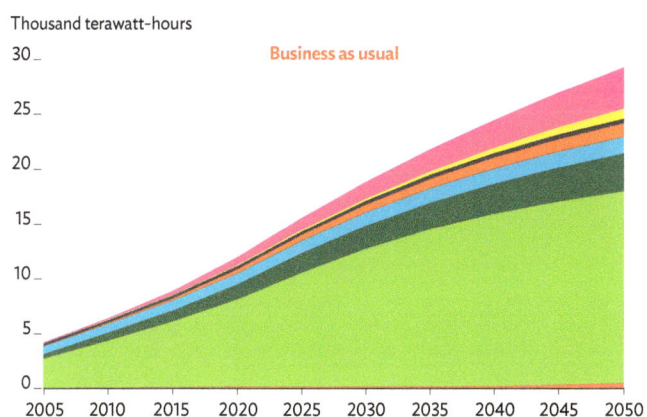

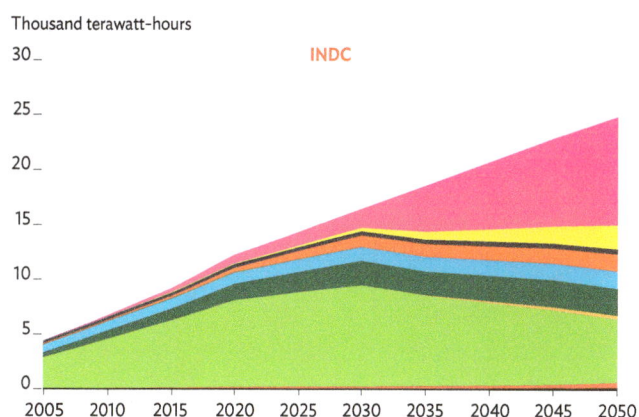

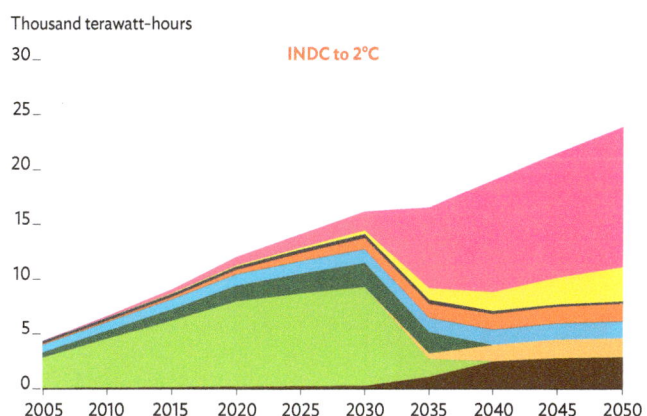

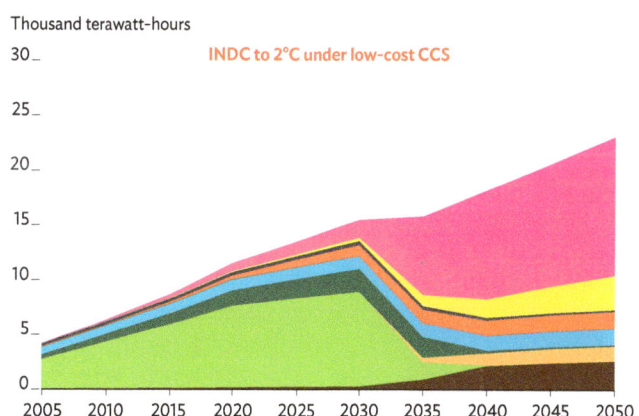

Legend:
- ▮ Biomass without CCS
- ▮ Biomass with CCS
- ▮ Gas with CCS
- ▮ Gas without CCS
- ▮ Coal with CCS
- ▮ Coal without CCS
- ▮ Oil
- ▮ Solar
- ▮ Hydro
- ▮ Wind
- ▮ Nuclear

°C = degree Celsius, CCS = carbon capture and storage, INDC = intended nationally determined contribution.
Source: Reis et al. 2016.
Click here for figure data

though a small amount of coal continues to be burned thereafter using CCS (Figure 2.3.3). In its place, wind expands dramatically, as do solar power, biomass with CCS, and gas with CCS.

The rise of renewables depends on their declining costs over time and on innovation induced by carbon markets. This innovation is the result of research, spillover, and learning by doing, and it affects both initial capital investment costs and variable operating costs. In terms of fixed initial capital costs, the progression over time and scenarios is presented in Figure 2.3.4. Solar photovoltaic and wind are found to have lower capital costs in 2050 than such fossil fuels as coal and gas.

By contrast, the initial capital costs for CCS are assumed to be fairly constant over time, so CCS is used less than in the results of other recent models. To explore the impact on the energy mix and sensitivity to CCS assumptions, a variant of the INDC to 2°C scenario was run. It shows the cost of CCS falling in line with the most optimistic projections currently available (Global CCS Institute 2012). Under this modified scenario, CCS for gas and biomass expands somewhat, but its utilization

2.3.4 Capital costs for energy technologies by scenario in 2050

- ■ 2010 capital costs
- ■ INDC
- ■ INDC to 2°C
- ■ INDC to 2°C under low-cost CCS

$/thousand kilowatts

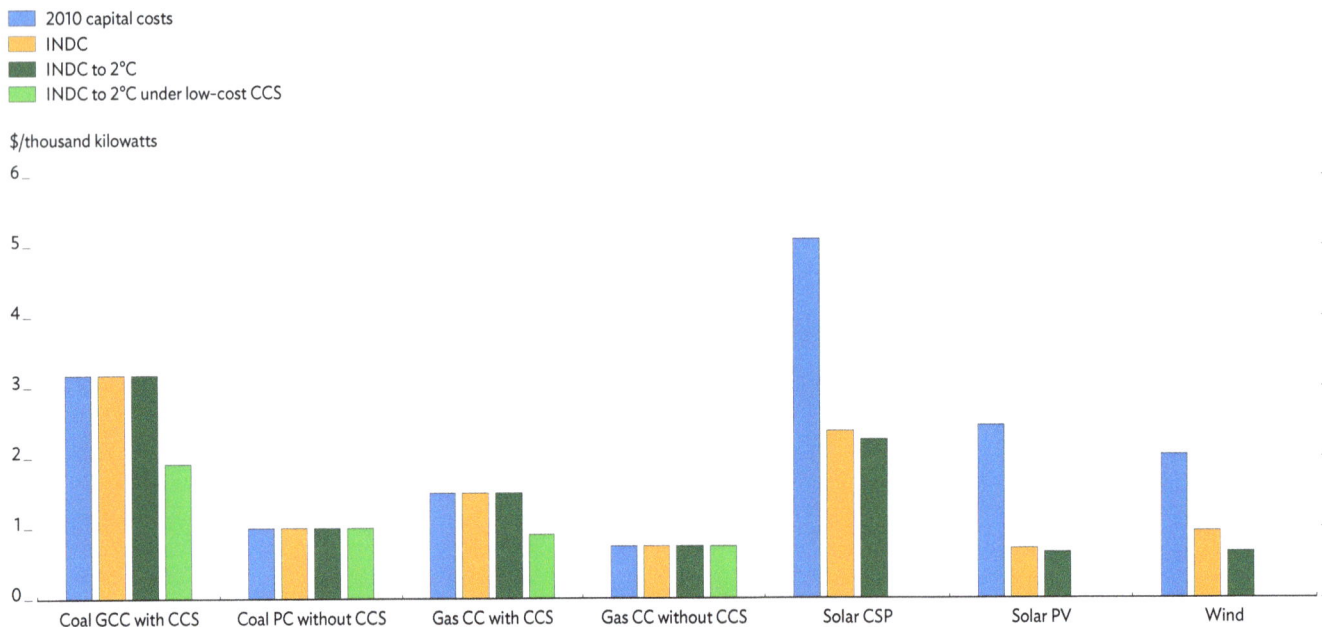

CC = combined cycle, CCS = carbon capture and storage, CSP = concentrating solar power, GCC = gasification combined cycle, INDC = intended nationally determined contribution, kW = kilowatt, PC = pulverized coal, PV = photovoltaic.
Source: Reis et al. 2016.
Click here for figure data

for coal is similar. Combined with earlier results, these findings imply that there is not much leeway for expanded coal capacity if the goals of the Paris Agreement are to be met. Moreover, dramatic improvements in the cost of CCS would do little to change this.

Electricity from renewable sources such as solar and wind is intermittent because installations produce electricity only when the weather cooperates. Therefore, as the share of variable renewables increases, energy storage becomes more important. Also, renewables may be located some distance from demand centers, as dictated by the availability of strong winds and empty land for solar panels. Renewable expansion as modeled therefore implies a greater need to balance variation in their production to solve problems of network congestion and the unpredictability of supply.

Mitigation from energy efficiency

Improving energy efficiency is a key part of any climate-compatible growth strategy. Energy efficiency is broadly defined to include the technical improvements of products and processes as well as structural and behavioral changes that reduce energy consumption.

Achieving energy access and economic diversification goals in Asia will entail a significant increase in energy consumption (Box 2.3.1). Primary energy demand in developing Asia is projected to increase by 2% under business as usual, which is faster than the projected world average growth rate of 1.6%. Slowing this growth rate is an important opportunity for reducing emissions. Reductions can be achieved by

2.3.1 Energy access and climate change in Asia

Around 700 million people in Asia and the Pacific have no access to electricity. Access to reliable and affordable energy is essential for development, job creation, and poverty reduction. The challenge for Asia is to ensure affordable and clean energy access for all, thus fulfilling Sustainable Development Goal 7, without compromising climate change targets. This will be challenging because Asian countries have reserves of fossil fuels that are, in the short term, the least expensive path to expanding energy access.

In the longer term, clean energy is the preferred option for ensuring energy access. In many countries particularly in the Pacific, less than half of the population is connected to electricity mains. As island nations often face high costs for imported fuel to run generators, renewable energy is an attractive alternative to meet energy access targets.

The cost of extending the national electricity grid to rural regions is often quite high. For such localities, off-grid or mini-grid solutions powered by renewables offer a cost-effective alternative. The national electricity grid fails to reach two-thirds of Myanmar's population, and the country is planning to install off-grid solar home systems and mini-grids in rural communities.

Solving the energy access problem is a priority for the region. Asia needs to prioritize the deployment of renewables and ensure that its energy access goals do not run counter to its climate change ambitions. As Asia accounts for most of the growth in future emissions, it is important that the region embark now on a clean-energy trajectory.

designing power grids for fewer technical losses, factories and transport systems for more efficient energy use, and buildings for better cooling, as well as by promoting energy-saving behavior. Climate policy can encourage all of these types of changes.

Mitigation scenarios foresee a large reduction in the amount of energy produced and used in regional economies. The 2°C scenarios cut primary energy use in 2050 nearly by half from business as usual and by a quarter from the INDC scenario. This is achieved mostly through improved energy efficiency.

Energy intensity patterns follow a similar trajectory. Even the business as usual scenario foresees improving energy intensity, or less energy required per unit of GDP, but the mitigation scenarios accelerate this substantially. Taking GDP growth into account, energy intensity by 2050 is 34% lower in the INDC to 2°C scenario than it would be under business as usual (Figure 2.3.5).

Because energy efficiency improvement means that more economic output is generated with less energy input, it helps to speed economic growth. Using energy more efficiently boosts productivity, lowers production costs, and strengthens competitiveness. Many energy-efficiency measures have relatively fast payback periods. The uptake of these economically viable energy-efficiency investments has been previously estimated to accelerate economic growth by 0.25–1.10 percentage points per year, with large associated increases in employment. Because energy-efficiency improvement is more labor intensive than equivalent investments in fossil fuel supply, it creates up to 3 times more jobs per dollar invested (IEA 2014).

2.3.5 Energy intensity in developing Asia under the modeled scenarios

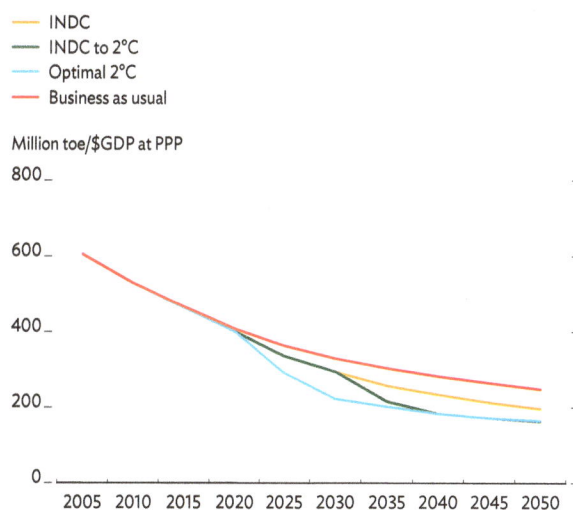

°C = degree Celsius, GDP at PPP = gross domestic product at purchasing power parity, INDC = intended nationally determined contribution, toe = ton of oil equivalent.
Source: Reis et al. 2016.
Click here for figure data

Mitigation from land use

Developing Asia has experienced dramatic land transformation. More than half of Asian land area is under agriculture, much higher than the global average of 37%. This pattern is accelerating. Southeast Asia, including Indonesia, has the highest deforestation rate of any major tropical region, and 5 of the world's 10 most endangered forests are in the Asia and the Pacific. Much of this deforestation is in peat swamp forests that store thousands of tons of carbon per hectare in their soils, and this carbon is released when water levels fall because of fires after forest clearance or other causes of desiccation. Further, peatland and forest fires cause respiratory and other illnesses.

Land-use change has both environmental and social consequences. While forests have contributed to economic growth, their benefits have been inequitably distributed. Growth predicated on deforestation has been highly unsustainable and has significantly increased Indonesia's carbon footprint. In 2015, the World Bank estimated economic losses from peatland and forest fires in Indonesia at close to $16 billion (World Bank 2016). At 8% of GDP, this figure includes the costs of direct damage and response to fires as well as losses to crops, forests, houses, and infrastructure. Low-carbon growth alters this dynamic by avoiding deforestation and undertaking afforestation to effect additional carbon sequestration. Peatland is rehabilitated to avoid desiccation and fires. In addition, agricultural emissions are avoided by changing

2.3.6 Forest cover changes under modeled mitigation scenarios relative to business as usual

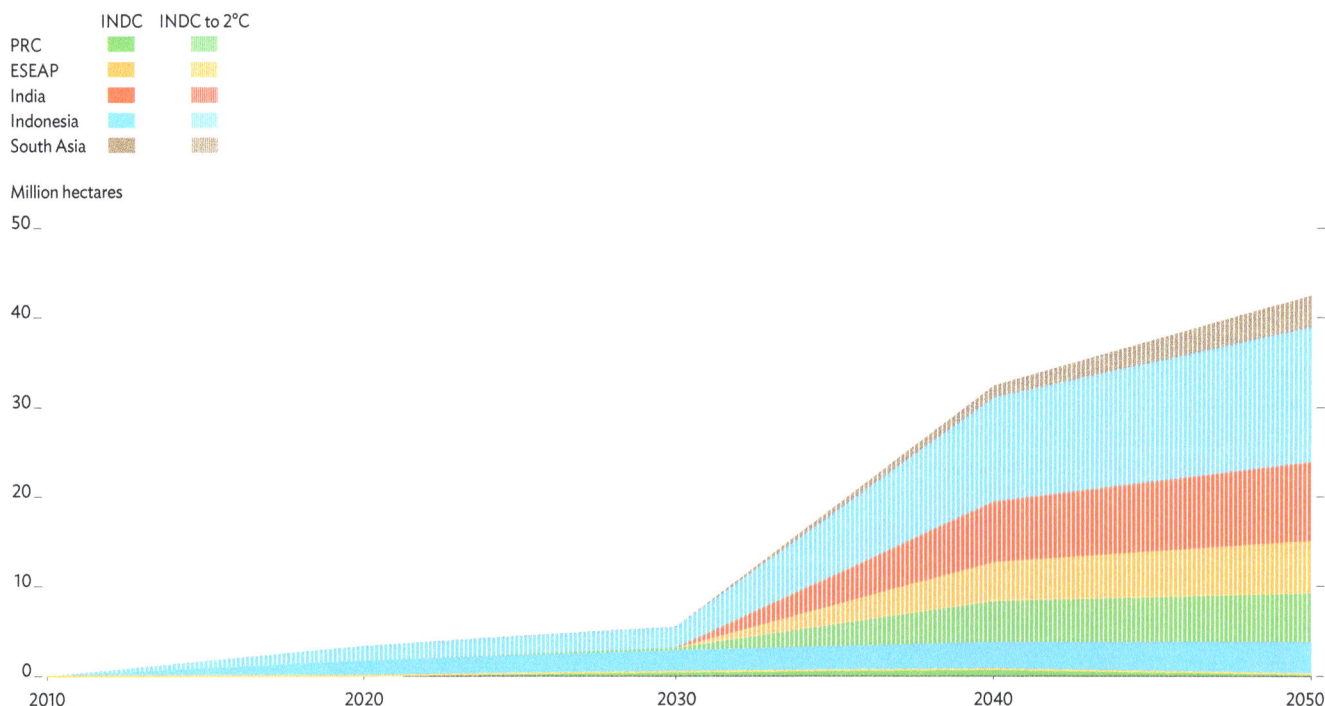

°C = degree Celsius, ESEAP = East and Southeast Asia and the Pacific, INDC = intended nationally determined contribution, PRC = People's Republic of China.

Notes: Values are additive between the INDC scenario and the INDC to 2°C scenario. East and Southeast Asia and the Pacific includes American Samoa, Brunei, Cambodia, Fiji, French Polynesia, Guam, Kiribati, the Lao People's Democratic Republic, Malaysia, the Marshall Islands, the Federated States of Micronesia, Mongolia, Myanmar, New Caledonia, the Northern Mariana Islands, Palau, Papua New Guinea, the Philippines, Samoa, Singapore, Solomon Islands, Thailand, Timor-Leste, Tonga, Vanuatu, Viet Nam, Taipei,China, and Hong Kong, China. South Asia includes Afghanistan, Bangladesh, Bhutan, the Maldives, Nepal, Pakistan, and Sri Lanka.

Source: Reis et al. 2016.

Click here for figure data

residue management practices, and methane emissions may be reduced by altering irrigation management, particularly in rice paddies. Reducing emissions from forest destruction, land degradation, agriculture, and other activities independent of energy production can contribute nearly 20% of the mitigation in INDCs to 2030.

As avoided deforestation is a low-cost mitigation strategy, its adoption saves money as well as forest cover. By 2050, the INDC to 2°C scenario produces 45 million additional hectares of forest, most of it in Indonesia and the rest of Southeast Asia (Figure 2.3.6). The INDC scenario produces a much smaller addition of 5 million hectares of forest by that time. Mitigation measures applied to rice and livestock production can improve productive efficiency at the same time that they reduce emissions.

Market opportunities for Asia in a mitigating world

The changes described in the previous sections reflect new patterns of demand for energy products and services. Dramatic expansion of wind and solar power will mean new markets for wind turbines and solar panels. Greater deployment of intermittent power sources will create more demand for energy storage. A greater focus on energy efficiency will develop new markets for energy-efficient equipment, appliances, and lighting. Asia is well placed to exploit these opportunities such that they spur economic growth while advancing climate change goals.

A substantial and thriving green economy already exists, with Asian companies playing important roles. Global sales of green goods and services amount to $2.9 trillion a year (FTSE Russell 2016). Developing Asia is already a large exporter of low-emissions products and services and, in some economies, a significant innovator. This strong existing green sector can pave the way for low-emissions pathways by taking advantage of reduced costs and readily available technologies. Trade data show developing Asia already accounting for 35% of global climate change mitigation exports, a slightly smaller percentage than Europe but substantially higher than that of the US or Latin America (Figure 2.3.7). Within the region, the PRC is the leading exporter, followed by the Republic of Korea, the Philippines, and India (Figure 2.3.8).

Developing Asia also has a good track record in technological innovation to mitigate climate change. This is a strong indicator of the region's potential, as more innovative economies are likely to be better placed to capture markets in new technologies. Data on patenting activity allowed an assessment of the extent to which nations currently demonstrate innovative capacity and in which technologies.

2.3.7 Regional shares of global climate change mitigation technology exports, 2013

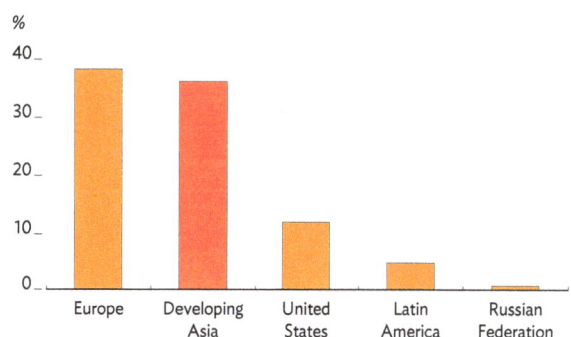

Sources: European Patent Office; United Nations. UN Comtrade online database (accessed 19 September 2016).
Click here for figure data

2.3.8 Selected economies' shares of climate change mitigation technology exports versus all exports, 2013

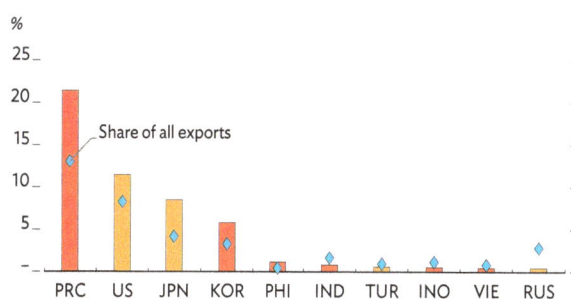

IND = India, INO = Indonesia, JPN = Japan, KOR = Republic of Korea, PHI = Philippines, PRC = People's Republic of China, RUS = Russian Federation, TUR = Turkey, US = United States, VIE = Viet Nam.
Source: United Nations. UN Comtrade online database (accessed 19 September 2016).
Click here for figure data

2.3.9 Regional share of high-value climate change mitigation technology patents, 2013

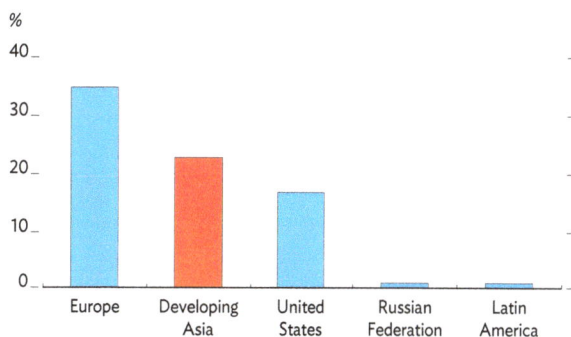

Note: Only high-value patents, defined as having been filed in two jurisdictions, are considered.
Sources: European Patent Office 2016; UN Comtrade online database.
Click here for figure data

2.3.2 Methodology for assessing future Asian competitiveness and opportunities in climate change mitigation

The green innovation index (GII) is a measure of a country's green innovation performance in a sector. The GII is defined as

$$GII_{is} = \frac{p^g_{is}\big/p_{is}}{\Sigma_i\, p^g_{is}\big/p_{is}}$$

where p^g_{is} is the number of green patents and p_{is} is the total number of patents in sector s of country i. The GII is a technology's share of patents in a country over that technology's share of patents in the world. Normalizing against broader patenting activity corrects for idiosyncrasies in patenting behavior in particular sectors or countries (Fankhauser et al. 2012).

Different values of the GII can be interpreted in the following manner for a given technology:
- GII = 1 shows the country with no particular advantage or disadvantage over the rest of the world with regard to innovation. The share of patents in the country is equal to the global average.
- GII >1 shows the country specialized in innovating the technology. The share of patents in the country exceeds the global average. This corresponds to better long-term prospects of capturing value from design.
- GII <1 shows a country less well placed than the global average in innovating in the technology.

The index of revealed comparative advantage (RCA), a measure of comparative advantage in a sector, is a sector's share of exports from a country over that sector's share of exports in the world:

$$RCA_{is} = \frac{e_{is}\big/\Sigma_i e_{is}}{\Sigma_i e_{is}\big/\Sigma_s \Sigma_i e_{is}}$$

where e_{is} is the size of exports from sector s in country i.

The RCA has following interpretations for a given technology:
- RCA = 1 shows the country with no particular export advantage or disadvantage over the rest of the world. The share of exports in the country is equal to the global average.
- RCA >1 shows the country specializing in exporting that technology. This is likely to correspond to better long-term prospects of capturing global market share and value from trade and manufacturing.
- RCA <1 shows a country at an export disadvantage as the share of exports from the country is below the global average.

Taking together, the assessments of exports and innovation in Asia allow a strengths-weaknesses-opportunities-threats assessment of specific sectors. As shown in Figures 2.3.10 and 2.3.11, plotting revealed comparative advantage and an index of green innovation on the x and y axes creates a grid whereby
- the top right corner of such a plane corresponds to better green growth prospects (strengths), with a sector innovating from a current position of competitive strength;
- the bottom left corresponds to weaknesses, with a sector exhibiting strength in neither innovation nor its current export position;
- the top left quadrant corresponds to opportunities, with a sector scoring well on innovation but poorly on comparative advantage, allowing the country to exploit its innovation to spur manufacturing and export in the sector; and
- the bottom right quadrant corresponds to threats, with a sector scoring poorly on innovation but well on comparative advantage. As an exporter but not an innovator, the country is exposed to the risk of market-changing innovations from elsewhere in the world that can render current production redundant. To mitigate this threat, the country can either start engaging in frontier innovation or adopt appropriate technology transfer policies.

Source: Fankhauser, Kazaglis, and Srivastav 2016.

The region as a whole accounts for over 22% of global patents for climate-compatible technologies (Figure 2.3.9).

According to strengths-weaknesses-opportunities-threats assessment (Box 2.3.2), economies in developing Asia appear well placed in a host of climate change mitigation technologies (Figure 2.3.10). Breaking down regional strengths by specific technology suggests that efficient lighting, energy storage, solar energy panels, and renewables are key opportunities (Figure 2.3.11). The PRC has a strong comparative advantage in solar energy panels, of which it is the world's

2.3.10 Strengths-weaknesses-opportunities-threats assessment, 2012

Green innovation index

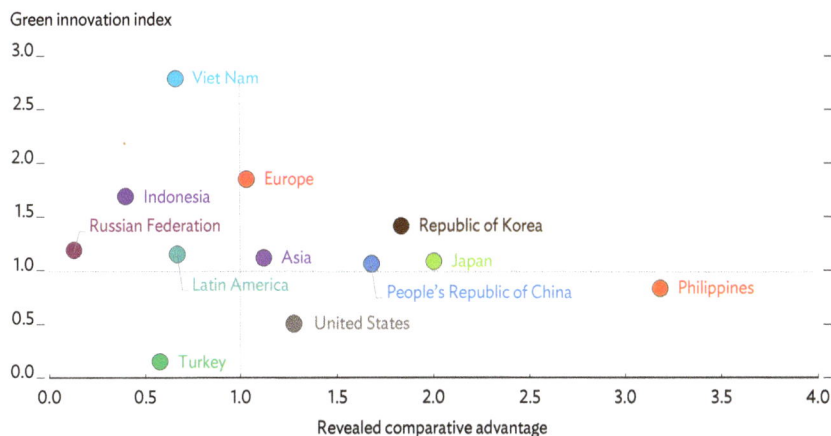

Note: 2012 data for green innovation index and revealed comparative advantage.
Source: Fankhauser, Kazaglis, and Srivastav 2016.
Click here for figure data

leading exporter. The Republic of Korea leads in patents for energy storage technology. India shows significant potential for incremental innovation by adapting existing technologies like wind power and smart-grid technologies to local needs. The Philippines excels in a number of low-carbon metrics and exhibits a comparative advantage in efficient lighting (Fankhauser et al. 2016).

These results show that economies in developing Asia are well placed to serve new markets created by climate change mitigation. Further, the region has innovation specialization and comparative advantage in a host of climate change mitigation technologies, indicating that there are gains from technology transfer, knowledge sharing, and trade within the region.

2.3.11 Strengths-weaknesses-opportunities-threats assessment of key low-carbon technologies for developing Asia, 2012

Green innovation index

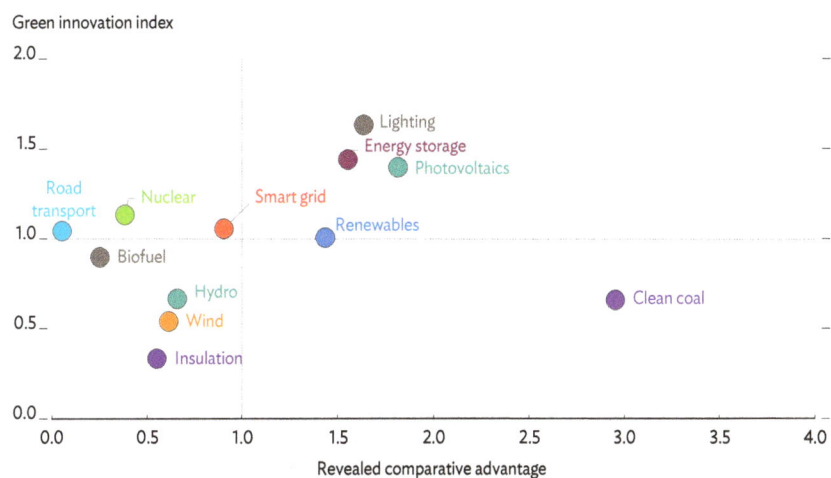

Note: 2012 data for green innovation index and revealed comparative advantage.
Source: Fankhauser, Kazaglis, and Srivastav 2016.
Click here for figure data

Unlocking the low-carbon transition

Achieving the global 2°C goal of the Paris Agreement requires a rapid reduction in GHG emissions. This has to be supported by a radical change in economic behavior and substantial investment in new low-carbon infrastructure, which in developing Asia is estimated to cost a net $10 trillion to 2050 in the energy sector. A strong policy framework is essential to bring about this transition.

One aspect of the change in economic behavior is replacing carbon-intensive energy with low-carbon energy sources and technologies. Low-carbon energy production can achieve nearly half of developing Asia's necessary emissions reduction. This strategy requires an enabling infrastructure, including energy storage and smart grids. The needed investment has to be supported by appropriate incentives from policy makers. These incentives can be designed to encourage energy efficiency as well, which can provide a further third of emissions reduction. Much of the remaining decline in emissions will have to come from land use, achieved by reducing forest destruction and land degradation, accelerating afforestation, and adapting agriculture to release less carbon. Fortunately, policy makers can draw on growing experience in this area, both globally and within the region (Box 2.4.1).

Asia can do its part to achieve the global 2°C goal with a four-pronged approach. Key policies include putting a price on carbon emissions, instituting appropriate regulations, supporting investment in clean and efficient energy, and fostering effective international action.

2.4.1 Toward livable cities—some Asian applications

As Asia prospers, its cities face new challenges with the convergence of several rising risks: climate change, vulnerability to natural disasters, worsening air pollution, growing demand for public services, and the rapid depletion of natural resources. As sector-specific approaches fall short, the government, the private sector, and civil society must coordinate to ensure the integrated management of transport and land, water, and energy use to effectively wed environmental stewardship with low-carbon, climate-resilient urban planning.

Many Asian cities have begun experimenting with a new framework that is scalable and balances economic viability with environmental sustainability and social equity in a flexible manner that responds to residents' vision of a livable city (ADB 2016c). A strategic development plan for Mandalay in Myanmar, for example, aims to strengthen spatial planning and building regulations to minimize the carbon and water footprints of human settlements and to address the carbon footprint of transport

using appropriate technologies, while reducing flood risk by improving solid waste collection and controlling development on natural floodplains. Rapidly urbanizing Mueang Songkhla in Thailand has launched four initiatives to counter environmental degradation, inefficient resource consumption, inequitable growth, and rising risk from climate change and natural disasters. These initiatives promote tourism, enhance land management while redeveloping low-income homes, improve environmental quality, and pursue innovative financing mechanisms to raise resources.

Following a regional approach, Cambodia, the Lao People's Democratic Republic, and Viet Nam have adopted integrated development planning to ensure that increased transport and trade flows along Greater Mekong Subregion corridors benefit selected towns. Environmental and economic infrastructure investments are oriented toward green growth and climate resilience, with a particular focus on poor communities.

Pricing carbon

Putting an appropriate price on carbon emissions is arguably the most important policy intervention to encourage low-carbon practices. At the core of the climate change problem is a fundamental market failure to reflect the full social, economic, and environmental costs of GHG emissions. Land-use arrangements and fossil fuel prices routinely fail to reflect the costs of damage from resulting carbon emissions, which encourages emitters to ignore their carbon output. In some cases, government subsidies on fuel and land use exacerbate this problem. The first step, therefore, toward arriving at an appropriate price for carbon emissions is to reduce or even eliminate these subsidies.

Carbon subsidies

Many Asian economies either implicitly or explicitly subsidize carbon emissions, with the bulk of subsidies going to the extraction and use of fossil fuels. Subsidies on emissions are equivalent to negative carbon prices. Not only do they perpetuate fossil fuel use, they undercut return on investment in clean energy production and efficient energy use. Withdrawing fuel subsidies can eliminate a substantial hurdle to low-carbon transition by allowing clean energy to be cost competitive. In addition, fossil fuel subsidies consume fiscal resources that could be devoted to financing the low-carbon transition (Table 2.4.1). The success of some countries—notably India, Indonesia, and Thailand—in reducing subsidies shows that reform is feasible.

Land use is also affected by subsidies. Forest concessions that grant private parties rights to logging and other uses can create incentives for deforestation. In many cases the state is not fully compensated from timber cleared from public lands, and the resulting economic rent incentivizes forest clearance and GHG emissions. For example, in Indonesia, where deforestation is the largest emitter of GHGs, the government's Corruption Eradication Commission (2015) estimated that state timber assets worth $61 billion–$81 billion were harvested from 2003 to 2014 without adequate payment to revenue-collecting authorities. The first step for many countries toward placing an appropriate price on carbon is to eliminate such subsidies. This will provide correct incentives for resource use while freeing up public funds to support the low-carbon transition.

2.4.1 Savings from fossil fuel subsidy reform, 2012

Item	India	Indonesia	Thailand
Total subsidies (% of GDP)	2.7	4.1	1.9
Cost of fully compensating bottom 40% of households for subsidy removal (% of GDP)	0.2	0.3	0.1
Net savings from subsidy reform (% of GDP)	2.5	3.8	1.8
Reduction of GHG emission by 2030 (% change)	1.3–1.8	5.1–9.3	2.8

Note: Substantial subsidy reform has taken place since 2012 in the countries listed.

Source: ADB 2016b.

Instruments for pricing carbon

Carbon pricing is the most efficient way to deliver emissions reductions. Placing a value or cost on emissions shifts preferences toward low-emissions products and processes and away from emissions-intensive inputs. Putting a price on carbon also encourages innovation in sustainable low-carbon technologies, which in turn creates efficiency gains over time (Reis et al. 2016, Calel and Dechezleprêtre 2016).

Globally, nearly 40 jurisdictions including countries, cities, states, and regions have adopted carbon pricing, covering around 12% of global emissions (Figure 2.4.1). These countries include the PRC, Kazakhstan, and the Republic of Korea. Carbon pricing is particularly important for Asia's largest emitters, which must substantially reduce coal consumption by 2030 to achieve their INDCs.

The success of policy instruments for carbon pricing depends on how they are designed and implemented. There are two generic methods of pricing carbon. Governments can induce firms to pay their carbon costs either through a carbon tax or by setting up emissions trading systems that cap total emissions and facilitate the buying and selling of emissions allowances. A uniform carbon price is established by either method. Increasingly, policy makers are experimenting with hybrid systems that combine elements of both approaches. The main features of these systems are as follows:

- A carbon tax fixes the carbon price but leaves the extent of emissions reduction to be determined by the market. This offers certainty over the cost of compliance, which is the tax rate, but leaves unknown the ultimate effect on emissions.
- An emissions trading system establishes the quantity of emissions allowed by issuing a fixed set of tradable emissions allowances that sum to a desired emissions maximum or cap—from which is derived the name "cap and trade." Allowances may be allocated to firms or auctioned to them. Each firm is required to comply with the emissions allowance it initially receives or else acquire allowances from other firms, either by purchase or trade. The carbon price is thus determined by the market. Although the initial allocation of emissions allowances may pose political and distributional challenges, they will not affect mitigation outcomes or social costs over the long run if the rules governing emissions caps and allowances are strictly enforced.
- Hybrid systems combine elements of both approaches. Examples include trading systems with a price floor and ceiling, or tax programs that accept emissions reduction units to lower tax liability.

The development of pricing mechanisms to address environmental pollutants emerged in the US in the late 1980s and 1990 (Stavins 1998). Most of them have been highly successful in reducing pollution while achieving substantial cost savings. A US emissions trading system to support the phasedown of leaded gasoline in the 1980s yielded cost savings of $250 million per year compared with traditional regulation. A sulfur dioxide trading program under the US Clean Air Act in 1990 helped to halve emissions with cost savings of $1 billion per year, but that market has since closed (Box 2.4.2). Nitrogen oxide trading in the eastern US succeeded in reducing emissions by almost a quarter, with estimated cost savings of 40%–47% percent.

These early trading systems offer practical lessons that can inform the design and operation of carbon pricing systems in Asia (Burtraw et al. 2005, Schmalensee and Stavins 2015). However, key design elements on which sectors to cover and on price flexibility need to be finely tuned to reflect local circumstances.

2.4.1 Evolution of carbon pricing instruments across the globe

Share of global GHG emissions (%)

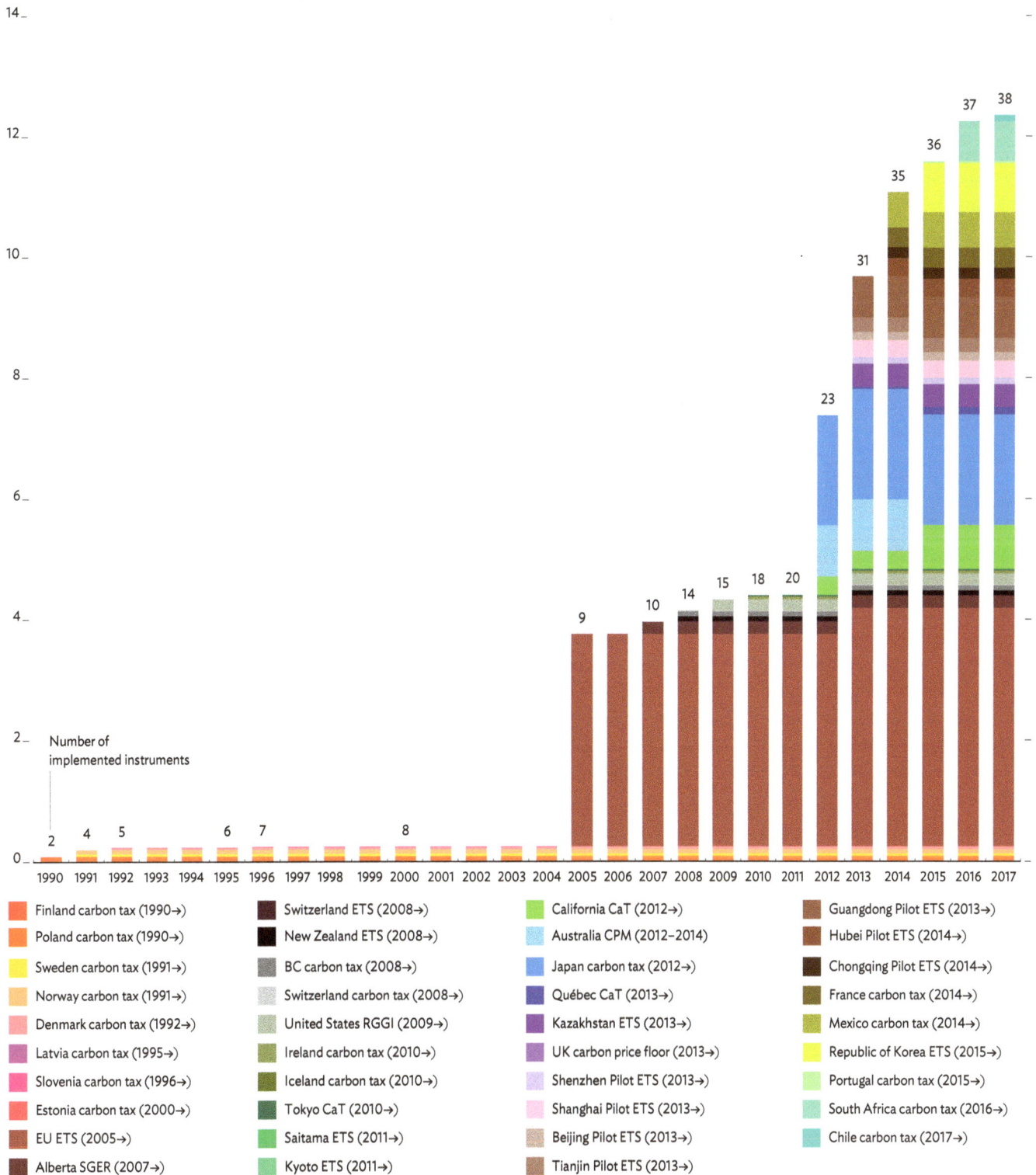

Finland carbon tax (1990→)	Switzerland ETS (2008→)	California CaT (2012→)	Guangdong Pilot ETS (2013→)
Poland carbon tax (1990→)	New Zealand ETS (2008→)	Australia CPM (2012–2014)	Hubei Pilot ETS (2014→)
Sweden carbon tax (1991→)	BC carbon tax (2008→)	Japan carbon tax (2012→)	Chongqing Pilot ETS (2014→)
Norway carbon tax (1991→)	Switzerland carbon tax (2008→)	Québec CaT (2013→)	France carbon tax (2014→)
Denmark carbon tax (1992→)	United States RGGI (2009→)	Kazakhstan ETS (2013→)	Mexico carbon tax (2014→)
Latvia carbon tax (1995→)	Ireland carbon tax (2010→)	UK carbon price floor (2013→)	Republic of Korea ETS (2015→)
Slovenia carbon tax (1996→)	Iceland carbon tax (2010→)	Shenzhen Pilot ETS (2013→)	Portugal carbon tax (2015→)
Estonia carbon tax (2000→)	Tokyo CaT (2010→)	Shanghai Pilot ETS (2013→)	South Africa carbon tax (2016→)
EU ETS (2005→)	Saitama ETS (2011→)	Beijing Pilot ETS (2013→)	Chile carbon tax (2017→)
Alberta SGER (2007→)	Kyoto ETS (2011→)	Tianjin Pilot ETS (2013→)	

BC = British Columbia, CaT = cap-and-trade program, CPM = carbon pricing mechanism, ETS = emissions trading system, EU = European Union, GHG = greenhouse gas, RGGI = regional greenhouse gas initiative, SGER = specified gas emitters regulation, UK = United Kingdom.

Note: Only the introduction or removal of an ETS or carbon tax is shown. Emissions are given as a share of global GHG emissions in 2012. Annual changes in global, regional, national, and subnational GHG emissions are not shown in the graph. Data on the coverage of the city-level Kyoto ETS are not accessible; its coverage is therefore shown as zero.

Source: Kossoy et al. 2015.

2.4.2 Successful cap and trade: sulfur dioxide trading in the United States

Sulfur dioxide trading first came into existence with the US Clean Air Act amendments of 1990. It was an emissions trading program to address acid rain. The stated purpose was to reduce annual sulfur dioxide emissions in the US by 10 million tons from the 1980 level.

The first phase, from 1996 to 1999, saw free allocation and significant emissions reductions from 262 highly polluting coal-fired power plants. The second phase, which began in 2000, placed an aggregate national emissions cap of 8.95 million tons per year on some 3,200 power plants.

The program was a great success by almost all measures, cutting emissions by half. The market response evolved over time (Chan et al. 2012). Burtraw and Szambelan (2009) noted that the large and dirty plants covered in Phase 1 reduced emissions by much more than those that joined in Phase 2, by 57% compared with 14%. Existing plants were allocated permits in proportion to past emissions, but new entrants were obliged to purchase them on the market or through auctions.

A range of studies compared the economic cost of the program with hypothetical regulations that would have achieved the same target through direct regulation. They found that the market-based measure saved 43%–90% on costs (Burtraw and Szambelan 2009). Although fuel prices and exogenous technical change played their parts in reducing compliance costs, the emissions trading program sparked a search for new and cheaper abatement options, such as the increased use of low-sulfur coal.

The costs of the program were estimated at $500 million, while the health benefits from reduced pollution were estimated to be 100 times higher at $50 billion (Chan et al. 2012).

The political economy of emissions permits allocated for free is complex. Free allocation has sometimes generated over-allocation and initial windfall profits because regulators have less prior knowledge about emissions and abatement potential than do industry players. Many systems result in carbon prices that are much lower than initially anticipated by the regulator, sufficient to encourage operational change like switching from coal to gas but not high enough to encourage larger changes in investment behavior. In addition, mitigation ambitions have been modest to date, keeping actual carbon market prices low.

Meanwhile, carbon pricing must be predictable to reduce risk in investment in low-carbon technologies, yet volatile prices have beset many emissions trading systems. So-called price collars that limit price fluctuations to within predetermined minimums and maximums are useful in emissions trading systems that are affected by fluctuating prices, as they provide some price stability. Hybrid systems have been introduced toward achieving more stable prices and have become more common in the latest carbon pricing instruments (Kossoy et al. 2015). Examples include the floor and ceiling prices in California's Cap-and-Trade Program and the reserve of allowances in the Republic of Korea's emissions trading system. Both mechanisms require permits to be auctioned. A stabilizing innovation that still allows free permit allocation is to establish a market stability reserve. The emissions trading system of the European Union is exploring the idea, which entails adjusting the supply of permits in a predefined way according to market conditions.

Recent developments in developing Asia

Carbon pricing systems are already being rolled out in Asia. Though still in its nascent stages, carbon pricing in the PRC has produced globally significant developments. The seven pilot systems are, when taken together, the largest national carbon pricing initiative in the world (Table 2.4.2). The success of these pilot systems has encouraged them to become more stringent and broaden their coverage. Shenzhen is planning to include transport, for example, and Guangdong is considering more industrial sectors, buildings, and transport. Hubei is adding new companies, and Chongqing has reduced its cap faster than expected. Plans are now being made to expand beyond these regions, and details have begun to emerge of a system scheduled for launch in 2017.

Kazakhstan launched its emissions trading system in January 2013, covering half of emissions there. In the first phase, the system stabilized capped entities' emissions at 2010 levels. In the second phase, it implemented further reductions by 1.5%. In the third phase, it set an absolute emissions cap of 746.5 million tons of carbon dioxide from 2016 to 2020. The penalty for noncompliance is about €30 per ton of carbon dioxide.

These new systems build on experience with the Clean Development Mechanism, an international carbon trading system established under the Kyoto Protocol. Under the mechanism, eligible countries could sell emissions reductions if the emissions in a certified project or installation fell below an agreed baseline. Developing Asia, and the PRC in particular, were leading participants, accounting for about three-quarters of contracted emissions reductions at the peak of the market. India accounted for the second highest contracted emissions reductions under the mechanism. However, after a short boom in the late 2000s, demand for Clean Development Mechanism credits dried up following the financial crisis and the end of the Kyoto commitment period in 2012, which created uncertainty about the market's future.

Given the patchwork of different carbon pricing instruments that is emerging globally, their impact on the competitiveness of low-carbon industries has been a source of concern, particularly in Asia. In theory, different carbon prices could induce companies to move production or redirect their investment to locations where costs are lower. However, a careful assessment of the evidence to date suggests there has been no major redirection of production or investment in response to carbon pricing (Dechezleprêtre and Sato 2014). The risk is limited to sectors that are both emissions- and trade-intensive.

2.4.2 Pilot emissions trading systems in the People's Republic of China

Carbon pricing system	2015 carbon price ($/tCO$_2$e)	Emissions covered (GtCO$_2$e)
Shanghai	<10	1.00
Chongqing	<10	1.75
Guangdong	<10	1.80
Tianjin	<10	2.25
Hubei	<10	2.40
Shenzhen	<10	2.50
Beijing	10	2.60

GtCO$_2$e = billion tons of carbon dioxide equivalent, tCO$_2$e = ton of carbon dioxide equivalent.

Source: Kossoy et al. 2015.

Instituting standards and regulations

Carbon pricing complements regulations and standards to spur the adoption of new technologies and technological improvements. The diffusion of low-carbon and energy-efficient products often needs to be actively facilitated. Inaccurate or insufficient information regarding the performance of efficient or clean technologies may cause underinvestment in them. Transaction costs associated with investing and installing new equipment may similarly deter investment in energy efficiency. Experience is growing on how regulatory measures are best deployed, including in developing Asia.

Renewable energy regulation

Switching to low-carbon and renewable energy is the single strategy by which developing Asia can mitigate climate change the most. However, Asia needs to do more than its current energy plans call for to align with the 2°C threshold. Whereas current energy plans for major economies in the region target 2%–3% annual growth in primary energy from renewable sources, the results presented earlier show that 4%–7% average annual growth is required to 2050 (Figure 2.4.2). This can be achieved with the right conditioning policies.

A number of policies have been applied in Asia to support renewables (Table 2.4.3). Most of them focus on deployment to increase clean energy output rather than on research and development to stimulate innovation. Quantity-based support systems like renewable portfolio standards revolve around obligations on electricity companies to generate a certain portion of their supply from renewable sources. These standards exist in much of Asia but may currently stipulate only low shares from renewables, and they are absent from India and Indonesia.

Meanwhile, standardized producer purchase agreements exist in much of Asia to make it easier to contract renewable power producers. The most prominent and arguably most successful renewables support policy is a price-based system. Feed-in tariffs (FITs) guarantee clean-energy producers a fixed price and, often, guaranteed offtake. Investors appreciate the certainty that a fixed price offers. FITs tend to be more successful at boosting renewable energy uptake than other instruments such as portfolio standards (Dong 2012). On the other hand, successful tariffs are sometimes overly generous and create excessive economic rents. This is particularly the case for rapidly evolving technologies like solar cells, for which regulation tends to lag behind the latest cost developments.

FITs are becoming more common in Asia (Table 2.4.4). Thailand introduced renewable electricity FITs in 2007, the PRC added a solar feed-in policy to its existing set of FITs in 2011, and India introduced FITs for all renewables in 2013. However, not all systems are fully implemented, and some may be too strict, instead of being too generous.

2.4.2 Planned versus optimal annual growth in renewable primary energy supply in selected Asian countries

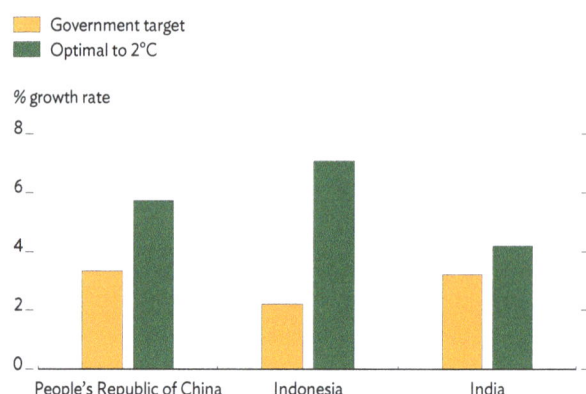

°C = degree Celsius.
Note: Government targets for renewable energy are expressed as shares of total primary energy supply.
Sources: Renewables 2016 Global Status Report (accessed 10 September 2016); PRC State Council (www.gov.cn) (accessed 14 September 2016); Reis et al. 2016.
Click here for figure data

2.4.3 Broader renewable energy support measures in developing Asia

Renewable power support policy	India	PRC	Indonesia	Malaysia	Philippines	Thailand	Viet Nam
Net metering	✓				✓		
Renewable portfolio standards		✓		✓	✓	✓	
Standard producer purchase agreement	✓	✓	✓	✓		✓	✓
Equity support	✓	✓	✓			✓	✓
Debt financing	✓	✓				✓	✓
Tax incentives	✓	✓	✓	✓	✓	✓	✓

PRC = People's Republic of China.
Sources: ADBI 2015; ASEAN Centre for Energy 2013.

Either prices are too low or the guaranteed price period is too short to have a significant impact. To avoid the risk of mispricing the feed-in rate, countries increasingly resort to competitive procurement systems, wherein fixed quantities of renewable energy capacity or output are purchased through auctions. The use of auctions reduces the risk of both underpricing and excessive rents. The PRC and India have pioneered renewable auctions in developing Asia.

Among other measures, net metering, which allows reverse sales into the grid by households and other actors with small-scale renewable power generation, is absent from much of Asia. However, some forms of financial incentives beyond FITs exist in many countries, including tax incentives, favorable finance, and equity support. At the same time, the scale and coverage of most such incentives are still insufficient to attract substantial investment.

2.4.4 Feed-in tariffs in operation in developing Asia				
Country	Solar	Wind	Hydropower	Biomass
PRC	✓	✓	✓	✓
India	✓	✓	✓	✓
Indonesia			✓	✓
Malaysia	✓		✓	✓
Philippines	✓	✓	✓	✓
Viet Nam		✓		
Thailand	✓	✓	✓	✓

PRC = People's Republic of China.
Source: Winston and Strawn 2014.

Energy performance standards and labeling

Minimum energy performance standards (MEPS) stipulate acceptable energy usage for appliances, lighting, industrial equipment, and other energy-consuming devices. MEPS have an advantage in relatively low administrative costs, but they run the risk that standards will not be set at the economic optimum.

The PRC has been a leader in implementing MEPS, first adopting them in 1989 and now covering a wide range of products including washing machines, refrigerators, air conditioners, and lighting. MEPS implementation and labeling varies widely across markets. MEPS apply to a broad range of products in India, Malaysia, Viet Nam and Taipei,China but to a narrower range in other markets such as the Philippines, covering only heating and lighting, and Thailand, covering refrigeration, heating, and air-conditioning.

Together with MEPS, labeling is a complementary measure that helps consumers make economic and eco-conscious decisions by stating appliances' cost savings and carbon footprints. The PRC has instituted mandatory labeling for computers and a host of other electronics in response to the strong uptake of these devices in recent years.

That the region includes some of the world's largest manufacturers of energy-using appliances and equipment suggests that there is scope for regional initiatives to raise and harmonize standards to "best available technology" level. Current initiatives include the global Collaborative Labeling and Appliance Standards Program, called CLASP, which seeks to share policy information and develop standards in Asia, and Energy Star labels, which are used in multiple Asian countries. However, much untapped opportunity remains for significant and low-cost gains from extending the deployment of standards across developing Asia.

Fuel efficiency standards and transport regulation

Low-carbon policy for transport can build on a transition to electric vehicles, stronger fuel economy standards, and strategies to encourage modal shifts towards public transport, walking, and cycling—as well as further reducing demand for transport through urban consolidation and building cities that are more compact. Many of these objectives are best achieved through regulations that complement pricing measures.

Developing Asia's vehicle emissions standards, where present, generally aim to reduce noxious air pollution rather than GHG emissions. Measures that have helped reduce GHG emissions include India's introduction in 2011 of a mandatory fuel efficiency standard and labeling system, the Bharat stage emissions standards, which mandated the phasing out of two-stroke engines and a transition toward the use of compressed natural gas. The PRC is among the few economies in the world—alongside Canada, Japan, and the US—to have imposed fuel efficiency standards not only on small vehicles but also on larger ones (Kodjak 2015). To achieve mitigation, other economies in Asia can focus more on GHG and fuel efficiency standards that aim to reduce emissions from both passenger and heavy goods vehicles, as do the GHG standards of the European Union.

Energy audits and energy service companies

Mandatory energy audits and benchmarking programs are important to changing energy consumption behavior. In Indonesia, the Ministry of Industry has introduced energy conservation plans and audits in all major industries, requiring, for example, that furnaces and boilers be well maintained. While several Asian countries have energy audits, their implementation, documentation, and monitoring is often insufficient.

Energy service companies help firms, households, and other agents improve energy efficiency and realize cost savings. Currently, the PRC has the biggest and most developed market for such companies in Asia. Other Asian countries have government-backed energy service companies but are still developing their markets. Instituting stricter MEPS and other standards would help promote the development of such companies in the private sector.

Building codes

Buildings are responsible for a significant portion of energy use in developing Asia, accounting in Southeast Asia, for example, for about 40% of energy use (IEA 2014). Low-cost energy efficiency measures in Asia include reduced demand for heating and cooling through greater rollout of insulation measures, improved air-conditioning systems, and better designs for on-site energy generators. Stricter building codes and standards can require these changes toward energy efficiency.

Industrial energy management practices

There is a role for regulation in industry to complement market-oriented measures by mandating the use of efficient equipment and energy management practices. These regulations can help overcome barriers related to long-lived assets and the high transaction costs associated with changing equipment.

The PRC has implemented technology mandates through its Iron and Steel Industrial Development Policy. The policy requires, for example, all new blast furnaces to adopt efficient top gas pressure recovery turbines and pulverized coal injection. Coking ovens used in steelmaking have to include coke dry quenching equipment, and all coke ovens and blast furnaces have to employ gas recovery.

In India, the "perform, achieve, and trade" mechanism, while a market-based measure, includes baseline and subsector targets for industries to reduce energy consumption toward achieving government-specified targets for particular facilities. These targets can also be met by purchasing permits.

Investing in clean energy

Governments in developing Asia have limited resources to invest in climate projects. The low-carbon transition has to be financed primarily by the private sector. However, evidence shows that capital flows to low-carbon opportunities are hampered by imperfections and misperceptions in financial markets. Clean energy investments tend to be prone to risk, as their returns are conditioned on government policies that may change. Moreover, climate-compatible investments require greater initial capital cost with payback over longer periods. To compensate, the public sector must share the risk faced by private business and provide supplementary finance to low-carbon projects. Much can be achieved by redirecting existing resources, making investment in new technologies less risky, and lining up finance.

Reduce investment risks

Clean energy investments tend to be risky. They require more capital up front than do conventional investments, and their returns depend on government policies that are subject to change. The problem is compounded by a financial sector that is inherently conservative and lacks experience and trust in new technologies. Regulatory complexity, remoteness, and the resulting higher costs of connection can reinforce negative risk perceptions. Attracting private investment thus requires the public sector to reduce risk, particularly by supporting the piloting of clean technologies.

An obvious first step toward reducing policy risk is to change the parameters of low-carbon policy making. At the strategic level, agreed climate targets anchored in legislation can help to make policy more predictable and reassure investors. Scrutiny by independent technocratic bodies can further allay concerns about political interference (Fankhauser 2013).

Such institutional arrangements can be complemented, at least in the short term, by financing instruments that allow private investors to share with other parties the real or perceived risk of low-carbon projects. If risks can be shared with public bodies, the returns are more likely to be sufficient for private investment and may even attract capital to green projects from groups that are generally averse to backing low-carbon projects, such as pension funds.

There is a particular need for greater equity investment in the early stages of project development and a wider use of instruments to deal with political and policy risk. This can include guarantee systems (for example, to cover initial losses), financial instruments that combine equity and debt features, and loans that are subordinated to the rights of senior lenders (Vivid Economics 2014). Toward generating clean power, for example, governments may offer risk guarantees and take equity stakes. Toward improving energy efficiency, energy service companies may promote technology diffusion.

Although these are well-known investment products offered by many development institutions oriented toward the private sector, rolling them out for low-carbon technologies at a larger scale will require some institutions to ramp up their ability to cover the risks associated with these investments. In some instances it may require the creation of new financing vehicles such as dedicated green funds or green investment banks, which are likely to become part of the climate finance landscape. Bangladesh is one country already exploring such options, driven by a desire to attract more climate finance.

2.4.3 Investment in renewable energy by region, 2004–2015

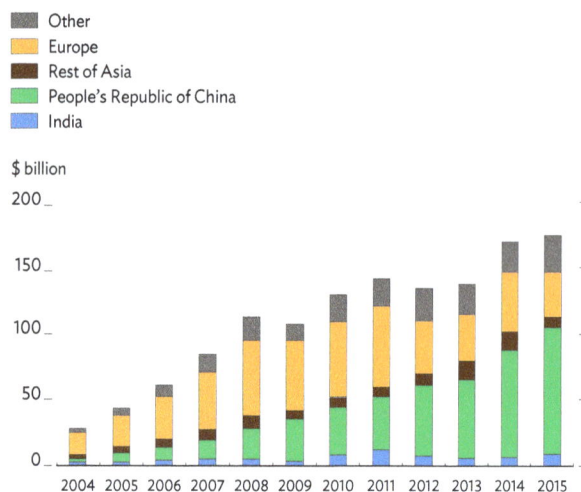

Source: UNEP 2016.
Click here for figure data

Facilitate greater climate finance

As noted above, achieving the 2°C scenario requires additional net investment of $300 billion annually in energy supply from 2015 to 2050, on top of the reference scenario. The total investment in renewables and carbon capture and storage (CCS) facilities will need to be $430 billion annually in developing Asia.

There is progress in ramping up such investment but not enough. Over recent years, global investment in renewables has been on the rise, and Asian investments have risen faster than the global average (Figure 2.4.3). More than half of global renewable investment in 2014 and 2015 was in Asia, with most of this in the PRC. Renewable investment in developing Asia has grown almost 14 times over from 2004 to 2015, approaching $150 billion in 2015.

The growth rate of asset finance investment in renewables varies much more within developing Asia (Figure 2.4.4). The PRC has enjoyed exceptional amounts invested. India, Pakistan, Thailand, Viet Nam, and Taipei,China are growing, while investment is declining in others. Outside of the PRC, the dollar value of asset investments is still small relative to GDP. This underscores that additional investment in clean energy remains low in much of developing Asia outside of the PRC.

In recent years, wind and solar have come to dominate renewable investment in Asia (Figure 2.4.5). Investment in solar reached $97 billion in 2015 and wind $54 billion. Investment in solar has ballooned to 37 times the investments made in the early 2000s, while wind grew by 16 times.

2.4.4 Asset finance investment in renewable energy in selected economies in developing Asia, 2015

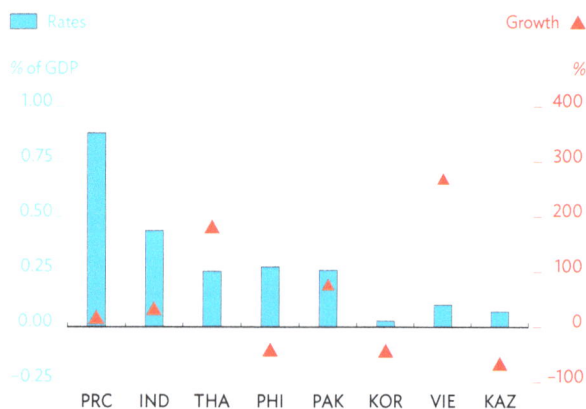

IND = India, KAZ = Kazakhstan, KOR = Republic of Korea, PAK = Pakistan, PHI = Philippines, PRC = People's Republic of China, THA = Thailand, VIE = Viet Nam.
Source: UNEP 2016.
Click here for figure data

Asia receives as well a substantial share, roughly one-quarter, of all public climate finance. The PRC, India, and Indonesia are the top recipients of climate finance, and 62% of all public climate finance approved in Asia since 2003 has been for mitigation (Barnard et al. 2015).

Yet, despite increased capital flows, low-carbon investments are still difficult to finance. They require outsized initial capital outlays and have long payback periods, making them relatively risky. Countries can, however, channel private finance by offering incentives such as interest subsidies, co-investment by government-backed institutions (including public–private partnership and joint investment by different levels of government), and guarantees for climate bonds. In 2014, global public climate finance stood at $148 billion, complementing private climate finance at $243 billion (CPI 2015).

Technologies like offshore wind and CCS have considerably higher upfront costs than do, for example, gas-fired power plants, though lower operating costs typically compensate for the higher capital costs.

Credit programs aimed at small borrowers, such as energy efficiency credit lines for small and medium-sized enterprises, can encourage local banks to extend further credit to those pursuing small projects in solar power or energy efficiency.

2.4.5 **New financial investment in clean energy in Asia**

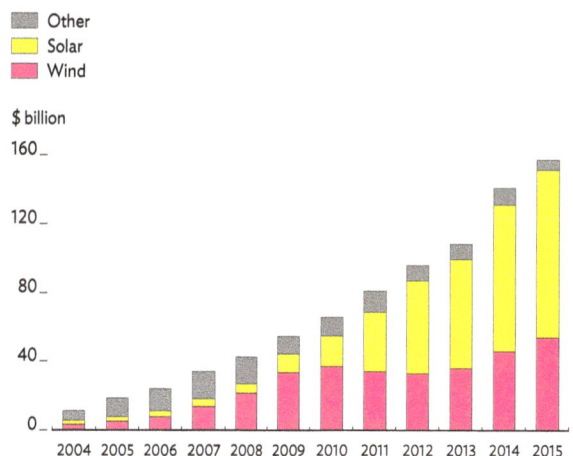

Source: UNEP 2016.
Click here for figure data

Fostering rapid international action

Because climate change is a global problem, and each economy receives only a subset of the climate benefits it creates through mitigation, climate change requires global solutions. Mitigation can be cheapest to achieve in economies that are less developed, but these are precisely the economies that have the fewest resources available to put toward mitigation and often the lowest capacity to deploy new energy-efficient technologies. International cooperation is therefore essential to achieve rapid emissions reduction at low cost.

Harmonization of carbon prices

From a theoretical standpoint, a global carbon pricing system can achieve mitigation most efficiently by encouraging emissions reductions where they are least costly. However, developing the institutional infrastructure and building the political consensus for a global carbon pricing system will take many years. In the meantime, the development of national and regional carbon pricing programs is a priority. Over time, these regional trading systems may become increasingly linked and start to resemble a global carbon market.

Global carbon pricing will likely evolve from national systems along a track of intensifying linkages and harmonization. Foreseeing this trajectory, the United Nations Framework Convention on Climate Change has developed its Framework for Various Approaches and its New Market Mechanism to develop international standards on emissions accounting, monitoring, and trading.

Carbon trading systems can be directly linked, with participants trading with one another, or indirectly linked, with participants trading only through a third party. However, the scale and complexity of integration will increase as more carbon markets in different jurisdictions become linked.

The 2015 Paris Agreement includes the Sustainable Development Mechanism, the successor to the Clean Development Mechanism. Much like its predecessor, the Sustainable Development Mechanism allows parties to fulfil their own mitigation requirements by reducing emissions elsewhere. However, the new mechanism is much more comprehensive, as it potentially allows for trading among all parties to the Paris Agreement, not among only a subset of more advanced economies as under the Clean Development Mechanism. The Paris Agreement further contains provisions to link national pledges under a system that trades a new class of carbon assets: internationally transferred mitigation outcomes. The system allows countries to meet mitigation targets by funding emissions reductions outside their borders. Such linkages will help equalize marginal abatement costs. It is likely that countries with low-cost abatement options, such as Indonesia and Myanmar, where deforestation is the prime driver of emissions, will have significant potential for attracting financing. The financial gains from selling excess carbon credits should exceed the cost of emissions reduction to make the system economically attractive. Internationally transferred mitigation outcomes provide a more direct route for transferring mitigation outcomes that does not depend on markets, as a country can simply finance and manage abatement project elsewhere in the world. This has a crucial role to play in the global effort against climate change because the INDCs of several developing countries have conditional targets that rely critically on assistance from developed nations.

Technological cooperation

Many of the most important elements of the low-carbon transition depend on the adoption or increased use of new technologies, particularly for energy generation and consumption: advanced biofuels, smart grids, new energy storage, CCS, and new technologies for energy efficiency in industries, transport, and households. Substantial investment in research and development is needed to make these technologies ripe for adoption. Some of this research will be upstream on basic technological improvement, but an important share will also be applied research to refine more mature technologies to local conditions. As such research investments are amenable to economies of scale, cooperation that combines research efforts can bring faster innovation, which is important for scaling out technologies that take many years to develop. Cooperation further helps to build absorptive capacity toward speeding the deployment of innovations.

Some Asian economies are becoming leaders in investment in renewable energy research. In 2015, research and development spending in the PRC reached $2.8 billion, a world record and, in terms of research intensity relative to GDP, far ahead of all other regions (Figure 2.4.6). Even in aggregate, Asia has a renewable energy research intensity in line with that of the US. In addition, research investment growth is faster in both the PRC and the rest of developing Asia than in the developed world. Nevertheless, it remains far below the $8 billion presented earlier as the annual average investment necessary in developing Asia to keep global warming within 2°C.

Moreover, these trends mask substantial disparity. Renewable research expenditure is concentrated in the PRC and other leading Asian countries, but India displays a pattern typical of much of Asia, with expenditure on research as a share of GDP lower than the global average. International cooperation within Asia can help participants with less capacity for innovation to benefit from those that have invested in improving technologies.

Getting advanced technologies deployed often requires long lead times, as conditions must be met for successful commercialization. For example, CCS must first be found to work through small-scale pilots run for technology development, and then demonstrated on a larger scale to win investor confidence before finally being deployed commercially (ADB 2013). A supportive regulatory environment must also be established to spell out long-term subsurface storage rights, regulatory approaches for carbon dioxide and CCS pipelines, and legal liability. Similarly, the deployment of advanced cellulosic biofuel production, which generates fuel from agricultural residues, depends upon establishing suitable supply chains that link vast numbers of farmers, collectors, transporters, and processors. Technical cooperation can help to shorten preparatory periods by replicating successful models and adaptations.

Shortening the long lead times for developing and deploying advanced energy technologies is of critical importance to reaping the large social returns possible from investment in mitigation policies. These technologies take decades to develop to the point of wide commercialization, and may take decades longer if countries attempt to develop and deploy them in isolation. As the previous section showed, accelerating ambitious mitigation to keep warming within 2°C can cut those costs by a quarter by 2050, and double their returns. Achieving such potential depends on rates of advanced energy adoption and energy system transformation that are simply not possible without both immediate action and international cooperation.

The analysis finds that the costs of the low-carbon transition can be modest compared with the large benefits possible from reduced climate change losses and improved air quality. At the same time, realizing the full potential of low-carbon growth at fairly low cost requires rapid action. A dramatic transition in energy and land use will not happen by itself. It requires a policy framework that strongly supports the uptake of low-carbon solutions. At the core of this framework is the need to put a realistic price on GHG emissions, but it also requires conducive regulations, stronger support for low-carbon innovation, a concerted push toward low-carbon investment, and international cooperation.

Reducing the risks of climate change unequivocally serves Asia's self-interest, as economies in the region are among the most vulnerable in the world to climate change. Developing Asia will flourish in a low-carbon world. The region has potential to sell billions of dollars' worth of carbon credits. Its industries are exceptionally well positioned to be global leaders in low-carbon technology, and its rich natural environment can be protected for future generations.

2.4.6 Corporate and government renewable energy research expenditures, 2015

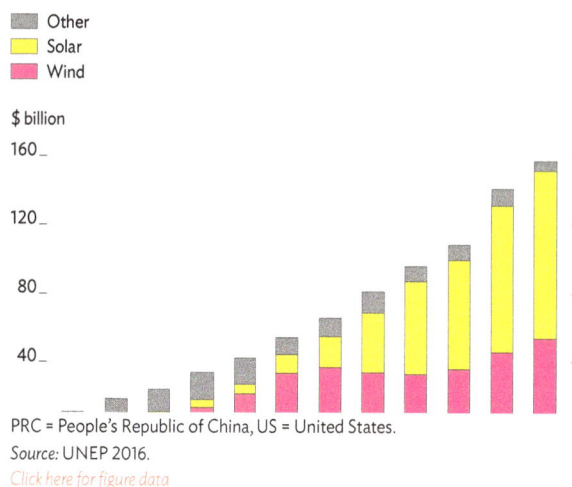

PRC = People's Republic of China, US = United States.
Source: UNEP 2016.
Click here for figure data

Annex: Developing Asia's intended nationally determined contributions

Economy	Unconditional emissions pledges	Conditional emissions pledges	GHG intensity goal	Business as usual details
Central Asia				
Armenia		• Limit emissions to 0.07 tons per capita annually by 2050 • Limit aggregate emissions to 633 $MtCO_2e$ from 2015 to 2050		2010 GHG emissions at 2.14 tons per capita
Azerbaijan	Reduce emissions by 35% below BAU by 2030			Emissions currently about 40% below 1990 levels
Georgia	Reduce emissions by 15% below BAU by 2030	Reduce emissions by 25% below BAU by 2030	Reduce emissions intensity per unit of GDP by about 34% from 2013 to 2030	BAU emissions at 38.42 $MtCO_2e$ in 2030, based on 2013 projections, so the 15% target means 32.66 $MtCO_2e$ in 2030, and 25% means 28.32 $MtCO_2e$
Kazakhstan	Reduce emissions by 15% by 2030	Reduce emissions by 25% by 2030		Base year unspecified but current emissions down 80%–85% from 1990
Kyrgyz Republic	• Reduce emissions by 11.49%–13.75% below BAU by 2030 • Reduce emissions by 12.67%–15.69% below BAU by 2050	• Reduce emissions by 29.00%–30.89% below BAU by 2030 • Reduce emissions by 35.06%–36.75% below BAU by 2050		0.079% of total world population but only 0.023% share of global GHG emissions from fossil fuel combustion, so per capita GHG emissions less than one-third of world average as 90% of electricity supply is hydroelectric
Tajikistan	Emissions not to exceed 80%–90% of 1990 level by 2030	Emissions to be 65%–75% below 1990 level by 2030		1990 reference year at 25.5 $MtCO_2e$
Turkmenistan		Stabilize or begin to reduce emissions by 2030		2030 BAU at 135,833 $MtCO_2e$
East Asia				
PRC	Reduce emissions intensity by 60%–65% below 2005 levels by 2030	CO_2 emissions to peak by 2030		2014 baseline for CO_2 emissions
Korea, Rep. of	Reduce emissions by 37% below BAU by 2030			782.5 $MtCO_2e$ in 2020, 809.7 $MtCO_2e$ in 2025, and 850.6 $MtCO_2e$ in 2030
Mongolia	Reduce emissions by 14% below BAU by 2030	Reduce emissions from deforestation by a further 5% by 2030		2014 baseline for CO_2 emissions
Taipei,China[a]	Emissions to be 50% below BAU by 2030			BAU emissions in 2030 estimated to be 428 $MtCO_2e$, and current emissions at 277.2 $MtCO_2e$
South Asia				
Afghanistan		Reduce emissions by 13.6% below BAU by 2030		46,482.20 $GgCO_2e$ in 2020, 53,180.64 $GgCO_2e$ in 2025, and 61,034.25 $GgCO_2e$ in 2030, all including LULUCF
Bangladesh	Reduce emissions by 5% below BAU by 2030	Reduce emissions by 15% below BAU by 2030		2011 base year at 64 $MtCO_2e$, so 234 $MtCO_2e$ in 2030 excluding LULUCF
Bhutan[b]	Remain carbon neutral with emissions not exceeding carbon sequestration by forests			Forestry sequestration estimated at 6.3 $MtCO_2e$

continued next page

Continued

Economy	Unconditional emissions pledges	Conditional emissions pledges	GHG intensity goal	Business as usual details
India		Reduce emissions intensity by 33%–35% by 2030 from 2005 baseline		Energy intensity at 18.16 grams of oil equivalent per rupee of GDP in 2005, but with no clear statement on emissions intensity baseline
Sri Lanka	Reduce emissions by 7% from BAU by 2030: 4% from energy and 3% from other sectors	Reduce emissions by 23% below BAU by 2030		Breakdown provided of mitigation efforts across different sectors
Maldives	Reduce emissions by 10% below BAU by 2030	Reduce emissions by 24% below BAU by 2030		2030 emissions projected to be triple those in 2010
Nepal[b]	80% of electrification through renewable energy sources for an appropriate energy mix			29,347 $GtCO_2e$ in 1994 (without LULUCF), 24,541 $GtCO_2e$ in 2000, and 30,011 $GtCO_2e$ in 2008; 0.027% share of global GHG emissions, with 1% of energy from renewable sources
Pakistan[b]	Reduce emissions after they peak based on calculations and pledges made then			No emissions baseline but will make pledges when reliable data on peak emissions are available
Southeast Asia				
Brunei Darussalam[b]	• Reduce energy consumption by 63% below BAU by 2030 • Increase share of renewables to provide 10% of power generation by 2035			No baseline emissions specified
Cambodia		• Reduce emissions by 27% below BAU by 2030 • Reduction of 3,100 $GtCO_2e$ from baseline of 11,600 $GtCO_2e$ by 2030		Second National Communication projections generated using a model for planning long-range energy alternatives, default emission factors, and activity data from a wide range of sources
Indonesia	Reduce emissions by 29% below BAU by 2030	Reduce emissions by 41% below BAU by 2030		BAU, based on historical trajectory 2000–2010 with projected energy increases and no mitigation, estimated at 2.881 $GtC0_2e$ in 2030
Lao PDR	Increase share of small-scale renewable energy to 30% of energy consumption by 2030, estimated to reduce emissions by 1,468,000 $ktCO_2e$ by 2025			BAU is based on emissions level in 2000.
Malaysia	Reduce emissions intensity by 35% below 2005 level by 2030		Reduce emissions intensity by 45% below 2005 level by 2030	2005 emissions intensity at 0.531 tons of CO_2 equivalent per RM1,000
Myanmar[b]	• By 2030, boost hydropower capacity by 9.4 gigawatts to achieve rural electrification using at least 30% renewable sources • Expand forested area to 30% by 2030			No emissions baseline specified
Philippines		Reduce emissions below 70% of BAU by 2030		Baseline scenario from historical GDP 2010–2014 and annual average of growth at 6.5% in 2015–2030, and average annual population growth at 1.85%; co-benefits recognized and climate impacts considered

continued next page

Continued

Economy	Unconditional emissions pledges	Conditional emissions pledges	GHG intensity goal	Business as usual details
Singapore	• Reduce emissions intensity by 36% below 2005 baseline by 2030 • Stabilize emissions with aim to peak by around 2030			GHG emissions in 2030 projected at 0.113 kgCO$_2$e per Singapore dollar at 2010 prices
Thailand	Reduce emissions by 20% by 2030	Reduce emission by 25% below BAU by 2030		BAU in 2030 at 555 MtCO2e
Viet Nam	Reduce emissions by 8% below BAU by 2030	• Reduce emissions by 25% below BAU by 2030 • Reduce emissions intensity by 30% below 2010 level by 2030		2010 emissions at 246.8 MtCO$_2$e, 2020 emissions at 474.1 MtCO$_2$e, and 2030 emissions at 787.4 MtCO$_2$e
The Pacific				
Cook Islands		Reduce emissions by 81% from 2006 level by 2030		2006 baseline emissions of 69,574 tCO$_2$e
Fiji	Reduce emissions by 10% below BAU by 2030 based on a 2013 baseline	Reduce emissions by 30% below BAU by 2030		• CO$_2$ emissions from electric generation in 2013 at 340 Gg • 2013 baseline energy sector CO$_2$ emissions close to 1500 Gg
Kiribati	• Reduce emissions by 13.7% below BAU by 2025 • Reduce emissions by 12.8% below BAU by 2030	Reduce emissions by 61.8% below BAU by 2030		Based on projections from historical data 2000–2014
Marshall Islands	• Reduce emissions by 32% below 2010 level by 2025 • Reduce emissions by 45% below 2010 level by 2030			Projections taken from 2010 baseline of 185 GtCO$_2$e
Micronesia, Fed. States of	Reduce emissions by 28% below 2000 level by 2025	Reduce emissions by 35% below 2000 level by 2025		Emissions in 2005 at 150,000 MtCO$_2$e
Nauru[b]		• Spend $50 million on solar power system and demand that management reduce emissions • Spend $5 million on smaller 0.6 megawatt solar system		Economic growth assumed at 2.2% per annum and projection of CO$_2$ emissions increasing from 57 kt per annum in 2014 to around 80 kt per annum in 2030
Palau	Reduce energy sector emissions by 22% below 2005 level by 2025			BAU based on 3.72% GDP growth per year per capita
Papua New Guinea[b]		100% renewable energy by 2030, contingent on funding		Emissions increase at around the 3%–4% per annum suggesting that 2014 emissions of 5 Mt per year could increase to around 8 Mt per year by 2030; CO$_2$ emissions could reach 18 Mt CO$_2$ annually in 2030
Samoa[b]	100% of electricity generated using renewables by 2017, and maintained to 2025			Base year 2014 with 26% of electricity generated from renewable energy sources
Solomon Islands	Emissions to be 12% below BAU by 2025 and 30% below BAU by 2030	Emissions to be 27% below BAU by 2025 and 45% below BAU by 2030		Reference year 2015, when GHG emissions were estimated at 20 MtCO$_2$e; BAU projection based on extrapolation of historic data 1994–2010; emissions estimated to be reduced by 18,800 tCO$_2$e annually by 2025 and by 31,125 tCO$_2$e annually by 2030

continued next page

Continued

Economy	Unconditional emissions pledges	Conditional emissions pledges	GHG intensity goal	Business as usual details
Tonga[b]	70% of electricity generation from renewable sources by 2030			In 2015 renewable energy accounting for approximately 9% of electricity generation
Tuvalu	Emissions of energy sector to be 60% below 2010 level by 2025	Emissions reductions in other sectors such as waste and agriculture		2010 emissions at about 20 $GtCO_2e$
Vanuatu		Renewable energy target to eliminate emissions from electricity generation and reduce emissions from the energy sector as a whole by 30% below BAU		Emissions from electricity at about 130 Gg in 2010 and estimated to increase under BAU by 3% per annum to 240 Gg by 2030
Developed Asian economies				
Australia	Reduce emissions by 26%–28% below 2005 level by 2030			2005 baseline
New Zealand	Reduce emissions by 30% below 2005 level by 2030, corresponding to 11% below 1990 levels by 2030			Based on 2005 levels of GHG emissions, which corresponds to a reduction of 11% from 1990 levels
Japan	• Reduce emissions by 26% from 2013 level by 2030 • Reduce emissions by 25.4% from 2005 level by 2030			2013 GHG emissions at 0.29 $KgCO_2e/\$$ of GDP in 2013, and at 11 $MtCO_2e$ per capita

BAU = business as usual, CO_2 = carbon dioxide, CO_2e = carbon dioxide equivalent, Gg = gigagram, GHG = greenhouse gas, $GtCO_2e$ = gigaton of carbon dioxide equivalent, $KgCO_2e$ = kilogram of carbon dioxide equivalent, kt = kiloton, Lao PDR = Lao People's Democratic Republic, LULUCF = land use, land-use change, and forestry, Mt = metric ton, $MtCO_2e$ = metric ton of carbon dioxide equivalent, PRC = People's Republic of China.

Note: Intended nationally determined contributions submitted as of 5 September 2016, with Timor-Leste, Uzbekistan, and Hong Kong, China not yet having submitted.

[a] Taipei,China is not a signatory to the United Nations Framework Convention on Climate Change or the Kyoto Protocol, and is therefore under no formal obligation to reduce carbon.

[b] No specific target set for emissions reduction.

Sources: Jotzo and Kemp 2016; United Nations Framework Convention on Climate Change Intended Nationally Determined Contributions, various countries. http://www4.unfccc.int/Submissions/INDC/Submission%20Pages/submissions.aspx (accessed 21 September 2016).

Background Papers

Alano, E. and M. Lee. 2016. Forthcoming. *Natural Disaster Shocks and Macroeconomic Growth in Asia: Evidence for Typhoons and Droughts.* Asian Development Bank.

Asuncion, R. C. and M. Lee. 2016. *Impacts of Sea Level Rise on Economic Growth in Developing Asia.* Asian Development Bank.

Eskander, S. M., S. Fankhauser, and S. Jha. 2016. *Do Natural Disasters Change Savings and Employment Choices? Evidence from Bangladesh and Pakistan.* Asian Development Bank.

Fankhauser, S., A. Kazaglis, and S. Srivastav. 2016. *Green Growth Opportunities for Asia.* Asian Development Bank.

Jotzo, F. and L. Kemp. 2016. *INDCs and Low-carbon Growth Strategies in Developing Asia.* Asian Development Bank.

Lee, M., M. L. Villaruel, and R. Gaspar. 2016. *Effects of Temperature Shocks on Economic Growth and Welfare in Asia.* Asian Development Bank.

Reis, L. A., J. Emmerling, M. Tavoni, and D. Raitzer. 2016. *The Economics of Greenhouse Gas Mitigation in Developing Asia.* Asian Development Bank.

Sovacool, B. 2016. *Co-benefits and Trade-offs of Green and Clean Energy: Evidence from the Academic Literature and Asian Case Studies.* Asian Development Bank.

References

Ahmed, M. and S. Suphachalasai. 2014. *Assessing the Costs of Climate Change and Adaptation in South Asia.* Asian Development Bank.

Albert, S., J. Leon, A. Grinham, J. Church, B. Gibbes, and C. Woodroffe. 2016. Interactions between Sea-level Rise and Wave Exposure on Reef Island Dynamics in the Solomon Islands. *Environmental Research Letters* 11(5).

Anthoff, D., R. J. Nicholls, and R. S. J. Tol. 2010. The Economic Impact of Substantial Sea Level Rise. *Mitigation and Adaptation Strategies for Global Change* 15.

Antilla-Hughes, J. K. and S. Hsiang. 2013. *Destruction, Disinvestment, and Death: Economic and Human Losses Following Environmental Disaster.* http://papers.ssrn.com/sol3/papers.cfm?abstract_id=2220501

ADB. 2012. *Addressing Climate Change and Migration in Asia and the Pacific.* Asian Development Bank.

———. 2013. *The Economics of Climate Change in the Pacific.* Asian Development Bank.

———. 2016a. *Asian Development Outlook 2016: Asia's Potential Growth.* Asian Development Bank.

———. 2016b. *Fossil Fuel Subsidies in Asia: Trends, Impacts, and Reforms— Integrative Report.* Policy Report. Asian Development Bank. http://www.adb.org/publications/fossil-fuel-subsidies-asia-trends-impacts-and-reforms

———. 2016c. *GrEEEn Solutions for Livable Cities.* Asian Development Bank.

ADBI. 2015. *Managing the Transition to a Low-Carbon Economy—Perspectives, Policies, and Practices from Asia.* Asian Development Bank Institute.

ASEAN Centre for Energy. 2013. *ASEAN Guideline on Renewable Energy Support Mechanisms for Bankable Projects.*

Baez, J., D. Kronick, and A. Mason. 2013. Rural Households in a Changing Climate. *World Bank Research Observer* 28(2).

Barnard, S., S. Nakhooda, A. Caravani, and L. Schalatek. 2015. Climate Finance Regional Briefing: Asia. *Climate Finance Fundamentals* 8. December.

Boden, T., G. Marland, and R. J. Andres. 2015. *Global CO$_2$ Emissions from Fossil-Fuel Burning, Cement Manufacture, and Gas Flaring: 1751–2013.* Carbon Dioxide Information Analysis Center, Oak Ridge National Laboratory, US Department of Energy, doi 10.3334/CDIAC/00001_V2015.

Burke, M., S. Hsiang, and E. Miguel. 2015. Global Non-linear Effect of Temperature on Economic Production. *Nature* 527(7577). http://www.nature.com/nature/journal/v527/n7577/full/nature15725.html

Burtraw, D., D. A. Evans, A. Krupnick, K. Palmer, and R. Toth. 2005. Economics of Pollution Trading for SO$_2$ and NO$_x$. *Annual Review of Environment and Resources* 30.

Burtraw, D. and S. J. Szambelan. 2009. *US Emissions Trading Markets for SO$_2$ and NO$_x$.* Discussion Paper 09-40. Resources for the Future.

Calel, R. and A. Dechezleprêtre. 2016. Environmental Policy and Directed Technological Change: Evidence from the European Carbon Market. *Review of Economics and Statistics* 98(1).

Chan, G., R. Stavins, R. Stowe, and R. Sweeney. 2012. *The SO$_2$ Allowance Trading System and the Clean Air Act Amendments of 1990: Reflections on Twenty Years of Policy Innovation.* Harvard Environmental Economics Program, Harvard Kennedy School.

Choi, C. 2016. Does Economic Growth Really Reduce Disaster Damages? Index Decomposition Analysis for the Relationship between Disaster Damages, Urbanization and Economic Growth and Its Implications. *International Journal of Urban Sciences* 20(2).

Cinco, T. A., R. G. de Guzman, A. M. D. Ortiz, R. J. Delfino, R. D. Lasco, F. D. Hilario, E. L. Juanillo, R. Barba, and E. Ares. 2016. Observed Trends and Impacts of Tropical Cyclones in the Philippines. *International Journal of Climatology.*

Corruption Eradication Commission. 2015. *Preventing State Losses in Indonesia's Forestry Sector: An Analysis of Non-tax Forest Revenue Collection and Timber Product Administration.* Jakarta.

CPI. 2015. Global Landscape of Climate Finance. Climate Policy Initiative.

Dechezleprêtre, A. and M. Sato. 2014. *The Impacts of Environmental Regulations on Competitiveness.* Policy Brief, Grantham Research Institute on Climate Change and Environment. London School of Economics and Political Science.

Dong, C. G. 2012. Feed-in Tariff vs. Renewable Portfolio Standard: An Empirical Test of Their Relative Effectiveness in Promoting Wind Capacity Development. *Energy Policy* 42(C).

Drijfhout, S., S. Bathiany, C. Beaulie, V. Brovkin, M. Calussen, C. Huntingford, M. Scheffer, G. Sgubin, and D. Swingedouw. 2015. Catalogue of Abrupt Shifts in Intergovernmental Panel on Climate Change Climate Models. *Proceedings of the National Academy of Sciences of the United States of America* 112(43).

Emmerling, J., L. Drouet, L. A. Reis, M. Bevione, L. Berger, V. Bosetti, S. Carrara, E. De Cian, G. de Maere d'Aertrycke, T. Longden, M. Malpede, G. Marangoni, F. Sferra, M. Tavoni, J. Witajewski-Baltvilks, and P. Havlík. 2016. The WITCH 2016 Model—Documentation and Implementation of the Shared Socioeconomic Pathways. *FEEM Working Paper* No. 42.2016. http://ssrn.com/abstract=2800970

EPA. 2016. *Valuing Mortality Risk Reductions for Policy: A Meta-analytic Approach.* US Environmental Protection Agency. February.

European Patent Office. 2016. http://www.epo.org/news-issues/technology/sustainable-technologies/clean-energy/europe.html

Fankhauser, S. 2013. A Practitioner's Guide to a Low-Carbon Economy: Lessons from the UK. *Climate Policy* 13(3).

Fankhauser, S. and T. McDermott. 2014. Understanding the Adaptation Deficit: Why Are Poor Countries More Vulnerable to Climate Events than Rich Countries? *Global Environmental Change* 27.

Fankhauser, S. and N. Stern. 2016. *Climate Change, Development, Poverty and Economics.* http://pubdocs.worldbank.org/en/728181464700790149/Nick-Stern-PAPER.pdf

FTSE Russell. 2016. *New Green Revenues Model from FTSE Russell Tracks Global Transition to a Green Economy.* http://www.ftserussell.com/files/press-releases/new-green-revenues-model-ftse-russell-tracks-global-transition-green-economy

Global CCS Institute. 2012. Potential cost reductions in CCS in the power sector. https://hub.globalccsinstitute.com

Gütschow, J., L. Jeffery, R. Alexander, B. Hare, M. Schaeffer, M. Rocha, N. Höhne, H. Fekete, P. van Breevoort, and K. Blok. 2015. INDCs Lower Projected Warming to 2.7°C: Significant Progress but Still above 2°C. *Climate Action Tracker Update.* http://climateactiontracker.org/assets/publications/CAT_global_temperature_update_October_2015.pdf

Hallegatte, S., M. Bangalore, L. Bonzanigo, M. Fay, T. Kane, U. Narloch, J. Rozenberg, D. Treguer, and A. Vogt-Schilb. 2016. *Shock Waves: Managing the Impacts of Climate Change on Poverty.* World Bank.

Hanson, S., R. Nicholls, N. Ranger, S. Hallegatte, R. Corfee-Morlot, C. Herweijer, and J. Chateau. 2011. A Global Ranking of Port Cities with High Exposure to Climate Extremes. *Climatic Change* 104(1).

Hijoka, Y., E. Lin, J. J. Pereira, R. T. Corlett, X. Cui, G. E. Insarov, R. D. Lasco, E. Lindgren, and A. Surjan. 2014. Asia. In V. R. Barros et al., eds. *Climate Change 2014: Impacts, Adaptation, and Vulnerability. Part B: Regional Aspects. Contribution of Working Group II to the Fifth Assessment Report of the Intergovernmental Panel on Climate Change.* Cambridge University Press.

Hunter, L. 2007. *Climate Change, Rural Vulnerabilities, and Migration.* Population Resource Bureau. http://www.prb.org/Publications/Articles/2007/ClimateChangeinRuralAreas.aspx

IEA. 2014. *Regional Energy Efficiency Policy Recommendations—Southeast Asia Region.* International Energy Agency.

IPCC. 2013. *Climate Change 2013—The Physical Science Basis.* Cambridge University Press. Intergovernmental Panel on Climate Change.

———. 2014. *Climate Change 2014: Impacts, Adaptation, and Vulnerability.* Cambridge University Press. Intergovernmental Panel on Climate Change.

Kodjak, D. 2015. Policies to Reduce Fuel Consumption, Air Pollution, and Carbon Emissions from Vehicles in G20 Nations. *ICCT Briefing Paper.* International Council on Clean Transportation.

Kossoy, A., G. Peszko, K. Oppermann, N. Prytz, N. Klein, K. Blok, L. Lam, L. Wong, and B. Borkent. 2015. *State and Trends of Carbon Pricing 2015.* World Bank.

Meyer, A. 2000. Contraction & Convergence: The Global Solution to Climate Change. *Schumacher Briefings.* UIT Cambridge Ltd.

Moss, R., J. Edmonds, K. Hibbard, M. Manning, S. Rose, D. van Vuuren, T. Carter, S. Emori, M. Kainuma, T. Kram, G. Meehl, J. Mitchell, N. Nakicenovic, K. Riahi, S. Smith, R. Stouffer, A. Thomson, J. Weyant, and T. Wilbanks. 2010. The Next Generation of Scenarios for Climate Change Research and Assessment. *Nature* 463.

NEDA. 2013. *Reconstruction Assistance on Yolanda (RAY): Build-Back-Better.* National Economic and Development Authority. http://yolanda.neda.gov.ph/reconstruction-assistance-on-yolanda-ray-build-back-better/

Raitzer, D., F. Bosello, M. Tavoni, C. Orecchia, G. Marangoni, and J. Samson. 2015. *Southeast Asia and the Economics of Global Climate Stabilazation.* Asian Development Bank.

Schmalensee, R. and R. Stavins. 2015. Lessons Learned from Three Decades of Experience with Cap-and-Trade. *NBER Working Paper* No. 21742. National Bureau of Economic Research.

Shaw, C., S. Hales, P. Howden-Chapman, and R. Edwards. 2014. Health Co-benefits of Climate Change Mitigation Policies in the Transport Sector. *Nature Climate Change* 4.

State Council, the People's Republic of China. 2016. *China Sets Targets for Local Renewable Energy Use.* http://english.gov.cn/news/top_news/2016/03/04/content_281475301129002.htm (accessed 15 September 2016).

Stavins, R. N. 1998. What Can We Learn from the Grand Policy Experiment? Lessons from SO_2 Allowance Trading. *The Journal of Economic Perspective* 12(3).

Townshend, T., S. Fankhauser, R. Aybar, M. Collins, T. Landesman, M. Nachmany, and C. Pavese. 2013. How National Legislation Can Help to Solve Climate Change. *Nature Climate Change* 3.

UNEP. 2016. *Global Trends in Renewable Energy Investment 2016.* United Nations Environment Programme.

UN Comtrade. 2016. UN Comtrade Database. http://comtrade.un.org/

Vivid Economics. 2014. *Financing Green Growth.*

Westphal, M. I., G. A. Hughes, and J. Brömmelhörster, eds. 2013. *Economics of Climate Change in East Asia.* Asian Development Bank.

World Bank. 2013. *Building Resilience: Integrating Climate and Disaster Risk into Development. Lessons from World Bank Group Experience.*

———. 2016. *The Cost of Fire: An Economic Analysis of Indonesia's 2015 Fire Crisis.* http://pubdocs.worldbank.org/en/643781465442350600/Indonesia-forest-fire-notes.pdf

Winston & Strawn. 2014. *Feed-In Tariff Handbook for Asian Renewable Energy Systems.* Winston & Strawn LLP.

World Meteorological Organization. 2016. *Global Climate Breaks New Records January to June 2016.* http://public.wmo.int/en/media/press-release/global-climate-breaks-new-records-january-june-2016

3

ECONOMIC TRENDS AND PROSPECTS IN DEVELOPING ASIA

Central Asia

Subregional growth is now forecast at 1.5% in 2016 and 2.6% in 2017, down from the 2.1% and 2.8% projected in *Asian Development Outlook 2016* because of weakness in Azerbaijan, Kazakhstan, and Turkmenistan. Higher inflation in Kazakhstan raises the subregional inflation forecast to 11.5% from 10.8% for 2016 and to 6.4% from 5.9% for 2017. The current account deficit is now projected at 5.0% of GDP in 2016, up from 3.9% on larger deficits in Georgia, Kazakhstan, and Turkmenistan, and at 3.9% in 2017, up from 3.0% on larger deficits in Georgia and Kazakhstan.

Subregional assessment and prospects

The growth forecast for Central Asia in 2016 is revised down from 2.1% to 1.5% as the subregion continues adjusting to lower global commodity prices and recession in the Russian Federation. Lower export revenues following a drop in oil and gas prices in 2015 continue to constrain growth in the subregion's energy exporters: Azerbaijan, Kazakhstan, Turkmenistan, and Uzbekistan (Figure 3.1.1). Higher fiscal deficits in these economies have made cuts in public investment unavoidable while limiting increases in social transfers. From the supply side, agriculture, mining, transport, and services performed well across the subregion in the first half of 2016, but weak external demand and declining remittances adversely affected trade and manufacturing.

The revised growth projection for 2016 reflects more pessimistic forecasts for the subregion's hydrocarbon exporters in view of depressed oil and natural gas prices, low external demand outside the subregion, and cuts in public investment. Their aggregate growth is projected to slow from 2.9% in 2015 to 1.3% in 2016 before recovering to 2.6% in 2017. Much of the projected recovery in 2017 assumes higher revenue sufficient to augment public investment, as well as greater currency stability to limit the pass-through of depreciation to domestic prices and consequent fluctuation in domestic demand.

Most of the subregion's hydrocarbon exporters have adjusted government budgets to mitigate the lagged adverse effects of weak oil prices, often cutting public investment while trying to maintain social expenditures and eventually allowing higher budget deficits (Box 3.1.1). In March 2016, Kazakhstan amended the central government budget to raise expenditure by 7.8% over the original budget approved in November 2015. By contrast, Azerbaijan pursued restrictive fiscal policy in the first half of 2016. In Turkmenistan, the fiscal deficit is projected

3.1.1 GDP growth, Central Asia

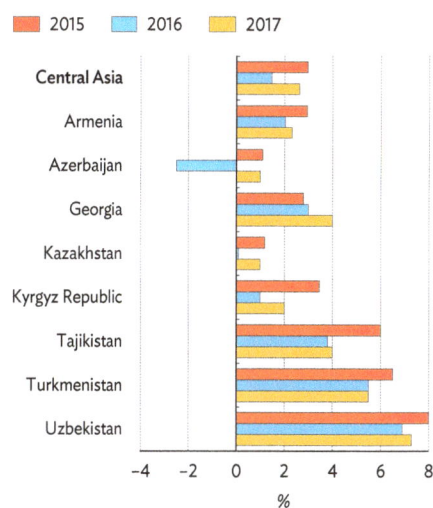

Source: Asian Development Outlook database.
Click here for figure data

The subregional assessment and prospects were written by Dominik Peschel. The section on Kazakhstan was written by Aigul Umurzakova and the part on other economies by Muhammadi Boboev, Iskandar Gulamov, Grigor Gyurjyan, Jennet Hojanazarova, George Luarsabishvili, Gulkayr Tentieva, and Nail Valiyev. All authors are with the Central and West Asia Department of ADB.

3.1.1 Hydrocarbon exporters under fiscal pressure

In tandem with falling global oil prices, GDP growth in Central Asia's hydrocarbon exporters fell from 5.2% in 2014 to 2.9% in 2015. The rate is projected to decline further to 1.3% in 2016 before recovering to 2.6% in 2017. The drop in oil prices in 2015 has also created pressure for fiscal consolidation.

The box figure shows estimates of the oil price at which the fiscal balance is zero for Azerbaijan, Kazakhstan, and Turkmenistan (no estimates are available for Uzbekistan). Fiscal adjustment to lower oil prices is projected to be gradual. While the central governments of the three hydrocarbon exporters spent slightly more as a share of GDP in 2015, the central government primary balance swung in Kazakhstan from a surplus equal to 1.3% of GDP in 2014 to a deficit of 4.9% in 2015, and in Azerbaijan from a surplus of 3.0% to a deficit of 3.2%. Turkmenistan's budget flipped less dramatically, from a surplus of 0.9% of GDP in 2014 to a deficit of 0.7% in 2015.

Hydrocarbon exporters in the subregion have traditionally channeled revenues from oil and natural gas exports into public investment, mostly construction. While hydrocarbon exports remained virtually unchanged by volume during 2011–2015, averaging 3.1 million barrels per day or its equivalent, the average Brent crude oil price fell from 2014 to 2015 by 47%, and the World Bank's natural gas price index by 34%. Central government capital expenditure

consequently declined from 2014 to 2015 in Azerbaijan by 1.3 percentage points of GDP to 9.2%, in Kazakhstan by 0.6 points to 2.0%, and in Turkmenistan by 1.1 percentage points to 6.6%. These cuts in investment have curbed the outlook for medium-term growth.

Fiscal breakeven oil price estimates for three large hydrocarbon exporters, Central Asia

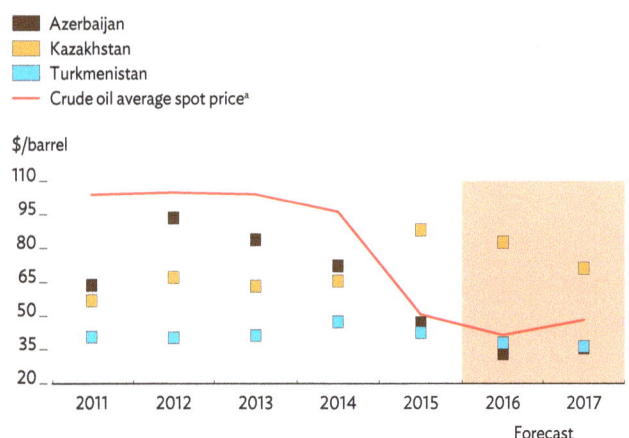

a Simple average of Brent, Dubai, and West Texas Intermediate.
Sources: International Monetary Fund and World Bank via Haver Analytics; ADB estimates.
Click here for figure data

to widen to 2.0% of GDP in 2016 as higher social spending offsets lower public investment. Uzbekistan continued to implement development programs worth $1.9 billion in the first half of 2016.

Less variation in growth is projected for the subregion's energy importers: Armenia, Georgia, the Kyrgyz Republic, and Tajikistan. Expansion will likely slow from 3.6% in 2015 to 2.6% in 2016 before recovering to 3.2% in 2017. Falling remittances have constrained growth in these economies (Box 3.1.2) and Uzbekistan. The growth forecast for Central Asia as a whole in 2017 is revised down slightly, from 2.8% in *Asian Development Outlook 2016* (*ADO 2016*) to 2.6%, taking into account slower growth now projected for Turkmenistan.

The inflation forecast for Central Asia in 2016 is raised to 11.5% from the 10.8% projected in *ADO 2016*, reflecting higher-than-expected inflation in Kazakhstan (Figure 3.1.2). The subregion's two biggest economies, Kazakhstan and Azerbaijan, continue to face double-digit inflation. Against the background of rising fiscal pressures and current account deficits, Kazakhstan adopted a floating exchange rate regime in August 2015, as did Azerbaijan in December. Sharp currency depreciation followed, fueling inflation. By the end of August 2016, the Azerbaijan manat had lost 38% of its value against the US dollar, and the Kazakh tenge had lost 42%. The resulting impact on prices, mostly for imported goods, has exacerbated inflation, which in Azerbaijan averaged 11.3% in the first half of 2016, and in Kazakhstan 13.1% from August 2015 to

3.1.2 Inflation, Central Asia

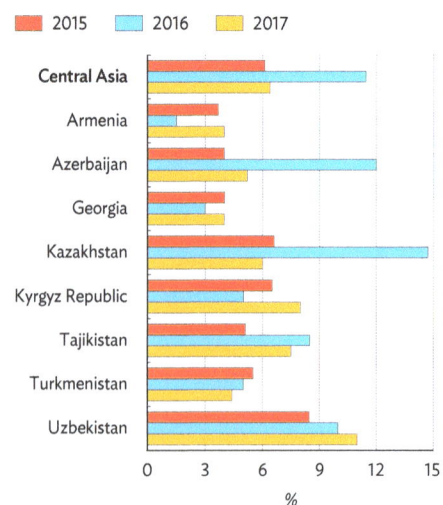

Source: Asian Development Outlook database.
Click here for figure data

3.1.2 Energy importers suffering declines in remittances

Remittances are key to growth in Central Asia's energy importers: Armenia, Georgia, the Kyrgyz Republic, and Tajikistan. From 2011 to 2014, remittances were especially high in Tajikistan, averaging 45.2% of GDP, and the Kyrgyz Republic, averaging 29.9%. They were lower but still significant in Armenia, averaging 18.3% of GDP, and Georgia, averaging 11.5%. Recession in the Russian Federation, which provides the bulk of remittances, has caused remittances to the subregion's energy importers to fall in aggregate from 24.6% of GDP in 2013 to 17.6% in 2015, a figure projected to slide further to 16.3% in 2016 (box figure). Remittance inflows were still falling at double-digit rates in Armenia and Tajikistan in the first half of 2016 but appeared to stabilize in Georgia and the Kyrgyz Republic, the latter of which has enjoyed since mid-2015 free movement of labor within the Eurasian Economic Union.

Despite lower remittances, average GDP growth in the subregion's energy importers slowed only modestly in 2015, to 3.6% from 4.7% a year earlier. Lower oil prices helped bring inflation down below expectations in 2015, keeping the cost of energy imports low and supporting domestic demand. Consequently, private consumption grew in 2015 by 11.9% year on year in Georgia and by 6.9% in the Kyrgyz Republic. It fell, however, by 5.0% in Armenia and probably even more in Tajikistan, where the plunge in remittances slashed disposable income by 10.0%. While remittances to the group are projected to keep falling as a share of GDP, except in the Kyrgyz Republic, continued moderate inflation in 2016 should limit the adverse impact on consumption.

Remittances to energy importers, Central Asia

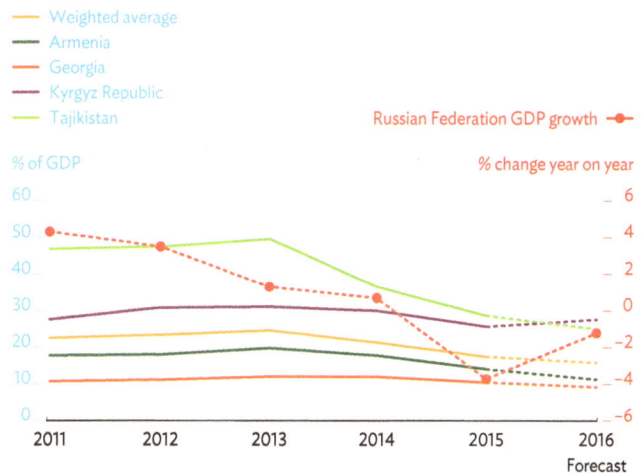

Note: The average is weighted by gross national income in current US dollars following the World Bank Atlas method.
Sources: World Bank. World Development Indicators online database; International Monetary Fund. World Economic Outlook; ADB estimates.
Click here for figure data

July 2016. Inflation in the subregion's energy-importing economies other than Tajikistan is now projected to be less than forecast in *ADO 2016*, mostly due to declining food prices and continued low energy costs. The inflation forecast for the Kyrgyz Republic is trimmed because its accession to the Eurasian Economic Union had a much smaller effect on prices than anticipated.

The average inflation rate across the subregion is projected at 6.4% in 2017, or 0.5 percentage points higher than forecast in *ADO 2016*, again because of higher inflation in Kazakhstan. This revision assumes that pass-through from earlier currency depreciation diminishes over time.

The current account deficit for Central Asia in 2016 is now projected at 5.0% of GDP, or 1.1 percentage points higher than forecast in *ADO 2016* (Figure 3.1.3). The revision reflects higher deficits now projected for Georgia, Kazakhstan, and Turkmenistan. While the change in the forecast is small, the current account balances of Central Asia's energy exporters remain highly dependent on oil prices. As most of their currencies have depreciated significantly, raising prices for imported goods faster than those for domestic goods, the resulting decline in import volumes is helping to contain current account deficits. Meanwhile, weaker domestic demand in general in these countries has further constrained imports.

In 2017, the subregion's current account deficit is projected to narrow to 3.9% of GDP. This is higher than the 3.0% forecast in *ADO 2016*, reflecting larger current account deficits now projected for Georgia and Kazakhstan.

3.1.3 Current account balance, Central Asia

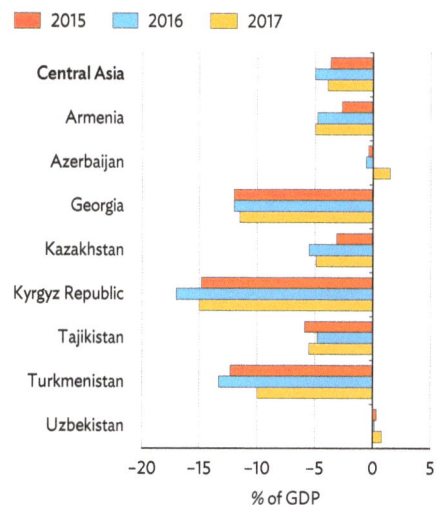

Source: Asian Development Outlook database.
Click here for figure data

Kazakhstan

Weak petroleum prices and the continued impact of currency depreciation on import prices cut growth to 0.1%, sharply accelerated inflation in the first half of 2016, and doubled the current account deficit from the same period in 2015. With similar trends expected for the rest of the year, the 2016 growth forecast is cut to 0.1%, while projections for inflation and the current account deficit are revised up for both 2016 and 2017.

Updated assessment

Growth slowed to 0.1% in the first half of 2016 from 1.7% in the same period of 2015 as declining exports and weak domestic demand cut industrial production. Industry contracted by 1.8% as lower mining and utility output reversed 0.9% expansion in the same period of 2015. Agriculture rose by 2.7% on higher livestock production. Services showed no growth, down from 3.2% a year earlier as sharp currency depreciation curbed household purchasing power, reducing trade and shrinking output in information and communication technology services.

Demand-side data for 2016 are limited to the first quarter, when consumption rose by 1.7%, less than half the 4.1% rise in the same period of 2015 because of higher prices for goods other than food, of which most are imported (Figure 3.1.4). Growth in public consumption slowed to 2.5% from 4.2% in the first quarter of 2015, reflecting small declines in health care, education, defense, science, and transport. Investment expanded by 1.7%, less than the 2.0% in the same period of 2015 because of lower public investment. Real exports fell by 9.2%, and real imports by 4.5%, in the 12 months ending March 2016. This compares with declines of 5.7% for real exports and 9.7% for real imports during the 12 months ending in March 2015.

The average monthly wage rose by 13.9% in the first half of 2016 in nominal terms, but the real wage index fell by 1.8% because of inflation. Real income dropped by 5.6% in the first half of 2016, much more than the 0.9% decline in the same period last year. The unemployment rate edged up to 5.1% in June 2016 from 5.0% a year earlier.

In response, the government raised both expenditure and budget transfers from the National Fund of the Republic of Kazakhstan (NFRK) in 2016. Budgeted transfers this year are 20.8% above last year's actual transfers, contributing to an 18.4% rise in total budget revenues, despite a 4.7% decline in tax receipts. Total expenditure rose by 16.7% against the background of relatively high inflation. The budget deficit is slated to remain at 2.0% of GDP in 2016, with the deficit excluding transfers rising from 7.5% of GDP to 8.7% (Figure 3.1.5). Social spending remains a priority, with these outlays rising by more than 13.7% over the same period in 2015. Civil servants' salaries increased on average by 30.0% on 1 January 2016. At the same time, central government investment fell to 6.8% of expenditure in the first half of 2016 from 8.5% in the same period of 2015. The macroeconomic impact of this spending will depend on the size and design of countercyclical measures and the rate of return on investments in infrastructure.

3.1.4 GDP growth by demand components

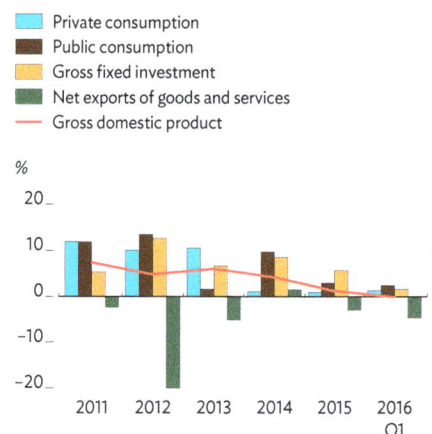

Q = quarter.
Source: Republic of Kazakhstan. Ministry of National Economy. Committee on Statistics.
Click here for figure data

3.1.5 Fiscal indicators

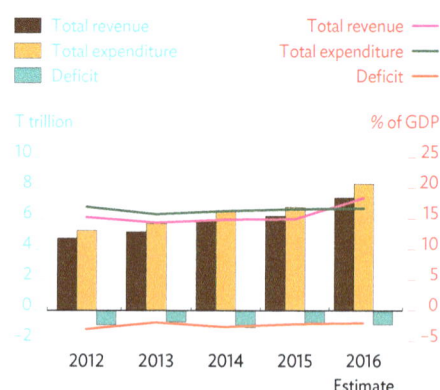

Sources: Ministry of Finance of the Republic of Kazakhstan; ADB estimates.
Click here for figure data

Average annual inflation tripled to 16.4% in January–August 2016 from 4.9% in the same period of 2015, reflecting price increases in the 12 months ending in August 2016 of 9.6% for services, 13.7% for food, and 26.7% for other goods, mostly imports (Figure 3.1.6). In August, inflation reached 17.6% year on year, a fivefold increase from 3.8% in August 2015, mainly because of sharp currency depreciation since the move that month from a narrow exchange rate corridor to a floating regime (Figure 3.1.7). The monetary policy shift from targeting the exchange rate to targeting inflation has yet to prove effective under high dollarization and the lagged effects of commodity price changes.

The National Bank of Kazakhstan, the central bank, lowered its base interest rate from 15.0% to 13.0% on 11 July 2016. Broad money grew by 40.6% from June 2015 to June 2016, up from –2.5% a year earlier, reflecting a 5.1% rise in gross international reserves to $30.4 billion as of 1 July 2016. The narrower monetary base (currency in circulation plus commercial bank reserves) rose by 16.7% over the period. The central bank continues to intervene on the foreign exchange market, with net purchases amounting to $3.0 billion from January to July 2016, compared with $17.7 billion in the whole of 2015 and $18.1 billion in 2014.

Bank credit fell by 1.7% in the 6 months to 30 June 2016, with domestic bank lending falling by 2.9% while foreign currency loans rose by 0.6% to equal 34.5% of total credit (Figure 3.1.8). At the same time, Kazakh tenge deposits started to recover. Since the beginning of 2016, foreign currency deposits declined by 12.0% while tenge deposits rose by 43.8%, reducing the share of deposits in foreign currency from 69.9% in January to 57.6% at the end of June. This development suggests that the central bank's de-dollarization measures have had an impact.

Kazakhstan's current account remained in deficit in the first half of 2016, with the deficit estimated to equal 5.2% of GDP, double the 2.6% in the same period last year before currency depreciation. Exports fell by 30.9%, less than the 42.2% decline in the first half of 2015. Imports fell by 28.4%, nearly double the 14.4% decline in the first half of 2015, mainly reflecting the fall in tenge purchasing power for imports. The trade surplus was $4.8 billion, down by 36.6% from the first half of 2015. Services imports declined by 1.0%, much less than the 8.6% decline in the same period of 2015. Moreover, the deficit in the income account narrowed to 21.1% from 44.9% in the first half of 2015, reflecting less income payable on direct investments.

Prospects

The growth forecast for 2016 is trimmed to 0.1% in light of the unexpectedly sharp slowdown in the first half of the year, continuing declines in industry, and weakening private domestic demand. The growth forecast for 2017 is kept at 1.0%. The pickup is likely because of the expected size and impact of countercyclical programs, the anticipated start of oil production at the Kashagan field, and an expected slowdown in consumer price increases.

Fiscal policy will likely be expansionary in the full year 2016. Additional expenditures are covered by large transfers to the budget from the NFRK projected at almost T3.7 trillion (equal to 50.1% of budgeted revenue), including a rise in the guaranteed transfer from

3.1.6 Monthly inflation

- Food and nonalcoholic beverages
- Clothing and footwear
- Housing, water, electricity, gas, and other fuels
- Furnishings, household equipment, and maintenance
- Transport
- All goods and services

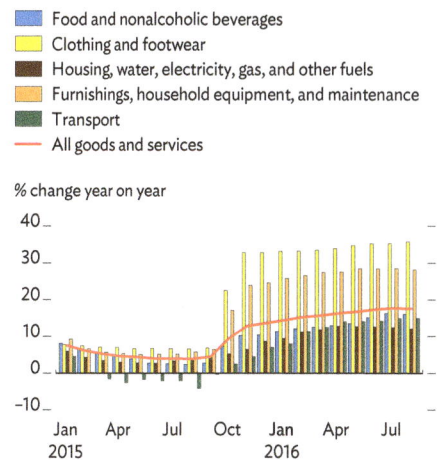

Source: Republic of Kazakhstan. Ministry of National Economy. Committee on Statistics.
Click here for figure data

3.1.7 Exchange rate

- US$/tenge
- US$/ruble
- Brent crude oil price
- Real effective excluding oil trade
- Real effective

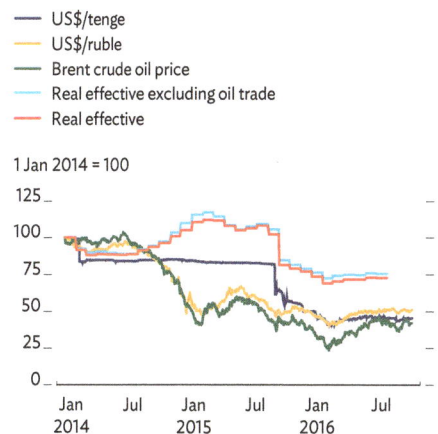

Sources: National Bank of the Republic of Kazakhstan; Bloomberg (accessed 8 September 2016).
Click here for figure data

3.1.8 Dollarization in the banking system

- Share of loans
- Share of deposits

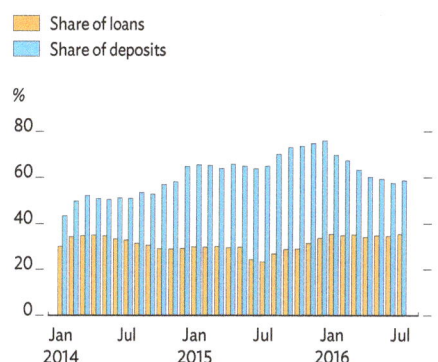

Source: National Bank of the Republic of Kazakhstan.
Click here for figure data

the NFRK of T480.0 billion. A budget amendment in March raised the additional targeted transfer from the NFRK for anti-crisis measures by 42.4% to T807.5 billion. The funds, available through reallocated spending, aim to assist small and medium-sized firms, provide loans for a program to construct individual homes, and support infrastructure projects. As of 1 July 2016, collections of the main taxes, including the corporate income tax, value-added tax, and export duty, were on track or exceeding plans.

The forecast for annual average inflation in 2016 is raised to 14.7% from 12.6% in *ADO 2016*, reflecting the impact of continuing currency depreciation on import prices. Gains from more competitive exports thanks to currency depreciation are expected to be limited. In 2017, inflation is projected to slow to 6.0%, or 1.4 percentage points higher than forecast in *ADO 2016*, reflecting a weakening of the pass-through of nominal currency depreciation to domestic prices.

Monetary conditions have eased somewhat since the reduction in the base interest rate to 13.0% in July. In particular, bank liquidity has improved as foreign currency deposits continue to be converted into tenge, among other factors. However, inflationary pressures appear to remain high in the second half of 2016.

By 1 July 2016, nonperforming loans had edged down to 7.9% of outstanding loans from 8.0% at the beginning of 2016. As part of de-dollarization, the central bank and the government introduced a number of measures such as an interest rate rise for tenge deposits from 10.0% to 14.0% and a cut from 3.0% to 2.0% for foreign currency deposits. Government support for small and medium-sized enterprises through interest rate discounts has helped raise the approval rate for new lending. However, continued macroeconomic risks have kept business activity lackluster as commercial bank loans have fallen as a share of GDP because of stagnant lending to households and enterprises. Credit is expected to expand in 2017, when greater exchange rate and macroeconomic stability should mitigate credit, currency, and liquidity risks while raising the value of collateral, thereby lowering lending costs.

The current account deficit is forecast at 5.5% of GDP in 2016, revised up from 3.5% in *ADO 2016*, and at 4.9% in 2017, revised up from 3.1% (Figure 3.1.9). Exports are projected to fall by 30.9% this year, reflecting a 3.6% decline in oil production in the first half. Imports are expected to contract by 28.4% as tenge depreciation weakens consumer purchasing power while the potential for import substitution is small. Trade is projected to recover in 2017, with exports rising faster than imports as oil prices recover slightly.

3.1.1 Selected economic indicators, Kazakhstan (%)

	2016		2017	
	ADO 2016	Update	ADO 2016	Update
GDP growth	0.7	0.1	1.0	1.0
Inflation	12.6	14.7	4.6	6.0
Current acct. bal. (share of GDP)	−3.5	−5.5	−3.1	−4.9

Source: ADB estimates.

3.1.9 Current account components

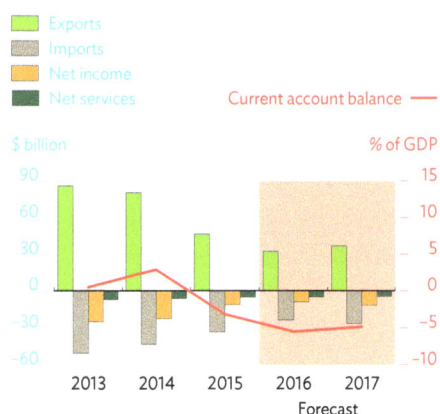

Sources: Republic of Kazakhstan. Ministry of National Economy. Committee on Statistics; ADB estimates.
Click here for figure data

Other economies

Armenia

The economy grew by 2.8% in the first half of 2016, down from 3.1% in the same period of 2015. Industry excluding construction grew by 6.8%, reflecting strong expansion in mining, quarrying, electricity production, and manufacturing. Construction continued to limit growth, declining by 4.8%. Less favorable weather cut expansion in agriculture to 0.3% in the first half of 2016 from 19.3% in the first half of 2015 and 13.2% for the full year. Growth in services rose to 2.1% from 1.4% a year earlier. Growth accelerated in transport and communications but stayed negative in remittance-supported retail trade.

On the demand side, a narrower deficit in net exports of goods and services likely remained the only contributor to GDP growth aside from public consumption in the first half of 2016. Private consumption declined by an estimated 4.0%, reflecting a 22.6% drop in remittances, with remittances from the Russian Federation plunging by 35.9%.

As developments in the first half of 2016 broadly aligned with expectations—and as reduced remittances, adverse weather in the second quarter of 2016, and lower international prices for exports of copper, molybdenum, and other nonferrous metals will likely trim growth in the rest of the year—growth forecasts remain unchanged from *ADO 2016*.

Lower commodity prices coupled with weaker domestic demand and a broadly stable exchange rate brought deflation that persisted through the first 7 months of 2016 to average 1.5%, versus inflation at 5.0% in the same period a year earlier. Deflation stood at 1.3% year on year in July 2016, versus 4.2% inflation in July 2015. In response, the central bank gradually eased its policy rate from 8.75% at the end of 2015 to 7.25% in August 2016. Higher food prices caused by bad weather may revive inflation later in 2016, but soft domestic demand and lower gas and electricity tariffs should help keep inflation low. The inflation forecast is reduced for 2016 but unchanged for 2017.

Concerned about rising public debt, the government resumed fiscal consolidation in 2016 while continuing to address social and capital investment needs. It aims to reduce the fiscal deficit to 3.5% of GDP in 2016 from 4.8% in 2015 and stabilize the ratio of debt to GDP over the medium term.

The current account deficit narrowed to 9.1% of GDP in the first quarter of 2016 from 13.9% a year earlier, mainly on a smaller deficit in goods and services. Despite worsening terms of trade and a less favorable external environment, exports rose by 21.7% quarter on quarter, reflecting higher earnings from commodities and manufactured goods, while weak domestic demand cut imports by 4.1%. The forecast of the current account deficit is thus reduced by 0.4 percentage points for 2016 but remains unchanged for 2017.

Azerbaijan

GDP contracted by 3.4% in the first half of 2016, reversing 5.7% growth in the same period of 2015. Sharp declines in export revenue and domestic demand explain the contraction. With tighter fiscal policy, capital investment plunged by 37.0% in the first half of 2016, and

3.1.2 Selected economic indicators, Armenia (%)

	2016		2017	
	ADO 2016	Update	ADO 2016	Update
GDP growth	2.0	2.0	2.3	2.3
Inflation	3.8	1.5	4.0	4.0
Current acct. bal. (share of GDP)	−5.2	−4.8	−5.0	−5.0

Source: ADB estimates.

construction by 33.6% following 11.5% growth in the same period in 2015; activity outside the oil sector contracted by 6.1% overall despite gains of 1.0% in trade and tourism. Accordingly, this *Update* forecasts deeper contraction in 2016 than projected in March, reflecting greater impact than expected from weak oil prices.

On the demand side, high inflation weakened household spending and constrained consumption. Restrictive fiscal policy in the first half of 2016 limited government outlays to 37.0% of planned expenditure for the year, further curbing demand. Sales of $1 billion in foreign bonds to finance Stage 2 expansion of the Shah Deniz gas field freed up public funds to cover a shortfall in social expenditure, and government spending is expected to rise during the rest of the year. However, economic activity will likely remain constrained by tighter monetary policy and cuts in bank lending. The growth forecast for 2017 is nevertheless unchanged, assuming higher oil prices and some recovery in domestic demand.

Inflation reached 10.6% year on year in July 2016 as prices rose by 12.0% for food, 15.5% for other goods, and 4.7% for services. Inflation reflected mainly the continuing effect of sharp currency depreciation during 2015. To curb inflation, the central bank repeatedly raised its policy interest rate, which quintupled to 15.0% in September 2016 from 3.0% in July 2015. However, shallow financial intermediation limits the central bank's ability to curb inflation. This year, a 38% increase in water supply tariffs in May and a 16% increase in power supply tariffs in July will likely fuel inflation slightly during the second half, while an expected stabilization of the local currency and prices for imported goods should sharply reduce inflation in 2017, as previously forecast.

From January to May 2016, exports fell by 5.9% while imports plunged by 18.3% as imports of vehicles and machinery fell sharply. The trade surplus halved to $1.7 billion from $3.6 billion in the same period of 2015. As developments in the external sector align with earlier expectations, the current account forecasts for 2016 and 2017 are maintained, with a deficit in 2016 converting to a surplus in 2017.

Georgia

Following growth at 2.8% in 2015, GDP expanded by 2.6% in the first quarter of 2016 as fiscal stimulus boosted domestic demand and as mining expanded by 29.0%, construction by 25.7%, and tourist-industry businesses such as hotels and restaurants by 11.7%. Foreign direct investment (FDI) in the quarter nearly doubled year on year to $376 million, going mainly into transport and communications, energy, and finance. Growth is estimated to have averaged 2.9% in the first half, up from 2.6% in the same period of 2015. Supported by buoyant tourism, continuing fiscal stimulus, and strengthening business confidence, growth is expected to accelerate in the rest of 2016 and 2017, with both projections revised up by 0.5 percentage points.

On the demand side, a stressed external sector remains the main constraint on growth but is expected to be offset by strong FDI and additional spending on infrastructure. Net exports will continue to constrain GDP as persistent weakness in trading partners lowers demand for Georgian exports.

3.1.3 Selected economic indicators, Azerbaijan (%)

	2016		2017	
	ADO 2016	Update 2016	ADO 2016	Update
GDP growth	−1.0	−2.5	1.0	1.0
Inflation	12.0	12.0	5.2	5.2
Current acct. bal. (share of GDP)	−0.6	−0.6	1.5	1.5

Source: ADB estimates.

3.1.4 Selected economic indicators, Georgia (%)

	2016		2017	
	ADO 2016	Update 2016	ADO 2016	Update
GDP growth	2.5	3.0	3.5	4.0
Inflation	5.0	3.0	4.0	4.0
Current acct. bal. (share of GDP)	−9.5	−12.0	−9.2	−11.5

Source: ADB estimates.

In the run-up to parliamentary elections in October 2016, the government plans to roll out an ambitious, growth-enhancing plan to develop public infrastructure in the second half of 2016 that embraces road and transport projects and urban redevelopment that supports tourism. Budget revenue exceeded projections in the first half of 2016, but spending also outpaced recent norms.

Average annual inflation in the 12 months through August 2016 declined to 3.8% from 4.0% at the end of 2015. Inflation has ebbed since the end of the first quarter of 2016 because currency weakness in Georgia's main trading partners has curtailed imported inflation. The Georgian lari continued to depreciate through February 2016, mainly for external reasons as a slowdown gripped the subregion, but has since strengthened by about 7%. In view of the decline in imported inflation, the inflation forecast is reduced for 2016 but not 2017.

In the first half of 2016, the current account deficit reached an estimated 12.5% of GDP, up from 12.0% in 2015. It was financed mainly by FDI. Merchandise exports are estimated to have fallen by 12.4% year on year in the first half of 2016, largely because the lari strengthened, while imports rose by 29.9%. Remittances declined by 1.6% year on year as those from the Russian Federation, Georgia's largest source, dropped by 15.1% but were largely offset by growth in remittances from Europe. In view of the worsening trade balance, projections for the current account deficit are raised for both 2016 and 2017.

Kyrgyz Republic

In the first 7 months of 2016, GDP contracted by 2.2%, reversing 6.6% growth in the same period of 2015 as industry fell by 15.6%, despite expansion in agriculture by 2.1% and in construction by 4.7% supported by a 4.1% increase in investment. Outside the gold sector, GDP rose by 1.6%. The decline in industry reflected output contractions of 29.0% in textiles, 26.6% in apparel, and 10.6% in electricity generation. On the demand side, private consumption is estimated to have grown slightly as retail sales buoyed by higher remittances boosted trade by 5.3%.

Recession in the Russian Federation has been the main cause of falling output. However, recent developments suggest some stabilization. Remittances from the Russian Federation grew by 10.3% year on year in January–June 2016. Kyrgyz exports to the Russian Federation in the first half of 2016 remained comparable to a year earlier. The forecasts for improved growth are maintained, assuming some recovery in the second half of 2016 and some improvement in 2017 in the Russian Federation and other trading partners.

Though core inflation in the first 7 months of 2016 was 2.3%, average inflation was only 0.8% because of a 6.0% drop in food prices and 10.4% appreciation of the Kyrgyz som. Transitional price adjustments following accession to the Eurasian Economic Union were less than expected. Inflation will likely accelerate in the second half of this year on seasonal factors but still average for the year only half the 10.0% projected in *ADO 2016*. The inflation forecast is unchanged for 2017, assuming gradual tariff adjustments.

3.1.5 Selected economic indicators, Kyrgyz Republic (%)

	2016		2017	
	ADO 2016	Update	ADO 2016	Update
GDP growth	1.0	1.0	2.0	2.0
Inflation	10.0	5.0	8.0	8.0
Current acct. bal. (share of GDP)	−17.0	−17.0	−15.0	−15.0

Source: ADB estimates.

Pressure on the economy has begun to moderate, and the government has strived to keep the 2016 fiscal deficit at 4.5% of GDP in 2016, well below the *ADO 2016* forecast of 9.1%. The government aims to limit the deficit by restraining expenditure and improving tax policies and administration. From 2017, it plans to continue fiscal consolidation despite a scheduled presidential election.

Imports fell by 7.3% during January–June 2016, largely reflecting declines in imports of vehicles, fuel, and wood products. However, exports plunged by 28.4%, mainly as exports of gold and of livestock and other agricultural products fell sharply, leaving a trade deficit of $1.3 billion. As these forecasts align with those in *ADO 2016*, the current account forecasts are maintained for 2016 and 2017, with some improvement in the external environment shrinking the deficit.

Tajikistan

GDP grew by 6.6% in the first half of 2016, up from 6.4% in the same period of 2015. Industry expanded by 12.1% versus 14.2% a year earlier, reflecting increases of 50.0% in extraction, 8.1% in processing, and 3.4% in electricity. Aluminium exports in the first half of 2016 reached 73,500 tons, or 20% above in the same period of 2015. Construction grew by 18.9%, fuelled by public and foreign investment, while trade and services expanded by 3.4%. Good weather contributed to a 9.9% rise in agriculture.

Growth in retail trade and services is expected to remain modest in the second half of 2016 as disposable income and household consumption continue to decline. Shortfalls in revenue led the authorities to revise the state budget in June 2016, reducing both revenue and expenditure projections by $57 million, with cuts to education, health, and social protection but no change in infrastructure spending. This *Update* maintains the growth projections made in *ADO 2016* while noting macroeconomic risks from a rise in nonperforming loans and deteriorating indicators of financial sector health.

Inflation averaged 5.7% in the first 7 months of 2016, reflecting efforts to reduce liquidity through foreign exchange controls and auctions of Treasury bills and of securities issued by the National Bank of Tajikistan, the central bank. During this period, the Tajik somoni depreciated by 10.7% against the dollar and 17.5% against the ruble despite currency interventions by the central bank. To curb inflation, it raised its refinancing rate from 9.0% to 11.0% in July 2016. This *Update* maintains inflation forecasts made in *ADO 2016* but notes that inflation could accelerate further if currency controls stymie domestic production and imports, thereby driving up prices for both.

Currency depreciation in the first half of 2016 helped drive public and publicly guaranteed external debt to 35.9% of GDP, up from 27.8% at the end of 2015. Continuing depreciation could risk breaching the 40% legal limit on external debt. Gross international reserves increased in the first 6 months of 2016 by 32.3% as the government purchased domestically produced gold and gold prices rose.

Employee compensation, the main component of remittances, dropped by 24.5% in the first quarter of 2016, contributing to a 22.1% fall in remittances year on year in the first half. Imports consequently fell by 4.8% in the half, while exports grew by 4.4%, but the current

3.1.6 Selected economic indicators, Tajikistan (%)

	2016		2017	
	ADO 2016	Update	ADO 2016	Update
GDP growth	3.8	3.8	4.0	4.0
Inflation	8.5	8.5	7.5	7.5
Current acct. bal. (share of GDP)	−4.8	−4.8	−5.5	−5.5

Source: ADB estimates.

account deficit nevertheless grew in the first quarter to equal 3.3% of GDP, slightly above the 3.0% recorded a year earlier. Uncertain as the outlook is—as lower remittances from the Russian Federation and Kazakhstan could curb imports, countering the effects of possibly lower exports caused by slower growth in the People's Republic of China and Kazakhstan—this *Update* retains the *ADO 2016* forecasts for the current account deficit in 2016 and 2017.

Turkmenistan

Despite fiscal consolidation after revenues from oil and natural gas exports plunged because of lower global energy prices, GDP grew by 6.1% in the first half of 2016, albeit more slowly than the 9.1% recorded in the first half of 2015. The government continued to support the private sector, encouraging import-substitution and export-promotion outside the hydrocarbon economy, where most of the growth occurred. Expansion was greatest in services, which grew by 12.3%, reflecting gains of 9.9% in transport and 16.0% in trade. Agriculture grew by 6.9% and industry by 2.1%, with construction rising by 4.4%. On the demand side, fiscal consolidation prompted by the decline in revenue from oil and gas exports led the government to trim some public investment programs. Investment nevertheless grew by 5.7% in the period. In view of continuing fiscal consolidation intended to rationalize and prioritize public spending, and of a freeze on new large-scale projects, this *Update* now revises downward the growth forecasts for both 2016 and 2017.

Lower public spending, restrictive monetary policy, and administrative price controls have contained inflation, and higher domestic production of food and other goods has replaced some imports. To resist pressure for a new devaluation and to curtail parallel markets, the government has imposed stringent foreign exchange controls. These measures have allowed the Turkmen manat to remain stable against the US dollar since January 2015. In view of these developments, inflation is now projected 1.6 percentage points lower in 2016 and 2017 than forecast in *ADO 2016*.

Although the government has slowed investment spending and started phasing out subsidies, the fiscal balance is projected to move from approximate balance in 2015 to a deficit in 2016 equal to nearly 2.0% of GDP, reflecting higher social spending. The budget deficit is expected to narrow to 1.0% of GDP in 2017.

The current account deficit is projected to widen this year more than forecast in *ADO 2016*, with a forecast 15.4% decline in exports mostly offset by a 16.7% fall in imports. Imports of high-tech machinery and equipment and of foreign services will remain substantial as they are needed for ongoing large-scale investments into hydrocarbons. Strong FDI, estimated at 13% of GDP in 2016, will continue to support the development of the hydrocarbon industry and related infrastructure. As higher exports are likely with some recovery in global oil and gas prices, the current account deficit is projected to narrow in 2017 as forecast earlier. Although foreign reserves are projected to remain at a comfortable 24 months of import cover, the economy remains vulnerable to a protracted period of low energy prices and/or lower demand from its major customers for energy imports.

3.1.7 Selected economic indicators, Turkmenistan (%)

	2016		2017	
	ADO 2016	Update	ADO 2016	Update
GDP growth	6.5	5.5	7.0	5.5
Inflation	6.6	5.0	6.0	4.4
Current acct. bal. (share of GDP)	-12.3	-13.3	-10.0	-10.0

Source: ADB estimates.

Uzbekistan

The government reported GDP growth at 7.8% in the first half of 2016, down from the 8.1% recorded in the same period of 2015, reflecting a weaker external environment and slower growth in industry. On the supply side, growth was driven by expansion at 12.9% in services and 17.5% in construction, which benefited from continued implementation of state housing and infrastructure development programs. A 5-year service sector development program and buoyant activity in finance and telecoms supported the growth in services. Industry including construction expanded by a reported 6.7%, down from the 8.1% reported a year earlier. While detailed output data are not available, weaker growth in energy and metals and decline in machinery likely explained the slowdown, despite substantial gains in food processing, construction materials, and chemicals. Agriculture expanded by 6.8% versus 6.5% a year earlier, reflecting higher production of fruit and vegetables. In April 2016, the Russian Federation and Uzbekistan agreed to expand bilateral trade in agricultural produce, prompting the government to announce a major horticulture development program.

On the demand side, investment was the main source of growth, with gross fixed capital formation estimated to have risen by 11.8% in the first half of 2016 over the same period of 2015 as the government continued implementing development programs worth $1.9 billion. Total gross fixed capital investment was reported at $7.8 billion. The government also reported foreign investment rising in the first half of 2016 by 20% year on year to $1.8 billion. As developments broadly correspond to forecasts in *ADO 2016*, growth forecasts for 2016 and 2017 are unchanged.

Despite higher public investment, the government kept the consolidated fiscal surplus equal to 0.1% of GDP in the first half of 2016. More than 60% of expenditure went to social objectives, mainly education and health, including a new program for child and maternal health.

The government reported inflation averaging 2.5% in the first 6 months of 2016, which was within the monetary authority's target range. As the trends affecting the consumer price index persist as described in *ADO 2016*—higher government spending, continued hikes in administered prices, and currency depreciation vis-à-vis US dollar, partly offset by lower import costs—this *Update* maintains the inflation forecasts for this year and next.

Finally, the government reported that exports of goods and services grew by 2.4% in the first half of 2016, and the balance of trade in goods and services recorded a surplus of $441.7 million. Although detailed external data are not available, exports of goods are believed to have declined in tandem with lower global prices for the country's export commodities (natural gas, gold, copper, and cotton) and slowing growth in its key trade partners: the Russian Federation, the People's Republic of China, and Kazakhstan. Cumulative bilateral trade with these three countries declined by 8.1% in US dollar terms. The projections for a slightly widening current account surplus are unchanged.

3.1.8 Selected economic indicators, Uzbekistan (%)

	2016		2017	
	ADO 2016	Update	ADO 2016	Update
GDP growth	6.9	6.9	7.3	7.3
Inflation	10.0	10.0	11.0	11.0
Current acct. bal. (share of GDP)	0.2	0.2	0.8	0.8

Source: ADB estimates.

East Asia

Economic indicators varied across East Asia in the first half of 2016. For the subregion as a whole, growth and inflation were lower and the current account surplus smaller than a year earlier. Growth will trend downward in 2016 and 2017 as individual economies see lower or stable growth this year, with some recovery in 2017. The current account surplus will narrow on faltering exports, and inflation will rise faster than previously forecast as price deregulation and rising costs for services push prices up in the subregion's largest economy.

Subregional assessment and prospects

Growth in the People's Republic of China (PRC) decelerated to 6.7% in the first half of 2016 despite strong fiscal and monetary support, with the slowdown sparing consumer-oriented and high-tech industries, construction, and services. Consumption was robust and provided the main impetus to growth in the PRC, but investment slackened and export growth remained weak despite renminbi depreciation against the dollar. In Mongolia, economic growth slowed to 1.4% as industry and services stagnated. In Hong Kong, China, growth was sharply curtailed as domestic demand lost momentum on prolonged weakness in the external sector, including reduced tourist arrivals, and volatile asset market movements continued to batter confidence. Taipei,China also suffered from widespread output stagnation, plummeting investment, and falling net exports, allowing no growth in the first 6 months of 2016. Growth recovered only in the Republic of Korea, where fiscal incentives and interest rate cuts fueled domestic demand and robust expansion in services outweighed faltering manufacturing output.

Price pressures remained subdued throughout the subregion in the first half. Inflation dropped well below the official target of 2.0% in the Republic of Korea. It cooled in Hong Kong, China, where it fell by 1 percentage point year on year. In Mongolia, stable food and fuel prices kept down price pressures. However, consumer price inflation rose in the PRC to 2.1% year on year, owing mainly to higher food prices and renminbi depreciation, and in Taipei,China, where it was fueled mainly by expansionary monetary policy and rising food prices.

On the external front, all subregional economies except Taipei,China recorded higher trade surpluses in the first half of 2016 as imports declined faster than exports. However, as net services receipts shrank,

3.2.1 GDP growth, East Asia

■ 2015　■ 2016　■ 2017

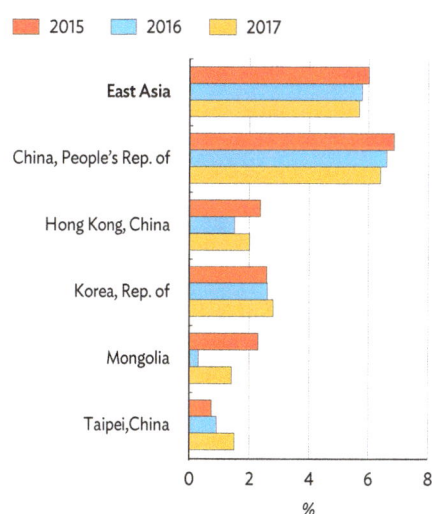

Source: Asian Development Outlook database.
Click here for figure data

The section on the PRC was written by Jurgen Conrad and Jian Zhuang and the part on other economies by Gemma Estrada, Benno Ferrarini, Xuehui Han, Marthe Hinojales, Nedelyn Magtibay-Ramos, Donghyun Park, and Norio Usui. Authors are with the East Asia and Economic Research and Regional Cooperation departments of ADB. Subregional assessment and prospects were written by Reza Vaez-Zadeh, consultant, Economic Research and Regional Cooperation Department.

current accounts relative to GDP deteriorated across the subregion except in Mongolia, where steeply lower imports narrowed the deficit. In the PRC, a sizeable decline in international reserves was the outcome of a substantially lower current account surplus and continuing net capital outflows triggered mainly by exchange rate uncertainties, private debt repayment overseas, and higher outbound direct investment.

Economic growth in East Asia will continue to trend downward from 6.1% in 2015 to 5.8% in 2016 and 5.6% in 2017 (Figure 3.2.1). Growth deceleration in the PRC will continue, but strong fiscal and monetary stimulus will limit the slowdown, with GDP rising by 6.6% in 2016 and 6.4% in 2017, faster than *ADO 2016* forecast. Growth deceleration will deepen in Hong Kong, China in 2016 on faltering domestic demand, with some recovery in 2017 as demand improves. The Republic of Korea will see growth stabilize this year and rise slightly in 2017, as accommodative monetary and fiscal policies mitigate the impact of tepid global demand and job losses from corporate restructuring. In Mongolia, falling household income and fiscal consolidation will lower growth to 0.3% in 2016, but some recovery is expected in 2017 as mine construction ramps up. Growth in Taipei,China will see a rising trend this year and next but remain low, held back by tepid domestic demand and persistent export weakness.

Inflation in East Asia will outpace the March forecast, rising at 1.9% in 2016 and 2.2% in 2017 (Figure 3.2.2). In the PRC, both headline and core inflation are expected to be higher than forecast in *ADO 2016*, reaching 2.0% in 2016 and accelerating to 2.2% in 2017 as administered prices are further deregulated and prices for services rise. Decade-long producer price deflation in the PRC will likely be reversed in 2017 as international commodity prices stabilize or increase. In the Republic of Korea, inflation is expected to accelerate moderately over the forecast period as global oil prices pick up and poor weather weighs on agricultural output, pushing up food prices. Weak domestic demand and lower fuel prices will moderate inflation in Mongolia and Hong Kong, China this year, but an uptick in growth and, in Mongolia, continuing currency depreciation will push inflation higher in both economies in 2017. Inflation in Taipei,China is forecast to turn positive in 2016 and edge up to 1.5% in 2017, exceeding the *ADO 2016* forecast as the authorities implement expansionary policies to stimulate growth.

The combined current account surplus will narrow from 4.0% of subregional GDP in 2015 to 3.1% this year and 2.7% next year, mainly on persistently weak exports and shrinking services receipts (Figure 3.2.3). In the PRC, exports are unlikely to pick up given tepid global growth and trade, and the deficit in the services account will widen as deregulation lags. Although imports will also decline, the current account surplus is expected to shrink relative to GDP in the forecast period. The deficit in Mongolia will widen more than previously forecast, reflecting lower ore quality in the main copper mine and higher machinery and fuel imports for mine construction. Elsewhere in the subregion, current account surpluses in 2016 and 2017 will be as forecast or slightly higher.

3.2.2 Inflation, East Asia

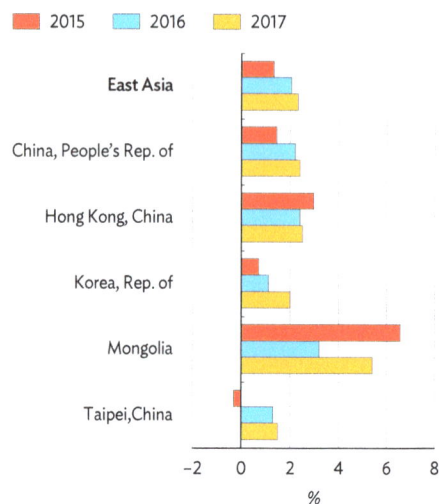

Source: Asian Development Outlook database.
Click here for figure data

3.2.3 Current account balance, East Asia

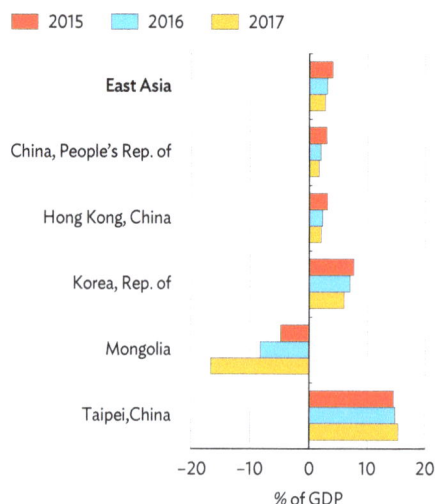

Source: Asian Development Outlook database.
Click here for figure data

People's Republic of China

Economic growth continues to slow but less than forecast in *ADO 2016* and not enough to threaten the government's growth target for 2016 of at least 6.5%. Inflation will rise but remain low in 2016 and 2017 even with the likely end of half a decade of producer price deflation. The authorities need to contain financial risks posed by high credit growth and recurring instability in the real estate market, while intensifying structural reform to unlock growth potential.

Updated assessment

Growth decelerated further from 6.9% year on year in 2015 to 6.7% in the first half of 2016 (Figure 3.2.4). The slowdown persisted despite strong fiscal and monetary support, which boosted investment in infrastructure and real estate. Still, growth continued to be driven mainly by services and consumption in line with government objectives (Box 3.2.1). Labor markets remained stable, as reflected in solid real wage growth and the creation of 7.2 million new urban jobs, as in the first half of 2015.

On the supply side, a severe winter moderated growth in agriculture from 3.9% year on year in 2015 to 3.1% in the first half of 2016. The secondary sector (comprising mining, manufacturing, electricity, and construction) expanded by 6.1% in the first 6 months of the year, slightly down from 6.2% in the same period in 2015. Mining all but stagnated while consumer-oriented and high-tech industries continued to expand briskly, and construction and related industries received an unexpected boost from infrastructure and housing investment. Services grew faster than industry, with most services, particularly real estate, retail trade, and hospitality services, expanding strongly. However, sector growth overall moderated from 8.3% in 2015 to 7.5% in the first half of 2016, dragged down by a weaker performance in the financial sector following equity market turbulence in mid-2015. Services contributed 60% to GDP growth and, as an indication of continued economic restructuring, expanded their share of GDP to 54.1% in the first half of 2016, or 1.8 percentage points higher than a year earlier and 14.6 percentage points above the industry share.

On the demand side, consumption contributed 73.4% to GDP growth (Figure 3.2.5), and consumer confidence remained upbeat, though real disposable income growth slowed to 6.5% year on year in the first half of 2016 from 7.4% in 2015. Government-led infrastructure investment expanded even more strongly than in 2015, and easy credit for developers and home buyers pushed housing sales and investment higher as the real estate market correction that started in 2014 petered out (Figure 3.2.6). However, much weaker manufacturing investment, particularly by private firms, dragged down overall investment growth. Key reasons for the softening of manufacturing investment include weak export growth, deteriorating business confidence, the need to reduce excess capacity in such capital-intensive industries as mining and steel, and meager investment opportunities for private companies in sectors that are still dominated by state-owned enterprises, such as electricity, oil and gas, railways, aviation, and telecommunications.

3.2.4 Economic growth

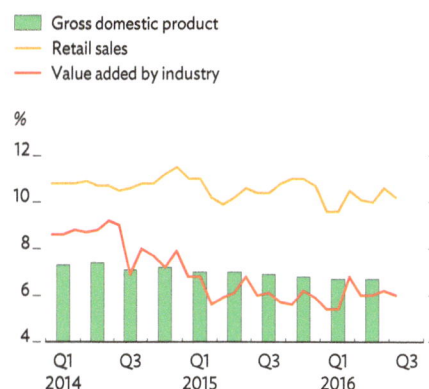

Q = quarter.
Source: National Bureau of Statistics.
Click here for figure data

3.2.5 Demand-side contributions to growth

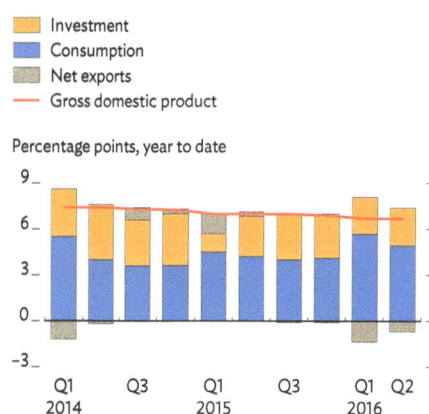

Q = quarter.
Source: National Bureau of Statistics.
Click here for figure data

3.2.6 Real estate markets

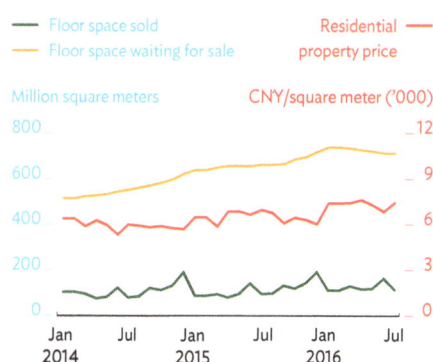

Sources: National Bureau of Statistics; National Development and Reform Commission; ADB estimates.
Click here for figure data

3.2.1 GDP statistics revised to meet international standards

In July 2016, the National Bureau of Statistics of the PRC adopted a new accounting method whereby research-and-development expenditures were no longer treated as intermediate input but as fixed capital formation. The new method aligns with the United Nations' international standards for national accounting—the System of National Accounts 2008, as revised in 2009—which was adopted by most members of the Organisation for Economic Co-operation and Development in 2010 and prompted their GDP series being revised up by an average of 2.2% in that year.

Using the new procedure, the PRC nominal GDP series since 1952 also came out higher, but revisions of real GDP in that period went both directions (box figure 1). As growth in

PRC spending on research and development has outpaced GDP growth in recent years (box figure 2), real growth rates since 1999 were all revised up, with those for the most recent 5 full years up by 0.06 percentage points on average. Similarly, GDP in the first quarter of 2016 was revised up by 1.3%, adding 0.04 percentage points to growth.

The new procedure yielded a higher share of GDP in 2015 for the secondary sector (mining, manufacturing, electricity, and construction), revised to 40.9% from 40.5% as the share of services in the same year was revised down to 50.2% from 50.5%. On the demand side, the share of consumption in GDP that year was revised down to 51.6% from 52.4% and that of capital formation revised up to 45.0% from 44.2%.

1 Adjustments to GDP value and growth

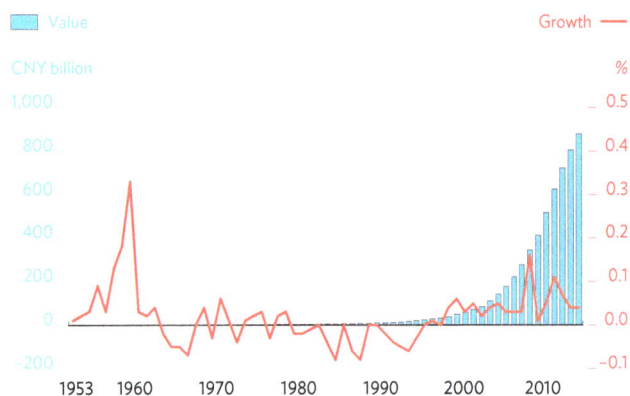

Source: National Bureau of Statistics.
Click here for figure data

2 Growth in research and development spending versus nominal GDP growth

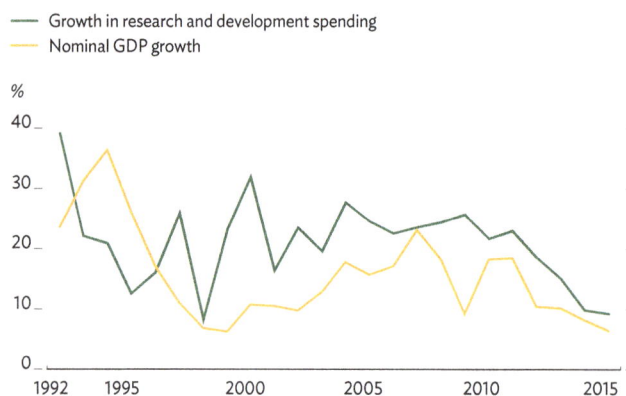

Source: National Bureau of Statistics.
Click here for figure data

Inflation remained below the government ceiling of 3.0% (Figure 3.2.7). Consumer prices increased by 2.1% year on year in the first 6 months of 2016, up from 1.3% in the first half of 2015, mainly on higher prices for pork and vegetables. Leaving aside food and energy, core inflation was 1.5%, the same as in the first 6 months of 2015. Producer price deflation slowed from 5.2% in 2015 to 3.9% in the first half of 2016 as the decline in global commodity prices, the main factor behind producer price deflation in the PRC since March 2012, halted and then reversed. The slowdown continued in July and August.

Fiscal policy became more expansionary in 2016, reflecting the government's keen interest in achieving a strong start to the Thirteenth Five-Year Plan, 2016–2020, which foresees average GDP growth at 6.5%. Consolidated expenditure by the central and local governments increased by 15.4% year on year in the first 6 months, outpacing the 11.8% growth recorded in the first half of 2015 and nominal GDP growth of 7.2% year on year in the same period of this year (Figure 3.2.8). Part of this increase likely reflects government efforts to reduce the traditional bunching of investment spending late

3.2.7 Monthly inflation

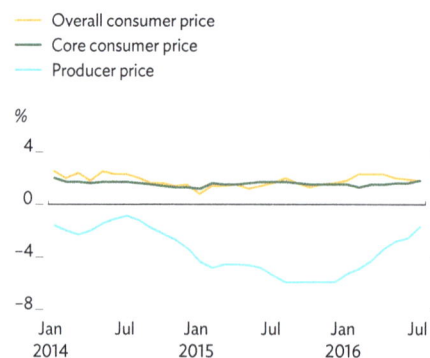

Sources: National Bureau of Statistics; People's Bank of China.
Click here for figure data

in the fiscal year. Consolidated budget revenue growth accelerated moderately to 7.4% on higher revenue from land sales. Growth in both revenue and expenditure was stronger at the local level. The consolidated budget balance turned from a surplus of 0.7% of GDP in the first half of 2015 to a deficit of 1.1% in the first half of 2016. Anecdotal evidence suggests that further strong spending support flowed off budget through policy banks and local government financing vehicles, contrary to the objective of incorporating off-budget spending into the consolidated budget.

Monetary policy remained accommodative in the first half of 2016. Policy and benchmark interest rates were unchanged, with interbank rates and bond yields remaining stable and low since the end of 2015 despite rising inflation and a number of bond defaults (Figure 3.2.9). The resulting credit expansion provided liquidity to absorb housing overhangs in many municipalities but also enabled ill-advised real estate investment in some smaller cities where the housing stock is still too high and created price bubbles in larger cities where supply could not meet increasingly speculative demand.

On average, money supply (M2) grew by 12.9% year on year in the first 6 months of 2016, only slightly below the 13.4% reported in the second half of 2015 (Figure 3.2.10). The stock of total social financing (a broader gauge of credit provided to nonfinancial enterprises and households from banks, nonbank financial institutions, and capital markets) expanded by an estimated 13.0%. Actual credit growth was likely even higher, as some credit provided by nonbank financial institutions is captured in neither money supply nor total social financing. Also, local governments now incur debt by issuing bonds that are not included in total social financing, rather than by borrowing through off-budget vehicles, which is included.

All this may suggest that leverage in the economy has further intensified, along with associated risk. However, the most active borrowers apart from real estate developers have been households and the public sector, both of which still enjoy scope to leverage. Together, they account for only two-fifths of overall debt, which stood at an estimated 250% of GDP at the end of 2015. The corporate debt burden is much higher, and it is not yet clear whether deleveraging has started, at least in some industries. Moreover, many companies are apparently hoarding funds rather than investing, a trend reflected in demand deposits rising much faster than time deposits.

Over the past year, the exchange rate regime changed from an undeclared US dollar peg to a managed float. The transition was not smooth, as the tardy emergence of policy intentions and technical details triggered exchange rate volatility and stronger capital outflow. However, since March 2016, the changes have been embraced by markets, allowing the People's Bank of China, the central bank, more flexibility in implementing both monetary and exchange rate policy. Amid increased volatility, the renminbi depreciated against the US dollar by 8.6% since July 2015, but this reflected US dollar strength more than renminbi weakness. In the same period, the renminbi softened by 7% in either nominal effective (trade-weighted) terms or real effective (inflation-adjusted) terms (Figure 3.2.11).

3.2.8 Fiscal indicators and nominal GDP

Q = quarter.
Sources: Ministry of Finance; National Bureau of Statistics.
Click here for figure data

3.2.9 Interest rates

Source: People's Bank of China.
Click here for figure data

3.2.10 Money supply and nominal GDP growth

Q = quarter.
Sources: National Bureau of Statistics; People's Bank of China.
Click here for figure data

Exports declined in the first half of 2016 by 6.9% year on year, as measured in US dollars. As in 2015, this mainly reflected weak global demand and exchange rate effects, with many exports purchased in currencies that lost value against the dollar, rather than any loss of PRC competitiveness. Lower commodity prices drove import value down by 9.9% despite higher commodity import volumes. The trade surplus as measured by customs statistics reached $269.2 billion, marginally larger than in the first half of 2015. The terms of trade (export prices relative to import prices) in the first 6 months of 2016 were 5.2% less favorable to the PRC than in the comparable period a year earlier. The current account surplus declined by 43% to $98.7 billion in the first half of 2016 from $173.2 billion in the previous year as the deficit in services account expanded substantially. Balance of payments data for the first quarter of 2016 confirm that higher outbound direct investment and repayment of foreign currency credits in anticipation of further renminbi devaluation caused net capital outflow to exceed the current account surplus. This reduced official reserves by $123.3 billion. Since then, net capital outflow has been smaller, and official reserves remained broadly unchanged at $3.3 trillion.

Prospects

The growth rate in the first half of 2016 was higher than *ADO 2016* forecast in March, and surprisingly strong fiscal and monetary stimulus will mitigate growth deceleration going forward. GDP growth forecasts are therefore revised up to 6.6% in 2016 and 6.4% in 2017 (Figure 3.2.12).

On the demand side, investment growth will further weaken following the housing sales and construction peak in May 2016, and as credit growth slows and investment in manufacturing, particularly in capital-intensive industries with excess capacity, continues to weaken (Figure 3.2.13). The government will continue to use infrastructure investment to smooth the effect of economic restructuring on the growth slowdown. However, as infrastructure investment accounts for only one-fifth of all investment, it cannot fully compensate for the falloff in investment elsewhere. Income growth will also moderate further, despite higher social spending by the government. Consumption growth will thus remain stable at best, and only if households further shake off their propensity to save. Finally, a gloomy international environment may weigh on exports as in previous years. On the supply side, widespread flooding in the southern provinces will hamper agriculture, industry will have to cope with slowing housing investment and weaker export demand, and year-on-year growth in services will be undercut by base effects arising from strong financial activity in 2015.

Headline and core inflation are expected to remain at current rates until the end of 2016 and accelerate only slightly in 2017 as administered prices are further deregulated and prices for services rise. The forecast for consumer price inflation is thus revised up to 2.0% in 2016 and 2.2% in 2017 (Figure 3.2.14). Strong credit growth harbors inflationary risks in the more distant future. Producer price deflation will further ameliorate by the end of 2016 and turn positive in 2017 as commodity prices stabilize or increase.

3.2.11 Exchange rates

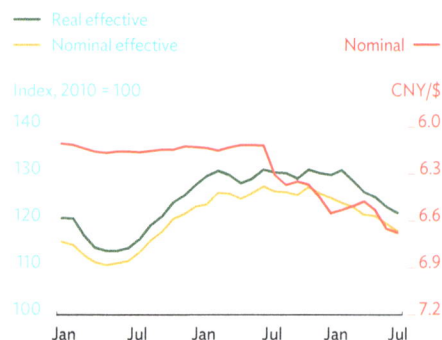

Sources: Bank for International Settlements; People's Bank of China.
Click here for figure data

3.2.12 GDP growth

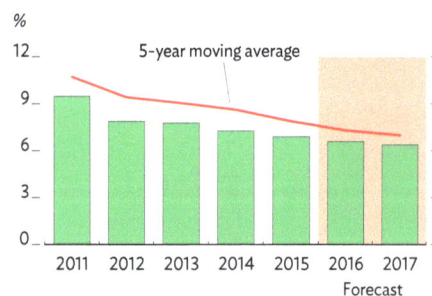

Source: Asian Development Outlook database.
Click here for figure data

3.2.1 Selected economic indicators, People's Republic of China (%)

	2016		2017	
	ADO 2016	Update	ADO 2016	Update
GDP growth	6.5	6.6	6.3	6.4
Inflation	1.7	2.0	2.0	2.2
Current acct. bal. (share of GDP)	2.7	2.0	2.5	1.7

Source: ADB estimates.

While exports are unlikely to pick up in light of lackluster global growth and trade, the share of exports with higher value added will continue to grow. The services deficit will widen further, especially in the absence of breakthroughs with service sector deregulation. The trade and current account surpluses will narrow over the forecast period. As moderate net capital outflow continues, the overall balance of payments will remain in deficit. This will further reduce official reserves, which nevertheless remain substantial, especially in light of the more flexible exchange rate policy than in the past. The PRC net foreign asset position will remain strong, with lower reserves matched by higher outbound investment. Foreign investment in domestic equity and bond markets has been facilitated since 2014 and will accelerate over the medium term as investors become more comfortable managing new exchange rate risks and warm to the relative ease of fund repatriation.

In response to declining foreign reserves, the central bank will likely have to further reduce regulatory reserve requirements to enhance liquidity in the banking system. At 17% for large banks, reserve requirements remain high by international norms. Interest rate cuts are less likely as rates are already low and further cuts would risk accelerating capital outflow. Because public debt is relatively low, fiscal policy offers more scope than monetary policy for providing stimulus. Budget deficits are thus expected to widen further over the forecast period.

The principal international risk to these projections arises from possible further worsening of the global investment climate and growth outlook, causing another dip in global commodity prices. Markets have calmed after the initial shock following the Brexit referendum, but Brexit has compounded what was already a very uncertain global economic outlook. The direct impact of Brexit on the PRC economy will likely be small and the damage through the trade channel manageable in the short run. However, Brexit may herald rising protectionism in global trade, with uncertain consequences over time.

The principal domestic risk is renewed instability in real estate. Recent increases in property and land prices derive mostly from some second tier cities, where in July 2016 average land prices were 50% above those seen a year earlier. These increases likely reflect speculation rather than economic fundamentals. Another property market slowdown would not only affect GDP growth but could also create a fiscal shock if government land auctions cool over the coming months, dragging down land sale revenues over the forecast period (land auctions precede sales revenues by 3–6 months). While it makes sense for the government to support the real estate market, as it has done since 2014, such support harbors the risk of delaying necessary adjustments, including tackling the persistently large housing overhang in many cities.

Another risk is consumer sentiment being undermined as income growth further decelerates and the labor market weakens under continuing industrial restructuring (Box 3.2.2). Although consumer confidence has remained strong, as have retail sales, real disposable income growth has lagged behind real GDP growth. For consumption to keep driving GDP growth, the household savings rate needs to decline further, but changes in savings behavior are difficult to predict.

3.2.13 Nominal growth in key components of fixed asset investment

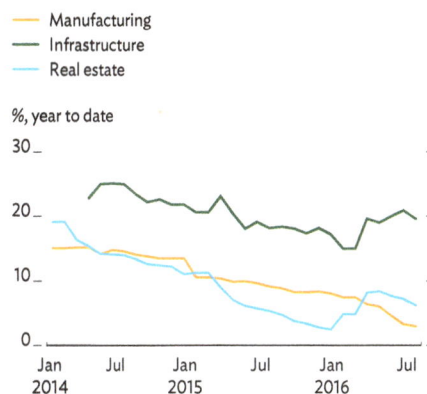

— Manufacturing
— Infrastructure
— Real estate

Source: National Bureau of Statistics.
Click here for figure data

3.2.14 Inflation

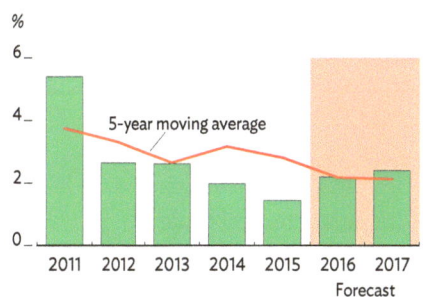

Source: Asian Development Outlook database.
Click here for figure data

3.2.2 A call for accelerated structural reform

Economic growth has decelerated since 2010. Rather than try to reverse the trend, the government aims to maintain a growth rate of 6.5% on average over the next 5 years. This rate may or may not be slower than the potential growth rate of the PRC economy, but a higher growth rate can be achieved in 2016 only with substantial fiscal and monetary support and at the cost of unrelentingly fast debt growth. Indeed, the government has managed growth and financial stability well over recent years, and it has enough external, fiscal, and monetary buffers and institutional leverage to manage financial and other risks into the future. However, unleashing the growth potential of the economy while safeguarding financial stability requires that the pace of structural reform be stepped up.

Economic reform has progressed in many areas since a comprehensive and ambitious reform agenda was presented in November 2013, albeit at a slower pace than the PRC leadership and many observers expected back then. Among the factors impeding implementation is the tendency to resort to the administrative management of economic development rather than reply on market mechanisms when stability is at stake. The emphasis on stability seems to have intensified, particularly since the stock market turmoil in mid-2015.

Moving forward, the need to unlock growth potential toward realizing the ambitions outlined at the third plenum is more urgent now than 3 years ago. Time is limited for the PRC to become wealthy before its population gets old. The labor force has peaked. Private sector investment, which is critical for economic restructuring and innovation, is still constrained by multiple factors, including government interference and the dominance of state-owned enterprises (SOEs). It is instructive in this regard that SOEs have been the private partner in half of the public–private partnership deals concluded since 2014, or more than 70% by value.

Renewed efforts are needed to refocus the third plenum agenda on bolstering potential growth and restoring investor confidence, which has suffered since 2013, albeit partly from a bleaker international environment. Clear progress is needed over the forecast period toward finding, as promised by the government in May 2016, a "comprehensive solution" for highly indebted "zombie companies," many of which are SOEs. Also needed are more concrete steps to stiffen competition for SOEs and otherwise improve their performance, and to reorganize fiscal relations between the central and local governments to ensure that local governments can effectively support urbanization, which is a key growth driver. Improving the allocation of financial resources is a further urgent need to mitigate the impact on growth from unavoidable deleveraging. This will be hard to achieve without pursuing more vigorous bank reform, implementing a comprehensive program of equity market development, and facilitating the development of nonbank financial services under risk-based regulation.

Moreover, slower economic growth, rapid credit expansion, and real estate price bubbles harbor risks to bank asset quality. Troubled loans classified as nonperforming or with overdue interest payments already account for almost 7% of the loan portfolio, and strong credit growth may mask more serious repayment problems, potentially undermining financial stability and investor confidence. Demand-side stimulus should thus be provided, if necessary, through fiscal rather than monetary policy, and coming primarily from the central government and its policy banks, not local governments. Further, any stimulus should be reflected in the budget, not implemented off budget.

Other economies

Hong Kong, China

GDP grew by 1.2% year on year in the first half of 2016, a considerable slowdown from 2.8% in the first half of last year. Weakness in the first quarter of 2016 reflected subdued global growth and sharp gyrations in global finance and money markets. The economy revived in the second quarter to grow by 1.7% year on year. Domestic demand lost momentum as prolonged weakness in the external sector and volatile asset markets continued to weigh on local confidence. Private consumption grew by only 0.9% in the first half against 5.9% in the same period last year, despite continued job creation and firm wage growth. Combined with persistent slowing in inbound tourism, this significantly dragged down retail sales, which saw in the first quarter their largest annual decline since the Asian financial crisis of 1997–1998. Gross fixed capital formation contracted by 7.2% in the first half as private machinery and equipment acquisition shrank in line with subdued business confidence, though building and construction picked up in the second quarter.

External demand helped offset slack domestic demand in the first half, with net exports contributing half of GDP growth. Goods exports resumed growth at 2.0% in real terms year on year in the second quarter, after declining for 4 consecutive quarters. Meanwhile, exports of services slowed their decline to 4.6% in the second quarter as drag eased from inbound tourism and regional trade and cargo flows. Imports declined faster, pushing the current account surplus up to the equivalent of 2.6% of GDP in the first half of 2016 from less than 0.1% a year earlier.

Inflation cooled after reaching an 8-month peak of 3.0% in February. It clocked at 2.6% during the first 7 months of 2016, or 1.0 percentage point lower than in the same period last year because of smaller increases for food and rent.

Growth forecasts are revised down for both 2016 and 2017 in light of weak growth in the first half of this year and likely economic headwinds. The latest business survey points to more cautious business spending, and the labor market shows some signs of slack in sectors related to tourism and consumption. Domestic demand is thus likely to remain weak in the second half of 2016 despite firm support from building projects and accommodative fiscal policy. Growth returned to visitor arrivals in July, at 2.6% year on year, suggesting gradual recovery in inbound tourism that may improve services exports and stabilize retail sales later this year. Inflation forecasts are pared as wage growth moderates and rents soften. Current account surpluses in 2016 and 2017 are now expected to be higher than previously forecast as exports and tourism appear to recover and continued weak domestic demand weighs on imports.

External downside risks persist. Any adverse development concerning monetary policy normalization in the US, growth moderation in the PRC, or deeper risk aversion globally could have negative spillover through both trade and finance channels, curbing growth by putting upward pressure on the local dollar, which is linked to the US dollar, or straining a consolidating property market.

3.2.2 Selected economic indicators, Hong Kong, China (%)

	2016		2017	
	ADO 2016	*Update*	*ADO 2016*	*Update*
GDP growth	2.1	1.5	2.2	2.0
Inflation	2.5	2.4	2.7	2.5
Current acct. bal. (share of GDP)	2.0	2.3	1.8	2.1

Source: ADB estimates.

Republic of Korea

Economic growth recovered from 2.6% in 2015 to 3.0% year on year in the first half of 2016, supported by domestic demand. Spurred by tax discounts for car purchases, private consumption expanded by 2.7%, well up from 1.6% in the same period last year. With a 4.0% increase in the smaller government contribution, total consumption expanded by 3.0%.

Investment grew by 5.0% on strong construction boosted by low interest rates, which outweighed weakness in other investment outlays. Led by residential construction, construction investment surged by 10.3% in the first half, a dozen times better than the 0.9% recorded in the same period last year.

However, business sentiment weakened by uncertainty in the domestic and global environments—and by 18 consecutive months of export decline—tamped down other investment outlays. In particular, investment in machinery and equipment, which accounted for 31.8% of gross fixed capital formation, contracted by 3.6% year on year against 5.4% expansion in the same period of 2015. Net exports continued to drag down economic growth as they declined by 11.1%, though less than the 14.5% drop in the first half of 2015.

On the supply side, industry propelled growth despite manufacturing expansion at just 2.0% year on year in the first half—faster than in the first half of 2015 but well below the 3.5% average over the past 5 years. Less robust manufacturing has hit employment in the sector, which added only 82,000 jobs in the first 6 months, compared with 143,000 in the same period a year earlier. The service sector performed better, growing by 2.8% in the first half and generating 270,000 new jobs.

Soft demand prompted aggressive monetary and fiscal responses to support growth. The Bank of Korea, the central bank, cut its policy rate to a record low of 1.25% in June, the first cut in a year. In addition, the government announced a $17 billion fiscal stimulus package in June to cushion the uncertain global outlook and support provincial economies at risk from ongoing corporate restructuring mandated by the Corporate Restructuring Promotion Act enacted in March. The government estimated that 60,000 workers could lose their jobs as the shipbuilding and shipping industries restructure, having been hard hit by sluggish global trade.

Growth is likely to remain subdued for the rest of the year against a backdrop of tepid global demand. Job loss from restructuring could weigh on domestic demand and pose an additional downside risk to growth in the second half, but accommodative monetary and fiscal policies should mitigate its impact. On balance, economic growth forecasts are unchanged from *ADO 2016*.

Consumer price inflation remained well below the central bank's target of 2.0% in the first half of 2016, averaging 0.9% in the year to July. As global oil prices pick up and poor weather weighs on agricultural output and pushes up food prices, inflation is expected to accelerate moderately to the forecast horizon.

The external current account surplus is now projected half a point higher in 2016, as imports are expected to continue to fall more than exports this year, weighed down by weak domestic demand. However, reviving domestic demand and an import recovery in 2017 should push the surplus lower next year, as projected.

3.2.3 Selected economic indicators, Republic of Korea (%)

	2016		2017	
	ADO 2016	Update	ADO 2016	Update
GDP growth	2.6	2.6	2.8	2.8
Inflation	1.4	1.1	2.0	2.0
Current acct. bal. (share of GDP)	6.5	7.0	5.5	6.0

Source: ADB estimates.

Mongolia

Economic growth slowed further to 1.4% in the first half of 2016. On the supply side, mining and agriculture lifted GDP by 2.5 percentage points, while industry and services pulled it down by 1.1 points. On the demand side, a drop in household consumption by 10.9% wiped out positive contributions from government consumption, gross capital formation, and net exports. Household income declined by 10.4% year on year in the second quarter, and unemployment edged up to 10.4% at the end of July from 8.3% at the end of 2015.

Average inflation from January to July stood at 1.7%. Stable food and fuel prices offset the inflationary impact of currency depreciation, expansionary fiscal policy, and monetary expansion as central bank quasi-fiscal activities, mainly loans to herders and subsidized mortgages, grew by an amount equal to 2.0% of GDP.

With government spending 32.6% higher than in the first 7 months of 2015 and revenue 3.1% lower, the fiscal deficit soared to equal 8.5% of 2015 GDP, significantly exceeding the full-year deficit target and the Fiscal Stability Law ceiling set at 4%. A budget amendment and a revised fiscal framework for 2016–2018 were approved in late August amid worsening fiscal pressures largely from off-budget expenditures, and several fiscal consolidation measures were enacted. The government nevertheless estimates that the fiscal deficit will reach 18.2% of GDP in 2016, up from 7.9% last year. Public debt is projected to exceed 90.0% of GDP by the end of the year, including central bank's liabilities.

Merchandise exports fell by 9.6% year on year from January to July 2016, while imports declined by 17.0%, yielding a higher trade surplus and a narrower current account deficit. This helped trim the overall balance of payments deficit to $46 million. Supported by newly issued external public debt, gross foreign exchange reserves stood at the end of June at $1.3 billion, or 3.2 months of import cover. As of the end of August, the Mongolian togrog had depreciated by 11.2% since January. This trend prompted the central bank to raise its policy rate in August by 4.5 percentage points to 15.0%.

A main driver of growth over the forecast period is the underground development of Phase 2 of the Oyu Tolgoi copper and gold mine. Another is agricultural rebound following the harsh winter of 2015–2016. On the demand side, gross capital formation driven by the mine project will boost growth, but falling household incomes and fiscal consolidation will constrain consumption in the near term. Net exports will subtract from growth as mine-related imports ramp up. On balance, growth is likely to be slightly more resilient in 2016 and 2017 than earlier forecast. Inflation is expected to ease this year then, reflecting currency depreciation, rise in 2017, both movements less than earlier forecast. The balance of payments will likely remain under pressure over the forecast period as the current account deficit widens and external debt is repaid. Lower ore quality at Oyu Tolgoi and rising imports for Phase 2 expansion will widen the current account deficit somewhat more than previously forecast. Volatility in global commodity prices, tighter external finance, and sizeable external debt repayments are the main risks to the forecast.

3.2.4 Selected economic indicators, Mongolia (%)

	2016		2017	
	ADO 2016	Update	ADO 2016	Update
GDP growth	0.1	0.3	0.5	1.4
Inflation	3.0	3.2	7.0	5.4
Current acct. bal. (share of GDP)	–8.0	–8.3	–15.0	–16.7

Source: ADB estimates.

Taipei,China

The economy stagnated in the first half of 2016 as manufacturing output and trade contracted and as other sectors showed barely any growth. On the demand side, strong growth in consumption, both government and private, was offset by falling investment and net exports. The growth in private consumption reflected car purchases benefiting from a government-sponsored trade-in program and increased restaurant and transportation expenditure associated with two big holidays. Delays in government investment pending the inauguration of a new president in May hurt private sector confidence and caused private investment to contract. Declining exports of goods and services pulled down net exports by 12.0% year on year in the first half of 2016, but net income from abroad rose by 9.7%, reflecting higher tourist arrivals, and foreign exchange reserves rose by 3.2% in the first half of 2016.

GDP growth forecasts are revised down for both 2016 and 2017. The decline in investment during the first half of the year, caused by the delayed implementation of the government budget, is unlikely to be compensated by larger government outlays or higher investment in technology and aviation in the second half of the year. Further, a continuing decline in export orders in the first half points to persistent weakness in exports, and growth in private consumption may stall as the effect of the car trade-in program wanes. These developments in the wake of lackluster growth in the first half of 2016 will tamp down growth going forward, outweighing the impact of a likely continuation of expansionary monetary policy.

This policy was one reason headline consumer inflation increased sharply in the first 6 months of 2016, another being higher prices for vegetables and fruit as agriculture suffered under unfavorable weather. Despite rising prices, the central bank responded to the sluggish economy by cutting the discount rate to 1.5% in March and 1.4% in June, having previously lowered it in September and December 2015. Assuming continued low fuel prices and further monetary easing to stimulate economic growth, inflation is forecast to edge up in 2016 and 2017 slightly more than foreseen in *ADO 2016*.

The forecasts of the current account balance are unchanged for this year and next. The decline in exports of goods and services is likely to be offset by a rise in net income as tourist arrivals continue to grow, pushing current account surpluses slightly higher than in 2015. However, the capital and financial account surplus in the first half of this year was 9.2% lower than a year earlier, pointing to possible deterioration in the overall balance of payments surplus in 2016 and 2017.

The main downside risks to the outlook are a steeper weakening of the global economy than is currently expected, perhaps triggered by Brexit, and rising cross-strait tensions, either of which could hurt trade. On the upside, the pace of investment may accelerate as the new government implements projects put on hold before the presidential election, spurring higher growth.

3.2.5 Selected economic indicators, Taipei,China (%)

	2016		2017	
	ADO 2016	Update	ADO 2016	Update
GDP growth	1.6	0.9	1.8	1.5
Inflation	0.7	1.3	1.2	1.5
Current acct. bal. (share of GDP)	14.8	14.8	15.3	15.3

Source: ADB estimates.

South Asia

Despite global headwinds, the subregional growth forecasts of 6.9% for 2016 and 7.3% for 2017 are maintained but with revisions for several individual economies. Exports and investment underperformed expectations in the first half of 2016 but were offset by higher consumption. The inflation forecasts of 5.2% for 2016 and 5.7% for 2017 are also maintained. Regarding the current account deficit, the forecast for 2016 is trimmed on an improved outlook for India, but the forecast for 2017 stands. Low oil prices underpin the favorable inflation and current account outcomes.

Subregional assessment and prospects

The economic outlook for South Asia remains strong, with growth on track to meet *ADO 2016* projections of 6.9% for 2016 and 7.3% for 2017 (Figure 3.3.1). Developments in the subregion reflect heavy weighting for India, where forecasts are maintained at 7.4% for 2016 and 7.8% for 2017. Growth in the first quarter was, at 7.1%, lower than expected with a decline in investment, but this outcome is not likely to be representative of the year. Growth in 2016 is now expected to rely more on increased consumer demand following double-digit wage and pension increases awarded by a pay commission that meets once every 10 years. With government acceptance, the award is likely to influence wages across the economy. A healthy monsoon is expected to spur higher rural spending after 2 years of poor weather. Expectations of revived investment arise from strong progress in restructuring bank balance sheets and reducing excessive leverage at large corporations, which could drive growth higher to 7.8% in 2017.

In Bangladesh and Pakistan, estimated growth in the 2016 fiscal year, to 30 June, exceeded the forecasts because robust performance in manufacturing and services more than compensated for unexpected weakness in agriculture. Increased consumption and public investment contributed to the better performance in Bangladesh in 2016. A slower growth forecast for 2017 is retained as agriculture growth is expected to moderate. Growth in Pakistan will outperform the *ADO 2016* projection for 2017 on improvements in energy supply, higher infrastructure investment in an economic corridor project, and a better security environment. Improved growth in these two large economies contrasts with Nepal, where the growth estimate for the 2016 fiscal year, which ended on 15 July, is below the forecast following disruption to supply

3.3.1 GDP growth, South Asia

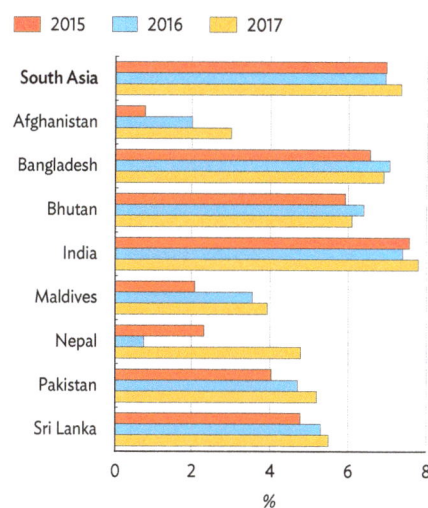

Source: Asian Development Outlook database.
Click here for figure data

The subregional assessment and prospects were written by Masato Nakane. The section on Bangladesh was written by Shamsur Rahman, Md. Golam Mortaza, and Barun K. Dey; India by Johanna Boestel and Abhijit Sen Gupta; Pakistan by Guntur Sugiyarto, Farzana Noshab, and Ali Khadija; and other economies by Sharad Bhandari, Rehman Gul, Tadateru Hayashi, Soon Chan Hong, Savindi Jayakody, Neelina Nakarmi, and Hasitha Wickremasinghe. Authors are with the Central and West, and South Asia departments of ADB.

and trade, delayed reconstruction of earthquake damage, and a poor monsoon. The economy is expected to recover in 2017 as forecast in *ADO 2016* on markedly accelerated reconstruction spending and a good monsoon able to lift agricultural output.

The growth forecast for Sri Lanka in 2016 is revised down to 5.0% from 5.3% on unexpected weakness in the second quarter, which held growth in the first half to 3.9%. Agriculture was depressed by dry weather in the first quarter and heavy rains and flooding in the second. However, a steep and unexpected slowdown in manufacturing and construction in the second quarter was the main cause of the weak half-year outcome. The growth forecast for 2017 is revised down to 5.5% from 5.8% in light of continued lackluster global demand and the need for fiscal policy adjustment. Growth prospects in Afghanistan remain as projected in *ADO 2016* as industry and services slowly revive in the wake of sharply reduced domestic demand following the withdrawal of international security forces in 2014, and assuming no deterioration in the political and security situation. Similarly, growth projections for Bhutan and the Maldives remain in line with *ADO 2016*.

Inflation in South Asia stands as projected in the *ADO 2016* at 5.2% in 2016 and 5.7% in 2017 (Figure 3.3.2). Inflation forecasts for India, the Maldives, and Sri Lanka are unchanged. Slightly lower inflation is forecast for Bangladesh and Bhutan in both 2016 and 2017. Pakistan and Nepal will likely experience slightly lower inflation than forecast for 2016 but now have slightly higher forecasts for 2017. The inflation forecast for Afghanistan in 2016 is revised up on the pass-through of a sharp currency decline in 2015 when emigration surged and trade was disrupted. While the exchange rate appears to have stabilized, the inflation forecast for 2017 is revised somewhat higher.

Although inflation in South Asia is much higher than in East or Southeast Asia, the subregion is enjoying lower inflation than several years ago mainly because of low global prices for oil and other commodities. While these prices are expected to strengthen in 2017, inflation outcomes are now underpinned by stronger demand-management policies.

The combined current account balance in South Asia is forecasted to be a deficit equal to 1.1% of aggregate GDP in 2016, revised down from 1.4% in *ADO 2016* (Figure 3.3.3). The forecast deficit for 2017 is retained at 1.6%. The 2016 improvement reflects a lower forecast deficit in India, revised to 1.4% of GDP from 1.6% on a smaller trade deficit as exports pick up. Afghanistan and Bangladesh are expected to see current account surpluses on better exports. Forecasts for Nepal's surplus are reduced because of disappointing remittances in 2016 and a wider trade deficit in 2017 as imports expand to supply sharply increased spending on earthquake reconstruction. Pakistan's modest current account deficit at 0.9% of GDP in 2016 is revised higher to 1.6% in 2017 on stepped up investment in its economic corridor project with the People's Republic of China and stronger growth. Only small revisions are in order for the relatively large current account deficits run by Bhutan and the Maldives as major government infrastructure investments continue. The forecast for the 2016 current account deficit in Sri Lanka is retained, but the forecast for 2017 is revised up on continued export weakness.

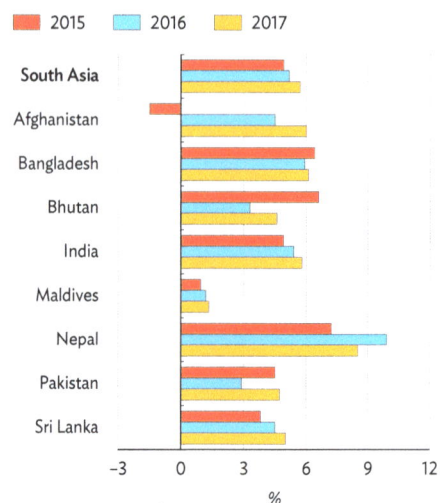

3.3.2 Inflation, South Asia

Source: Asian Development Outlook database.
Click here for figure data

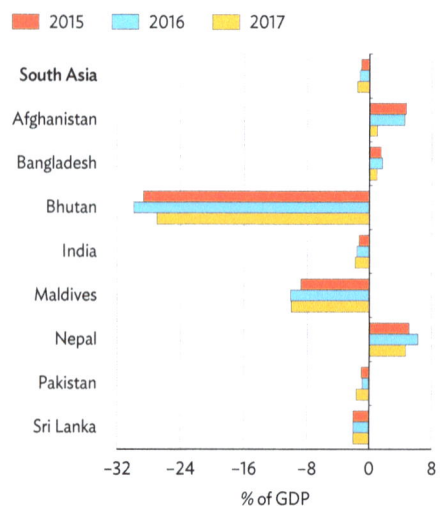

3.3.3 Current account balance, South Asia

Source: Asian Development Outlook database.
Click here for figure data

Bangladesh

Growth in FY2016 (ended 30 June 2016) exceeded expectations, aided by revived exports and sustained domestic consumption. Inflation was lower than projected, while larger exports and modest imports enlarged the current account surplus. This *Update* retains the *ADO 2016* growth projection for FY2017, revises downward the inflation projection, and forecasts a current account surplus instead of a deficit. For meeting the growth target of the Seventh Five-Year Plan, the timely completion of priority infrastructure projects is essential.

Updated assessment

GDP growth in FY2016 is officially estimated at 7.1%, which is higher than both the 6.6% growth recorded in FY2015 and the *ADO 2016* projection of 6.7% (Figure 3.3.4). Consumption continued to be the mainstay of growth as higher public sector salaries offset a decline in remittances. Despite some statistical discrepancy, net exports are likely to have contributed to growth.

Investment rose to equal 29.4% of GDP in FY2016 from 28.9% in the previous year on higher public investment. Private investment remained at the same level, by and large, despite some easing of infrastructure constraints and improvement in power supply, reflecting continued investor caution. Foreign direct investment rose slightly, mainly from reinvestment of earnings.

On the supply side, agriculture grew by 2.6% in FY2016, further decelerating from the previous year's 3.3% as expansion in staple crops and horticulture moderated. Industry saw growth rise to 10.1% from 9.7% in FY2015 as the export-oriented garment industry and manufacturing for the domestic market both performed well. Services growth was stronger at 6.7%. Higher public sector spending boosted the contributions of public administration, education, and health services, augmenting growth in trade and business services.

Average inflation declined to 5.9% in FY2016 from 6.4% in FY2015, slightly lower than projected in *ADO 2016*, as it was restrained by lower global commodity prices, steady domestic supply, and a stable exchange rate. Inflation declined to 5.5% year on year in June 2016 from 6.3% a year earlier, driven lower by food price inflation that dipped to 4.2% from 6.3%. Nonfood inflation accelerated to 8.7% before easing to 7.5% in June 2016, still up from 6.2% a year earlier. This reflected higher prices for natural gas and electricity and higher wages that sustained consumer demand (Figure 3.3.5).

With inflation pressures weakening, Bangladesh Bank, the central bank, lowered its repo and reverse repo rates by half a percentage point in January 2016 (Figure 3.3.6). The call money rate dropped to 3.7% in June 2016 from 5.8% a year earlier, reflecting the rate cut and very ample liquidity in the banking system. Treasury bill rates also declined. Banks' average lending rate declined markedly to 10.4% in June 2016 from 11.7% a year earlier. The deposit rate fell by a larger margin, slightly widening the interest rate spread to 4.9 percentage points. The ratio of nonperforming loans to all loans in the banking system improved to 9.9% in March 2016 from 10.5% a year earlier, as banks were allowed to reschedule overdue loans.

3.3.4 Demand-side contributions to growth

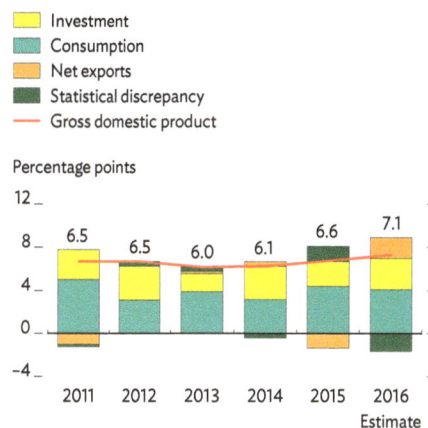

- Investment
- Consumption
- Net exports
- Statistical discrepancy
- Gross domestic product

Percentage points

6.5 6.5 6.0 6.1 6.6 7.1

2011 2012 2013 2014 2015 2016
Estimate

Note: Years are fiscal years ending on 30 June of that year.
Source: Bangladesh Bureau of Statistics. 2016. National Accounts Statistics. June.
Click here for figure data

3.3.5 Monthly inflation

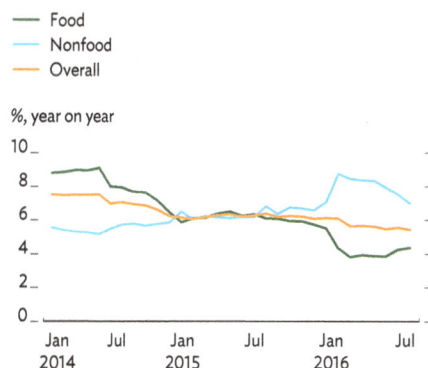

- Food
- Nonfood
- Overall

%, year on year

Jan 2014   Jul   Jan 2015   Jul   Jan 2016   Jul

Source: Bangladesh Bank. 2016. *Monthly Economic Trends.* August. http://www.bangladesh-bank.org
Click here for figure data

3.3.6 Interest rates

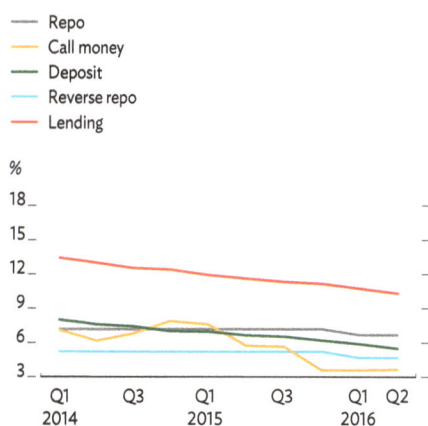

- Repo
- Call money
- Deposit
- Reverse repo
- Lending

%

Q1 2014   Q3   Q1 2015   Q3   Q1 2016   Q2

Q = quarter.
Source: Bangladesh Bank. http://www.bangladesh-bank.org
Click here for figure data

Broad money grew by 16.4% year on year in June 2016, rising from 12.4% in June 2015 and exceeding the FY2016 monetary program target of 15.0% (Figure 3.3.7). Private credit growth accelerated to 16.6% in June 2016 from 13.2% a year earlier, exceeding the FY2016 program target of 14.8% as credit demand, especially consumer credit, responded to lower lending rates. Growth in net credit to the government was lower at 3.6% in FY2016 as government borrowing through national savings certificates expanded. As banks' deposit rates declined under higher liquidity, savers sought these high-yielding savings instruments despite their minimum term of 3 years.

While below target, revenue collection rose to 10.3% of GDP from 9.6% in FY2015. Overall spending rose to the equivalent of 15.3% of GDP from 13.5% in FY2015, though current spending was nearly 10% below budget due to revenue shortfalls. Reduced subsidy payments thanks to lower oil prices helped to keep spending in check. In addition, a shortfall in annual development program spending helped to limit total spending and contain the fiscal deficit within its target of 5.0% of GDP. Domestic sources, about evenly split between national saving certificates and banks, financed just over 70% of the deficit.

Of the 48 nonfinancial state-owned enterprises in Bangladesh, 33 earned a combined profit of $2.5 billion in FY2016 as of 28 April 2016, and the remainder incurred a loss of $989.5 million. The consolidated net profit of these enterprises surged to $1.5 billion, exceeding by far the full year net profit of $555.7 million in FY2015 (Figure 3.3.8). The profit earned by the Bangladesh Petroleum Corporation tripled to $1.6 billion from $531.2 million as a 41% fall in global oil prices reduced its costs. The net profit of the Bangladesh Oil, Gas, and Mineral Resources Corporation contracted slightly to $118.3 million from $142.8 million, and that of the Bangladesh Telecommunications Regulatory Commission eased to $516.7 million from $537.7 million because it could not hold a planned spectrum auction. The Bangladesh Power Development Board (BPDB) cut its losses to $796.4 million (equal to 0.4% of GDP) from $936.9 million in FY2015, mostly through lower fuel bills. BPDB losses absorbed about one-third of government subsidy spending for the year.

Government spending on subsidies declined to $2.4 billion (1.1% of GDP) in FY2016 from $2.8 billion in FY2015, the savings reflecting the sharp fall in oil prices (Figure 3.3.9). The government was able to save on its subsidy allocations to Bangladesh Petroleum Corporation as it earned profit. The BPDB also required a lower subsidy—$700 million in place of the initial budgetary allocation of $1.0 billion and the previous year's actual subsidy spending of $1.2 billion—because of lower fuel costs and higher bulk and retail power tariffs. Agriculture continued to be the main subsidy destination, providing fertilizer, diesel, and electric power to farmers. Its allocations declined marginally to $900 million from $910 million in FY2015.

The government cut prices for furnace oil, used mostly by industry and power plants, by more than 30% to Tk42/liter, effective 1 April 2016. It also cut prices for diesel, kerosene, and regular and premium gasoline by 4.4%–10.4%, effective 25 April 2016. Despite these price reductions, the first since global oil prices began their marked decline, Bangladesh Petroleum Corporation is expected to maintain a strong profit margin

3.3.7 Contributions to broad money growth

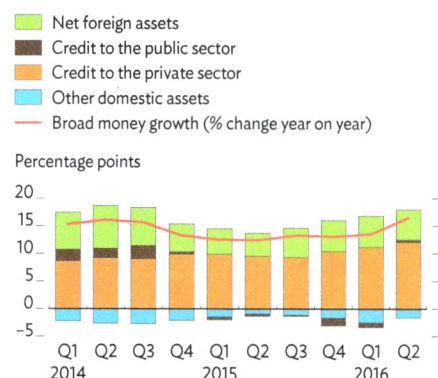

- Net foreign assets
- Credit to the public sector
- Credit to the private sector
- Other domestic assets
- Broad money growth (% change year on year)

Q = quarter.
Sources: Bangladesh Bank. 2016. Monthly Economic Trends. August. http://www.bangladesh-bank.org; ADB estimates.
Click here for figure data

3.3.8 Profits and losses at state-owned enterprises

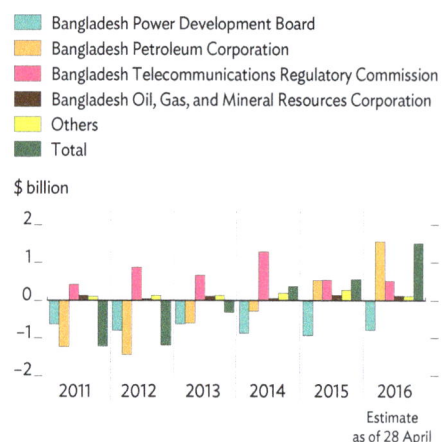

- Bangladesh Power Development Board
- Bangladesh Petroleum Corporation
- Bangladesh Telecommunications Regulatory Commission
- Bangladesh Oil, Gas, and Mineral Resources Corporation
- Others
- Total

Note: Years are fiscal years ending on 30 June of that year.
Sources: Ministry of Finance. Bangladesh Economic Review 2016; ADB estimates.
Click here for figure data

3.3.9 Government subsidies

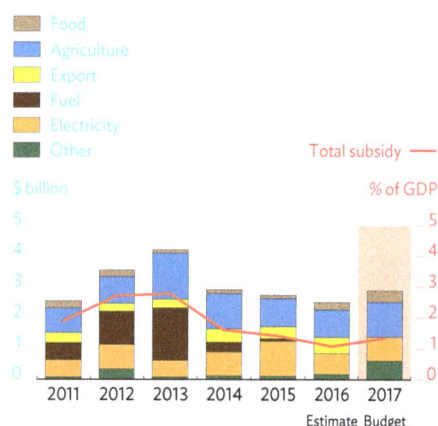

- Food
- Agriculture
- Export
- Fuel
- Electricity
- Other
- Total subsidy

Note: Years are fiscal years ending on 30 June of that year.
Sources: Ministry of Finance, Medium Term Macroeconomic Policy Statement 2015–16 to 2017–18; government budget document 2016–17; ADB estimates.
Click here for figure data

in the final 2 months of FY2016, allowing it to further offset losses incurred in previous years. To further stanch BPDB losses and reduce power and fuel subsidies, the government raised electricity tariffs in September 2015 by 6.9% for bulk consumers and 2.9% for retail consumers.

Exports rose briskly by 8.9% in FY2016, up from 3.1% in the previous year (Figure 3.3.10). After a slow start in the first quarter, export growth accelerated through the remainder of the year. Garment export earnings—accounting for about 82% of total export earnings—grew faster by 10.2% as buyer demand improved partly in response to progress in adopting better safety standards and worker rights in garment factories. Other factors were gradual migration to manufacturing higher-value apparel and the absence of production disruptions like those that lasted for several months a year earlier. Other exports also rebounded, growing by 7.8%.

Imports grew by 5.5% in FY2016. While food grain imports declined, growth in imports of consumer items was healthy. Expansion in imports of capital goods and intermediate items was modest.

Remittances declined by 2.5% to reach $14.9 billion in FY2016, even as the number of workers going abroad increased substantially. Slowing investment and construction in the Middle East in response to low oil prices have reduced wages, made it hard for employers to pay them, and caused layoffs. Weaker currencies were also a factor that limited workers' remittances.

The trade deficit narrowed by $691 million to $6.3 billion in FY2016 as expansion in export earnings outpaced that of import payments. Even with lower remittances, the improved trade deficit and smaller net outflows in the services and primary income accounts boosted the current account surplus by $831 million to $3.7 billion, or 1.7% of GDP (Figure 3.3.11). Slower growth in imports was the main factor that kept the current account from moving into the small deficit projected in March.

Combined capital and financial accounts including unclassified flows recorded a surplus of $2.1 billion in FY2016, slightly less than the $2.4 billion a year earlier. The large current account surplus nevertheless pushed the overall balance of payments up to a surplus of $5.0 billion, which brought the central bank's gross foreign exchange reserves at the end of June 2016 to $30.2 billion, or cover for 7.9 months of imports (Figure 3.3.12).

The Bangladesh taka–US dollar exchange rate was broadly stable in FY2016, reflecting the favorable current account position and the central bank's exchange rate objectives of building reserves and avoiding excessive rate volatility (Figure 3.3.13). The taka depreciated by 0.8% against the dollar at the end of June 2016 as remittance inflows declined. The taka appreciated in real effective terms by about 5% in FY2016 and by 25% over the past 3 years, implying lost competitiveness. However, Bangladesh maintains a large labor cost advantage over its competitors in the garment industry.

3.3.10 Contributions to export growth

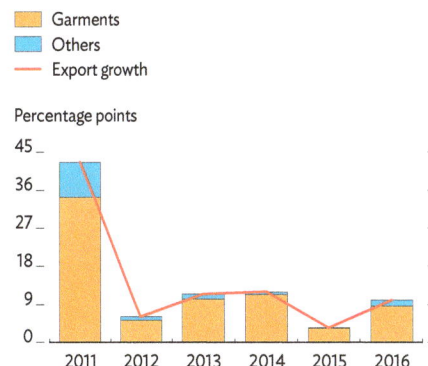

Note: Years are fiscal years ending on 30 June of that year. High export growth in 2011 largely reflects an increase in cotton prices by more than 40%.
Sources: Export Promotion Bureau; ADB estimates.
Click here for figure data

3.3.1 Selected economic indicators, Bangladesh (%)

	2016		2017	
	ADO 2016	*Update*	*ADO 2016*	*Update*
GDP growth	6.7	7.1	6.9	6.9
Inflation	6.2	5.9	6.5	6.1
Current acct. bal. (share of GDP)	−0.5	1.7	−1.0	1.0

Note: Years are fiscal years ending on 30 June of that year.
Source: ADB estimates.

3.3.11 Current account components

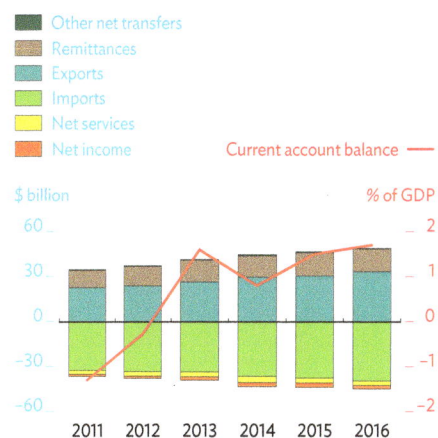

Note: Years are fiscal years ending on 30 June of that year.
Source: Bangladesh Bank. http://www.bangladesh-bank.org
Click here for figure data

Prospects

Forecasts for FY2017 rest on these assumptions: In line with the monetary policy statement published in late July 2016, the central bank will adopt measures to contain inflation while ensuring adequate credit flows to support higher private investment and growth. The government will accelerate its investment spending while strengthening efforts to attain its high revenue target.

GDP is expected to grow by 6.9% in FY2017, unchanged from *ADO 2016* (Figure 3.3.14). Agriculture growth in FY2017 is expected to moderate to 2.4% as low domestic rice prices discourage farmers' expansion of crop area. Industry growth is projected to edge up to 10.2% on sustained strong domestic demand and some improvement in power supply and easing of transport bottlenecks. Services growth is likely to be lower at 6.3% on more moderate expansion in agriculture, trade, transport, and public administration.

Consumption growth is expected to pick up, supported by higher public and private sector salaries as well as continued ready access to consumer credit. While remittances are unlikely to pick up in the near future, healthy export and employment growth is expected to be maintained with continued demand for the low-end garments and fast fashion products exported from Bangladesh.

An upturn in private investment is expected to begin in FY2017 with the continuation of political stability. A major catalyst is the completion of public sector energy and transport projects that reduce the cost of doing business. The new Dhaka–Chittagong and Dhaka–Mymensingh four-lane highways commissioned in July 2016 will save time, cut transportation costs, and ensure more timely shipments. Moreover, the government has fast-tracked several large infrastructure projects in the energy and transport sectors, providing impetus to business activity. The development of special economic zones, including some run by the private sector, further builds momentum for private investment.

The FY2017 budget aims to raise revenue equal to 12.4% of GDP for financing a larger annual development program and a major increase in other capital spending for speeding up the implementation of infrastructure projects (Figure 3.3.15). Current spending will grow to 9.6% of GDP with an increase in public sector salaries and modestly larger subsidies directed mainly to agriculture and social welfare. Capital spending is slated to rise to 7.8% of GDP with development expenditure amounting to 6.0% and other capital spending and net lending to state-owned enterprises increasing substantially to 1.8%. The deficit is targeted at 5.0% of GDP with about 60% financed by domestic borrowing. As in the past, prudent budget implementation should avoid exceeding the target deficit.

The implementation of the new Value-Added Tax Act, which had been scheduled for July 2016, was deferred until July 2017 to allow more time for the private sector to adapt their accounting systems and for greater outreach and education to small business. New revenue-enhancing tax measures in the FY2017 budget included raising rates on net wealth taxes, enhancing the minimum corporate tax, broadening the base of the existing value-added tax by bringing wholesale and retail traders into the tax net, increasing taxes on tobacco products,

3.3.12 Foreign exchange reserves

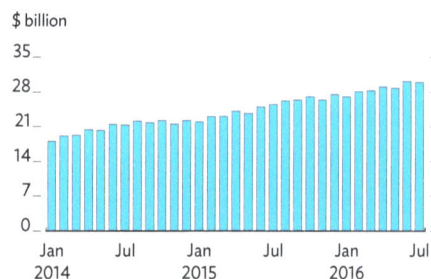

Source: Bangladesh Bank. 2016. Major Economic Indicators, Monthly Update. August. http://www.bangladesh-bank.org
Click here for figure data

3.3.13 Exchange rates

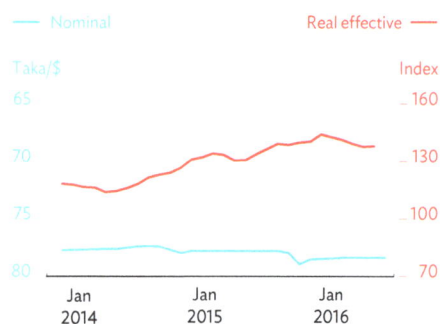

Source: Bangladesh Bank. 2016. *Monthly Economic Trends.* August. http://www.bangladesh-bank.org (accessed 29 August 2016).
Click here for figure data

3.3.14 GDP growth

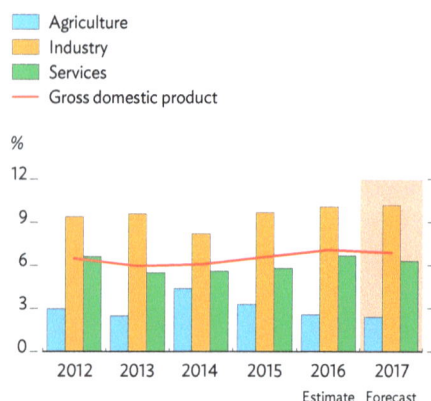

Note: Years are fiscal years ending on 30 June of that year.
Sources: Bangladesh Bureau of Statistics. 2016. *National Accounts Statistics.* June; ADB estimates.
Click here for figure data

and raising import duties on a large number of items. The rates of supplementary and regulatory duties were also increased.

In the monetary policy statement for the first half of FY2017, issued in late July 2016, the central bank focused on stabilizing inflation while supporting output and employment growth. The central bank thus kept its main policy rate unchanged at 6.75%. Inflation is expected to be 6.1% in FY2017, below the 6.5% forecast in *ADO 2016*. Despite price pressures from public and private sector wage increases and upward price adjustments for natural gas and electricity, a benign inflation outcome is anticipated in light of very modest increases in global food prices and more apparent elasticity in domestic supply response to domestic demand.

The revised forecast for export growth is 7.0% in FY2017, reflecting slower growth than projected in *ADO 2016* in the US and the euro area, the main textile markets. The import bill is revised to grow at 8.0% in FY2017. The revision takes into account modest import expansion in FY2016, when higher domestic production partly replaced imports. Imports of capital machinery are expected to pick up on higher investment, and a rebound in demand for raw materials and a projected increase in oil prices are also taken into account.

With the low oil price environment continuing, remittance inflows are likely to decline by 3.0% in FY2017. The imposition by Kuwait, Oman, and Saudi Arabia of taxes on remittances will further discourage them. Nonetheless, the current account is expected to show a surplus of 1.0% of GDP in FY2017 (Figure 3.3.16).

There are some assumptions for these projections: Sustained improvement in private investment will depend on the timely implementation of key infrastructure projects, and exports and investor confidence will require continued political stability. While concerted efforts have been taken toward climate and disaster resilience, weather remains a risk.

3.3.15 Fiscal indicators

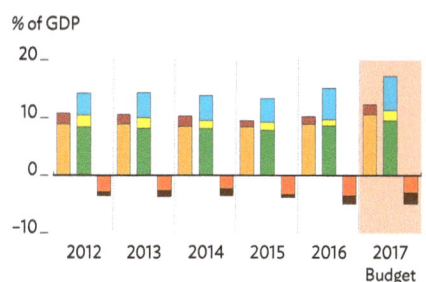

- Tax revenue
- Nontax revenue
- Current spending
- Capital spending and net lending
- Development spending
- Foreign financing
- Domestic financing

Note: Years are fiscal years ending on 30 June of that year.
Source: Asian Development Outlook database.
Click here for figure data

3.3.16 Current account balance

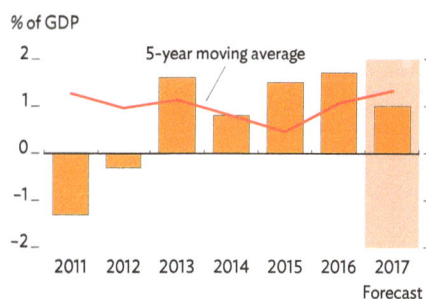

Note: Years are fiscal years ending on 30 June of that year.
Sources: Bangladesh Bank. http://www.bangladesh-bank.org; ADB estimates.
Click here for figure data

India

Growth is expected to stay high in FY2016 (ending 31 March 2017) on the strength of robust consumer demand from a general increase in wages that offsets a slowdown in investment. Inflation and the current account deficit are broadly in line with *ADO 2016* forecasts. The enactment of legislation to allow a national value-added tax was a milestone reform that will create a much more integrated and productive economy. Ongoing efforts to restructure bank balance sheets to revive lending and reduce excessive leverage at large corporations is setting the stage for a recovery in investment likely to drive growth higher in FY2017.

Updated assessment

GDP growth moderated to 7.1% year on year in the first quarter of FY2016 from 7.9% in the fourth quarter of FY2015 (Figure 3.3.17). Growth benefitted from a surge in government consumption, which grew by 18.8%. Excluding government consumption, GDP growth slowed to 5.7% as growth moderated in private consumption, investment, construction, and agriculture. The slowdown was exacerbated by an increase in the GDP deflator as nominal growth remained largely unchanged from the previous quarter.

Private consumption growth decelerated to 6.7% from 6.9% a year earlier, likely weighed down by weak rural demand after 2 consecutive years of weak monsoons. In contrast, government consumption recorded its highest growth in 7 quarters, reflecting high current expenditure. Fixed investment remained sluggish, contracting by 3.1% amid listless private investment and a slowdown in public investment, which was the major driver of investment in the first half of FY2015. Weak domestic demand caused imports to decline, such that net exports contributed positively to growth.

Weak rains in the past 2 years slowed agriculture growth to 1.8% in the first quarter of FY2016 as winter production of rice, coarse cereals, and pulses declined from the previous year (Figure 3.3.18). Growth in production other than field crops, including livestock, dairy, and forestry, also slowed.

Industry growth decelerated a bit to 6.0% in the first quarter of FY2016, primarily because mining contracted and construction was weak, with the latter reflecting muted growth in cement production and the consumption of finished steel. Manufacturing growth at 9.1% was respectable despite softening compared with the previous 3 quarters. The robust growth figure indicates strong corporate profitability as production volumes continued to be weak, as reflected by the index of industrial production (Figure 3.3.19).

Growth in services strengthened to 9.6%, largely reflecting strong growth in community, social, and personal services. The increase in personal services was driven by a sharp increase in government current expenditure. While growth in financial services remained stable, growth slowed in trade, hotels, transport, and communication services, as indicated by contraction in the ratios of net tonnage and passengers per kilometer carried by railways, weak expansion in hotels and restaurant services, and a slowdown in cargo handled at major ports.

3.3.17 Demand-side contributions to growth

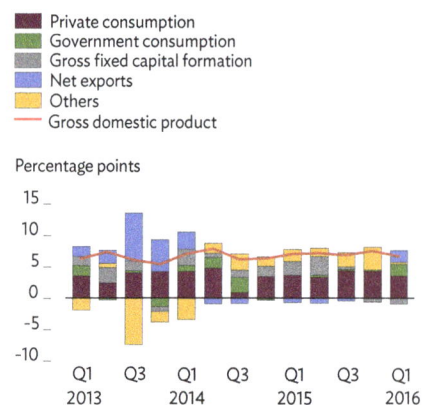

- Private consumption
- Government consumption
- Gross fixed capital formation
- Net exports
- Others
- Gross domestic product

Percentage points

Q = quarter.
Note: Years are fiscal years ending on 31 March of the next year.
Sources: Ministry of Statistics and Programme Implementation. http://www.mospi.nic.in; CEIC Data Company (accessed 1 September 2016).
Click here for figure data

3.3.18 Supply-side contributions to growth

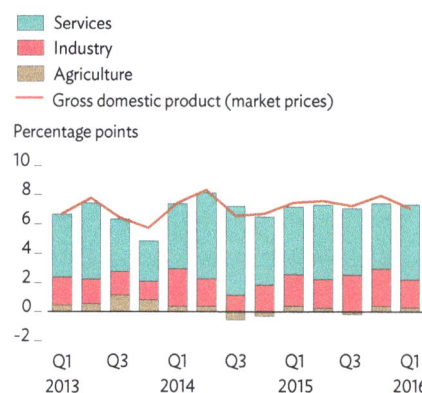

- Services
- Industry
- Agriculture
- Gross domestic product (market prices)

Percentage points

Q = quarter.
Notes: Years are fiscal years ending on 31 March of the next year. Sectoral output valued at market prices.
Sources: Ministry of Statistics and Programme Implementation. http://www.mospi.nic.in; CEIC Data Company (accessed 1 September 2016).
Click here for figure data

3.3.19 Manufacturing industrial production index

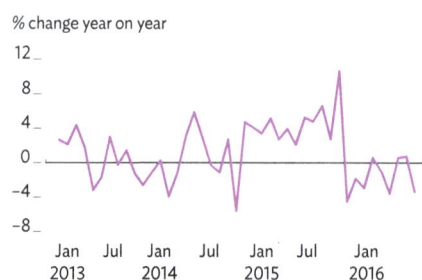

% change year on year

Source: CEIC Data Company (accessed 14 September 2016).
Click here for figure data

Inflation, which had decelerated to less than 5% in FY2015, inched higher in the first 4 months of FY2016, with much of the acceleration driven by an upsurge in some food prices, including vegetables, pulses, and sugar. August saw markedly better food supply, allowing overall inflation to fall by a full percentage point to 5.0% year on year and average 5.6% in the first 5 months of FY2016 (Figure 3.3.20). Fuel inflation eased in this period as more of the decline in global oil prices was passed on to consumers, unlike in FY2015 when the drop in oil prices was to a large extent offset by increases in excise duties. Core inflation, which excludes food and fuel, has continued its low trend. In August, the government agreed with the Reserve Bank of India, the central bank, that the consumer price inflation target in the next 5 years would be 4%. They also agreed on setting a range of plus or minus 2 percentage points. While the range is a ground-breaking monetary policy reform, the target of 4% would seem somewhat ambitious in light of historical trends in monthly consumer inflation.

Credit growth continued to be lackadaisical, dipping to below 10% in the first quarter of FY2016. The slowdown primarily reflected reduced lending by public banks to certain borrowers that pose high existing credit exposure, mainly in industry and among small enterprises, in light of overburdened balance sheets and high risk aversion. A review of asset quality undertaken by the central bank brought a near doubling of the nonperforming assets held by scheduled commercial banks, from 4.6% of gross advances in March 2015 to 8.7% in June 2016, as banks applied more appropriate standards that reclassified a substantial portion of restructured loans as nonperforming assets. Consequently, the ratio of restructured loans to all loans almost halved from 6.3% to 3.3% in the same period. The ratio of stressed advances increased only marginally from 10.9% to 12.0%. The bulk of the nonperforming assets and remaining restructured loans are concentrated in public sector banks, where the stressed asset ratio rose to 15.4% in June 2016, compared with 4.4% for private banks and 4.0% for foreign banks (Figure 3.3.21).

Parliament approved the Bankruptcy Code, which will help to create an institutional structure to deal with bankruptcy. It sets a time limit of 180 days within which resolution has to be completed. A streamlined legal framework for resolving bankruptcy is expected to improve the ease of doing business and boost the health of the banking sector.

The central government's fiscal deficit was targeted to decline from 3.9% in FY2015 to 3.5% in FY2016 (Figure 3.3.22). However, the fiscal deficit for April–July 2016 reached 73.7% of the targeted deficit for the year, up from 69.3% in FY2015. The higher deficit is a result of an uptick in current spending and subdued realization of nontax revenue. While tax revenue growth has been robust, driven by strong collections of excise, personal income, and service taxes, nontax revenue and nondebt capital receipts experienced sluggish growth on account of weak collections from dividends and disinvestment.

Current expenditure registered growth at 13.7%, well above the targeted growth rate. In contrast, capital spending remained weak from April to July 2016, contracting by 17.1% from the same period of the previous year. The lower capital spending possibly stems from slower

3.3.20 Inflation

- Overall
- Food
- Core

%, year on year

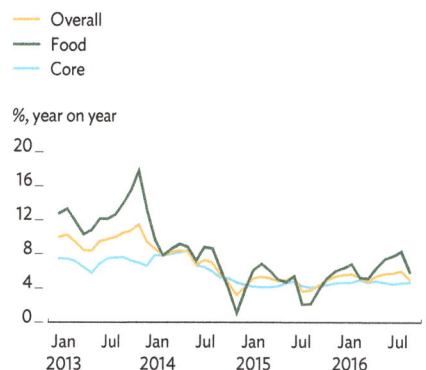

Sources: CEIC Data Company (accessed 14 September 2016); ADB estimates.
Click here for figure data

3.3.21 Nonperforming and restructured loans

- Restructured
- Nonperforming

%

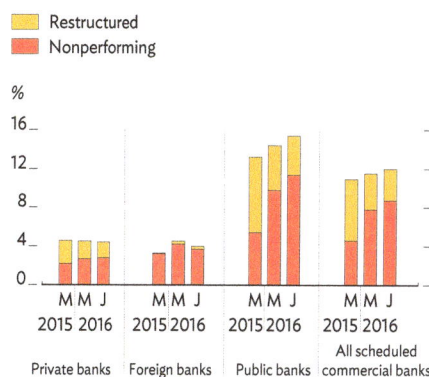

M = March, J = June.
Source: Reseve Bank of India.
Click here for figure data

3.3.22 Federal budget indicators

- Tax
- Nontax
- Other revenue
- Current
- Capital
- Fiscal balance

% of GDP

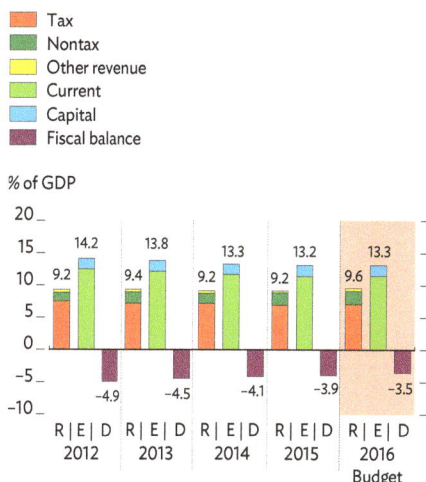

R = revenue, E = expenditure, D = deficit financing.
Note: Years are fiscal years ending on 31 March of the next year.
Source: Ministry of Finance Union Budget 2015–16. http://indiabudget.nic.in
Click here for figure data

nontax revenue growth and an upcoming large liability on account of hikes in government employee salaries and pensions.

The government has appointed a committee to review the intended path of fiscal consolidation in the future. The committee is expected to review the possibility of moving to a fiscal deficit range instead of a point target, thereby accommodating the policy flexibility needed to deal with dynamic situations.

In August, Parliament approved the legislation that will allow the introduction of the long-pending uniform goods and services tax (GST). By simplifying the tax regime, eliminating the cascading effects of taxes, and broadening the tax base, the GST is expected to boost GDP growth and revenue while lowering inflation. Moreover, the GST does away with the tax assessed when goods cross a subnational state border, ending a major inefficiency in the economy. However, some key issues are still to be finalized, including the determination of the rate structure, the list of exempted products, and how taxes will be shared between states and the center. These issues will make it a challenge for the government to meet its target of implementing this legislation at the beginning of FY2017.

A moderating monthly trade deficit helped the cumulative trade deficit from April to July 2016 decline by 41.2% from the previous year to $27 billion (Figure 3.3.23). The improvement in the trade deficit was a result of a 16.3% fall in imports. While oil imports were 25% lower than in the previous year, helped by lower prices, imports other than oil also contracted. Gold imports were considerably weaker on lower volumes in response to higher prices. Excluding oil and gold, there was a broad reduction in imports of capital goods such as machinery and transport equipment, as well as of consumable goods including electronics. Exports also contracted in this period, by 3.6%, though much of the decline was a drop in refined petroleum exports, with other exports remaining fairly stable. Slow recovery in the advanced economies means that export volume is improving at a slow pace as well. The services trade surplus from April to June 2016 moderated a bit to $16.2 billion, primarily on increased imports of services.

Net foreign direct investment inflows slowed a bit in the first 4 months, though they remained strong at $9.9 billion. Large portfolio inflows of foreign institutional investment in April were erased by net outflows in May and June reflecting heightened risk aversion globally. Despite the Brexit vote, portfolio inflows recovered strongly from July to September, driven by a global search for yield in the face of a sharp decline in interest rates in the major industrial economies. Net foreign institutional investment flows from April to September 2016 were, at around $6.5 billion, a marked contrast to the outflow of nearly $3.0 billion in the previous year (Figure 3.3.24). A rise in real interest rates and a stable currency continued to attract deposits from nonresident Indians, prompting flows of $1.3 billion in the first quarter of FY2016.

A healthy external balance and strong capital inflows have helped the Indian rupee remain relatively stable against the US dollar, depreciating by about 1% in the year to the end of August (Figure 3.3.25). However, a pickup in inflation pushed the rupee higher by its real

3.3.23 Trade indicators

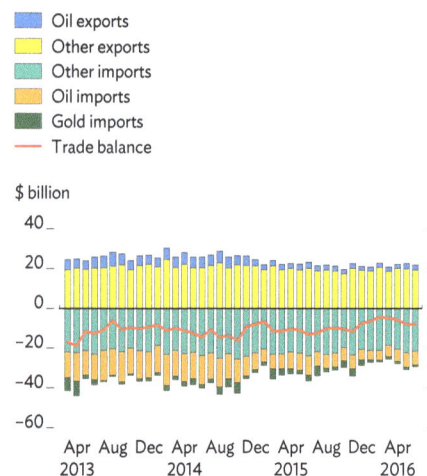

Legend:
- Oil exports
- Other exports
- Other imports
- Oil imports
- Gold imports
- Trade balance

Sources: CEIC Data Company (accessed 31 August 2016); ADB estimates.
Click here for figure data

3.3.2 Selected economic indicators, India (%)

	2016		2017	
	ADO 2016	Update 2016	ADO 2016	Update 2016
GDP growth	7.4	7.4	7.8	7.8
Inflation	5.4	5.4	5.8	5.8
Current acct. bal. (share of GDP)	−1.6	−1.4	−1.8	−1.8

Note: Years are fiscal years ending on 31 March of the next year.
Source: ADB estimates.

3.3.24 Portfolio capital flows

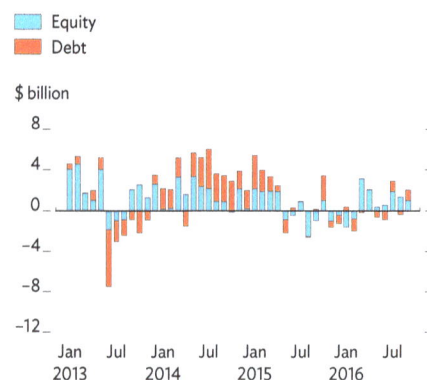

Legend:
- Equity
- Debt

Source: Security and Exchange Board of India.
Click here for figure data

effective exchange rate by just over 1% in this period. The central bank intervened on the foreign exchange market to stave off volatility by purchasing foreign assets, which caused reserve holdings to rise by $10 billion to over $365 billion in August 2016 (Figure 3.3.26).

Prospects

The forecasts in *ADO 2016* were predicated on growth improving modestly in the advanced economies, a healthy monsoon, subdued growth in government capital expenditure compared with FY2015, and the further resolution of structural bottlenecks. This *Update* takes into account a deceleration in economic activity in the major industrial economies, a healthy monsoon, and some forward movement on structural reform.

Despite growth in the first quarter of FY2016 declining to its lowest in 5 quarters, growth is expected to pick up in the remaining quarters of FY2016. Consumption is seen to be the major driver of growth as new investment project announcements have not been promising (Figure 3.3.27). A committee set up once every 10 years to review compensation for central government employees recommended a 16% increase in wages and a 23.6% hike in pensions, which have been approved by the government. This is likely to provide a strong fillip to urban discretionary demand, especially for consumer durables like automobiles and electronic goods. A healthy monsoon is going to provide a parallel impetus to rural demand, which has been sluggish because of 2 years of weak rains.

A strong recovery in investment continues to be challenged by low capacity utilization caused by lackluster demand (Figure 3.3.28) and subdued growth in bank credit to industry in response to the high proportion of stressed assets and high corporate leverage (Figure 3.3.29). However, signs of decline in the proportion of leveraged companies, moderation in the growth of stressed assets, and the central bank's further cutting of interest rates by 150 basis points from the start of 2015 are likely to provide some support to a measured recovery in private investment (Figure 3.3.30). Budgetary constraints will limit the scale of public investment, but sources of finance off the government balance sheet, such as the profits of the public sector enterprises, financing by insurance companies, and bonds raised by quasi-government entities, can fund investment.

A healthy monsoon is expected to push agriculture growth up beyond 4%, as the sown area to mid-September 2016 was 4.2% higher than in the previous year. The production of food grains in FY2016 is targeted to be 7.1% higher than last year. Higher consumption in both rural and urban areas is likely to provide an impetus to manufacturing growth, though low capacity utilization in the sector continues to be a concern.

Incremental data show manufacturing growth consolidating. The Nikkei manufacturing purchasing managers' index in August attained its highest level since July 2015 on account of strong new orders and lower input costs (Figure 3.3.31). The central bank's industrial outlook survey also indicates optimistic business sentiment, driven by improved outlooks for order books, capacity utilization, and

3.3.25 Exchange rate

Source: Bloomberg (accessed 31 August 2016).
Click here for figure data

3.3.26 International reserves

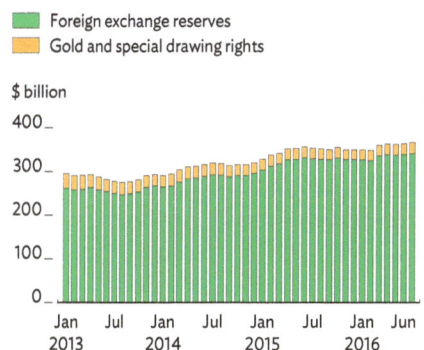

Source: CEIC Data Company (accessed 31 August 2016).
Click here for figure data

3.3.27 New investment projects announced

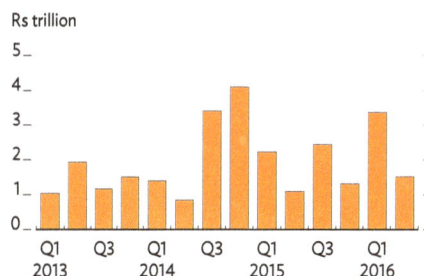

Q = quarter.
Source: Center for Monitoring Indian Economy.
Click here for figure data

employment. Construction is expected to get a boost from an array of measures announced in August 2016 that seek to ease rules to achieve quicker settlement of disputes in housing and to pump in liquidity to reinvigorate stalled projects.

Services, especially tradeable services, could witness some moderation with the growth slowdown in the advanced economies. Moreover, the surge in community, social, and personal services witnessed in the first quarter of FY2016 is unlikely to continue given the government's commitment to rein in the fiscal deficit.

Policy options for augmenting growth continue to be limited as inflation averages near the ceiling of the inflation target band, and with the government having exhausted from April to July 2016 more than 73% of the targeted deficit for the fiscal year. On balance, growth is expected to be 7.4% in FY2016, unchanged from the *ADO 2016* forecast.

An uptick in growth in the advanced economies and steady recovery in investment aided by a revival of public investment will likely accelerate growth in FY2017. Growth is likely to receive an impetus as well from improvement in manufacturing and construction. In sum, growth is forecast to pick up to 7.8% in FY2017, as projected earlier.

A healthy monsoon is likely to dampen food inflation in the second half of FY2016, which will also be lower on a base effect. However, any rise in global fuel prices is likely to be transmitted to consumers because the government is unlikely to alter its excise duty structure on petroleum products. Moreover, the government has decided to raise the price of kerosene, which it subsidizes, by a small amount each month to April 2017. This will prune the fiscal deficit but could have a small inflationary impact. Core inflation is likely to remain stable with the weakening of inflationary expectations, even though the rise in discretionary consumption from the hike in government salaries will have a marginal impact. In sum, inflation is forecast at 5.4% in FY2016, in line with *ADO 2016*.

Higher global commodity prices, and the anticipated rise in prices for some services as they start to be taxed at a higher rate under the proposed GST, could push inflation up in FY2017. Inflation is forecast at 5.8% in FY2017, again in line with *ADO 2016*.

Although the fiscal deficit from April to July 2016 exceeded 73% of the target for the entire year, as mentioned above, the government is likely to meet its target of pruning the fiscal deficit to the equivalent of 3.5% of GDP, albeit with some risk of slippage. Measures to improve the targeting of subsidies—such as expanding the scheme of cash transfers for cooking gas subsidies, the digitization of cards required to collect food subsidies, and the computerization of food supply chain— are expected to significantly plug leakage and rein in the subsidy bill. While the government has budgeted for the increase in expenditure on account of higher civil servant wages and pensions, the final outgo could be somewhat higher, raising some concern of slippage.

Targeted tax revenue growth at 11.2% seems achievable in light of current buoyancy in tax collection with hikes in excise duties and tax rates for services. By contrast, estimates of nontax revenue appear to be optimistic. Disinvestment has started on a low note with less than 10% of the targeted revenue raised in the first 4 months of FY2016.

3.3.28 Manufacturing capacity utilization

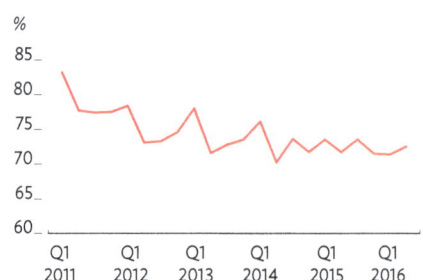

Q = quarter.
Source: Haver Analytics (accessed 2 September 2016).
Click here for figure data

3.3.29 Bank credit to businesses

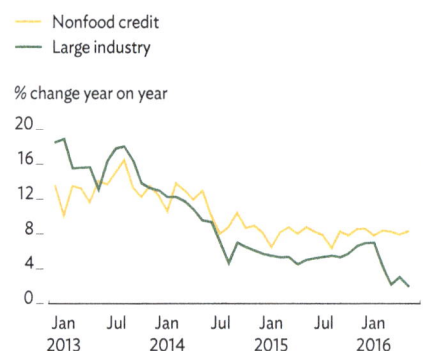

Source: Bloomberg (accessed 31 August 2016).
Click here for figure data

3.3.30 Policy interest rates

Sources: Bloomberg; CEIC Data Company (both accessed 31 August 2016).
Click here for figure data

Unless disinvestment proceeds pick up significantly in the second half, it could be a challenge to restrict the fiscal deficit to the target. The government has moved forward in selling its stake in some of the private companies, which could take up some slack in the shortfall in disinvestment proceeds, as this was not included in the budget estimates. The revenue target from telecom spectrum allocation is similarly on the ambitious side under current market conditions.

After 2 years of contraction, exports are expected to grow by 4% in FY2016. As the volume of most exports remained relatively steady in FY2014 and FY2015, the contraction primarily reflected lower prices. Somewhat higher commodity prices are expected to bolster export growth in FY2016. Imports are estimated to grow by 5% in FY2016. Somewhat higher crude oil prices in the second half of FY2016 are expected to push up oil imports, while improved manufacturing will raise demand for imports other than oil and gold. The invisible surplus could weaken a bit as slow growth in the advanced economies is likely to adversely affect the services surplus, especially in software services. Net remittances are also likely to be hit by soft growth in oil-exporting economies and a steady rise in outward remittances. Consequently, the current account deficit is expected to widen in 2016 to 1.4% from 1.3% a year earlier, which is slightly less than the 1.6% forecast in *ADO 2016* (Figure 3.3.32).

Exports are expected to grow by 7% in FY2017 as growth picks up in the advanced economies and increased crude oil prices improve export demand from oil-exporting economies. At the same time, higher oil prices and improved domestic demand are likely to push import growth to 9%. On balance, the current account deficit is expected to widen to 1.8% in FY2017, in line with *ADO 2016*.

While the 27.3% increase in foreign direct investment (FDI) inflows experienced in FY2015 would be difficult to replicate, FDI flows are likely to remain strong with the government liberalizing caps on FDI in several sectors and improving the ease of doing business. Investor interest is clearly evident in announcements in 2015 of $63 billion in greenfield FDI projects in India with an average size of $88 million, marking a major upswing in interest from earlier years (Figure 3.3.33).

Portfolio flows are likely to remain strong, though the bulk of the inflows is concentrated in equities. To stem the currency depreciation that occurred in the aftermath of the so-called "taper tantrum" in 2013, the central bank announced a swap facility with banks for their nonresident Indian deposits. These swaps are set to mature during September–November 2016, threatening to trigger an outflow of around $25 billion. However, the impact is likely to be muted as the central bank has entered into forward contracts of similar magnitude that will mature during this period, and the US dollars received from these contracts will be passed on to the banks, which will pass them on in turn to their customers.

3.3.31 Purchasing managers' indexes

— Manufacturing
— Services

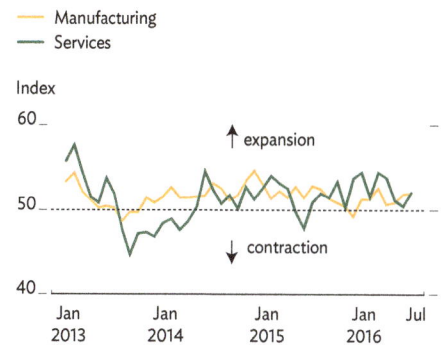

Note: Nikkei, Markit.
Source: Bloomberg (accessed 31 August 2016).
Click here for figure data

3.3.32 Current account components

- Exports
- Service receipts
- Net secondary income
- Imports
- Service payments
- Net primary income
- Current account balance —

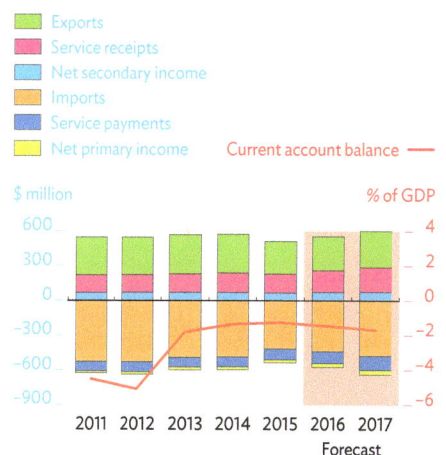

Note: Years are fiscal years ending on 31 March of the next year.
Sources: Reserve Bank of India; ADB estimates.
Click here for figure data

3.3.33 Announced greenfield FDI projects by investors

- Project value
- Average project size —

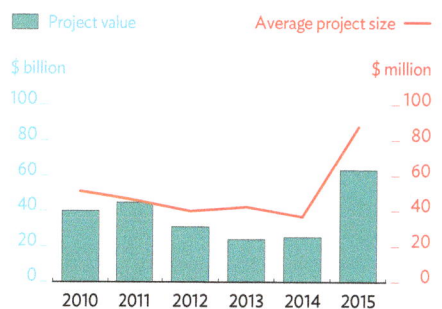

Source: United Nations Conference on Trade and Development. 2016. *World Investment Report 2016.*
Click here for figure data

Pakistan

Growth accelerated in FY2016 (ended 30 June 2016) on the cumulative impact of the government's macroeconomic and structural reform program, sharply lower oil prices, and improved security, outpacing the *ADO 2016* forecast despite a major crop failure. Inflation and the current account deficit were lower than expected, while foreign exchange reserves strengthened and the budget deficit shrank. This *Update* raises the projection for growth in FY2017. It also edges up the forecasts for inflation and the current account deficit mainly on the expectation of higher global oil prices.

Updated assessment

Preliminary estimates put GDP growth at 4.7% in FY2016, up from 4.0% in FY2015 and higher than the 4.5% projected in *ADO 2016* (Figure 3.3.34). Growth would have been even higher if massive failure of the cotton crop caused by excessive rain and pest infestation, and moderate declines for other crops, had not caused a 0.2% fall in agriculture, which accounts for about 20% of GDP. Strong performances in services and industry lifted growth overall. The government introduced a relief program for smallholder farmers that discounted input prices and waived sales tax on some of them.

Industry grew at 6.8%, mainly on a rebound in manufacturing and increased construction. Growth in large-scale manufacturing expanded by 4.6%, up from 3.3% a year earlier. Broad-based expansion featured a notable boost in automobile production that benefitted from the introduction of new models and special credit facilities offered by a provincial government, but also a surge in fertilizer production, increased gas supply, and much higher cement production to meet demand from a 13.1% rise in construction. Business confidence strengthened on improved credit, electricity and gas supply, and security, underpinning better performance across the economy. Rapid growth in industry spilled over to the large service sector, which supplies about 60% of GDP and expanded by 5.7%, up from 4.3% a year earlier. The upturn mainly reflected marked expansion in wholesale and retail trade and government services.

On the demand side, private consumption continues to drive growth, though estimates of how much expenditure components contribute to GDP growth have varied from year to year (Figure 3.3.35). Private consumption grew by 7.0% in 2016, and government consumption by 15.1%. Total investment grew by 5.7%, well below the 14.1% increase in FY2015, when both public and private consumption expanded by unusual margins. Net exports were a large offset to growth as a 41% drop in global oil prices improved Pakistan's terms of trade by nearly 10% and left enough spending power for a sizeable increase in other imports on top of an estimated 7% increase in oil imports by volume. Meanwhile, export volume fell by 4.5%. Fixed capital formation continued to languish, reflecting a legacy of persistent power and gas shortages that have constrained investment and growth (Figure 3.3.36). Government investment increased by 13.6% while public enterprise spending rose only slightly, marginally lifting total public sector fixed investment to 3.8% of GDP. Private investment grew by only 3.3%

3.3.34 Supply-side contributions to growth

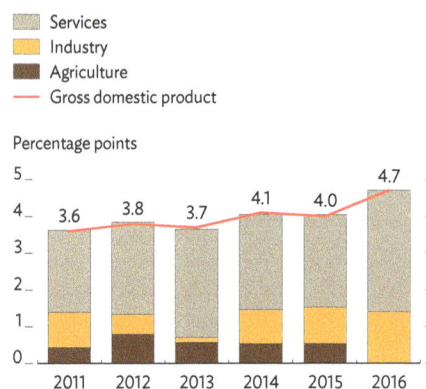

Note: Years are fiscal years ending on 30 June of that year.
Source: Ministry of Finance. Pakistan Economic Survey 2015-16. http://www.finance.gov.pk

3.3.35 Demand-side contributions to growth

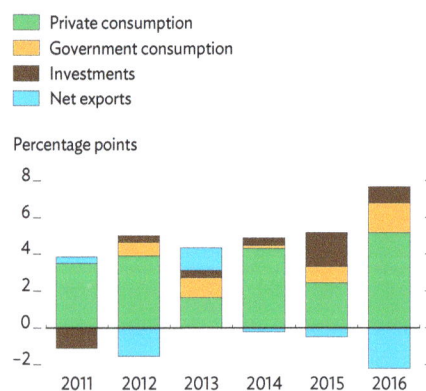

Note: Years are fiscal years ending on 30 June of that year.
Source: Ministry of Finance. Pakistan Economic Survey 2015-16. http://www.finance.gov.pk

3.3.36 Gross fixed investment

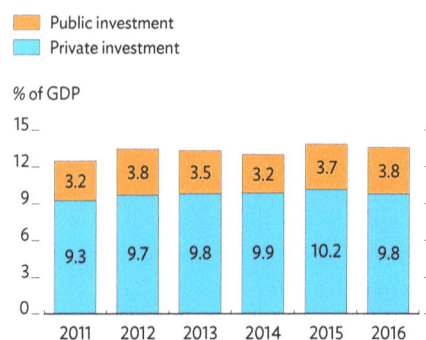

Note: Years are fiscal years ending on 30 June of that year.
Source: Ministry of Finance. Pakistan Economic Survey 2015-16. http://www.finance.gov.pk

despite a more upbeat economic environment, slipping to 9.8% of GDP from 10.2%.

Headline inflation averaged 2.9% in FY2016, down from 4.5% a year earlier and less than the 3.2% forecast in *ADO 2016*. Improvement came from the marked fall in oil prices, further easing of other global commodity prices, larger non-oil imports, steady supplies of key foodstuffs, and a stable exchange rate. The easing trend reversed during the year, however, with an upturn in food inflation, higher natural gas tariffs, and higher duties on certain imports (Figure 3.3.37). Mounting inflationary pressure was evident in core inflation, which increased from an average of 3.8% in the first half of the year to 4.5% in the second.

As inflation slowed, the State Bank of Pakistan, the central bank, eased monetary policy by reducing its policy rate by a total of 75 basis points in FY2016 to 5.75%, following cuts totaling 300 basis points in FY2015 (Figure 3.3.38). Banks passed through the reductions in full, bringing average rates on new lending to 7.6% in June 2016 from the 11.5% that prevailed 2 years earlier. Adjusted for inflation, average rates on new lending in FY2016 were 5.2%, or about 100 basis points less than a year earlier. Nominal deposit rates fell somewhat less than lending rates, and real deposit rates turned positive to average 2.3% in FY2016. With budget financing requirements markedly reduced and domestic economic conditions benign, credit to the private sector grew by Rs461 billion, double the Rs224 billion in FY2015. The positive trend in monetary developments was evident across the board—for savers, business, and the economy as a whole.

The general government deficit (consolidating federal and provincial budgets but excluding grants) improved to an estimated 4.4% of GDP in FY2016 from 5.4% a year earlier, achieved as planned by boosting revenue and containing expenditure. Federal Board of Revenue tax collection increased as targeted by 1.1 percentage points to 11.4% of GDP as additional excise, regulatory, and customs duties were implemented during the year to offset a shortfall in oil import duties. Total revenue increased to equal 15.4% of GDP from 14.4% a year earlier, as provincial taxes at near 1% and nontax revenue at about 3.% were broadly unchanged. Total expenditure was, at 19.8% of GDP, unchanged from FY2015, while the increase in current expenditure was reined in to 7.2% from 10.5%, such that it equaled 16.5% of GDP, essentially unchanged from a year earlier. Thus, revenue performance met the deficit reduction target but only by precluding any major expansion in the share of the public sector development program.

The current account deficit in FY2016 is estimated equivalent to 0.9% of GDP, little different from the 1.0% forecast in *ADO 2016* or the FY2015 outcome, though large changes in composition are noteworthy (Figure 3.3.39). The trade deficit increased from $17.2 billion to $18.5 billion because exports fell by $2.1 billion, or 8.6%, as declines hit the main export categories: food by 15.7%, textiles by 5.7%, and other manufactures by 13.9%. The 14% price decline during the fiscal year for globally traded commodities other than oil made a downdraft in exports inevitable, but lackluster export performance has dogged the economy in recent years because of high production costs and insufficient investment to modernize and diversify. The 37% fall in oil imports reduced oil

3.3.37 Inflation

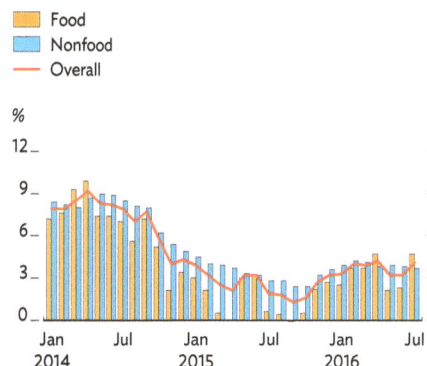

Source: State Bank of Pakistan. Economic Data. *Trend in Price Inflation.* http://www.sbp.org.pk (accessed 11 August 2016).
Click here for figure data

3.3.38 Interest rates

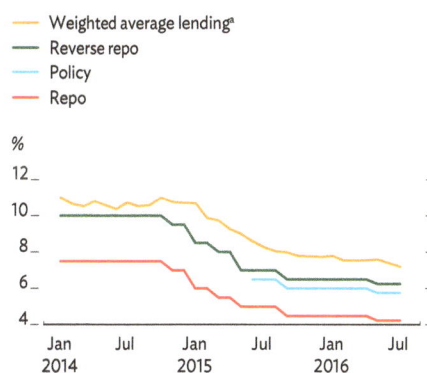

a On gross disbursements, the amounts disbursed by banks either in Pakistan rupees or foreign currency against loans during the month. It also includes loans repriced, renewed, or rolled over during the month. In case of running finance the disbursed amount means the maximum amount accepted by the borrower at any time during the month.
Source: State Bank of Pakistan. Economic Data. http://www.sbp.org.pk (accessed 11 August 2016).
Click here for figure data

3.3.39 Current account components

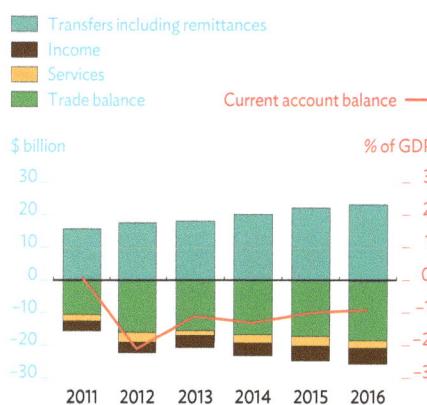

Note: Years are fiscal years ending on 30 June of that year.
Source: State Bank of Pakistan. 2016. *Monetary Policy Information Compendium.* July.
Click here for figure data

payments by $4.5 billion from a year earlier, accommodating a 12.7% increase in other imports even as the total import bill was trimmed by $811 million, or 2.0%. Although growth in worker remittances slowed markedly to 6.4% from 18.2% in FY2015, remittances were, at $19.9 billion, sufficient to offset the usual deficits in the services and primary income accounts. Even with the larger trade deficit, the current account deficit shrank by nearly $200 million to $2.5 billion.

Net inflows of $5.1 billion into the capital and financial accounts in FY2016 were little changed from a year earlier, sustained mainly by long-term flows from official lenders and, to a lesser extent, foreign direct investment, bringing the overall balance of payments to a $2.6 billion surplus. This surplus and the net use of $2.0 billion in International Monetary Fund (IMF) credit raised official central bank reserves by $4.6 billion to $18.1 billion, or cover for 4.3 months of imports (Figure 3.3.40).

The Pakistan rupee was broadly stable in FY2016, depreciating by 2.7% against the US dollar as the central bank intervened on the exchange market to build reserves and prevent appreciation. While the rupee in real effective terms appreciated by only 1.0% during the year, it climbed by about 20% over the previous 2 years as exports weakened substantially (Figure 3.3.41). Lower oil prices and strong remittances have underpinned the favorable external position in the past 2 years, but any reversal of these forces would highlight the need to strengthen competiveness and exports.

Prospects

The government significantly strengthened macroeconomic fundamentals and advanced a comprehensive program of structural reform under a 3-year program with the IMF that ended in September 2016. Inflation has been squashed to the low single digits, foreign reserves rebuilt, and the budget deficit markedly reduced. Tax reform was launched to improve revenue performance, and substantial progress achieved toward restructuring the power sector. Key challenges remain, however, regarding governance and security issues, reviving agriculture and improving its productivity, increasing exports and attracting investment, strengthening public enterprises, and improving the business and regulatory environment.

A major impetus to growth in FY2017 and beyond will be the implementation of $46 billion in spending on roads, railways, pipelines, and electric power in an economic corridor project linking Pakistan with the People's Republic of China (PRC), which was announced in April 2015. Fast-tracking will enable several energy projects to come onstream in FY2018. The planned reduction in the FY2017 budget deficit will further enhance funding for private sector credit and better enable it to meet rising domestic demand. As such—and assuming further improvement in energy supply and security, and likely recovery in cotton and other agriculture—the growth forecast for FY2017 is revised up to 5.2%.

The general government budget for FY2017 projects further reduction in the deficit to 3.8% of GDP achieved by adopting new revenue measures and streamlining current expenditure (Figure 3.3.42). Tax revenues are projected to increase by half a percentage point, raising the ratio of tax

3.3.40 Gross international reserves

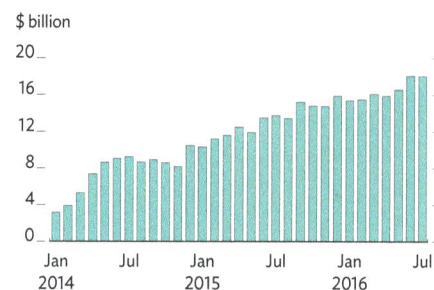

Source: State Bank of Pakistan. *Economic Data.*
http://www.sbp.org.pk (accessed 31 August 2016).
Click here for figure data

3.3.41 Exchange rates

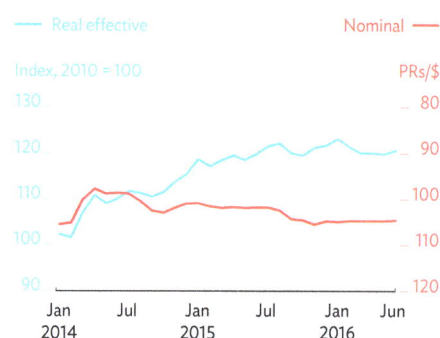

Source: State Bank of Pakistan. *Economic Data.*
http://www.sbp.org.pk (accessed 31 August 2016).
Click here for figure data

3.3.42 Government budget indicators

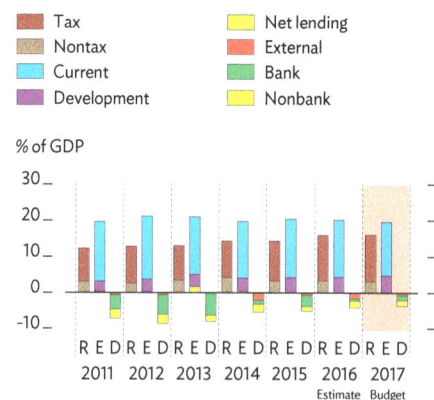

R = revenue, E = expenditure, D = deficit financing.
Notes: Years are fiscal years ending on 30 June of that year. Data refer to consolidated federal and provincial governments. Net lending includes statistical discrepancy. Nonbank includes privatization proceeds.
Source: Ministry of Finance. *Pakistan Economic Survey 2015–16.* http://www.finance.gov.pk
Click here for figure data

to GDP to 12.8% by eliminating more tax concessions and exemptions, expanding the withholding system as part of administrative reform to widen the tax base, and raising some excise taxes and customs duties (Figure 3.3.43). Including nontax and provincial tax revenue, total budgeted revenue amounts to 15.8% of GDP. Current expenditure is to be held to 15.8% of GDP, mainly by economizing on spending where possible and further reducing energy subsidies, to allow the public sector development program to expand by 18.4%.

Inflation is now expected to average 4.7% in FY2017. The upward revision takes into account expected oil price rises and stronger domestic demand in an economy under worsening supply constraints. It is tempered by the prospect of broad agricultural recovery and only modestly higher global food prices. The July 2016 monetary policy statement covering the first 2 months of FY2017 kept policy rates unchanged as the central bank continues its cautious forward-looking approach, expecting to hold inflation within the range of 4.5%–5.5%.

The current account deficit is expected to widen in FY2017 to about $5 billion, or 1.6% of GDP, which is higher than forecast in March. The revision reflects a somewhat greater increase in global oil prices than expected and continued expansion in other imports stemming from faster economic growth. Exports are expected to perform better during the year, increasing by nearly 5% as a recovery in cotton production underpins an upturn in textile sales, and as global prices for commodities other than oil reverse from a sharp decline to a modest increase. Exports are not expected to recover to the FY2014 level, however, as little if any improvement in global demand is expected, forestalling any major boost for food or manufacture exports. Construction cutbacks in the Gulf, where most Pakistani overseas workers are employed, will slow growth in remittances. However, remittances will likely be sufficient to hold in check deficits in trade and other payments in the current account.

The mobilization of larger inflows into the capital and financial accounts has been central to the 3-year economic program with the IMF, and these flows are projected to increase to $6.5 billion in FY2017, mainly with more foreign direct investment and continuing sizeable official flows (Figure 3.3.44). Thus, even with the projected widening of the current account deficit, the overall balance of payments should remain in surplus, augmenting official reserves. The corridor project with the PRC is expected to attract more foreign direct investment, and already in 2015 investors announced 40 greenfield projects worth $19 billion, or 4 times the norm in recent years. Although implementation will extend over several years, the large increase signaled the catalytic effect of the corridor project and success in making Pakistan a stable destination attractive to foreign investment. Moreover, the decision by Morgan Stanley Capital International to put Pakistan in its MSCI emerging market index from May 2017 will likely spur equity portfolio inflows.

Risks to the economic outlook in the short term are unexpectedly high oil prices or a marked slowing of remittances. Further down the road, the end of the IMF program could relax focus on monetary and fiscal discipline, especially with a parliamentary election scheduled for 2018, and distract attention from the structural reform agenda that is essential to maintaining sustainable and equitable growth.

3.3.3 Selected economic indicators, Pakistan (%)

	2016		2017	
	ADO 2016	*Update*	ADO 2016	*Update*
GDP growth	4.5	4.7	4.8	5.2
Inflation	3.2	2.9	4.5	4.7
Current acct. bal. (share of GDP)	–1.0	–0.9	–1.2	–1.6

Note: Years are fiscal years ending on 30 June of that year.
Source: ADB estimates.

3.3.43 Budget tax revenue collection

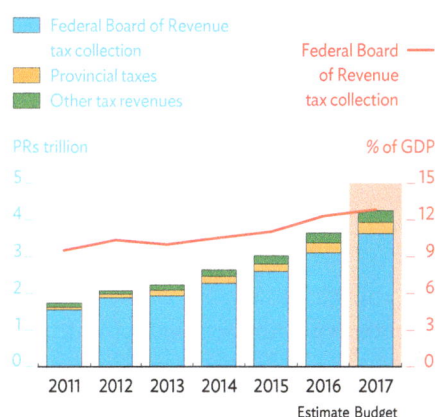

Note: Years are fiscal years ending on 30 June of that year.
Source: International Monetary Fund. 2016. *IMF Country Report* No. 16/207. June.
Click here for figure data

3.3.44 Capital and financial flows

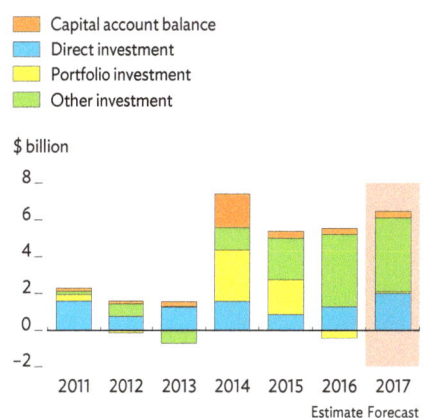

Note: Years are fiscal years ending on 30 June of that year.
Sources: State Bank of Pakistan, *Economic Data* (accessed 19 August 2016); ADB estimates.
Click here for figure data

Other economies

Afghanistan

Anecdotal evidence suggests that industry and services expanded in the first half of 2016. Investor and consumer confidence appear sustained as the authorities strive to deal with worsening insurgent violence. Concern nevertheless arises over deteriorating security, political uncertainty, and the economic outlook. Support from development partners was underpinned by governance and policy reform implemented under a staff-monitored program of the International Monetary Fund, which was successfully completed in May.

Initial reports indicate another good harvest following rains toward the end of winter. This contrasts with early projections of low production under unfavorable weather for most of the winter. However, agriculture is assessed to have reached its full potential and will not likely improve on its 2015 performance.

Inflation has accelerated since January 2016 after 9 consecutive months of deflation in 2015. Consumer price inflation rose sharply to 7.4% year on year in July. Food inflation reached 8.7%, mostly on rising prices for meat, bread, cereals, spices, sugar, and sweets, and nonfood inflation accelerated to 5.9%, bringing the 7-month inflation average to 4.4%. The main causes of the upsurge were steep currency depreciation in 2015 that pushed up import prices and trade disruptions affecting supply, especially of food. A start on improving connectivity to speed transit times and lower trade costs was the September inauguration of regular train service linking Afghanistan with the port city of Nantong in the People's Republic of China. Trade connectivity will be further enhanced with the completion of rail links with Chabahar, a deep seaport in Iran. Nonetheless, weather affects on agriculture, global commodity price developments, and supply disruptions will continue to determine price developments.

The afghani depreciated against the US dollar by 17% in 2015, reflecting in part downward pressure from sharply increased emigration. Foreign exchange sales reduced gross official reserves by about 6% to an estimated $6.8 billion in December 2015, still enough for 9 months of import cover. Downward pressure on the afghani dissipated in the first half of 2016, leaving the exchange rate and reserves largely unchanged from the end of 2015. The modest upturn in the economy helped, as did an apparent slowing of emigration as people who had sought to emigrate returned in frustration at the difficulties they encountered.

The International Monetary Fund approved in July a 3-year extended credit facility (ECF) aimed at advancing the country's economic reform agenda through policy and legislative action. The government is on track to meet its budget revenue target, the main quantitative target of the ECF, with the Ministry of Finance reporting a 35% increase in domestic revenues to AF70 billion in the first half of 2016, mainly from tax increases under a staff-monitored program and improved governance and compliance.

Assuming that the political and security situation does not worsen and the pickup in economic activity continues, this *Update* maintains the *ADO 2016* growth forecasts for 2016 and 2017. The ECF is expected

3.3.4 Selected economic indicators, Afghanistan (%)

	2016		2017	
	ADO 2016	Update	ADO 2016	Update
GDP growth	2.0	2.0	3.0	3.0
Inflation	3.0	4.5	3.5	6.0
Current acct. bal. (share of GDP)	2.0	4.5	-0.7	1.1

Source: ADB estimates.

to strengthen macroeconomic stability and support from development partners. In the wake of price pressures in the first half of the year, the forecast for inflation is revised up for 2016 and more so for 2017, in line with the ECF. The forecast for the current account including grants is also revised up, largely on a major revision of balance of payments data. The decline in the current account surplus is now expected to be slower than forecast in *ADO 2016*.

Bhutan

Robust economic expansion is supported by rapid growth in industry and services. One driver of growth in FY2016 (ended 30 June 2016) was the construction of three major hydropower projects, which has been under way for several years, and another was hydropower generation mainly for export, which rose by 14.8% from a year earlier. Tourism earnings declined by 9.5% to $69.4 million because of concerns over earthquakes in the Himalayas following the devastating quakes in Nepal in April and May 2015, and because tourist agencies often sell combined tours to Nepal and Bhutan. Nevertheless, the service sector is expected to be shored up by robust wholesale trade in construction goods and intensified government spending.

Banks expanded credit to the private sector by 15.5%, up slightly from FY2015, mainly for housing, construction, and service industries. The government's budgeted capital spending was revised up by 10%, largely on account of a grant increase for enhancing priority sectors outside of hydropower such as tourism, agro-processing, construction, small and cottage industries, and manufacturing. Fiscal and monetary policies are likely to remain broadly expansionary, bolstering aggregate demand. Torrential rains in July 2016 caused damage to infrastructure, estimated at $8.1 million as of 30 August, which may bring slight economic deceleration. Revised personal and corporate income tax rates should boost revenue collection and, along with an expected rise in dividends, mainly from hydropower, broaden budget revenue and boost funding for development programs. Barring further bad weather and a heavy damage assessment, Bhutan is likely to meet growth projections for FY2016 and FY2017 published in *ADO 2016* in March.

Inflation was broadly steady in FY2016, albeit slightly lower than projected in *ADO 2016*, as wholesale price deflation persisted in India, the major source of imports, but passed through to domestic prices only slowly. Inflation indexes remained low and stable for both food and other goods because of low import prices, ample supply, falling crude oil prices, and easing housing costs with the phasing out of import restrictions that made home construction expensive. The Bhutanese ngultrum, which is pegged to the Indian rupee, was broadly stable against the US dollar in FY2016, depreciating on average by 6.4% from a year earlier. The inflation estimate for FY2016 is somewhat below the forecast, and the forecast for FY2017 is revised down slightly in line with expected global commodity prices.

In the first half of FY2016, exports fell by 11% year on year because of a higher tariff on gypsum imposed by a major buyer and low prices for Bhutan's steel exports because of excess global capacity in the steel industry. Meanwhile, imports grew by nearly 12%, moderately widening

3.3.5 Selected economic indicators, Bhutan (%)

	2016		2017	
	ADO 2016	*Update*	ADO 2016	*Update*
GDP growth	6.4	6.4	6.1	6.1
Inflation	4.0	3.3	5.0	4.6
Current acct. bal. (share of GDP)	−28.8	−29.9	−27.0	−27.0

Source: ADB estimates.

deficits in the trade and current accounts. Import growth is expected to continue apace in the second half on strong aggregate demand before gradually easing in FY2017 as hydropower-related imports tail off with the scheduled completion of major projects in 2018. Gross international reserves remain adequate at $1.1 billion in June 2016, up by 16.7% from a year earlier. The projected current account deficit is revised up for FY2016 but seen to narrow in FY2017 as forecast earlier.

Maldives

Forecasts of mildly accelerating GDP growth are unchanged from those in *ADO 2016*. In the first 6 months of 2016, tourism remained broadly on track with projections published in March as arrivals grew by 1.8%, up from 1.3% a year earlier. Growth was led by higher arrivals from Europe, which provided about half of visitors and offset a continuing marked decline in tourist arrivals from the People's Republic of China. Occupancy, which indicates sector earnings, recovered to post positive but minimal growth after falling markedly over the same 6-month period in previous year. Continuing recovery in tourism is expected to be tepid but could benefit from the opening of new resorts in 2017—and perhaps from an unusually good peak season in October. Growth momentum in the construction-led industry sector appears to have been sustained as indicated by surges in imports of wood, cement, and machinery. As expected, industry growth is propelled by foreign-financed projects that provide public goods to support private sector expansion, as well as by continued resort development.

Potential downside risks to the forecast are a pullback in global tourism, growing political tensions that may threaten social strife, and the rising ratio of gross public debt to GDP, which could exacerbate macroeconomic uncertainty and undermine investor confidence.

The consumer price index fell by 0.8% in the year to June 2016, and inflation averaged only 0.3% in the first 6 months of 2016 as domestic price movements were subdued for such major items as the staple fish, other food, oil products, and transport. As diesel generally powers island water and electricity supply, domestic prices are likely to pick up gradually as global crude oil prices recover going into 2017. Inflation is expected to edge up in 2016 and 2017 as projected in *ADO 2016*, but inflationary pressures may intensify under expansionary fiscal policies that fuel higher consumption.

Prospects for external accounts are broadly unchanged. Import growth is expected to remain strong over the medium term on robust demand for infrastructure and other construction and as world commodity prices gradually recover. Export growth will remain minimal on poor and volatile fish catches. Travel receipts, and therefore the services balance, will climb broadly in line with the tepid pickup in tourist arrivals. Gross foreign exchange reserves increased by 10% to $623 million in June 2016 as usable reserves grew by 8% to $209 million, providing only 1.2 months of import cover. Projections for the current account deficit are revised slightly downward for both years, mainly to accommodate a base effect following revisions to data on the balance of payments in 2015 that indicated somewhat lower trade and current account deficits.

3.3.6 **Selected economic indicators, Maldives (%)**

	2016		2017	
	ADO 2016	Update	ADO 2016	Update
GDP growth	3.5	3.5	3.9	3.9
Inflation	1.2	1.2	1.4	1.4
Current acct. bal. (share of GDP)	−12.6	−10.1	−10.5	−10.0

Source: ADB estimates.

Nepal

GDP growth slowed in FY2016 (ended 15 July 2016) even more than forecast in *ADO 2016*. The depressed result following 5.7% growth achieved in FY2014 reflected lost income and productive capacity following large earthquakes in April and May 2015, delays in reconstruction, unrest in the Terai region bordering India that seriously disrupted trade and supply from September 2015 to February 2016, and an unfavorable monsoon for the second year running. Agriculture and services expanded only slightly, with trade, transport, and tourism (collectively 25% of GDP) either growing only marginally or contracting. The trade disruption and delays in reconstruction pushed manufacturing and construction down sharply.

The projection for economic recovery in FY2017 is unchanged, as reconstruction is expected to accelerate markedly, the adverse effects on trade and supply from the Terai unrest have receded, and the monsoon appears to be favorable. Rehabilitation and reconstruction picked up after the National Reconstruction Authority became operational in early 2016. As of 23 August 2016, it had enrolled 375,502 households (the occupants of 70% of the homes damaged in the April earthquake) to receive housing grants and had deposited the first tranche of NRs50,000 into the bank accounts of 106,884 applicants.

The budget for FY2017 envisages allocations 42% higher for recurrent expenditures and 95% higher for capital expenditures including earthquake rehabilitation and reconstruction. A deficit equal to 10% of GDP is slated to reverse a surplus of 1.4% in FY2016. However, as capital expenditure historically falls short to an average of 77% of allocation because of inadequate project planning and implementation, actual capital spending and the realized deficit will likely be smaller than projected in the budget. It will nevertheless stimulate growth.

The earthquakes and trade disruptions, coupled with weak agricultural production, exacerbated inflation, which rose sharply in FY2016 for food (44% of the consumer price basket) and other goods but a bit less than forecast in *ADO 2016*. The differential from inflation in India, to whose currency the Nepali rupee is pegged, rose to 4.7 percentage points on acute trade shortages, rendering exports less competitive.

The inflation forecast for FY2017 is revised up to 8.5% despite improved agricultural production and trade flows, and much higher government spending to rebuild will bring a surge in domestic demand. Monetary policy will thus need to restrain inflation and defend the currency peg even as it supports growth. The introduction of an interest rate corridor in FY2017 should improve the authorities' management of liquidity and the monetary transmission mechanism and, along with ample foreign exchange reserves, equip them to achieve their objectives.

Economic disruption and a stronger inflation-adjusted Nepali rupee contributed to a 29% decline in the dollar value of exports in FY2016. Imports fell by 7.1% from a higher base, and the trade deficit narrowed marginally to equal 30% of GDP in FY2016. Remittances were much smaller than forecast but still sustained a sizeable current account surplus estimated at 6.2% of GDP and pushed foreign exchange reserves up by nearly 20% to $9.7 billion, or cover for about 14 months of imports of goods and nonfactor services.

3.3.7 Selected economic indicators, Nepal (%)

	2016		2017	
	ADO 2016	Update	ADO 2016	Update
GDP growth	1.5	0.8	4.8	4.8
Inflation	10.5	9.9	8.2	8.5
Current acct. bal. (share of GDP)	10.3	6.2	6.4	4.6

Source: ADB estimates.

Exports will revive following the restoration of normal trade, though growth will likely remain sluggish on account of longstanding structural impediments such as inadequate infrastructure, energy shortages, and cumbersome business regulations, as well as the stronger currency. Imports should rebound markedly with the faster pace of reconstruction and higher consumer spending. Even with a significantly larger trade deficit, the expected return of healthy remittance expansion should sustain a current account surplus, albeit narrower than forecast in March.

Sri Lanka

In June 2016, the International Monetary Fund approved a 36-month extended arrangement under the Extended Fund Facility to support the country's economic reform agenda. The main efforts are to boost the tax ratio, reduce the budget deficit, rebuild foreign exchange reserves, and improve public financial management, including of state-owned enterprises.

GDP grew by 5.2% in the first quarter and then slumped to 2.6% in the second to hold growth in the first half of 2016 to 3.9% year on year. Agriculture was hit by dry weather that cut tea production in the first quarter and by heavy rain and flooding in the second quarter that markedly reduced agricultural output by 2.5% in the first half. However, the weak economic performance in the first half came mostly from an unexpected slowing of industry in the second quarter, mainly in manufacturing and construction. As other industry indicators show stronger performance, recovery is expected in the second half. The forecast for GDP growth in 2016 is nevertheless revised down by 0.3 percentage points. The forecast for growth in 2017 is similarly lowered because of tight monetary and fiscal policies to achieve economic reform objectives.

National consumer price index inflation rose in July to 5.8% year on year. Food inflation reached 6.7%, reflecting the second-quarter drop in agriculture, while nonfood inflation rose to 5.0%. On expectations that food production will revive under normal weather and that monetary tightening will curb demand pressures, inflation is expected to moderate in the second half of the year. On balance, *ADO 2016* forecasts for inflation are retained.

Exports shrank by 5.8% year on year in the first half of 2016, more rapidly than in 2015, with earnings falling in June for the sixteenth consecutive month. Most agricultural and industrial exports fell—tea and spices particularly hard—but textile and garment exports strengthened. Imports fell by 2.8% in contrast with the 5.5% expansion recorded in the first half of 2015, as growth in consumer imports, especially vehicles, was sharply reined in. The trade deficit grew by only 2.2% to $4.2 billion.

Tourist earnings continued their strong performance in the first half of 2016, and remittance inflows strengthened. Their combined earnings offset the trade deficit by a larger margin than in 2015. Accordingly, the *ADO 2016* forecast for the current account deficit is retained for 2016. It is widened for 2017, however, on oil prices rising more than expected earlier and possible adverse effects on exports from Brexit.

Gross official reserves fell by $2.0 billion to $5.3 billion in the 6 months to June but recovered to $6.5 billion in July, reflecting inflow from a sovereign bond issue. The exchange rate with the US dollar was largely stable.

3.3.8 Selected economic indicators, Sri Lanka (%)

	2016		2017	
	ADO 2016	Update	ADO 2016	Update
GDP growth	5.3	5.0	5.8	5.5
Inflation	4.5	4.5	5.0	5.0
Current acct. bal. (share of GDP)	−2.0	−2.0	−1.8	−2.0

Source: ADB estimates.

Southeast Asia

This subregion is on track to achieve the *ADO 2016* forecast for economic growth at 4.5% in 2016, marking a return to an upward growth trend after 3 years of deceleration. Growth is still seen trending higher in 2017, though not to the extent envisaged in March. Inflation in Southeast Asia this year is now projected at 2.0%, considerably below the earlier forecast, with inflation still expected to rise to 2.9% in 2017. The projection for the current account surplus in 2016 is raised to 3.4% of subregional GDP.

Subregional assessment and prospects

Six of the 10 economies in the Association of Southeast Asian Nations (ASEAN) are forecast to expand faster in 2016 than in 2015, nudging up aggregate growth to 4.5%, or 0.1 percentage points above the 2015 figure (Figure 3.4.1). This projection is unchanged from *ADO 2016* but masks revisions of most of the forecasts for individual economies. On the upside, the Philippines is performing better than expected on a surge of investment and strong expansion in consumption, prompting a 0.4 percentage point increase in its growth forecast to 6.4%. Thailand is recovering slightly faster than anticipated, helped by buoyant tourism, so its growth forecast is raised by 0.2 percentage points to 3.2%.

Against this, forecasts for 2016 are lowered for Indonesia, Malaysia, Singapore, and Viet Nam. For Indonesia, the biggest economy in this group, growth is now seen at 5.0% in 2016, improving on the 4.8% outcome in 2015 but 0.2 percentage points below the earlier projection because investment is rising at a more moderate pace than anticipated. The forecast for Viet Nam is lowered by 0.7 percentage points to 6.0% as drought cut agricultural output in the first half of 2016, and mining also contracted. Sluggish global growth has dampened prospects for Malaysia and Singapore, so their growth forecasts are trimmed. Brunei Darussalam, Cambodia, the Lao People's Democratic Republic (Lao PDR), and Myanmar are projected to meet their *ADO 2016* growth forecasts.

Infrastructure investment has played an important role in driving growth this year. Indonesia accelerated public investment and, through policy reform, improved the climate for private investment. However, a shortfall in revenue caused the government to prune expenditure and delay some projects, so the infrastructure expansion is more gradual than

3.4.1 GDP growth, Southeast Asia

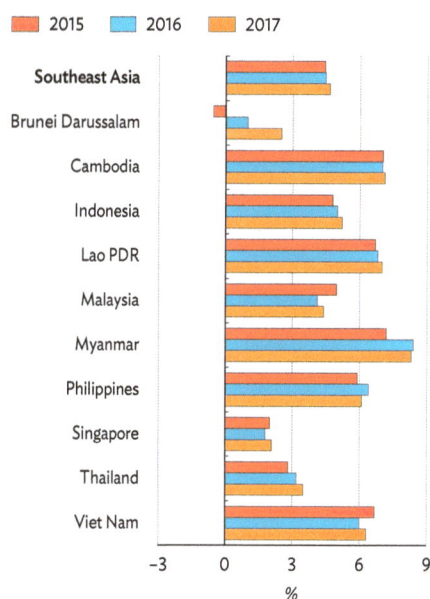

Lao PDR = Lao People's Democratic Republic.
Source: Asian Development Outlook database.
Click here for figure data

The subregional assessment and prospects were written by Jin Cyhn and Dulce Zara. The section on Indonesia was written by Priasto Aji and Emma Allen; Malaysia by Akiko Terada-Hagiwara and Shiela Camingue-Romance; the Philippines by Aekapol Chongvilaivan and Teresa Mendoza; Thailand by Luxmon Attapich; Viet Nam by Aaron Batten, Nguyen Luu Thuc Phuong, and Chu Hong Minh; and other economies by Peter Brimble, Jan Hansen, Shikha Jha, Samphors Khieu, Minsoo Lee, Soulinthone Leuangkhamsing, Rattanatay Luanglatbandith, Thi Da Myint, Pilipinas Quising, and Mai Lin Villaruel. Authors are with the Southeast Asia and Economic Research and Regional Cooperation departments of ADB.

anticipated in March. In the Philippines, growth in public construction soared by 31.6% in the first half of 2016. In Thailand, public fixed investment rose by almost 12%, and Singapore boosted its public fixed investment by an estimated 10%. Malaysia's public fixed investment turned to growth in the first half of 2016 after contracting in the first half of 2015.

Private fixed investment was patchy in the first half of 2016. In the Philippines and Thailand, private fixed investment improved on the same period in 2015, and in Viet Nam foreign direct investment remained strong. However, Malaysia posted slower growth in private fixed investment, which actually fell in Singapore. Private consumption, too, is mixed this year. Consumer spending grew by a rapid 7.2% in the Philippines in January–June on higher employment and remittances. It picked up in Indonesia and Thailand but decelerated in Malaysia, Singapore, and Viet Nam.

Next year, subregional growth is seen quickening to 4.6%, with 8 of the 10 economies posting faster growth than in 2016, albeit modest increases for most. This projection is 0.2 percentage points below that in *ADO 2016* owing to downward revisions for Indonesia, Singapore, and Viet Nam. Investment in Indonesia is seen staying on a lower growth trajectory than earlier projected. Its growth forecast for 2017 is lowered by 0.4 percentage points to 5.1%, but this will still be the best pace in 4 years. Forecasts for Singapore and Viet Nam are trimmed by 0.2 percentage points, to 2.0% and 6.3% respectively. For the Philippines, the 2017 growth forecast is edged up by 0.1 percentage points to 6.2%. Stronger subregional growth next year than in 2016 will stem from expected improving demand in the major industrial economies, higher prices for some export commodities, recovery in agriculture in countries hurt by drought this year, and rising investment in infrastructure.

Inflation is milder than projected in March, leading to downward revisions to forecasts for most economies. Subregional inflation is now seen at 2.0% in 2016, significantly lower than the 2.6% projected in March and well below inflation of 2.7% in 2015 (Figure 3.4.2). For Indonesia, the inflation forecast is lowered by 1.0 percentage point to 3.5% mainly because of a government decision in April to reduce fuel prices. Brunei Darussalam and Singapore are experiencing deflation again this year. In contrast, inflation remains near double-digits in Myanmar. Subregional inflation is still seen picking up to 2.9% in 2017 on higher global prices for food and fuel and on firmer domestic demand.

This *Update* raises the projection for Southeast Asia's current account surplus in 2016 by 0.6 percentage points to 3.4% of combined GDP (Figure 3.4.3). The decline in merchandise exports generally is slowing, and exports are rising in some countries. Imports remain weak in most economies in part due to lower global oil prices. Forecasts of current account surpluses in 2016 are revised up for Singapore, Thailand, and Viet Nam, while current account deficits are now seen to be narrower than earlier anticipated in Indonesia and the Lao PDR. A surge of imports into the Philippines prompts a downward revision in the forecasts of its current account surplus. For 2017, the aggregate current account surplus is seen narrowing to 2.7% of GDP, this forecast unchanged from March, on higher prices for oil and commodities and stronger infrastructure spending that will lift imports of capital equipment.

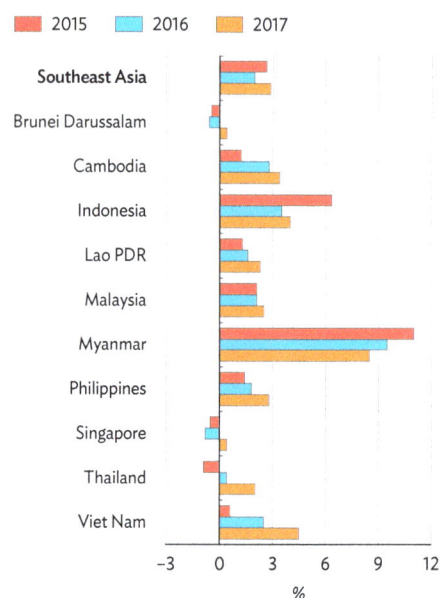

3.4.2 Inflation, Southeast Asia

Lao PDR = Lao People's Democratic Republic.
Source: Asian Development Outlook database.
Click here for figure data

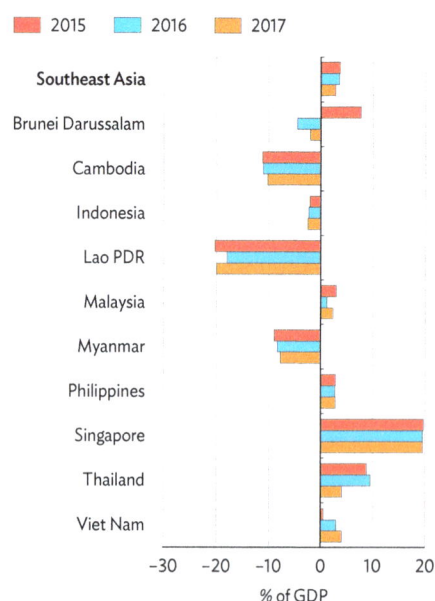

3.4.3 Current account balance, Southeast Asia

Lao PDR = Lao People's Democratic Republic.
Source: Asian Development Outlook database.
Click here for figure data

Indonesia

Stronger domestic demand generated slightly faster growth in Southeast Asia's biggest economy in the first half of 2016. Growth this year and next is seen trending higher but at a lower trajectory than envisaged in *ADO 2016* owing to a more moderate increase in investment than earlier anticipated. Inflation is milder than projected in March, so forecasts for 2016 and 2017 are lowered. Indeed, inflation in 2016 could be the lowest in 16 years. Current account deficits will be narrower than forecast in March.

Updated assessment

GDP growth accelerated to 5.2% year on year in the second quarter of 2016 from 4.9% in the first, putting expansion in the first half at 5.0% (Figure 3.4.4). Domestic demand grew faster in the first 6 months than in the same period in 2015, but the impetus to growth from net external demand waned.

Higher government investment in infrastructure and improvements in the climate for private investment drove a 5.3% increase in fixed capital investment in January–June, the best first-half result since 2013 but still not as strong as anticipated in March (Figure 3.4.5). Government consumption spending rose by 4.8%, considerably faster than first-half increases in recent years as the government improved its procurement performance. Growth in private consumption quickened to 5.0%, benefitting from higher minimum wages since early January, an increase in the tax-free income threshold last year, and decelerating inflation. Rural incomes, hurt by drought, got support from higher budget allocations for the government's Village Fund, which hires rural workers to build local infrastructure.

Net external demand made a small contribution to GDP growth in the first half, as a 4.0% decline in imports of goods and services in volume terms outpaced a 3.1% decline in the volume of exports.

By sector, services expanded by 6.2% and generated just over half of GDP growth. Significant contributions came from wholesale and retail trade, transportation, and rapidly expanding communications and finance. Social services posted modest expansion, with health services stimulated by government efforts to meet its targets for universal health care coverage by 2019 and higher budget allocations for health care more generally.

Growth in manufacturing picked up to 4.7%, the fastest since 2013. Subsectors that performed well included food processing, automotive industries, and electronics. The government's push to build more infrastructure and homes drove strong 7.0% growth in construction. Drought from El Niño hurt agriculture, which grew by only 2.5% in the first half. Mining contracted by 1.0%, though this was a smaller decline than in 2015.

Inflation was milder than anticipated partly because the government decided to reduce administered fuel prices by 11.5% in April. Year on year, inflation slowed to 2.8% in August and averaged 3.7% over the first 8 months of 2016 (Figure 3.4.6). Food price inflation remained relatively high, reflecting supply and distribution issues, but subsided after the government approved increases in food imports. Core inflation excluding the more volatile food and energy prices eased to 3.3% in August.

3.4.4 Demand-side contributions to growth

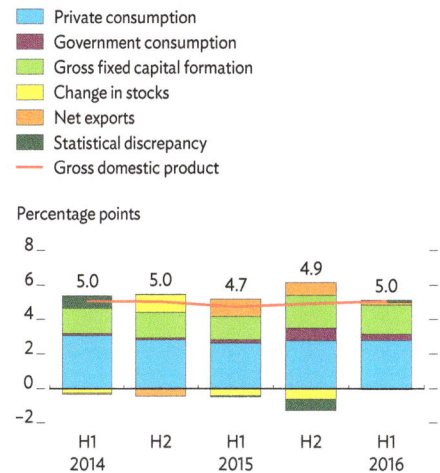

3.4.5 Fixed investment

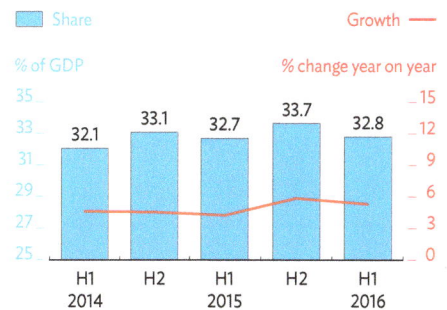

3.4.6 Policy and inflation rates

Monetary and fiscal policies stimulated economic growth in the first half. Bank Indonesia, the central bank, lowered its policy rate four times, from 7.5% in early January to 6.5% in June, as inflation eased and the global economic outlook deteriorated. The central bank also reduced rates on its deposit and lending facilities. Even so, growth in credit decelerated to 7.7% in July from 10.4% at the end of last year.

Budget disbursement rates improved on the sluggish performances of recent years. Capital spending by the central government jumped by 65% in the first half of 2016 from the same period in 2015 as the Ministry of Public Works and Housing accelerated its procurement. On the revenue side, tax collection fell by 2.4% from a year earlier, with only 34% of the revised budget target collected by 30 June. This put the budget in deficit in the first half equal to 1.8% of GDP.

Merchandise exports and imports continued to fall in January–June but at slower rates than a year earlier. Exports fell by 10.5% in US dollar terms on slack global demand compounded by an appreciation of the Indonesian rupiah in real effective terms. Prices for some export commodities—crude palm oil, coal, and tin—edged up from a year earlier. Merchandise imports also fell by 10.5% in US dollar terms. Imports of raw materials and capital goods declined while imports of consumer goods excluding fuel rose. The trade surplus narrowed by 10.6%, and the current account deficit widened by 12.0% to $9.4 billion, equal to 2.0% of GDP (Figure 3.4.7).

Inflows of portfolio and foreign direct investment more than offset the current account deficit to put the overall balance of payments in surplus by $1.9 billion. Net inflows of portfolio investment totaled $12.8 billion, down by 8.9% from a year earlier, and net foreign direct investment fell by 27.9% to $6.4 billion. Gross international reserves rose by $7.6 billion to $113.5 billion in the first 8 months, providing cover for 8.3 months of imports of goods and services and government debt payments. The rupiah appreciated by 3.9% against the US dollar in the first 8 months after having depreciated by 10.2% in 2015 (Figure 3.4.8).

Despite better economic growth this year, the number of people employed fell by almost 200,000 in the 12 months to February 2016 (Figure 3.4.9). The unemployment rate nevertheless fell to 5.5% because labor force participation declined. Employment rose in rural areas, which contributed to a slight decline in rural poverty to 14.1% in the 12 months to March 2016. Urban poverty also declined, to 7.8% in March. However, the weak urban labor market showed signs of wage stagnation for educated workers, with post-secondary graduates increasingly accepting positions for which they are overqualified. This trend coincides with low-skilled urban workers, particularly women, leaving the labor force.

Prospects

The government unveiled 13 policy packages from September 2015 to August 2016 to stimulate investment, strengthen competitiveness, and diversify the economy. Included in the policy packages are measures to reduce regulatory bottlenecks, secure the legal rights of investors, facilitate international trade, and promote infrastructure investment. Economic projections in this *Update* assume that these measures are implemented effectively.

3.4.7 Current account components

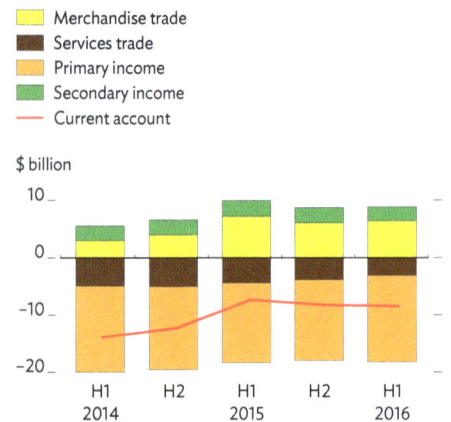

H = half.
Sources: Asian Development Outlook database; CEIC Data Company (accessed 2 September 2016).
Click here for figure data

3.4.8 Gross international reserves and exchange rate

Sources: Bloomberg; CEIC Data Company (both accessed 6 September 2016).
Click here for figure data

3.4.9 Change in the number of employed

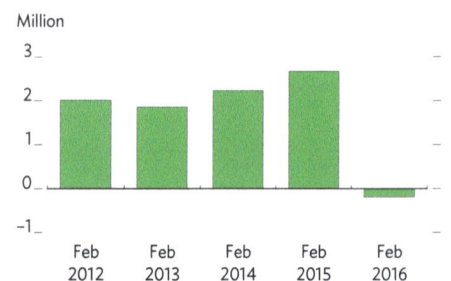

Source: Statistics Indonesia. https://www.bps.go.id (accessed 16 September 2016).
Click here for figure data

In June this year, the government revised the budget and widened the deficit target to 2.4% of GDP from 2.2%. A substantial shortfall in revenue has caused the government to cut operating expenditure and delay some projects. Public investment will be less vigorous in 2016 than projected in March, and government consumption spending will likely be dampened in the second half of this year. Revenue in 2016 is now expected to undershoot the original budget target by about 14%, and the government is expected to reduce spending by 7%. Officials have noted that the revenue shortfall will not affect infrastructure contracts that are already signed.

Aiming to boost revenue by $12.5 billion, the government launched in July a partial tax amnesty to encourage individuals and companies to repatriate funds held abroad. Funds repatriated before April 2017 will be taxed at concessional rates of 2%–5%. By mid-September 2016, just 14% of the amnesty revenue target had been realized. The draft 2017 budget retains the wider 2.4% deficit target and focuses spending on infrastructure, education, health, and food security.

Private investment is seen gathering momentum over the forecast period, benefitting from policy reform. Among other improvements, the reforms opened an additional 35 industries to foreign ownership and cut the time taken to secure business permits to 3 hours through a one-stop service facility. Data from the Investment Coordinating Board show that actual foreign direct investment—outside of certain industries including oil, gas, and banking—rose by 12.3% in the first half of 2016 from the same period last year. The government expects that funds repatriated under the tax amnesty will not only broaden the tax base but also lift investment. Funds repatriated under the tax deal must be invested in domestic financial markets or businesses for at least 3 years.

Nevertheless, the pickup in private investment is likely to be more moderate than earlier anticipated. One reason is that the outlook for trade and investment has been dampened by unexpectedly sluggish growth in the major industrial economies and global trade. Also, imports of capital goods have been lackluster this year, and domestic credit growth has been persistently weak (Figure 3.4.10). Cuts in the policy interest rate have not been fully reflected in lower bank deposit and lending rates. To address this issue, the central bank adopted in August the 7-day reverse repo rate as the new policy rate to make monetary policy transmission more effective. In September, the central bank lowered the new policy rate to 5.0% from 5.25%. Subdued inflation suggests that the authorities could further ease monetary policy to stimulate the economy.

Solid growth is projected for private consumption. Rural incomes will benefit from better prospects for agriculture and expectations of some recovery in export commodity prices in 2017. This year's increase in the minimum wage is positive for consumer spending, and subdued inflation helps. Consumer confidence has firmed since April (Figure 3.4.11).

From the production side, services are expected to maintain robust growth. Business surveys indicate a generally optimistic outlook for the rest of 2016. The purchasing managers' index has shown in most recent months signs of improving conditions for manufacturers, though this

3.4.1 Selected economic indicators, Indonesia (%)

	2016		2017	
	ADO 2016	Update 2016	ADO 2016	Update 2016
GDP growth	5.2	5.0	5.5	5.1
Inflation	4.5	3.5	4.2	4.0
Current acct. bal. (share of GDP)	-2.6	-2.3	-2.8	-2.4

Source: ADB estimates.

3.4.10 Credit growth

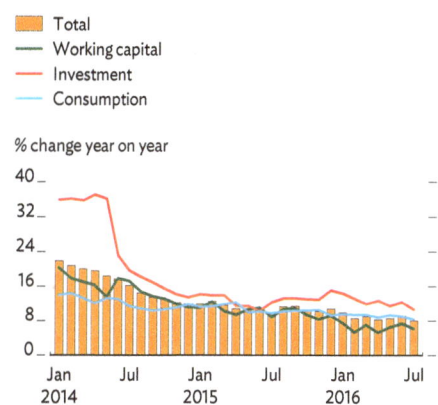

Source: CEIC Data Company (accessed 16 September 2016).
Click here for figure data

3.4.11 Consumer and business confidence indexes

Q = quarter.
Note: A score above 100 means that respondents are optimistic and vice versa.
Source: CEIC Data Company (accessed 16 September 2016).
Click here for figure data

has not generated new factory jobs (Figure 3.4.12). As for agriculture, drought under El Niño has eased but there is a risk that heavy rains could damage crops later in 2016. The outlook for agriculture is brighter in 2017, assuming improved weather.

On balance, economic growth is forecast to stay around 5.0% this year, edging up to 5.1% in 2017 as the policy reforms take hold and growth gathers momentum in the major industrial economies. Higher global commodity prices next year would further bolster investment and incomes. The GDP projections are lowered from *ADO 2016* because the pickup in investment has been more gradual than earlier anticipated.

Exports are forecast to remain weak through 2016 in light of subdued global demand, with some improvement seen for 2017. The reduced economic growth projections suggest that imports will be lower than expected earlier. Consequently, current account deficits will be narrower than forecast in March, though still widening from 2.1% of GDP in 2015. Inflows of foreign direct and portfolio investment should keep the overall balance of payments in surplus.

Inflation is now seen averaging 3.5% in 2016, revised down by a full percentage point from March. If realized, this will be the lowest inflation in 16 years. Higher global fuel and food prices in 2017 are projected to lift inflation to 4.0% on a year-average basis.

The government is addressing persistently high food price inflation that results from high logistics costs and nontariff trade barriers (Figure 3.4.13). The distribution of food staples such as rice, chilies, and chicken from producer to consumer involves long and costly marketing chains. For rice, the domestic price is double the international price. The government has strengthened its inflation task force, which can recommend suspending duties on imported commodities and take other steps to improve the availability and affordability of essential food in short supply. Further measures are being considered, such as price floors and ceilings for food staples and measures to prevent illegal stockpiling.

Risks to the forecasts are posed by the budget cuts and delays in infrastructure projects. Cuts in government expenditure could be extended if revenue from the tax amnesty falls short of expectations. Significant delays in implementing infrastructure projects would hurt business confidence as well as reduce the impetus to growth from public investment. Growth in private consumption would be jeopardized by prolonged weakness in the labor market. Deficits in the budget and the current account reinforce the importance of maintaining capital inflows, which would be put at risk by renewed volatility in global financial markets.

3.4.12 Manufacturing purchasing managers' index

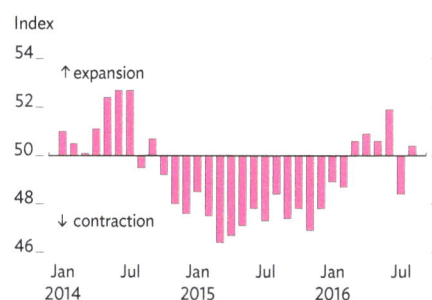

Note: Nikkei, Markit.
Source: Bloomberg (accessed 7 September 2016).
Click here for figure data

3.4.13 Inflation rates

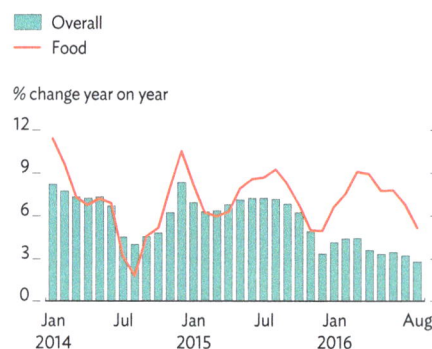

Source: CEIC Data Company (accessed 16 September 2016).
Click here for figure data

Malaysia

Heavily reliant on external trade, the economy has slowed for a second year because of weak demand for exports of hydrocarbons and manufactures and export prices that are mostly lower. Nevertheless, GDP is seen growing at a moderate pace this year, though slightly undershooting the *ADO 2016* forecast, with growth expected to pick up in 2017. Inflation in 2016 is lower than was anticipated in March and is projected to rise moderately in 2017. This *Update* retains the forecasts for the current account surplus to narrow in 2016 and expand again next year.

Updated assessment

Economic growth slowed for 5 consecutive quarters to June 2016 as external demand remained weak and domestic demand lost momentum. At 4.1% in the first half of this year over the first half of 2015, growth was the most subdued since GDP contracted in 2009 and compares with average growth of 5.3% over the past 5 years.

Private consumption grew by a relatively robust 5.8% and contributed most of the increase in GDP in January–June (Figure 3.4.14). Still, this increase was considerably slower than the 7.7% expansion in the first half of 2015. One reason is that the labor market has softened this year, with job vacancies falling sharply and the unemployment rate edging up to 3.4%. Also, rural incomes have been hurt by drought that caused agriculture to contract in the first half of 2016. As a result, consumer confidence is low.

Government consumption maintained solid growth at 5.2%, decelerating slightly from a year earlier. Public fixed investment grew by 1.1%, an improvement on the first half of 2015, when it contracted (Figure 3.4.15). However, growth in private fixed investment slowed to 4.0%, about half the pace of a year earlier. Fixed investment overall increased by a modest 3.2%.

Net external demand dragged on growth, as in 2015. Imports of goods and services rose by 1.6% in real terms in the first 6 months of 2016, faster than a 0.2% rise in exports of goods and services in real terms.

By sector, services held up relatively well, expanding by 5.4% against 5.7% in the first half of 2015 and generating most of the GDP growth from the supply side. Growth in wholesale and retail trade, information and communications, and business services drove the expansion in services. Construction performed strongly, expanding by 8.4% largely on higher civil engineering activity. However, growth in manufacturing slowed to 4.3%, and some domestically oriented production including automobiles recorded declines.

Production of crude oil and condensate was virtually flat in the first 6 months, though production of natural gas edged up. Mining overall recorded growth of 1.4%, well below the year-earlier pace. Agriculture contracted by 6.0% as drought under El Niño cut production of crude palm oil by 15% and natural rubber output by almost 10%.

Inflation accelerated early in 2016, in part the result of a temporary base effect but also reflecting government decisions to increase the excise tax on alcohol and tobacco and to reduce rebates on electricity tariffs (Figure 3.4.16). Pushing the other way, the statistical effect of

3.4.14 Demand-side contributions to growth

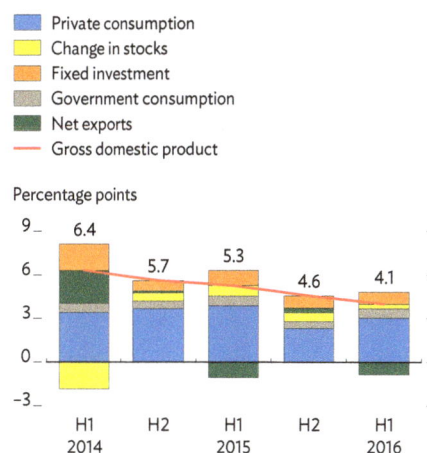

- Private consumption
- Change in stocks
- Fixed investment
- Government consumption
- Net exports
- Gross domestic product

H = half.
Source: Haver Analytics (accessed 7 September 2016).
Click here for figure data

3.4.15 Fixed investment growth

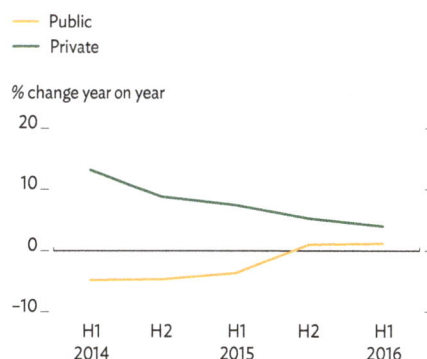

- Public
- Private

H = half.
Source: Haver Analytics (accessed 7 September 2016).
Click here for figure data

3.4.16 Inflation and policy rate

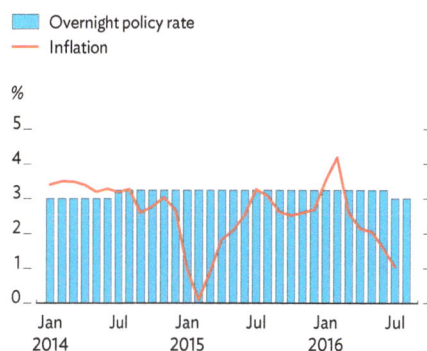

- Overnight policy rate
- Inflation

Sources: Haver Analytics; Bank Negara Malaysia. 2016. *Monthly Statistical Bulletin.* July. http://www.bnm.gov.my (both accessed 7 September 2016).
Click here for figure data

the goods and services tax introduced in April 2015 dropped out of the year-on-year inflation rate in the second quarter. Lower fuel prices this year have further dampened inflation, which averaged 2.3% over the first 8 months.

In the context of slowing economic growth and subdued inflation, Bank Negara Malaysia, the central bank, lowered its policy interest rate in July by 25 basis points to 3.0%. To inject liquidity into the financial system, the central bank in January reduced the reserve requirement ratio for banks from 4.0% to 3.5%. Demand for credit was lackluster (Figure 3.4.17). Growth in outstanding household loans decelerated to 6.0% year on year in June from 8.7% in June 2015, and growth in outstanding business loans slowed to 3.8% in June from 8.0% a year earlier. Broad money (M3) grew by 2.3% year on year in July.

Fiscal policy was expansionary in the first half. The government raised spending by 5.4% from the same period in 2015, with development expenditure boosted by almost one-third. Construction on major infrastructure projects pushed ahead even as government revenue from oil and gas and income taxes declined. Total revenue fell by 9.8% in the first 6 months. Consequently, the federal government's budget deficit doubled to 5.6% of GDP from 2.8% in the first half of 2015.

Trade and current account surpluses continued to narrow in January–June. Merchandise exports fell by 11.9% in US dollar terms on tepid global demand for Malaysian exports, including electronics and electrical products, and lower prices for oil and other export commodities compared with a year earlier (Figure 3.4.18). Sharp declines were recorded in exports to Japan, the People's Republic of China (PRC), the Republic of Korea, and Taipei,China, while shipments to the European Union and the US rose. Merchandise imports fell by 9.3% in US dollar terms. Lower imports of capital and intermediate goods reflected weakness in investment and exports, but imports of consumer goods rose slightly. These developments narrowed the trade surplus by 25% to $10.5 billion, and, together with deficits in services and income, sharply narrowed the current account surplus by almost 70% to $1.7 billion. As a ratio to GDP, the current account surplus fell to 1.2%.

The capital and financial accounts recorded net inflows of $3.8 billion in January–June compared with large net outflows of $7.0 billion in the first half of 2015. Malaysian net investment abroad fell by over half from a year earlier, to $3.6 billion. Net foreign direct investment inflows totaled $5.8 billion, partly due to foreign investors acquiring Malaysian power plants, and net portfolio investment recorded an inflow of $3.1 billion. Gross international reserves recovered by 2.3% to $97.5 billion in the first 8 months of this year, providing cover for 8.1 months of retained imports of goods and 1.2 times short-term debt (Figure 3.4.19).

The Malaysian ringgit appreciated by 3.8% against the US dollar from the end of 2015 to mid-September, after depreciating by 19% last year on weak exports, capital outflows, and concerns about the finances of the government-owned investment company 1Malaysia Development. External debt rose marginally to $210.5 billion over the 12 months to June 2016, equal to 70.0% of GDP. About 60% of the external debt was medium to long term.

3.4.17 Credit and money supply

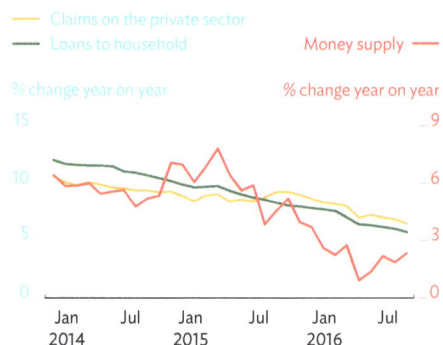

Source: Haver Analytics (accessed 7 September 2016).
Click here for figure data

3.4.18 Trade indicators

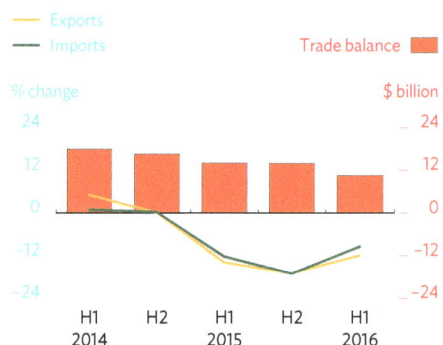

H = half.
Source: Haver Analytics (accessed 7 September 2016).
Click here for figure data

3.4.19 International reserves and exchange rate

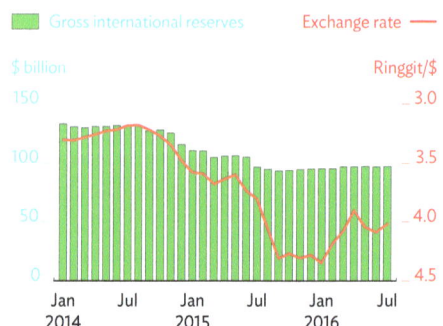

Source: Haver Analytics (accessed 7 September 2016).
Click here for figure data

Prospects

GDP growth in 2016 is now projected at 4.1%, slightly below the March forecast (Figure 3.4.20). Factors that slowed the economy in the first half—weak external demand stemming from decelerating growth in the PRC and unexpectedly slow recovery in the major industrial economies and, domestically, the softer labor market, lower earnings from hydrocarbons and other commodities, and contraction in agriculture—will continue through 2016. The government's leading indicator compiled in July pointed to modest economic growth in the months ahead. Next year, more robust recovery in the major industrial economies is still seen driving growth up to 4.4%.

Private consumption is expected to remain muted at least through this year. Growth in loans outstanding to households continued to slow in July even as bank interest rates declined after the reduction in the policy rate. Surveys have shown persistently dour consumer sentiment since late 2014, though the latest survey indicated a slight improvement (Figure 3.4.21). Sales of automobiles have slumped this year.

Measures taken by the government to cushion the slowdown in consumer spending have provided some support. Among other steps the government has reduced mandatory employee contributions to the national retirement fund, trimmed some personal income tax rates from January, and maintained cash transfers. Minimum wages were raised in July, though this affects a small percentage of employees.

Private consumption should start to strengthen in 2017 as the labor market firms and rural areas recover from the drought. Lower interest rates will help. Still, high household debt, equal to 89% of GDP, will continue to weigh on consumer spending.

Private investment is likely to stay subdued, particularly in manufacturing, energy, and agriculture, until external demand improves and prices for oil and other commodities trend higher. The business conditions index turned positive in the second quarter of 2016, but subsequent indicators have been more somber. In August, the purchasing managers' index signaled continuing deterioration in operating conditions for manufacturers, with declines in output and new orders deepening and job-shedding by manufacturers the worst in 3 years (Figure 3.4.22). Growth in industrial production slowed in July from June, and growth in outstanding business loans decelerated to 3.7% in July.

As for public investment, the government has committed to proceed with a number of major infrastructure works, notably road and rail networks, and it has a pipeline of development projects still to roll out under the Economic Transformation Programme and the Eleventh Malaysia Plan, 2016–2020. Most of the projects require private sector investment. In July, Malaysia and Singapore signed a memorandum of understanding to build a 350 kilometer high-speed rail line between Kuala Lumpur and Singapore. Building this large project will stimulate investment and construction over the medium term.

While the government is also committed to reining in its budget deficit, this year's target to narrow the fiscal gap to 3.1% of GDP is challenging in light of the first-half outcome. For 2017, the budget to be unveiled this October is expected to provide some additional support for

3.4.20　GDP growth

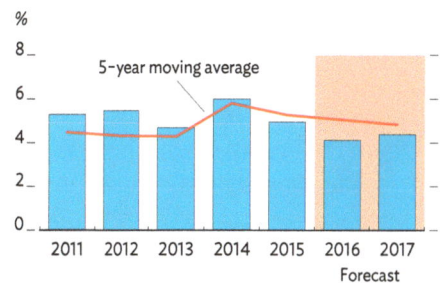

Source: Asian Development Outlook database.
Click here for figure data

3.4.21　Business and consumer confidence

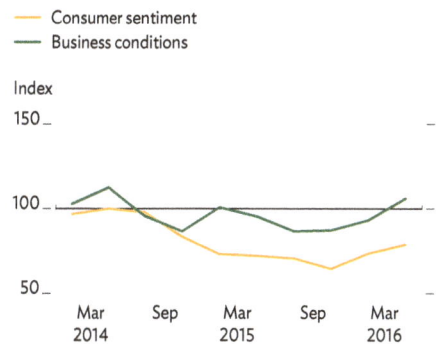

Note: Above 100 indicates improvement in business conditions and rising consumer confidence.
Source: CEIC Data Company (accessed 7 September 2016).
Click here for figure data

3.4.22　Manufacturing purchasing managers' index

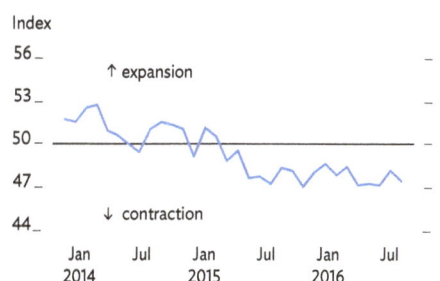

Note: Nikkei-Markit.
Source: Bloomberg (accessed 7 September 2016).
Click here for figure data

economic growth, including assistance to low-income households and to first-time buyers of modest homes, though the government is likely to be constrained from extensive fiscal stimulus by its pledge to shrink the deficit and public debt and to balance the budget by 2020.

Over the past 2 years, the government has taken two important steps to strengthen its fiscal position: introducing the goods and services tax to diversify the revenue base away from reliance on hydrocarbons, and reducing costly subsidies on fuel and other consumer items to free up budget resources for more productive purposes. These reforms have helped to shield the fiscal position from the slump in oil-related revenue. Nevertheless, as this revenue is likely to remain depressed for some time, fiscal consolidation may be delayed.

As inflation pressures have been weaker than earlier anticipated, the forecast for year-average inflation in 2016 is lowered to 2.1% (Figure 3.4.23). Higher global fuel and food prices in 2017 are seen, along with firmer domestic demand, lifting inflation to 2.5%. The outlook for moderate inflation suggests that monetary policy can remain accommodative to economic growth.

The disappointing economic performances of the major industrial economies this year and structural changes in the PRC continue to cloud the outlook for exports. In July, customs-recorded merchandise exports fell by 10.3% in US dollar terms, though this was a more moderate decline than in June. The semiconductor equipment book-to-bill ratios in North America and Japan, two of Malaysia's top export markets for electronic and electrical products, indicate sluggish demand. Exports of oil and liquefied natural gas face slack global demand, and exports of crude palm oil and rubber are curbed by both lower production because of drought and subdued demand. The outlook for export earnings improves for 2017 in anticipation of the major industrial economies growing faster and prices rising for oil and other commodities.

Merchandise imports fell by 10.5% in US dollar terms in July and are projected to fall for the whole year. Imports are seen rising in 2017 in tandem with modestly higher investment. This *Update* retains forecasts that the current account surplus will narrow to 1.2% of GDP in 2016 before increasing next year (Figure 3.4.24).

Risks to the outlook are posed by the slow recovery in the US, the euro area, and Japan. Further declines in exports would intensify the drag on GDP growth from net exports and delay the upturn in investment. Interest rate increases in the US could disrupt global capital flows. As Malaysia is an exporter of hydrocarbons, renewed weakness in oil and gas prices is a risk to its economy.

3.4.2 Selected economic indicators, Malaysia (%)

	2016		2017	
	ADO 2016	Update	ADO 2016	Update
GDP growth	4.2	4.1	4.4	4.4
Inflation	2.7	2.1	2.5	2.5
Current acct. bal. (share of GDP)	1.2	1.2	2.3	2.3

Source: ADB estimates.

3.4.23 Inflation

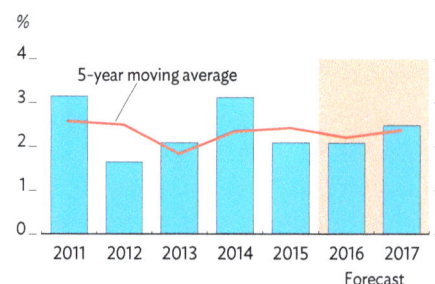

Source: Asian Development Outlook database.
Click here for figure data

3.4.24 Current account balance

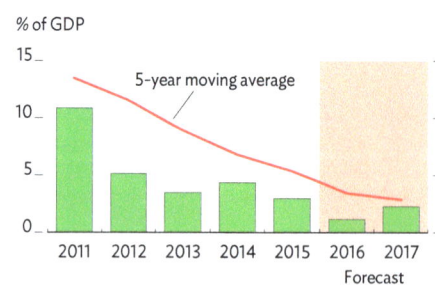

Source: Asian Development Outlook database.
Click here for figure data

Philippines

A surge in investment and strong consumption drove unexpectedly high GDP growth in the first half of this year. Growth is projected to moderate in the second half but will still exceed the March forecast for 2016 as a whole. The growth forecast for 2017 is nudged up as well. Despite the strong domestic demand, inflation will be lower this year than earlier anticipated. For 2017, though, the inflation forecast is raised slightly. Weak merchandise exports and buoyant imports indicate that current account surpluses will be smaller than forecast in *ADO 2016*.

Updated assessment

Strong investment and consumption powered economic growth to 6.9% in the first half of 2016, the fastest pace in 3 years (Figure 3.4.25). Domestic demand expanded by a rapid 12%, supported by election-related spending ahead of national polls in May. However, weakness in net external demand weighed on GDP growth.

Growth in fixed investment accelerated to 27.7% in the first half and made the biggest contribution to growth from the demand side. Private investment was buoyant, while public construction soared by 31.6%. The surge in fixed investment came on top of a double-digit increase in 2015 (Figure 3.4.26). As a ratio to GDP, fixed investment improved to 23.7%, the highest in over a decade, moving the Philippines closer to Southeast Asian norms (Figure 3.4.27).

Government consumption rose by 12.7% as outlays increased on education, health, and conditional cash transfers to 4.6 million poor families. Civil service salaries were raised early this year.

Robust growth in private consumption, at 7.2% in the first 6 months, stemmed from higher employment and remittances from Filipinos overseas and mild inflation. Remittances rose by 4.4% in US dollar terms and by 9.8% in Philippine pesos. Just over 750,000 new jobs were generated in the 12 months to January 2016, mostly in services. Construction and, to a lesser extent, manufacturing also generated more jobs. Drought from El Niño reduced employment in agriculture. The unemployment rate fell to 5.4% in July 2016 from 6.5% in July 2015, but underemployment remained high at 17.3%. Almost a quarter of the workforce is either unemployed or underemployed.

Buoyant investment and consumption spurred a near 20% rise in imports of goods and services in real terms, far outpacing a 7% rise in real exports. As seen in 2015, exports of services, particularly business process outsourcing (BPO), were brisk, but goods exports were soft.

Services and manufacturing were the key drivers on the supply side (Figure 3.4.28). Services, the biggest sector at 58% of GDP, expanded by 8.0% and generated two-thirds of GDP growth. Buoyant subsectors included BPO, retail trade, real estate, and transportation. Manufacturing grew by 7.2%, contributing one-fourth of total growth. Stronger performances were recorded in food processing, chemicals, and transportation and communication equipment. Construction grew by 11.6% on higher investment in public and private projects alike. However, agriculture including fisheries contracted by 3.3%, largely the result of the drought.

3.4.25 Demand-side contributions to growth

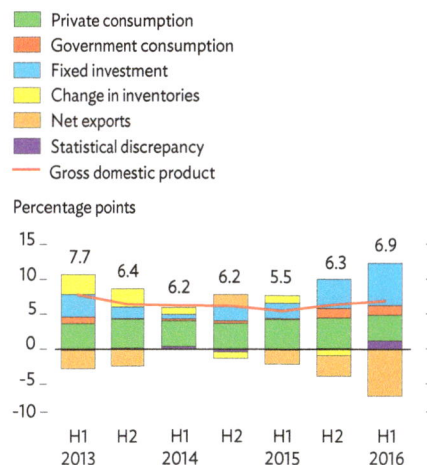

H = half.
Source: CEIC Data Company (accessed 13 September 2016).
Click here for figure data

3.4.26 Contributions to fixed investment growth

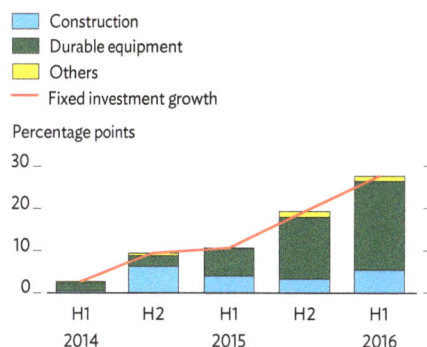

H = half.
Source: CEIC Data Company (accessed 13 September 2016).
Click here for figure data

3.4.27 Fixed investment

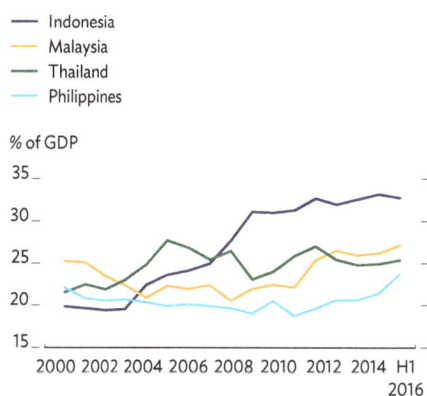

H = half.
Source: CEIC Data Company (accessed 13 September 2016).
Click here for figure data

Despite this disruption to food production and the surge in economic growth, inflation remained modest. On a year-on-year basis, it edged up by 1.8% in August 2016, and the average in the first 8 months was 1.5% (Figure 3.4.29). Lower global oil prices suppressed inflation, as did rice imports to augment domestic supplies. Bangko Sentral ng Pilipinas, the central bank, kept its policy settings steady, the overnight reverse repurchase rate at 3.0% based on an interest rate corridor adopted in June 2016. Growth in credit to the private sector accelerated to 15.4% year on year in July, from 12.1% at the end of 2015, and growth in liquidity (M3) over this period picked up to 13.1% in July from 9.4%.

Reflecting strong fiscal stimulus, the fiscal deficit widened to 1.7% of GDP in January–June from 0.9% in all of 2015. Government spending excluding interest rose by 16.6%, while tax collections increased by 10.0%.

In the external accounts, merchandise exports fell by 5.2% in US dollar terms, with declines in electronics, garments, chemicals, machinery, and transport equipment, as well as in minerals and agricultural products except sugar. By contrast, merchandise imports rose by 18.3%. Capital goods imports soared by 55.7%, reflecting the strong investment. Imports of consumer goods and raw materials also posted significant increases, though lower global oil prices trimmed the bill for oil imports. The trade deficit widened by 72.1% to $16.4 billion. Earnings from services, notably BPO and tourism, and remittance inflows increased in the first half, but the wider trade gap shrank the current account surplus to $778 million, equal to 0.5% of GDP, from a surplus of 3.7% of GDP a year earlier. In the financial account, portfolio investment outflows partly offset higher direct investment. This put the overall balance of payments in surplus by $634 million.

Gross international reserves rose by 6.4% to $85.8 billion in the 8 months to August, or cover for 10 months of imports. The peso depreciated against the US dollar by 0.8% to mid-September. External debt declined to the equivalent of 26.2% of GDP by June from 28.9% in 2013.

Prospects

Vigorous economic growth is expected to continue through 2016, though at a more moderate pace in the second half as the impact of election spending fades. Based on the strong performance in January–June, the forecast for full-year growth is raised by 0.4 percentage points to 6.4%. Prospects have also improved for 2017, so the growth forecast for next year is raised to 6.2% (Figure 3.4.30).

The new government that took office on June 30 outlined a 10-point economic agenda that will be reflected in the 2017–2022 Philippine Development Plan. It will maintain and strengthen the major economic policies of the previous administration by increasing investment in infrastructure and human capital, improving the investment climate, and sustaining efforts to reduce corruption and red tape. An anti-red tape team was created in July to cut processing time for permits, clearances, and other documents from government offices. Reform proposals include a more progressive tax system with lower corporate and personal income tax rates, and relaxed restrictions on foreign direct investment.

3.4.28 Supply-side contributions to growth

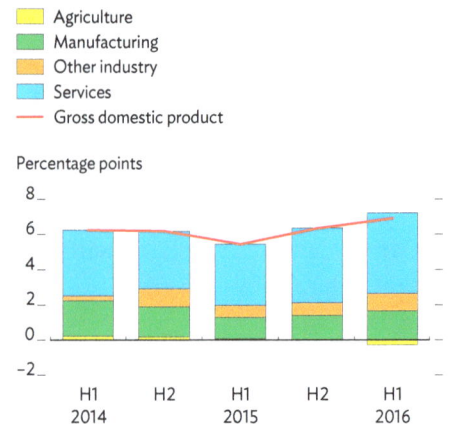

- Agriculture
- Manufacturing
- Other industry
- Services
- Gross domestic product

Percentage points

H = half.
Source: CEIC Data Company (accessed 13 September 2016).
Click here for figure data

3.4.29 Contributions to inflation

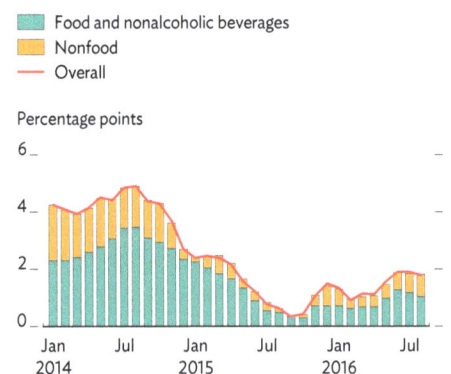

- Food and nonalcoholic beverages
- Nonfood
- Overall

Percentage points

Source: CEIC Data Company (accessed 13 September 2016).
Click here for figure data

3.4.30 GDP growth

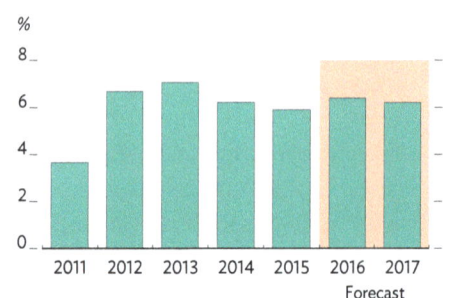

%

Forecast

Source: *Asian Development Outlook* database.
Click here for figure data

Among other early steps, the administration issued an executive order that mandates freedom of information to enhance transparency and accountability in the executive branch, and it aims to extend this to all branches of the government, pending Congressional approval. Budget execution is to be strengthened by improving project planning and approval, and infrastructure construction is to be accelerated.

The government committed to stronger efforts to develop rural and regional areas. Despite solid economic growth that averaged 6.2% in the past 6 years, poverty nationwide remains high—though, at 26.3%, it has eased from 28.8% in 2006. Poverty rates are higher in the Visayas and Mindanao (Figure 3.4.31). The government's target is to reduce poverty to 17% by 2022. A major cause of poverty is inadequate employment. Moreover, economic growth is centered on the cities. Among the country's 18 regions, only three—Metro Manila and two adjacent regions in Luzon—generate nearly two-thirds of GDP (Figure 3.4.32).

The budget proposed for 2017 targets an 11.6% rise in spending over the 2016 budget, with significant increases for infrastructure, education, health, and social protection. Investment on infrastructure is raised to equal 5.4% of GDP from the 5.1% allocated in 2016, covering projects such as schools, railways, ports, and road networks, with attention to improving connections between lagging regions and growth centers. For agriculture, projects include farm-to-market roads and irrigation systems. The budget aims to accelerate the roll-out of public–private partnership (PPP) projects. This additional expenditure is accommodated by widening the deficit target to 3.0% of GDP from the previous administration's ceiling of 2.0%. The deficit ceiling for 2016 is raised from 2.0% of GDP to 2.7%.

To compensate for revenue foregone by reducing income tax rates, the government is considering broadening the value-added tax base, raising oil excise taxes and indexing them to inflation, and streamlining fiscal incentives to investors, among other measures. It will crack down on tax evasion. Such actions to bolster revenue will be vital, given the low ratio of tax revenue to GDP, at 13.6% in 2015. The target is to raise it to 14.5% in 2017. A stronger fiscal position would pave the way for further reducing national government debt, which fell in June 2016 to 43.0% of GDP, its lowest in over a decade (Figure 3.4.33).

Private investment looks set to remain robust. Foreign direct investment almost doubled to $4.2 billion in the first 6 months. Imports of capital goods have recorded double-digit growth this year, and in July credit to business rose by a vigorous 17.4% year on year. The investment climate will improve further provided the government follows through on commitments to encourage foreign investment, reduce the cost of doing business, accelerate PPPs, and address infrastructure bottlenecks.

Rising employment, incomes, and remittances will support growth in private consumption. Consumer confidence rose to record highs in a survey conducted in July (Figure 3.4.34). Growth in remittances has eased this year, but source diversity has cushioned the impact of a slowdown in the Middle East, where a quarter of overseas Filipinos work.

Net external demand is projected to remain a drag on GDP growth. Prospects for exports to the major industrial economies have deteriorated since March with soft economic growth in those markets.

3.4.31 Poverty incidence

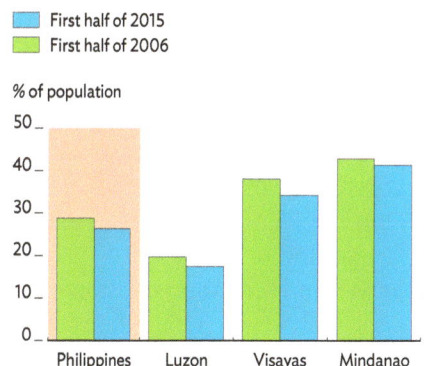

Source: Philippine Statistics Authority.
Click here for figure data

3.4.3 Selected economic indicators, Philippines (%)

	2016		2017	
	ADO 2016	Update	ADO 2016	Update
GDP growth	6.0	6.4	6.1	6.2
Inflation	2.3	1.8	2.7	2.8
Current acct. bal. (share of GDP)	2.7	2.0	2.8	1.8

Source: ADB estimates.

3.4.32 Contributions to GDP, 2010–2015 average, %

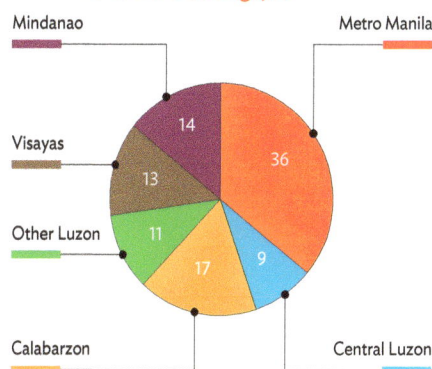

Calabarzon = Cavite, Laguna, Batangas, Rizal, and Quezon.
Source: Philippine Statistics Authority.
Click here for figure data

Merchandise exports fell in most product categories in January–July. As noted above, though, exports of services are relatively strong. Demand from the major industrial economies in 2017 is projected to improve over 2016. However, strong domestic consumption and investment point to buoyant imports again next year.

By sector, services, manufacturing, and construction will be the key growth drivers over the forecast period. Services will continue to be buoyed by growth in BPO revenue, estimated by its industry association to have increased by 16% to $22 billion last year and projected to rise by 14% in 2016. Tourism is buoyant as well, with international visitor arrivals rising by 13.7% to 3 million in the first half of 2016.

Growth in manufacturing will benefit from the strong consumer base and expansion in construction. The manufacturing purchasing managers' index in August showed that growth in new orders and output continued into the second half of 2016. Improved economic prospects next year for the US and Japan, the Philippines' two biggest export markets, are positive for export-oriented manufacturing. These countries are also significant sources of foreign direct investment. Construction will gain from expansion in infrastructure including PPPs. Building permit approvals show the number of construction projects rising by 20.2% year on year in the second quarter of 2016. An easing of the drought in the second half of this year augurs well for some recovery in agriculture in 2017.

Inflation is now forecast to average 1.8% this year, lower than projected in *ADO 2016* as the drought affected food prices less than anticipated (Figure 3.4.35). There is a risk that typhoons and La Niña could disrupt food supplies and push inflation up later in 2016. Next year, inflation is seen rising to average 2.8%, this forecast revised up slightly from March in tandem with projections for domestic demand and global oil prices. Inflation could be higher if the government increases excise taxes on oil products but probably still within the official target range of 2%–4%. In these circumstances, the central bank is expected to maintain an accommodative monetary stance.

The forecasts for current account surpluses are lowered to 2.0% of GDP in 2016 and 1.8% in 2017 in light of soft merchandise exports, strong imports, and this *Update's* upwardly revised projections for oil prices.

Unexpectedly weak economic outcomes in major export markets would pose risks to the outlook. The impact of Brexit on the Philippines is expected to be small as the United Kingdom accounted for only 0.9% of Philippine merchandise exports and 0.5% of imports in 2010–2015. Prospects for the European Union are more relevant because it takes 12% of exports.

Maintaining the domestic reform agenda will be vital to sustaining the solid economic performance. Risks from volatility on global financial markets are cushioned by the improved macroeconomic fundamentals and a robust banking sector. The current account has been in surplus since 2003, international reserves are high, the ratio of external debt to GDP has trended lower, and that of public debt has fallen, with nearly two-thirds now denominated in pesos.

3.4.33 Government debt and fiscal balance

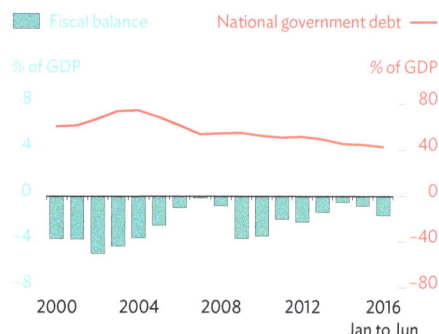

Source: CEIC Data Company (accessed 13 September 2016).
Click here for figure data

3.4.34 Consumer confidence

Source: Bangko Sentral ng Pilipinas.
Click here for figure data

3.4.35 Inflation

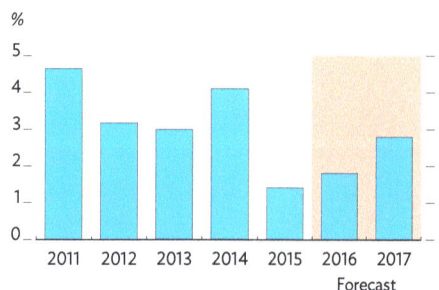

Source: Asian Development Outlook database.
Click here for figure data

Thailand

Government expenditure and buoyant tourism played important roles in driving moderately stronger growth in the first half of 2016. GDP growth for the year as a whole is expected to slightly exceed the *ADO 2016* forecast, and for 2017 is still seen picking up to 3.5%. Inflation has returned after 15 months of declining consumer prices but will likely be lower this year than earlier projected. Robust growth in tourism is, together with weak imports, generating a larger current account surplus than projected in March.

Updated assessment

Economic growth quickened to 3.4% in the first half of 2016 on robust government spending, some improvement in private consumption, and, from the supply side, strong expansion in tourism and a smaller contraction in agriculture (Figure 3.4.36).

Growth depended heavily on government expenditure, as in 2015. Public fixed investment rose by 11.8% in the first half of 2016, following a sharp rebound of almost 30% last year. The government boosted investment in water management, roads, residential construction, and electricity distribution. Government consumption expenditure rose by 5.0%, the highest increase since 2012, partly the result of higher public service salaries and social transfers, including for health services.

After 2 years of decline, private fixed investment rose by 1.1% in January–June (Figure 3.4.37). It benefited from government incentives for housing, including low-interest loans for purchases, and opportunities provided by the public infrastructure programs. Private investment in buildings increased by 2.2%, but investment in machinery and equipment edged up by just 0.8%.

Growth in private consumption was, at 3.1%, still modest but the highest first-half increase in 3 years. Consumption spending got support from government stimulus that included incentives for spending on domestic travel during the Thai New Year in April 2016. Virtually flat consumer prices in the first half also helped. Rural incomes, which slumped last year on drought and low commodity prices, have seen some gains this year from improved agriculture and fishery prices and government funding for village projects. Nevertheless, wage growth is anemic, and employment fell by 0.9% in the second quarter of 2016 from the same period in 2015.

Net external demand contributed to GDP growth in the first half with vigorous expansion of inbound tourism and lower goods imports. Exports of services, mainly tourism, jumped by 15.4% in real terms. By contrast, exports of goods fell by 0.8% in real terms, though this was a more moderate decline than in 2015. Reflecting persistently lackluster domestic demand and sluggish growth in manufacturing, imports of goods and services fell by 3.5%.

Services grew by 5.0%, generating the vast bulk of the GDP increase from the supply side. The number of international tourists rose by 12% year on year to 16.6 million in the first half of the year, spurring double-digit expansion in the hotels and restaurants subsector, which singlehandedly added as much to GDP growth as construction, manufacturing, and utilities combined (Figure 3.4.38).

3.4.36 Supply-side contributions to growth

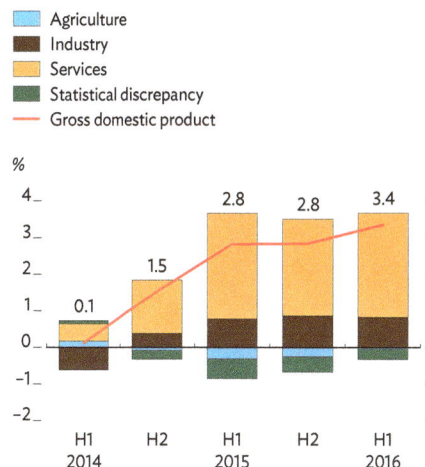

H = half.
Source: Office of the National Economic and Social Development Board, http://www.nesdb.go.th (accessed 15 August 2016).
Click here for figure data

3.4.37 Fixed investment growth

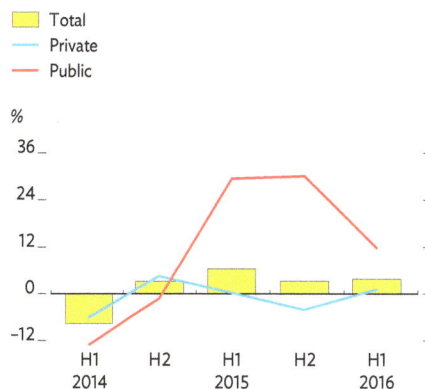

H = half.
Source: Office of The National Economic and Social Development Board, http://www.nesdb.go.th (accessed 15 August 2016).
Click here for figure data

3.4.38 Tourist arrivals

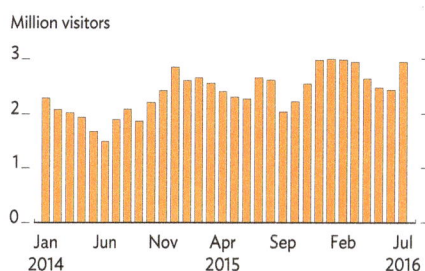

Source: CEIC Data Company (accessed 9 September 2016).
Click here for figure data

Manufacturing posted modest growth at 0.9%, similar to the pace in 2015. Subdued domestic and external demand has weighed on manufacturing for several years. Construction gained from government infrastructure works and from homebuilding to expand by 9.3% in the first half of 2016.

Agriculture contracted by 0.8%, which was considerably less than last year's 3.8% decline under drought and low commodity prices. The drought continued into 2016 but has eased since midyear. A 10.8% recovery in fisheries production helped to slow the contraction in agriculture.

After declining for 15 consecutive months, the consumer price index posted slight increases from April to August 2016 (Figure 3.4.39). The drought rekindled food price inflation, and fuel prices steadied. The consumer price index nevertheless posted a marginal 0.02% decline in the first 8 months of 2016. Core inflation remained positive during January–August, increasing by an average of 0.7%.

The Bank of Thailand, the central bank, kept its policy interest rate at 1.5%, having lowered it by 50 basis points in 2015. Growth in credit to the private sector decelerated to 4.0% year on year in July 2016 from 5.5% at the end of 2015, even as major commercial banks reduced lending interest rates in April.

As noted above, fiscal policy supported growth. Government budget disbursement rose by 10.5% in the first 9 months of FY2016 (ending 30 September 2016) from the same period a year earlier, with disbursement of capital expenditure up by one-third. Revenue rose by 10.0% in the first 9 months when the government booked B48.2 billion from auctioning telecommunications spectra. The fiscal deficit for FY2016 is expected to equal 3.0% of GDP. At midyear, public debt was manageable at 42.8% of GDP.

Thailand is posting large trade and current account surpluses for a third year in a row despite an extended slide in merchandise exports. In the first 6 months of 2016, merchandise exports fell by 2.2% to $103.3 billion, the lowest half-year export earnings since 2010. Demand from major trading partners, notably the People's Republic of China, is subdued, and prices are weak for export commodities such as rice, natural rubber, and petrochemical products. Merchandise imports fell steeply by 11.1% to $80.2 billion, also the lowest since 2010, on lower prices for imported oil and commodities as well as reduced demand for raw materials for export-oriented manufacturing. Lower imports pushed the trade surplus up by 50.3% to $23.0 billion, while rising inbound tourism generated a surplus in services trade (Figure 3.4.40). The current account surplus jumped by 71.4% to $25.0 billion, equal to 12.6% of GDP.

After accounting for a $6.4 billion net outflow on the financial account, the overall balance of payments recorded a surplus of $17.7 billion. Outward investment from Thailand doubled to $8.9 billion in the first half as investors sought cheaper assets abroad and some manufacturers relocated to take advantage of lower wages. Further, the government has loosened regulations to facilitate outward investment. Inflows of foreign direct investment totaled $483 million in the first half.

3.4.39 Inflation and policy interest rate

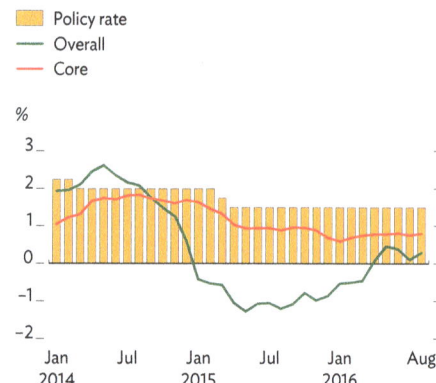

Source: CEIC Data Company (accessed 9 September 2016).
Click here for figure data

3.4.40 Trade indicators

H = half.
Source: CEIC Data Company (accessed 27 July 2016).
Click here for figure data

3.4.41 GDP growth

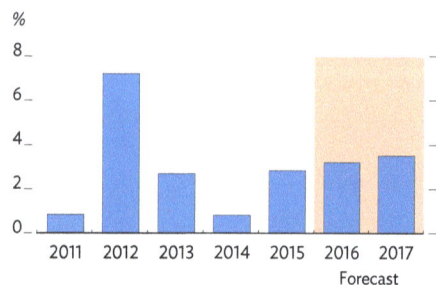

Source: Asian Development Outlook database.
Click here for figure data

Gross international reserves rose to $180.2 billion in July 2016, cover for 10 months of imports of goods and services and over 3 times short-term external debt. The strong external position underpinned a 3.9% appreciation of the Thai baht against the US dollar from the end of 2015 to mid-September.

Prospects

A referendum in August approved a new constitution, paving the way for national elections expected in late 2017. The forecasts below assume that the elections and transition to a new government go smoothly, and that planned public infrastructure projects proceed without significant delay.

In light of the unexpectedly high first-half GDP outcome, this *Update* raises the growth forecast for 2016 by 0.2 percentage points to 3.2% (Figure 3.4.41). Growth is still seen quickening in 2017 to 3.5% on the implementation of large infrastructure projects and better prospects for private investment.

Government expenditure will remain an important growth driver. The government plans to invest $54 billion under its transport infrastructure development strategy to 2022, bidding out in the second half of 2016 project contracts that include constructing double-track rail lines, expanding Bangkok's mass rapid transit system and international airport, and upgrading seaports. The action plan for FY2017 calls for bidding and contract signing for a further 20 major transportation projects valued at more than $20 billion, to be funded from the budget and by state-owned enterprises and private sector partners.

The budget for FY2017 provides for a 6.6% increase in government capital expenditure, though it trims total spending by 1.5% from the expanded FY2016 budget that included proceeds from auctioning telecommunications spectra. The budget deficit in FY2017 is set at B390 billion, or 2.6% of estimated GDP.

Private investment is expected to improve in tandem with the projected pickup next year in demand from the major industrial economies and the implementation of the transportation infrastructure projects. Buoyant tourism will spur further investment in hotels and transportation. The government's rollout of measures to stimulate private investment includes augmented tax deductions for private investment in power plants, telecommunications, waste treatment, and other infrastructure. In August, the cabinet approved a proposal for small businesses and community enterprises to borrow at very low interest rates from the Government Savings Bank.

Nevertheless, excess manufacturing capacity, lackluster growth in credit, and subdued global trade suggest that recovery in private investment will be gradual (Figure 3.4.42). Upgrading to products with more value added will require much higher investment in research and development. The government is addressing this issue, but achieving results will take time. The cabinet has approved proposals to offer corporate tax exemptions for up to 13 years to firms that invest in certain high-tech and innovative industries, and the government will establish a B10 billion fund to help finance research and development in targeted industries. Cooperation between the public and private sectors has produced the Thailand 4.0 initiative, a plan to spur activities with

3.4.4 Selected economic indicators, Thailand (%)

	2016		2017	
	ADO 2016	Update	ADO 2016	Update
GDP growth	3.0	3.2	3.5	3.5
Inflation	0.6	0.4	2.0	2.0
Current acct. bal. (share of GDP)	7.5	9.5	4.0	4.0

Source: ADB estimates.

3.4.42 Manufacturing capacity utilization

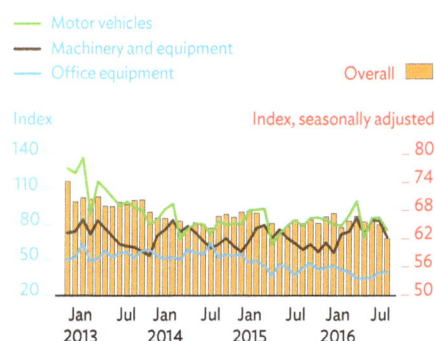

Source: CEIC Data Company (accessed 9 September 2016).
Click here for figure data

3.4.43 Private consumption and investment

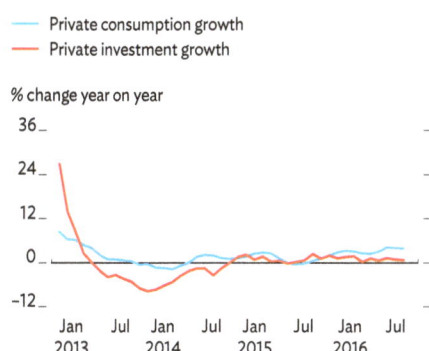

Note: Seasonally adjusted 3-month moving average.
Source: CEIC Data Company (accessed 9 September 2016).
Click here for figure data

higher value added. It includes the Eastern Economic Corridor special economic zone and incentives such as tax breaks and landownership privileges to attract investment in advanced fields like robotics, biotechnology, and digital industry.

Economic indicators were mixed at the start of the second half of this year. The manufacturing production index fell by 5.1% year on year in July, and the purchasing managers' index in August indicated sluggish conditions for manufacturers. Tourism remained a bright spot in July as arrivals rose by 10.8% from the same month in 2015. In August, though, several explosions, mainly in the southern provinces, caused some tourists to cancel or delay visits. Judging from past experience, the damage to tourism is likely to be short lived provided that security conditions stabilize. An easing of the drought this year points to some recovery in agriculture in the second half of 2016 and a better outlook for 2017.

Private consumption was subdued in July, growing at the slowest pace in 5 months (Figure 3.4.43). It is seen improving next year as recovery in agriculture and scheduled tax breaks raise disposable incomes. Consumer confidence showed signs of improvement in the latest survey (Figure 3.4.44). Even so, high household debt will continue to suppress growth in consumption as a significant part of household incomes goes to servicing debt. Household debt as a ratio to GDP eased to 81.1% in March from 81.6% at the end of 2015, but the ratio of nonperforming household loans edged up.

Merchandise exports in July fell by 4.5% in US dollar terms and are forecast to decline in the whole of 2016 before stabilizing in 2017. Exports will benefit from higher growth expected in the major industrial economies and higher prices expected for some export commodities. Against this, slower growth in the People's Republic of China will limit the recovery in exports. Merchandise imports fell by 8.6% in July and are expected to decline for the whole year. Imports are seen rebounding in 2017 as the large infrastructure projects get under way, private investment improves, and global oil prices rise. Unexpectedly weak imports this year mean the current account surplus will overshoot the *ADO 2016* projection, but it will narrow in 2017, as forecast in March, with rising imports (Figure 3.4.45).

Inflation is seen inching up toward the end of 2016. Year-average inflation is now forecast at 0.4%, a touch below that projected in March (Figure 3.4.46). Next year, higher global oil and food prices will likely combine with firming domestic demand to prod inflation to an average of 2.0%. Low inflation and the moderate economic recovery suggest that monetary policy will remain accommodative to growth.

Domestic risks to the outlook come from delays to government infrastructure projects and from political and security uncertainties ahead of the national elections. Further bad weather would hamper recovery in agriculture and rural incomes.

3.4.44 Consumer confidence and business sentiment indexes

— Consumer confidence in the next 3 months
— Business sentiment for the next 3 months

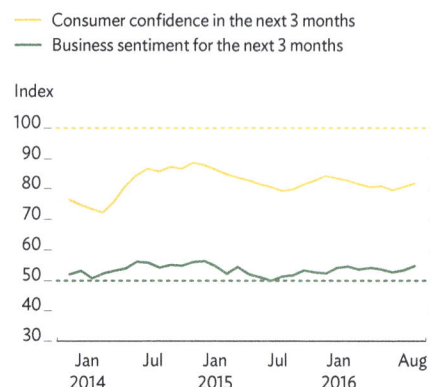

Note: A reading of less than 50 denotes a deterioration in business sentiment, while a reading of less than 100 denotes deterioration in consumer confidence.
Source: Bank of Thailand. http://www.bot.or.th (accessed 9 September 2016).
Click here for figure data

3.4.45 Current account balance

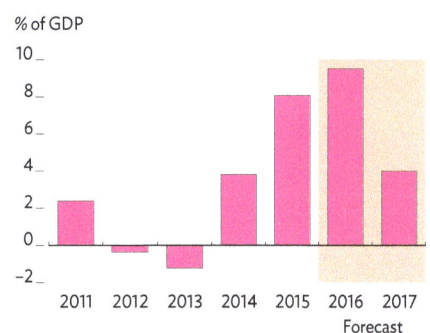

Source: Asian Development Outlook database.
Click here for figure data

3.4.46 Inflation

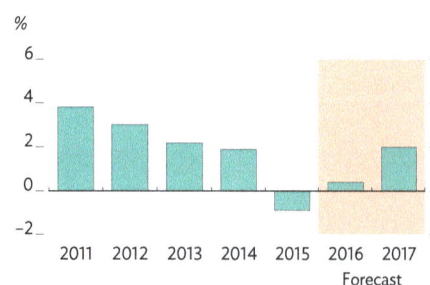

Source: Asian Development Outlook database.
Click here for figure data

Viet Nam

Manufacturing, construction, and services expanded robustly in the first half of 2016, driven by inflows of foreign direct investment (FDI), but GDP growth was weighed down by weak performances in agriculture and mining. Although the economy is expected to pick up in the second half, *ADO 2016* growth forecasts for the year as a whole and for 2017 are nevertheless revised down. Inflation has stirred, as expected, but is forecast to remain moderate. External accounts have improved such that the current account is now seen posting a surplus through the forecast period.

Updated assessment

Contraction in agriculture and mining, which together account for just over one-quarter of GDP, moderated economic growth to 5.5% in the first half of 2016 (Figure 3.4.47). Agriculture shrank by 0.2% owing to severe drought in the Mekong Delta and the Central Highlands. Mining contracted by 2.2% as low global mineral prices discouraged production at aging mines and oilfields.

Other sectors maintained robust expansion in the first half. Manufacturing expanded by 10.1% as new foreign-invested factories ramped up production. Construction grew by 8.8% on strong investment in real estate and growth in credit. Industry overall recorded growth at 7.1%. Growth in services quickened to 6.3%, the drivers being wholesale and retail trade and telecommunications. Tourism rebounded with arrivals up by 25.4% from a year earlier.

On the demand side, private consumption expanded by 7.0% in the first half, decelerating from the pace recorded a year earlier as drought hurt rural incomes. Growth in public consumption was sustained at 7.2%. Investment strengthened, with gross capital formation up by 10.0% on strong credit growth and rising FDI. Disbursements of FDI rose by 15% to a record $7.3 billion. However, solid growth in domestic demand was partly offset by a decline in net external demand, driven largely by an increase in services imports.

While inflation remained low, averaging 1.9% year on year in the first 8 months, it quickened to 2.6% by August on higher fees for public hospitals and schools and on food prices pushed up by drought (Figure 3.4.48). Real estate prices rose only slightly, held in check by supply of newly completed apartments, hotels, and retail spaces. Transportation costs eased with lower oil prices. Core inflation, excluding food, averaged a moderate 2.2% in the first 8 months.

In this context, the State Bank of Viet Nam, the central bank, kept policy interest rates steady, as it has done since late 2014. Broad money supply rose by 18.4% year on year in June. Credit grew by a buoyant 17.6% year on year in June, close to the government's 2016 target band of 18%–20% (Figure 3.4.49). At this pace, credit expanded by about 3 times the rate of increase in nominal GDP. Growth in lending by state-owned commercial banks is reported to substantially outpace that of private sector banks. Much of the new credit is for real estate and personal purposes including mortgages, raising concerns over the quality of the loans.

3.4.47 Supply-side contributions to growth

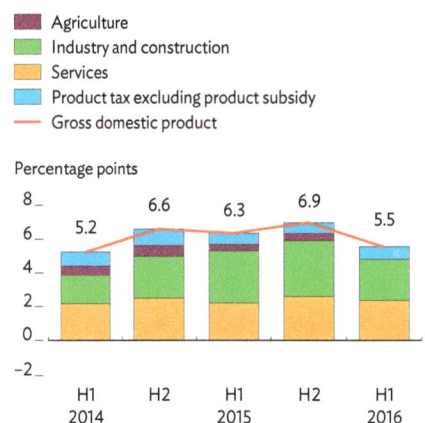

- Agriculture
- Industry and construction
- Services
- Product tax excluding product subsidy
- Gross domestic product

H = half.
Source: General Statistics Office of Viet Nam.
Click here for figure data

3.4.48 Monthly inflation

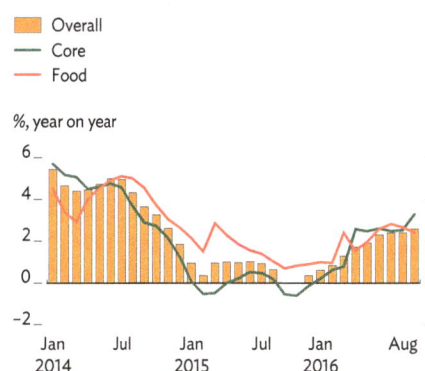

- Overall
- Core
- Food

Note: Core excludes food inflation.
Source: General Statistics Office of Viet Nam.
Click here for figure data

3.4.49 Credit and money supply growth

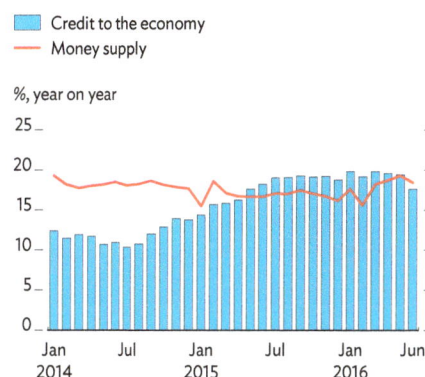

- Credit to the economy
- Money supply

Sources: State Bank of Viet Nam; ADB estimates.
Click here for figure data

Fiscal policy tightened, albeit modestly, in the first half. The government held the rate of increase in budget expenditure to 4.1%, below the 10.0% recorded in the first half of 2015. Revenue increased by 6.9% to equal 25.4% of GDP, largely reflecting higher collection of personal income taxes and dividends from state-owned enterprises. As a result, the fiscal deficit excluding off-budget items narrowed to 3.0% of GDP from 3.7% in the first half of 2015.

External accounts improved in the first half. Merchandise exports rose in US dollar terms by an estimated 5.7% as compiled for the balance of payments, decelerating from 9.2% growth a year earlier but still a good outcome compared with many other economies this year. Customs data show that mobile phones and other electronic products were again the main source of growth in exports. These products now account for 29% of all exports, up from 11% in 2011 (Figure 3.4.50). Despite the drought, the value of exports of farm and aquaculture products was little changed from a year earlier. Lower costs for oil and gas products, and moderating demand for pesticide and fertilizer, saw merchandise imports decline by an estimated 1.1% in US dollar terms.

These developments produced a large merchandise trade surplus estimated to equal 8.2% of GDP, while strong growth in imports of services widened the deficit in services trade. The current account recorded a surplus estimated at 6.2% of GDP (Figure 3.4.51), and the capital account also recorded a substantial surplus thanks largely to FDI inflows. That put the overall balance of payments in surplus. Foreign exchange reserves increased to a more comfortable level estimated at 2.5 months of imports of goods and services, up from 2.0 months at the start of the year.

The Viet Nam dong has held steady against the US dollar so far this year following the central bank's adoption of a more flexible exchange rate regime and daily announcements of the reference rate (Figure 3.4.52).

Spurred by the relaxation of restrictions on foreign investment in domestic shares, the VN-Index of share prices rose by 16.0% over the first 8 months of this year, its strongest performance since 2008.

Structural reform is making progress but at a slow pace. The government partly privatized 58 state-owned enterprises in the first 7 months of 2016. This mostly involved the sale of minority stakes, which is likely to limit the potential for better performance at these companies. The central bank continues to support mergers between small private banks and state-owned commercial banks. The government has set what appears to be an ambitious target, aiming to consolidate commercial banks now numbering 34 into about 15 by the end of next year.

The central bank reported that nonperforming loans (NPLs) declined by midyear to 2.6% of banks' outstanding loans, achieved largely by transferring bad loans to the Viet Nam Asset Management Company and thereby excluding them from the data. This company—established by the government in 2013 to acquire, restructure, and sell NPLs—is hampered by its limited capital base and lack of a clear legal framework for resolving NPLs. By the end of August, it had purchased an estimated $11.5 billion of bad debts but sold or recovered only 15% of this amount.

3.4.50 Exports by product

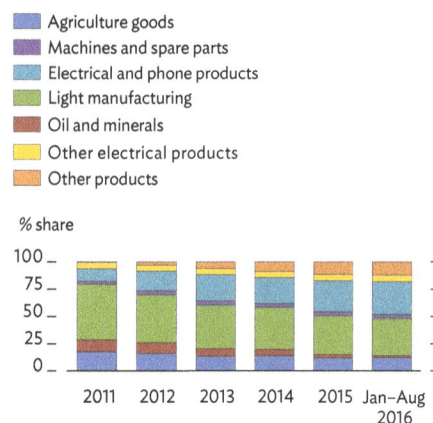

Source: General Statistics Office of Viet Nam.
Click here for figure data

3.4.51 Current account indicators

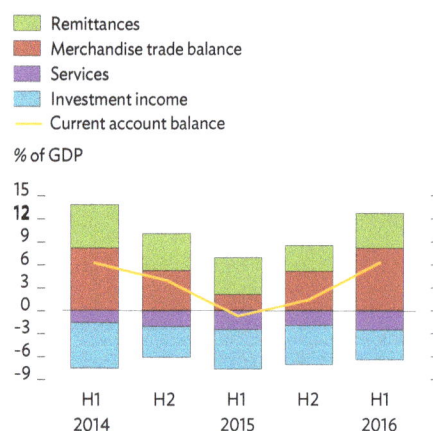

H = half.
Sources: State Bank of Viet Nam; International Monetary Fund; ADB estimates.
Click here for figure data

3.4.52 Exchange rate

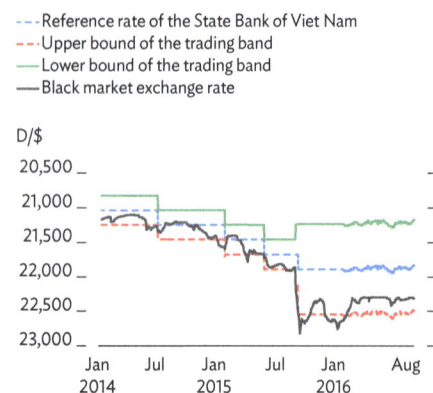

Sources: State Bank of Viet Nam; International Monetary Fund; ADB observations.
Click here for figure data

Prospects

Economic growth is forecast to pick up in the second half of this year but still undershoot *ADO 2016* projections, owing domestically to weakness in agriculture and mining and externally to a more subdued global outlook brought about by unexpectedly soft growth in the major industrial economies. This *Update* lowers the forecasts for GDP growth in Viet Nam to 6.0% this year and 6.3% in 2017 (Figure 3.4.53).

Buoyant FDI inflows are expected to drive higher growth in manufacturing and construction through the rest of the forecast period. FDI commitments in the first 8 months of 2016 rose by 7.7% to $14.4 billion (Figure 3.4.54). Much of this investment is directed to manufacturing, generating the steep rise in production and exports of mobile phones, electronics, and other products. The contribution of foreign-invested firms in all exports climbed from 54% in 2011 to 70% in 2015. The expansion of manufacturing is underpinned by a series of international and bilateral trade and investment agreements concluded by Viet Nam over the past 2 years that will progressively grant exporters greater access to large consumer markets in Europe and the Republic of Korea.

The manufacturing purchasing managers' index in August showed a ninth consecutive monthly improvement in business conditions for manufacturers (Figure 3.4.55).

Investment on infrastructure will contribute to expected robust growth in construction in the months ahead. The government plans to accelerate disbursements of capital expenditure on national infrastructure programs, with 70% of the 2016 target to be achieved in the second half. As for mining, the forecasts assume that declines in mineral and crude oil production have bottomed out this year.

Services are projected to maintain their growth momentum, supported by increases in private consumption and inbound tourism. Consumption spending is benefitting from growth in employment and development in the private sector. The number of new companies registered in January–August rose by 20% from the same period in 2015. The government aims by 2020 to double the number of private enterprises to at least 1 million.

Agriculture is likely to record a better performance in the second half of this year than the first, assuming a continuation of improved weather experienced in July and August. Still, severe drought and saltwater intrusion across key agricultural areas suggest that the sector's output will be flat for the year as a whole. GDP is projected to get a modest lift in 2017 from recovery in agriculture and expanded aquaculture and forestry.

The gradual quickening of inflation is seen continuing through the forecast period. This year, inflation is rekindled by higher fees for public education and health care and food prices driven up by the drought. By the end of 2016, inflation is likely to reach 4% year on year, but the modest price pressures in the first half prompt a downward revision in the year-average inflation forecast by half a percentage point to 2.5%.

Next year, higher global fuel prices and some strengthening in domestic economic growth from 2016 are seen lifting inflation half a percentage point above the *ADO 2016* forecast to average 4.5% (Figure 3.4.56).

3.4.53 GDP growth

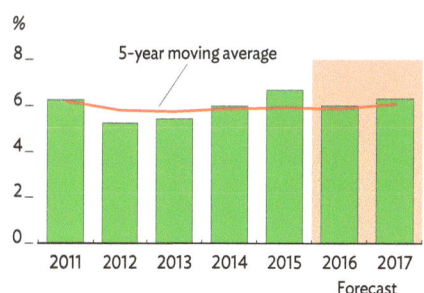

Source: Asian Development Outlook database.
Click here for figure data

3.4.54 Foreign direct investment

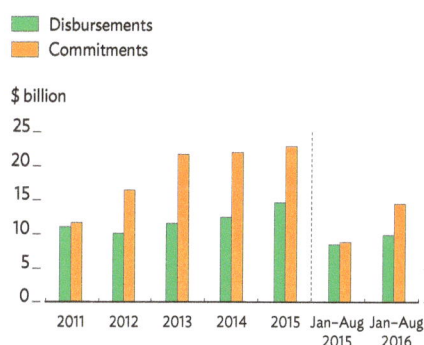

Source: General Statistics Office of Viet Nam.
Click here for figure data

3.4.55 Purchasing managers' index

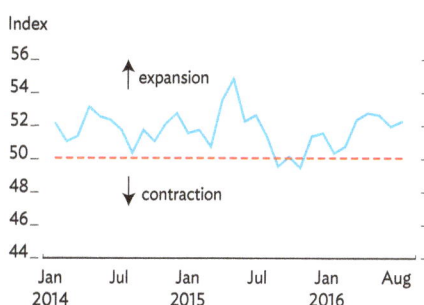

Note: Nikkei, Markit.
Source: Bloomberg (accessed 14 September 2016).
Click here for figure data

Monetary and fiscal policies are expected to support economic growth. Credit expansion looks set to approach the central bank's growth target of 18%–20% this year, and the gradual and moderate upturn in inflation suggests that central bank interest rates could be kept around current levels for some time. Concerns over the impact of buoyant credit on lending quality are likely to continue being addressed through targeted macroprudential measures rather than broad increases in interest rates.

In line with annual public expenditure patterns, budget execution is seen accelerating toward the end of the year, acting as a spur to economic growth in the second half. The challenge will be to contain the budget deficit to the official targets of 5% of GDP in 2016 and 4% in 2017. Government plans to step up spending on infrastructure would seem to require it to impose much tighter control on recurrent expenditure, including for administration and public sector personnel, to meet the deficit targets. Administration costs as a share of total budget spending have risen from an average of 8% in 2007–2009 to 11% in 2013–2016.

Medium-term fiscal consolidation, achieved by strengthening revenue collection and trimming unessential spending, will likely be required to ensure the sustainability of public debt, which is seen mounting to a record 63.5% of GDP this year, including government-guaranteed liabilities.

Trade performance is expected to remain relatively strong. New factories continue to increase the production of high-tech and consumer electronics for export. Recovery in agriculture and an expected upturn in prices for some commodities will help exports next year. On the back of a surprisingly strong outcome in the first half of this year, forecasts of the current account are revised to rising surpluses equivalent to 3.0% of GDP in 2016 and 4.0% in 2017 (Figure 3.4.57).

Risks to the forecasts are further downgrades in the outlook for the major industrial economies or unexpectedly slow growth in the People's Republic of China, an increasingly important trading partner. Domestically, further bad weather would hurt agriculture and push up food prices. Delays in fiscal consolidation cloud the outlook for debt sustainability and economic stability.

Over the medium term, risks come from slow progress on structural reform, notably of state-owned enterprises. Banks face challenges in meeting by the end of 2018 the more stringent capital adequacy standards of the Second Basel Accord. Some domestic banks are able to attract injections of capital from foreign institutions. However, raising adequate capital to meet the new requirements may be a struggle for banks with deficient accounting standards or opaque ownership structures. Further, it will be vital for the authorities to implement macroprudential measures to contain risks in the banking system that stem from increased lending for property and mortgages.

3.4.5 Selected economic indicators, Viet Nam (%)

	2016		2017	
	ADO 2016	Update	ADO 2016	Update
GDP growth	6.7	6.0	6.5	6.3
Inflation	3.0	2.5	4.0	4.5
Current acct. bal. (share of GDP)	-0.2	3.0	0.0	4.0

Source: ADB estimates.

3.4.56 Inflation

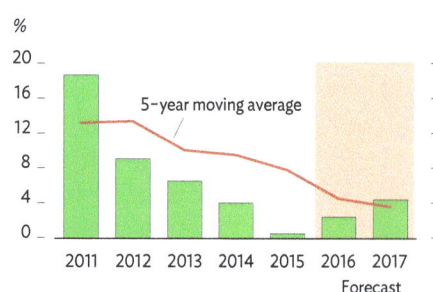

Source: Asian Development Outlook database.
Click here for figure data

3.4.57 Current account balance

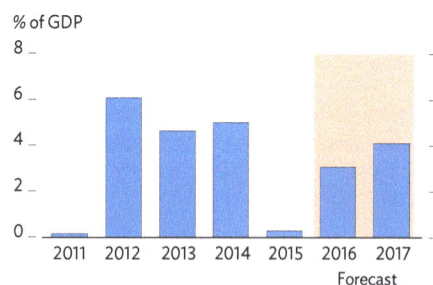

Source: Asian Development Outlook database.
Click here for figure data

Other economies

Brunei Darussalam

Updated official data show the economy contracting by 0.6% in 2015. It was the third consecutive year of decline caused by subdued production of oil and natural gas, though the pace of contraction moderated as hydrocarbon output started to recover. Production continued to pick up in the first quarter of 2016, generating a 3.6% rebound in GDP. Crude oil output rose by 8.6% to 135,200 barrels per day in January–March, and that of liquefied natural gas rose by 13.5% to 1.04 billion cubic feet per day.

Sectors other than hydrocarbons sagged in the first quarter. Services contracted by 0.7%, mainly on falls in government and transportation services. Construction, textiles, and agriculture declined by double digits. On the demand side, household consumption rose by 5.2%, but government spending, investment, and net exports fell. Investment from the People's Republic of China (PRC) rose sharply to $86 million in the first 4 months of 2016, according to PRC officials. Companies from the PRC are building a $50 million plant to make carbon steel pipe, to be completed in 2017, and jetties for a $2.5 billion oil refinery and aromatic cracker. Construction is scheduled to start next year on the refinery.

The first quarter GDP growth rate is unlikely to be sustained through 2016 because it is partly a base effect, the economy having started to improve after a sharp contraction in the first quarter of 2015. Also, government spending is constrained by lower global oil and gas prices that have slashed revenue. The budget for this fiscal year allocates $390 million for infrastructure investment but cuts total government spending by 12.5%. On balance, *ADO 2016* forecasts are maintained for modest GDP growth in 2016 and a pickup in 2017 assisted by higher hydrocarbon production and prices.

Deflation has persisted for longer than expected, with the consumer price index falling by 0.6% in the first half of 2016 following declines in the 2 previous years. Prices have slipped this year for housing and utilities, transportation, and food. Consumer prices are now forecast to decline in 2016 before nudging higher in 2017 as global oil and commodity prices firm and domestic demand strengthens. The Brunei dollar, which is pegged to the Singapore dollar, appreciated by 4% against the US dollar in the first 8 months of 2016.

Merchandise exports fell by 31.5% in US dollar terms in the first half of 2016, reflecting weak oil and gas prices. Imports declined by 8.7%. Having plunged by more than half in 2015, the trade surplus slid further in the first 6 months of this year to $1.1 billion. Current account deficits are now forecast for next year as well as this year, for which the gap is projected to be wider than anticipated in March. Nevertheless, gross international reserves had risen by midyear to $3.8 billion, cover for 15 months of merchandise imports.

Cambodia

Economic developments so far in 2016 have unfolded broadly as expected in *ADO 2016*. Exports from the important garment and footwear industry rose by 9.4% in the first half, almost double the pace in the same period of 2015. Tourist arrivals rose by 3.4% in January–July, marking deceleration

3.4.6 Selected economic indicators, Brunei Darussalam (%)

	2016		2017	
	ADO 2016	Update	ADO 2016	Update
GDP growth	1.0	1.0	2.5	2.5
Inflation	0.2	−0.6	0.4	0.4
Current acct. bal. (share of GDP)	−1.3	−4.5	2.0	−2.0

Source: ADB estimates.

from growth at 4.9% a year earlier. Better weather since June following an extended drought suggests modest recovery in agriculture this year.

Fiscal policy supports economic growth. Government spending rose by 15.6% in the first half of 2016, a turnaround from 10.9% contraction in the first half of 2015. Wage increases for the civil service contributed to the boost in budget outlays. Although revenue jumped by 24.1% as the government continued to improve tax collection, the budget deficit excluding grants is targeted to widen to 4.3% of GDP in 2016.

Growth in credit to the private sector moderated to 28.1% year on year in June 2016 from 33.9% in June 2015, still indicating buoyant domestic demand. Credit to construction, real estate, and related activities—about one fifth of the total—moderated to 33.0% in June from the rapid 41.9% expansion seen in June 2015. Growth in money supply (M2) slowed to 18.0% year on year in June from 20.6% in June 2015.

To boost resilience in finance and dampen rapid lending growth, the central bank introduced last December a liquidity cover ratio for banks and microfinance institutions that complies with the Third Basel Accord on bank regulation. Then it announced in March, effective in 2018, a doubling of minimum capital requirements for commercial and specialized banks and a sharply higher capital requirement for microfinance institutions.

Forecasts for economic growth this year and next are retained from *ADO 2016*. Solid domestic demand and higher food prices lifted average inflation to 2.7% year on year in the first 6 months of 2016, a little higher than anticipated. Based on the first-half outcome and this *Update's* higher projections for global oil prices, inflation forecasts are nudged up for 2016 and 2017.

Merchandise exports rose by an estimated 12.3% in US dollar terms in the first 6 months, faster than the 9.4% recorded in the first half of 2015, while growth in merchandise imports slowed to 7.3% from 17.0%. The current account deficit excluding official transfers is still seen little changed from 2015 this year and narrowing in 2017. Gross official reserves rose to $5.8 billion at midyear, or cover for 4.9 months of imports of goods and services.

Lao People's Democratic Republic

The economy is on track to meet *ADO 2016* forecasts of slightly higher economic growth this year and next. Electricity generation from the growing number of hydropower plants and the Hongsa lignite-powered plant is trending up. Construction on new hydropower projects, residential and commercial buildings, and facilities in special economic zones is contributing to GDP growth. Better weather in 2016 has improved prospects for agriculture, though the risk remains that monsoon rains could cause floods. Gold output from the two major mines rose by 15% in the first half of 2016, but copper production declined by 4%. Tourist arrivals also fell by 4% in this period.

A new cabinet appointed in April 2016 pledged to improve governance and economic management. One of its early decisions, to suspend logging and curb smuggling with a crackdown on exports of unprocessed logs, could dampen incomes in some places in the near term, as well as exports. The government has renewed efforts to

3.4.7 Selected economic indicators, Cambodia (%)

	2016		2017	
	ADO 2016	Update 2016	ADO 2016	Update
GDP growth	7.0	7.0	7.1	7.1
Inflation	2.5	2.8	3.0	3.4
Current acct. bal. (share of GDP)	−11.1	−11.1	−10.0	−10.2

Source: ADB estimates.

improve revenue collection and is scrutinizing expenditure more closely. The fiscal deficit could nevertheless widen more than projected earlier, in part from weakness in government revenue caused by low prices for both mineral exports and oil imports, as well as by spending on a series of international meetings hosted in 2016 as the chair of the Association of Southeast Asian Nations in 2016.

Inflation rose from 0.9% year on year at the start of this year to 1.9% in August, averaging a low 1.3% in the first 8 months and prompting year-average inflation forecasts to be trimmed by 0.2 percentage points for this year and next. The Lao kip appreciated by 0.7% against the US dollar from the end of 2015 to September, but it depreciated by 3.4% against the Thai baht. Growth in M2 money supply slowed to 11.2% year on year in June 2016 from 14.7% in 2015, but growth in credit accelerated to 22.5% in June from 16.8% last year. The central bank directed commercial banks to reduce interest rates on kip deposits from 1 September 2016 to put downward pressure on lending rates and stimulate borrowing in kip.

Merchandise exports, comprising electricity, minerals, forestry and agricultural products, and some manufactures, edged up by 1.3% in US dollar terms in the first 4 months of 2016 from the same period in 2015. Merchandise imports fell by 10.5% in US dollar terms, in part reflecting lower costs for imported oil and other commodities. With the trade deficit for January–April down by 25.3% to $827.5 million, the current account deficit is now seen narrowing a little more than expected in March, before widening again in 2017 if a proposed new railway from Vientiane to the People's Republic of China is at a stage that requires sizeable imports of materials and equipment and if global oil prices rise as projected. Gross international reserves fell by midyear to $765.2 million, or cover for less than 2 months of imports.

Myanmar

Floods have damaged agriculture again this year, but the economy is expected to record solid growth overall, spurred by wide-ranging reform and expansionary fiscal and monetary policy. Monsoon rains and flooding in July and August 2016 disrupted the lives of nearly half a million people and damaged crops, including rice production on the Ayeyarwady Delta. The heavy rains hit as agriculture, which contributes almost 30% of GDP and more than 60% of employment, was still recovering from a severe battering in 2015 from a cyclone and intense monsoon rains. Moreover, a temporary ban on certain logging practices to re-establish the country's forests will likely curb forestry output in the near term. Looking to boost prospects for agriculture over the longer run, the government is reforming the land-titling system and returning previously confiscated land to farmers.

Manufacturing has been sluggish as foreign investment approvals have dropped, but services have maintained robust expansion. Growth in telecommunications is being spurred by investments to extend networks to rural areas and build and maintain telecoms towers. The Central Bank of Myanmar issued new rules that allow mobile network operators to offer financial services, which should benefit the 75% of the population without access to banking services.

3.4.8 Selected economic indicators, Lao People's Democratic Republic (%)

	2016		2017	
	ADO 2016	Update	ADO 2016	Update
GDP growth	6.8	6.8	7.0	7.0
Inflation	1.8	1.6	2.5	2.3
Current acct. bal. (share of GDP)	−17.0	−16.0	−20.0	−19.0

Source: ADB estimates.

Tourist arrivals could jump by 25% this year to a record 6 million, according to a Ministry of Hotels and Tourism forecast.

Three public companies have listed on the new Yangon Stock Exchange, and more are preparing to list. Five securities firms are licensed to trade on the market. The Securities and Exchange Commission of Myanmar has started to prepare for foreign investors and local joint ventures to access the stock market following the expected approval soon of a new company law.

The government that took office in April after national elections in November 2015 unveiled in July a broad set of economic principles that establish the overarching goals of inclusive and sustainable economic development, national reconciliation, equitable development, natural resource protection, and job creation. Key policy priorities include fiscal prudence, reforming state-owned enterprises, building human capital, improving infrastructure, and developing agriculture, the private sector, and financial services. In September, the US announced plans to lift sanctions on Myanmar and restore Generalized System of Preferences trade benefits to the country.

Inflation eased early in 2016 after accelerating to 16.2% in October 2015 on higher food prices, rapid growth in credit, and depreciation of the Myanmar kyat. In the first 4 months of FY2016 (ending 31 March 2017) inflation averaged 10.9%. The kyat regained some ground against the US dollar early in FY2016 before starting to soften again.

GDP growth is still expected to pick up to 8.4% in FY2016 from an estimated 7.2% in FY2015, though the forecast is at risk from the impact of the floods and sluggish global growth. *ADO 2016* forecasts for growth, inflation, and the current account are retained pending data updates.

3.4.9 Selected economic indicators, Myanmar (%)				
	2016		2017	
	ADO 2016	Update	ADO 2016	Update
GDP growth	8.4	8.4	8.3	8.3
Inflation	9.5	9.5	8.5	8.5
Current acct. bal. (share of GDP)	−8.3	−8.3	−7.7	−7.7

Source: ADB estimates.

Singapore

GDP growth in the second half of this year is expected to ease from the 2.1% pace seen in the first half. Construction performed relatively well in the first 6 months, bolstered by investment in public projects. Most service subsectors recorded modest growth, and manufacturing grew slightly in the April–June quarter after 6 quarters of contraction. On the demand side, growth got support from increases of about 10% in both government consumption spending and public fixed investment. By contrast, private consumption increased by a moderate 3.7% while private fixed investment fell by 3.5%, largely on weakness in private housing investment. External demand picked up in April–June after contracting in the first 3 months. The labor market has softened as growth in employment slowed to 1.3% in the 12 months to June 2016 from about 2% in 2015 and the unemployment rate inched up to a seasonally adjusted 2.1% in mid-2016.

In August, the government said that externally oriented sectors such as finance and insurance had slowed and it expected construction would slow as well. Moreover, it added, the improvement in manufacturing in April–June may not be sustained under subdued global conditions. Indeed, manufacturing production dropped by 3.6% in July, the sharpest fall this year, and domestic exports other than oil plunged by 10.6% that month. The purchasing managers' index in

July indicated further contraction in manufacturing. These factors, together with the downward revision in growth projected for the major industrial economies, prompt a shaving of Singapore's growth forecasts, with a modest pickup in growth still expected in 2017.

The consumer price index fell by 0.8% in the first 8 months of 2016, the result of declining prices for housing and utilities, private transportation, and communications. The completion of more housing and the softening in the labor market are helping to suppress inflation. The fall in consumer prices over the year as a whole is now expected to be a bit steeper, with inflation returning in 2017 at an average rate of 0.8%. Core inflation, which excludes accommodation and private road transportation, was 1.0% in July.

In light of sluggish economic growth and low core inflation, the Monetary Authority of Singapore eased its stance in April by setting a zero rate of appreciation for the Singapore dollar in nominal effective terms, a change from its previous setting for gradual appreciation. The Singapore dollar appreciated by 4% against the dollar in the 8 months through August.

Merchandise exports fell by 9.3% in the first half of 2016 in US dollar terms, while imports fell by 10.9%. The merchandise trade surplus narrowed as the services deficit widened. Nevertheless, the current account surplus expanded by 1.7% to $28.8 billion on a narrowing primary income deficit and is now forecast slightly higher for the whole year.

3.4.10 **Selected economic indicators, Singapore (%)**

	2016		2017	
	ADO 2016	Update	ADO 2016	Update
GDP growth	2.0	1.8	2.2	2.0
Inflation	−0.6	−0.8	0.4	0.8
Current acct. bal. (share of GDP)	18.8	19.5	19.5	19.5

Source: ADB estimates.

The Pacific

Growth across the Pacific is slowing on average more than anticipated in *ADO 2016* as extreme weather and fiscal concerns have affected most of the larger Pacific economies. However, several of the smaller economies are outperforming expectations thanks to strong tourism and stimulus from capital project construction. Growth is seen to nudge up in 2017 with rebounding exports and broader economic recovery. As activity revives, inflation is expected to trend upward. The subregional current account surplus is projected to rise slowly as commodity prices strengthen.

Subregional assessment and prospects

Average growth in the Pacific is now expected to fall from 7.2% last year to 2.7% in 2016 (Figure 3.5.1). This forecast is 1.1 percentage points lower than the *ADO 2016* projection in March. Weaker growth largely reflects continuing fiscal contraction in Papua New Guinea (PNG)—the Pacific's largest economy, accounting for almost 60% of subregional output. The PNG government projects a larger revenue shortfall from weak tax and nontax receipts, prompting cuts in government expenditure that further limit economic stimulus from public investment spending.

Weather-related disturbances have further slowed subregional growth. In Fiji, growth is down sharply from 2015 because of economic damage and losses from two cyclones at the start of the year. The adverse effects of El Niño have reduced growth prospects in the North Pacific, with droughts harming agriculture in the Federated States of Micronesia and tourism in Palau.

By contrast, economies in the South Pacific have performed above expectations, as has Timor-Leste. Growth in the Cook Islands, Samoa, and Tonga in FY2016 (ended 30 June 2016) surpassed projections thanks to unexpectedly strong tourism. Samoa received an additional strong boost from fisheries, and Tonga benefitted from recovery in agriculture and stimulus from construction on major infrastructure projects.

The 2016 growth projection for Timor-Leste is revised up following the government's approval of a rectification budget in July that raised capital spending. In Vanuatu, tourism has held up better than expected despite the temporary cancellation of international air services by major regional carriers, prompting an upward revision to the 2016 growth projection.

3.5.1 GDP growth, the Pacific

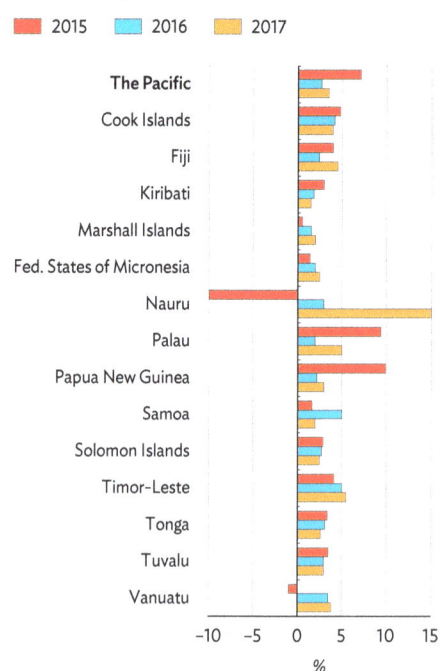

Source: Asian Development Outlook database.
Click here for figure data

The writeup on the Pacific economies was prepared by Yurendra Basnett, Caroline Currie, Christopher Edmonds, David Freedman, Malie Lototele, Rommel Rabanal, Roland Rajah, Shiu Singh, Cara Tinio, Laisiasa Tora, Norio Usui, and Johannes Wolff of the Pacific Department of ADB.

Growth in 2017 is now projected to rise to a weighted average of 3.5%, or 0.4 percentage points higher than projected in *ADO 2016*. The main factor behind the rise is stronger recovery anticipated in the PNG economy, fueled by expected recovery in prices for its export commodities. Most of the other domestic trends highlighted above are seen to persist into next year. The 2017 growth outlook for the economies of Fiji, the Federated States of Micronesia, Palau, and Solomon Islands is weaker, while the Cook Islands and Samoa enjoy prospects brighter than the projections made in *ADO 2016*.

Average inflation across the Pacific is now expected to accelerate from 3.9% in 2015 to 4.7% this year, or 0.2 percentage points higher than projected in March (Figure 3.5.2). Although surprisingly modest consumer price increases prompt reduced inflation projections for the Marshall Islands, Samoa, Timor-Leste, and Tuvalu, these revisions are more than offset by rising inflation in Fiji, Kiribati, PNG, and Tonga. Continuing currency depreciation is adding to price pressures in PNG, while domestic inflation is rising in Fiji and Tonga due to supply bottlenecks following Cyclone Winston. In Fiji, a recent increase in taxes on alcohol and tobacco also contributes to higher inflation.

In 2017, subregional inflation is projected to rise to 5.5% mainly on price increases anticipated for imported food and fuel. This projection is 0.8 percentage points higher than in *ADO 2016*. Price pressures are likely to intensify in PNG from increased public spending related to national elections in June and July 2017 and to preparations in Port Moresby toward hosting Asia-Pacific Economic Cooperation meetings in 2018.

Although merchandise trade deficits are common across the Pacific, the subregion's combined current account has been in surplus in recent years, largely reflecting Timor-Leste's large royalties from offshore petroleum operations and, more recently, high fishing license revenues collected by Pacific nations whose exclusive economic zones include prime fishing grounds for tuna. The Pacific's combined current account surplus is seen to expand in 2016 to the equivalent of 7.2% of subregional GDP from 4.6% last year but then to narrow to 5.8% in 2017 (Figure 3.5.3). These projections are higher than those in *ADO 2016* mainly because of the strong performance of Petroleum Fund investments in Timor-Leste and an improved outlook for net exports in PNG, which outweigh the effect of disappointing fishing license revenues in the North Pacific.

Fiji

Following 5 consecutive years of economic growth, the economy is on target for a sixth such year in 2016, making this the longest period of sustained growth since Independence in 1970.

The growth forecast for 2016 is revised down, however, as the full extent of economic damage and losses from tropical cyclones Winston in February and Zena in March are taken into account. Despite the cyclones, a rise in consumption is evident from loans to private households and registrations of new and used cars. Higher consumption was supported by a value-added tax rate cut from 15% to 9%, the release of $133 million in Fiji National Provident Fund members'

3.5.2 Inflation, the Pacific

■ 2015   ■ 2016   ■ 2017

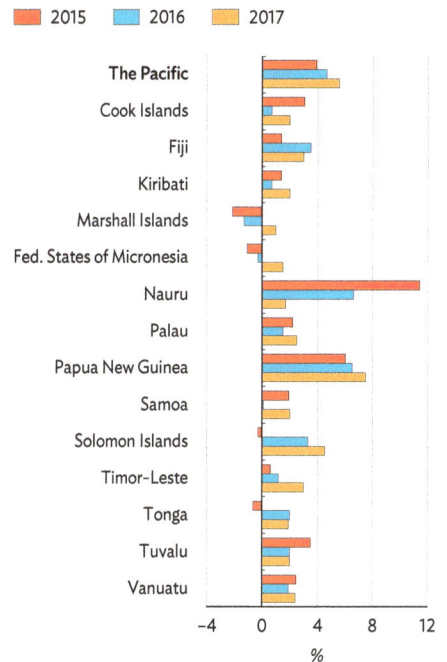

Source: *Asian Development Outlook* database.
Click here for figure data

3.5.3 Current account balance, the Pacific

■ 2015   ■ 2016   ■ 2017

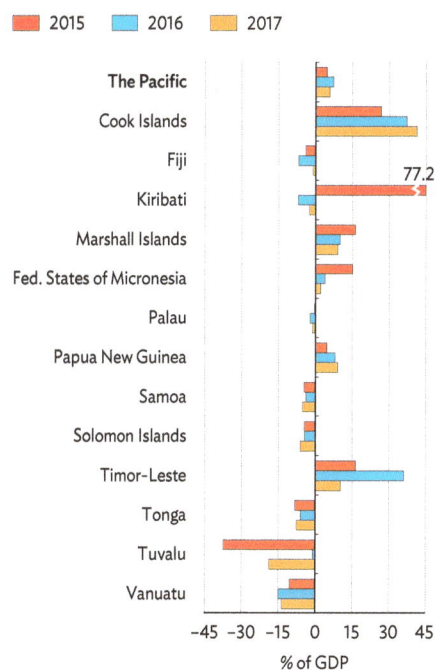

Source: *Asian Development Outlook* database.
Click here for figure data

savings (equivalent to 3% of GDP) to assist recovery, the government's $45 million Help for Home program, and strong remittance inflows, up by nearly 6% year on year in the first half of 2016.

Tourism was largely unaffected by the cyclones. Visitor arrivals in the year to July 2016 were 4.9% higher year on year. Arrivals from Australia and New Zealand, the two largest source markets, increased by 6.0% and 29.4%, respectively. Tourist arrivals from the People's Republic of China grew strongly from a small base. Opportunities for more tourist arrivals opened up as Fiji Airways launched new routes to Singapore in April and San Francisco in June.

The outlook for growth in 2017 remains positive, as forecast in *ADO 2016*. Transport and tourism are expected to lead growth, alongside construction as the restoration of damaged public infrastructure and private property gets under way.

While international prices remain subdued, domestic food prices have increased because of supply disruptions from the cyclones. Taking into account as well increased duties on alcohol, cigarettes, and other tobacco products announced in the FY2017 budget (Box 3.5.1), this *Update* raises the inflation forecast for 2016 by half a percentage point. The forecast for 2017 is unchanged.

International reserves remain adequate, providing as of the end of August an estimated 5.3 months of import cover. New loans from development partners totaling $100 million (equivalent to 2% of GDP) were approved in June to support reserves.

The current account deficit is expected to widen in 2016. Exports are projected to decline by 1.4% as imports increase by 8.5% on higher demand for imported food and for construction materials to use in cyclone rehabilitation. The current account deficit is projected to narrow in 2017 by more than projected in *ADO 2016* on higher inflows from tourism and transport services, remittances, and development assistance.

Papua New Guinea

Growth in Papua New Guinea continues to face headwinds from weakness in global prices for its export commodities and unfavorable weather caused by El Niño in 2015. Agriculture is expected to rebound to production levels achieved immediately before El Niño, but sustained growth in the sector is constrained by inadequate infrastructure and a weak business environment.

The growth forecast for 2016 is almost halved, mostly because of cuts to government capital expenditure this year. Another reason for the downward revision is the late restart and slow recovery of production at the Ok Tedi gold and copper mine. Although coffee and cocoa production and exports are seen to be picking up following El Niño, other agricultural output has not yet fully recovered.

The growth forecast for 2017 is revised up to accommodate lagged effects as mining and agriculture return to full production. The forecast assumes modest recovery in global commodity prices and favorable weather in 2017. Spending related to national elections scheduled for July 2017 is expected to spur economic activity starting late in 2016.

3.5.1 Selected economic indicators, Fiji (%)

	2016		2017	
	ADO 2016	Update	ADO 2016	Update
GDP growth	2.7	2.4	4.5	4.5
Inflation	3.0	3.5	3.0	3.0
Current acct. bal. (share of GDP)	–7.0	–7.0	–4.4	–1.2

Source: ADB estimates.

3.5.1 New fiscal year adopted

The Government of Fiji has adjusted its fiscal planning period from the calendar year to a fiscal year that begins on 1 August. This is intended to improve budget planning by placing annual budget preparation after the cyclone season. The FY2017 budget was approved on 22 June 2016 and covers the period from 1 August 2016 to 31 July 2017. However, growth figures in this *Update* are for calendar years.

The government has started consolidating its fiscal position toward achieving a balanced budget by 2020. After the 2016 *Mid-Year Fiscal and Economic Outlook* identified a revenue shortfall of $579 million, equivalent to 2.8% of GDP, the government passed a supplementary budget to hold the fiscal deficit to 3.8% of GDP in 2016 and address the revenue shortfall through $288 million in expenditure cuts and $291 million in additional financing. The supplementary budget sought to protect outlays for social commitments, key infrastructure, and law and order. Expenditure cuts reportedly focus on nonessential capital projects and recurrent expenditure such as car hire and travel.

Recently revised national accounts estimates show that the three largest sectors of the economy in 2013 were agriculture, forestry, and fishing at 20.2% of GDP, mining and quarrying 13.2%, and wholesale and retail trade 12.4%. Further, the revisions show that the fiscal deficit and debt stock are lower relative to GDP than had previously been estimated. Similarly lower was the share of government spending dedicated to its priority sectors for medium-term development: health, education, key infrastructure, and law and order.

The forecast for inflation in 2016 is revised up by half a percentage point primarily because of anticipated increases in international oil prices and continued currency depreciation. The PNG kina exchange rate continues to be managed by the Bank of Papua New Guinea. The higher inflation forecast reflects increased prices reported in the first quarter of 2016 for medical services at 17.1%, motor vehicles at 2.4%, transport at 2.2%, and household appliances at 2.0%. Imported inflation increased by 0.9% over the same period, mostly driven by higher food import prices. The inflation projection for 2017 is also revised up on the expectation of further currency depreciation, gradual increases in global oil prices, higher spending related to the upcoming national elections, and the stronger outlook for economic growth. Risks to the inflation forecasts are unexpectedly high imported inflation, government spending above fiscal targets, and unforeseeable supply shocks caused by adverse weather.

The projection for the current account surplus is more than doubled for 2016 and is significantly higher for 2017, largely in anticipation of higher output of liquefied natural gas. In the second quarter of 2016, the current account recorded a surplus of $1.3 billion (equivalent to 6.4% of GDP), up from $978 million in the same quarter in 2015. This increase followed higher exports of liquefied natural gas and agricultural commodities, coupled with an import slowdown. The surplus in the current account in the second quarter of 2016 more than offset deficits in the capital and financial accounts stemming primarily from higher outflows related to investment. These outflows have reflected mounting foreign currency balances in the accounts of mineral companies and net loan repayment by the government.

Gross foreign exchange reserves stood at $1.6 billion on 29 July 2016, down from $1.9 billion at the end of December 2015. Slowing imports, rising exports, and planned foreign borrowing may ease the pressure on foreign exchange reserves seen since 2015. Commercial banks in PNG generally report that foreign exchange inflows increased in the first 2 quarters of 2016, which helped meet some of the backlog of requests for foreign exchange.

3.5.2 **Selected economic indicators, Papua New Guinea (%)**

	2016		2017	
	ADO 2016	*Update*	*ADO 2016*	*Update*
GDP growth	4.3	2.2	2.4	3.0
Inflation	6.0	6.5	6.0	7.5
Current acct. bal. (share of GDP)	3.8	7.9	7.2	9.0

Source: ADB estimates.

Recently released results from the 2009–2010 Household Income and Expenditure Survey estimate that 39.9% of PNG residents live below the upper poverty line, defined as income of K3,500 per adult per year, and 26.5% live below the food poverty line, defined as expenditure sufficient to buy 2,200 calories per day. The highest poverty incidence was found in densely populated areas of the highlands.

The survey results show no statistically significant difference in poverty incidence by gender of the household head. However, there was a strong relationship between poverty and the educational attainment of the household head. Households headed by an unschooled person comprised 35%–43% of the poor. Households headed by individuals with wage employment were significantly less likely to be poor. Notwithstanding important methodological differences between this survey and previous poverty estimates, the recent survey results show little progress in reducing poverty in PNG.

Solomon Islands

Growth forecasts for Solomon Islands in both 2016 and 2017 are revised down by 0.3 percentage points from the forecasts published in March in *ADO 2016*. This largely reflects a similar downward revision to the growth estimate for 2015, to 2.9%. Fiscal expansion and private investment will continue to augment domestic demand but at a slowing pace, while declining net exports will continue to weigh on growth.

Economic performance in 2016 has been mixed. After contracting in 2015, export earnings have been higher than expected as international prices increased for key exports, notably round logs and palm oil. However, supply problems are expected to keep export volumes relatively weak. Meanwhile, growth in credit to the private sector slowed in the first half of 2016 but, at 14.2% year on year, remained consistent with relatively robust investment.

Fiscal policy has continued to add to domestic demand. The 2015 budget deficit equivalent to 1.2% of GDP indicated a significant expansionary shift following years of fiscal surpluses. In May, the government passed a supplementary budget adding expenditure equivalent to 1.9% of GDP to an already expansionary budget primarily to fund additional scholarships. This threatens to deplete government cash buffers that are crucial to budget stability, though the Ministry of Finance and Treasury has announced its intention to take steps to contain the fiscal deficit.

Inflation forecasts are revised down for both years from those in *ADO 2016*. Inflation has been lower than expected, at 2.9% year on year in the second quarter, as lower prices for imports offset relatively high domestic price inflation. Strong domestic demand, elevated money supply growth, and modest rises in global commodity prices are expected to add to inflationary pressures in 2017.

Forecasts for current account deficits in both years are also revised down. The change reflects unexpectedly high export earnings while import costs stayed broadly in line with earlier projections. Foreign exchange reserves have changed little since the beginning of the year and remain substantial, providing 10.3 months of import coverage.

3.5.3 Selected economic indicators, Solomon Islands (%)

	2016		2017	
	ADO 2016	Update	ADO 2016	Update
GDP growth	3.0	2.7	2.8	2.5
Inflation	4.4	3.3	5.7	4.5
Current acct. bal. (share of GDP)	−5.9	−4.4	−7.2	−6.1

Source: ADB estimates.

Risks to the outlook include shocks to demand for Solomon Island exports, changes in log production, and climate-related disasters. Downside risks continue to come mainly from external developments, particularly in the People's Republic of China, the country's major export destination. That said, the continued recovery of export commodity prices could provide a significant boost. Logging remains mostly an upside risk to the forecast, having defied predictions of imminent decline in recent years. However, the longer logging output remains elevated, the higher the risk that the industry's eventual decline will be sudden and disruptive. Uncertainty related to the pace at which actual government spending expands has also increased. Developments will depend on the success of efforts to contain the fiscal deficit.

Timor-Leste

The forecast for GDP growth in 2016 excluding the large offshore petroleum sector is revised up by half a percentage point because capital investment will likely increase following the approval of a rectification budget. The forecast for growth in 2017 remains unchanged. The projected current account surplus for 2016 is sharply increased in light of strong performances by Petroleum Fund investments, but the forecast for the surplus in 2017 is now lower to reflect a likely decline in petroleum income and a larger deficit in goods and services trade.

Government spending, the main driver of the domestic economy, increased in the first 7 months of 2016 by 16.0% year on year. Spending on capital investment, salaries and wages, and transfer payments rose significantly to account for 81.6% of government spending in the period, with transfer payments accounting for 48.6%. Of these payments, 62.8% went to the Special Administrative Region of Oe-Cusse Ambeno. Payments to veterans of the fight for independence were 57.2% higher than in the same period of 2015 and amounted to 15.9% of all transfer payments.

The 2016 budget law restructured Timor-Leste's Infrastructure Fund as an autonomous agency under the minister of planning and strategic investment, and a new legislative framework for the fund was subsequently approved. In July, the National Parliament approved a rectification budget with additional appropriations for capital investment that increased the budget from $1.56 billion to $1.95 billion. The additional appropriations cover the government's contribution to the recently approved Tibar Bay port project and increased expenditures on road upgrades and on the Tasi Mane project to develop a supply base, petroleum refinery, liquefied natural gas plant, and related industries on the south coast. Tibar Bay is being developed as a public–private partnership. The concession agreement with the private partner was signed in June 2016, but construction is not expected to start until 2017 at the earliest.

Petroleum taxes and royalties in the first 7 months of 2016 came in at only 22.8% of the budget forecast because of lower international oil prices. The Petroleum Fund balance rose by 3.4% during January–July to reach $16.8 billion, or about $13,800 per capita. Fund investments have performed well in 2016, yielding a gross return of 5.1% over this

3.5.4 Selected economic indicators, Timor-Leste (%)

	2016		2017	
	ADO 2016	Update	ADO 2016	Update
GDP growth	4.5	5.0	5.5	5.5
Inflation	2.0	1.2	3.0	3.0
Current acct. bal. (share of GDP)	26.1	36.1	11.8	10.2

Source: ADB estimates.

period, which equaled 96.2% of the budget forecast for the full year.
Non-oil revenues have also performed strongly, rising by 26.2% in the
first half of 2016 on higher customs and excise revenues.

Strong budget execution added liquidity to the banking sector.
In the first half of the year, deposits were up by 46.2% year on year, and
the money supply expanded by 27.0%. Private sector credit, mainly for
agriculture, construction, trade, and tourism, rose in the first quarter
by 8.7% year on year. However, most of the additional liquidity held by
private banks was placed in foreign assets.

Merchandise imports fell in the first 6 months of 2016 by 1.7% year
on year as prices for imported fuel fell, but services imports rose in the
first quarter by 4.3% year on year, resulting in a moderate worsening of
the trade deficit in that quarter. Declining import prices for rice, cooking
oil, and other foods induced consumer deflation in the first half of 2016
at an annual average of 0.2%. Prices appear to have fallen more in Dili
than in the rest of Timor-Leste, though measurement outside of Dili
is limited. The 2016 inflation forecast is revised down, but the forecast
for 2017 is maintained.

Vanuatu

The growth forecast for 2016 is revised up by 1 percentage point because
tourism has performed better than expected in light of problems
affecting arrivals by air. Economic recovery from Cyclone Pam, which
hit in March 2015, continues. After experiencing delays in 2015, major
reconstruction and infrastructure projects are now providing an
important boost to domestic economic activity. The forecast for growth
in 2017 is unchanged, assuming recovery and construction stay strong.

Tourism has been challenged by regional airlines' cancellation of
services to Vanuatu early in the year over runway safety concerns.
With emergency repairs completed in early May, both Qantas, which
codeshares flights with state-owned Air Vanuatu, and Virgin Australia
had by June resumed flights to Port Vila. Air New Zealand says it
is awaiting details for a permanent solution to runway problems.
Reduced services caused visitor arrivals by air to fall year on year in
the early part of 2016 but by less than anticipated. Cruise ship visits
have remained elevated in 2016, with arrivals up by around 30% over
previous years. However, benefits to the local economy from cruise
ships depend crucially on passengers venturing ashore and consuming
local goods and services, which may be affected by extensive
construction in Port Vila. Further signs of tourism recovery are evident
in the midyear reopening of two major hotels following reconstruction
and renovation.

The 2016 budget was approved in May after being delayed by
snap elections and the formation of a new government in January.
The government targets a small net operating surplus equal to 0.1%
of GDP. However, the overall budget balance, which includes capital
investment financed largely by development partners, targets a
deficit at 16.7% of GDP to finance plans for major reconstruction and
infrastructure projects. In June, Parliament approved additional
supplementary appropriations equal to 1.6% of GDP, primarily to cover a

3.5.5 Selected economic indicators,
        Vanuatu (%)

	2016		2017	
	ADO 2016	Update	ADO 2016	Update
GDP growth	2.5	3.5	3.8	3.8
Inflation	1.9	1.9	2.4	2.4
Current acct. bal. (share of GDP)	−15.0	−15.0	−11.0	−13.5

Source: ADB estimates.

financing package for Air Vanuatu and additional funding for school fee exemptions.

Inflation in the first quarter of 2016 was 2.0% year on year, which was broadly in line with expectations. Low international commodity prices should help keep inflation subdued despite domestic pressures arising from continued economic recovery and buoyant construction. At its March meeting, the central bank lifted its policy rate by 100 basis points, unwinding some of the large rate cut it adopted in the aftermath of Cyclone Pam. The forecasts for inflation this year and next are unchanged.

The current account deficit forecast for 2016 is also unchanged. The import bill rose sharply, by 32.7% year on year, in the first quarter, reflecting strong growth in imports of food and construction materials. This more than offset lower costs for imported fuel. Higher import costs have also been offset by unexpectedly strong tourism earnings. Merchandise exports have performed well thus far in 2016, in line with recovery expectations following the 2015 cyclone. The forecast for the current account deficit in 2017 is revised up on an expected continuation of high imports.

North Pacific economies

Growth projections for FY2016 (ending 30 September 2016) are revised down for two of the three North Pacific economies. El Niño caused drought that reduced agricultural output in the Federated States of Micronesia and adversely affected tourism to Palau. This *Update* maintains the projection of weak growth in the Marshall Islands. Tourism and public investment funded by development assistance are seen to continue to drive growth in these island economies.

Marshall Islands

The latest estimates suggest that growth was a modest 0.5% in FY2015, reversing an earlier estimate showing a decline of 0.5%. Stimulus from fishery and agriculture performance that exceeded forecasts and the renewed consideration of compact-related infrastructure projects accounted for the upward revision. GDP growth is forecast to improve in FY2016 and FY2017, as projected earlier, with the expected implementation of infrastructure projects funded by compact infrastructure grants and development partner assistance.

Inflation is forecast lower, with price declines early in FY2016 suggesting deflation this year. Inflation will likely return in FY2017 but below the *ADO 2016* forecast. The forecast for the current account surplus in FY2016 is reduced in line with lower fishing license fee collections this year. The surplus is seen to narrow further in FY2017 on higher import costs, as forecast earlier.

Subsidies to state-owned enterprises (SOEs) were estimated to have increased in FY2015 to $11.5 million, equivalent to 6.2% of GDP. This is considerably higher than capital spending of $7.4 million that year. The SOE Act, approved in October 2015, loosened prohibitions against public officials serving on SOE boards, which exacerbates risks of political intervention and conflict of interest in SOE management.

3.5.6 Selected economic indicators, Marshall Islands (%)

	2016		2017	
	ADO 2016	Update	ADO 2016	Update
GDP growth	1.5	1.5	2.0	2.0
Inflation	2.0	−1.3	2.5	1.0
Current acct. bal. (share of GDP)	11.1	10.0	8.9	8.9

Source: ADB estimates.

Social security liabilities also pose major fiscal risks. A 2014 actuarial valuation identified $228 million in unfunded liabilities in the social security fund, equal to 122% of GDP that fiscal year. Under the current system, fund depletion is forecast by FY2023. In response, the new administration intends to prioritize SOE and social security fund reform.

Federated States of Micronesia

When the government updated its Infrastructure Development Plan in FY2015, infrastructure grants through the Compact of Free Association with the US became available after a hiatus of 4 years. The resumption of public investments has helped the economy attain 1.4% growth in FY2015, following 3 years of economic contraction. Stimulus from construction under compact infrastructure grants will support growth in the near term.

Drought early this year caused the FY2016 growth projection to be trimmed by half a percentage point. Further, the repeal of Public Law 14-48 means compact infrastructure grants will now bypass the national government and go directly to states, whose limited capacity to implement projects is expected to slow public investment. This prompts a downgrade of the FY2017 growth projection by a full percentage point.

Strong revenues from fishing license fees, amounting to $65.0 million, helped the government to maintain a fiscal surplus last year. It deposited $38.0 million into the Compact Trust Fund, lifting the balance to $57.8 million at the end of FY2015 but still short of the target. The repeal in FY2015 of long-standing reform to taxes and tax administration is expected to undercut the government's fiscal position.

Weak global commodity prices are likely to bring another year of deflation in FY2016, as forecast earlier, but recent fuel price movements suggest inflation returning in FY2017 above the earlier forecast.

Current account surpluses are now seen to decline sharply in FY2016 and FY2017, largely reflecting lower projections for remittances, budget grants, and fishing license revenues. Given scheduled decrements in compact grants to FY2023, maintaining fiscal sustainability will remain a challenge over the medium and long term, as will state and national governments' coordination and execution of development projects.

Palau

Revised estimates show the economy grew by 9.4% in FY2015, well above the earlier estimate of 6.7%. Growth reflected a dramatic increase in tourist arrivals, in particular of visitors on package tours from the People's Republic of China. However, the challenges to sustaining such high increases in visitor arrivals became clear this year, prompting government measures to slow tourist inflows and encourage Palau's development as a high-end ecotourism destination.

Tourist arrivals were 21% lower in the first 5 months of FY2016 than in the same period in FY2015 because drought restricted water supplies to hotels and harmed a popular attraction, reducing demand. Also, flight reductions caused by aircraft maintenance issues affected a major tour operator in Hong Kong, China. These developments prompt a 1 percentage point downgrade to the FY2016 growth forecast.

3.5.7 Selected economic indicators, Federated States of Micronesia (%)

	2016		2017	
	ADO 2016	Update	ADO 2016	Update
GDP growth	2.5	2.0	3.5	2.5
Inflation	−0.3	−0.3	0.3	1.5
Current acct. bal. (share of GDP)	19.5	3.8	30.1	2.0

Source: ADB estimates.

3.5.8 Selected economic indicators, Palau (%)

	2016		2017	
	ADO 2016	Update	ADO 2016	Update
GDP growth	3.0	2.0	7.0	5.0
Inflation	1.5	1.5	2.5	2.5
Current acct. bal. (share of GDP)	−2.3	−2.3	−1.3	−1.3

Source: ADB estimates.

The projection for FY2017 is downgraded by 2 percentage points despite the planned opening of new hotels.

Tax revenues have increased on earlier growth in tourism, lifting the ratio of tax to GDP to about 20%. This helped the government realize a budget surplus equivalent to 5.9% of GDP in FY2015. However, unfunded liabilities in the civil servant pension fund now exceed half of GDP and are a growing concern. The government planned to transfer revenues from environmental protection fees to the pension fund, but Congress did not endorse the proposal.

Inflation is seen to remain low, as projected in *ADO 2016*. Projections of current account deficits are also unchanged as increased imports of construction materials for tourism ventures, and lower tourism revenues, offset lower spending on fuel imports.

South Pacific economies

The growth outlook in the South Pacific has improved on robust tourism, remittance inflows, and construction, with Samoa also benefitting from new deep-sea fishing operations. Low global fuel and food prices have stemmed imported inflation across the South Pacific, though supply disruptions from cyclone damage pushed up domestic prices in Tonga.

Public debt is estimated to have increased in FY2016 (ended 30 June 2016) in all three economies, to the equivalent of 24.8% of GDP in the Cook Islands, 52.6% in Samoa, and 58.3% in Tonga. Debt levels are expected to remain stable in FY2017 in all three economies under planned fiscal consolidation.

Cook Islands

Revised GDP estimates show that the economy grew in FY2015 by 4.8%, reversing the previous estimate of a small decline. Greater activity in agriculture, commerce, tourism, and transport drove growth higher. Preliminary estimates suggest the economy has sustained this rate of growth in FY2016, outpacing earlier expectations of stagnation. Growth largely resulted from higher visitor arrivals, which rose by 11% in the year, partly aided by the launch of a new Jetstar Airways service between Auckland and Rarotonga in March 2016. Interest rates have been relatively stable despite continued declines in credit to the private sector. Commercial bank lending fell by 2.5% year on year to March 2016. Projected growth for FY2017 is likewise revised up to reflect improved prospects for public and private investment, as well as vibrant tourism with the addition of another flight, Virgin Australia's Auckland–Rarotonga nonstop service in June.

The government is estimated to have achieved a fiscal surplus in FY2016 equivalent to 2.3% of GDP, revised from a deficit projected earlier. Revenues were higher than expected on strong economic performance, while spending was lower as public investment spending was restrained. The FY2017 budget plans for the government to run a small deficit equivalent to 3.7% of GDP. The government is drafting legislation to establish the Cook Islands Sovereign Wealth Fund for investing windfall earnings from natural resource exploitation for the benefit of future generations.

3.5.9 Selected economic indicators, Cook Islands (%)

	2016		2017	
	ADO 2016	Update	ADO 2016	Update
GDP growth	0.0	4.2	0.2	4.0
Inflation	1.8	0.7	2.0	2.0
Current acct. bal. (share of GDP)	37.3	37.3	41.3	41.3

Source: ADB estimates.

Inflation in FY2016 is estimated to have run below the forecast in *ADO 2016* because of unexpectedly low import price rises. Inflation in FY2017 is seen to rise, as earlier projected, with expected movements in international food and fuel prices. The current account position remains in line with earlier forecasts, showing a large surplus in FY2016 driven by tourism receipts. Another large surplus is anticipated in FY2017.

Samoa

The estimate for growth in Samoa in FY2015 is revised up by 0.2 percentage points, to 1.6%. The first 3 quarters of FY2016 saw the start of two deep-sea fishing operations, an upgrade of the main international airport, and investments in hotels. These initiatives have contributed to robust growth in transport, tourism, construction, and electricity and water supply. Accordingly, growth in FY2016 is estimated to have been substantially higher than the *ADO 2016* forecast. Projected growth in FY2017 is likewise revised up on expectations of continuing strong performance in fisheries, tourism, and construction, though the recent decline in manufactured goods other than food is expected to continue.

The estimated FY2016 fiscal deficit was kept in line with budget plans through minor spending reallocation. The FY2017 budget targets a deficit equivalent to 3.5% of GDP. The Central Bank of Samoa continued its accommodative monetary policy to support economic growth while the government undertook fiscal consolidation. Private sector credit grew by 9.1% year on year to March 2016.

Consumer prices rose very modestly in FY2016, below the *ADO 2016* forecast, as increases in import costs were lower than anticipated. Inflation in 2017 is expected higher, as projected in March on rising international prices for fuel and food.

Foreign exchange reserves declined but remained reasonable at 4.8 months of import cover in March 2016. The current account deficit in FY2016 is estimated to be slightly smaller than forecast, reflecting higher tourism revenues. Conversely, the current account deficit in FY2017 is now projected to be slightly larger than forecast earlier as projections of inward remittances are revised down.

Tonga

Estimated growth exceeded the forecast for FY2016, driven by recovery in agriculture, the implementation of major projects such as the renovation of the International Dateline Hotel and the construction of the government office complex St. George's Palace, remittance receipts unexpectedly up by 24.8%, and private sector lending up by 14.5%. Tourism was strong as international arrivals increased by almost 15.0%. The growth projection for FY2017 is revised down slightly to account for a base effect from surprisingly good growth in FY2016, but the economy is expected to enjoy continued support from vibrant construction and tourism, as well as increased commerce related to preparations for the South Pacific Games.

Downside risks to this outlook are disasters and cost overruns in South Pacific Games preparations that could weaken the government's fiscal position and add to public debt. The tourism outlook is positive,

3.5.10 Selected economic indicators, Samoa (%)

	2016		2017	
	ADO 2016	Update	ADO 2016	Update
GDP growth	2.0	5.0	0.5	2.0
Inflation	2.0	0.1	2.0	2.0
Current acct. bal. (share of GDP)	−4.3	−3.9	−5.1	−5.3

Source: ADB estimates.

3.5.11 Selected economic indicators, Tonga (%)

	2016		2017	
	ADO 2016	Update	ADO 2016	Update
GDP growth	2.8	3.1	2.7	2.6
Inflation	−0.3	2.0	0.5	1.9
Current acct. bal. (share of GDP)	−1.9	−6.0	−3.2	−7.6

Source: ADB estimates.

with Fiji Airways having commenced direct flights in April 2016 from
Nadi in Fiji to Vava'u in Tonga.

The FY2016 fiscal deficit is estimated to be in line with budget
forecasts. The FY2017 national budget plans a 10% increase in
expenditure over the FY2016 budget. Planned expenditures are
increased to construct storage facilities to augment Tonga's fuel
reserves, as well as to expand support to vulnerable groups through,
for example, welfare payments and services and lifeline electricity tariffs
for low-income users. Spending on preparations for the South Pacific
Games also increases expenditures, but this will be partly financed by
development partners.

The National Reserve Bank of Tonga, the central bank, maintained
an accommodative monetary policy in FY2016. Lending rates averaged
7.8% in May 2016, down from 8.5% in June 2015. Credit to the private
sector increased by 14.5% in FY2016, strongly outpacing the 8.6%
growth recorded in the previous fiscal year.

Estimated inflation in FY2016 is higher than forecast, reflecting
impacts of Cyclone Winston on domestic supply chains that exceeded
early estimates. The inflation projection for FY2017 is revised up
to accommodate possible lingering effects from this disruption,
particularly on food prices in Vava'u.

The FY2016 current account deficit is estimated to be triple the
amount forecast earlier on higher merchandise imports driven by
the implementation of major projects and strong private demand that
more than offset robust remittance and tourism inflows. The deficit is
seen to widen further in FY2017, above the earlier forecast, with the
commencement of other projects, notably preparations for the South
Pacific Games.

Small island economies

The completion of large construction projects funded by development
partners will likely slow economic growth in Kiribati and Tuvalu,
while continued recovery in phosphate exports and revenues from
the Australia-run Regional Processing Centre will support growth
in Nauru. Kiribati and Tuvalu continue to see strong revenues from
fishing license fees, though revenues have moderated from the record
highs of 2014 and 2015. In the first 7 months of the current year, Tuvalu
received A$28.6 million against a budget of A$31.5 million for the
whole year, while Kiribati collected A$62.0 million against a budget of
A$100.0 million.

Kiribati and Tuvalu

Growth in Kiribati is expected to moderate in 2016 as forecast in
ADO 2016. The 2017 forecast is reduced by half a percentage point as
major projects wrap up and the waning El Niño depresses fishing in
its exclusive economic zone. Inflation is still expected to ease in 2016
before rising in 2017, but forecasts for both years are slightly increased
in response to some upward pressure from higher fiscal spending
and possibly more costly imports with a depreciating Australian
dollar, which all three small island economies use as their currency.

3.5.12 Selected economic indicators,
        Kiribati (%)

	2016		2017	
	ADO 2016	Update	ADO 2016	Update
GDP growth	1.8	1.8	2.0	1.5
Inflation	0.3	0.7	0.8	2.0
Current acct. bal. (share of GDP)	15.0	-7.0	-10.0	-2.6

Source: ADB estimates.

Kiribati's current account is now expected to run a deficit in 2016, not the surplus projected earlier, as its trade deficit widens and net income transfers fall off with a projected decline in fishing license revenue. A narrower current account deficit is forecast for 2017 as the merchandise trade deficit eases with the end of imports of materials for projects.

For Tuvalu, forecast growth in 2016 is revised down by half a percentage point as delays affect the implementation of infrastructure projects, but maritime projects funded by development partners are expected to maintain growth as forecast in 2017. Inflation is now seen to moderate in 2016 with import costs lower than expected because of prevailing global commodity prices. It is expected to remain modest in 2017, as forecast. The current account deficit is now projected to narrow much more sharply in 2016 on a lower import bill and high fishing license revenues. The deficit forecast for 2017 is maintained, however, in anticipation of increased imports of construction materials for upcoming infrastructure projects financed by development partners.

Risks to the outlook for both Kiribati and Tuvalu include climate-related disasters, further unexpected falls in fishing license revenues, and commodity price shocks. These risks are particularly acute as both countries' fiscal buffers are small relative to their exposure to these potential shocks.

The Government of Kiribati, elected early this year, is intent on continuing reform to diversify away from the economy's reliance on volatile fisheries revenues and strengthen its resilience to shocks. Kiribati has improved the Revenue Equalization Reserve Fund (RERF) by using strong fishing license revenues to replenish fund resources by A\$50 million in 2015 and A\$70 million in 2016, appointing new fund managers, and adopting a more conservative policy on asset allocation. Further, it placed fiscal surpluses of A\$76.0 million in 2014 and A\$66.4 million in 2015 in a savings account for eventual transfer to the RERF. With these investments, the RERF balance is projected to increase to A\$775.8 million by the end of 2016. This is equal to about \$5,580 per capita, increasing RERF resources per capita by 12.8% in real terms since 2014.

In Tuvalu, the government achieved a substantial fiscal surplus in 2015 supported by strong fishing license fees, license fees for the dot-tv internet domain, and assistance from development partners. It was the fourth consecutive year of fiscal surpluses, enabling the government to build up fiscal buffers. A small fiscal deficit is projected for 2016, however, because of recovery spending after Cyclone Pam. As part of its effort to adapt to climate change, the government secured, in partnership with the United Nations Development Programme, a grant of \$36 million from the Green Climate Fund to strengthen coastal protection on three islands.

3.5.13 Selected economic indicators, Tuvalu (%)

	2016		2017	
	ADO 2016	Update	ADO 2016	Update
GDP growth	3.5	3.0	3.0	3.0
Inflation	3.5	2.0	2.0	2.0
Current acct. bal. (share of GDP)	−21.4	−1.2	−18.7	−18.7

Source: ADB estimates.

Nauru

The growth outlook for Nauru depends on the phosphate industry and activities supporting the Regional Processing Centre. Phosphate exports rose to 160,000 tons in FY2016 (ended 30 June 2016), up by 56.8% year on year, but remain deeply depressed because of damage to the moorings at Nauru's seaport, its primary gateway for international cargo. Growth in FY2016 was in line with the forecast and, with the completion of port repairs, is projected to be much higher in FY2017, also as forecast earlier. Growth in domestic demand has been substantial in recent years but is expected to stabilize as government spending and activity at the Regional Processing Centre plateau. Inflation is projected to ease, as forecast earlier, in FY2016 and much further in FY2017 as growth in aggregate demand slows and port repairs end.

Nauru held national elections in July that returned the governing coalition, which bodes well for existing economic plans. The FY2017 budget targets balance. With revenues from the Regional Processing Centre and fishing licenses reaching a plateau, the government introduced measures to raise revenues, including a turnover tax on small businesses, and a profits tax on larger businesses. Setting aside recent windfalls to help finance public service delivery in the future, it allocated A$10.4 million to the Nauru Intergenerational Trust Fund.

3.5.14 Selected economic indicators, Nauru (%)

	2016		2017	
	ADO 2016	Update	ADO 2016	Update
GDP growth	3.0	3.0	15.0	15.0
Inflation	6.6	6.6	1.7	1.7
Current acct. bal. (share of GDP)	...	...	...	...

... = data not available.
Source: ADB estimates.

STATISTICAL APPENDIX

Statistical notes and tables

This statistical appendix presents selected economic indicators for the 45 developing member economies of the Asian Development Bank (ADB) in three tables: gross domestic product (GDP) growth, inflation, and current account balance as a percentage of GDP. The economies are grouped into five subregions: Central Asia, East Asia, South Asia, Southeast Asia, and the Pacific. The tables contain historical data for 2013–2015 and forecasts for 2016 and 2017.

The data were standardized to the degree possible to allow comparability over time and across economies, but differences in statistical methodology, definitions, coverage, and practices make full comparability impossible. The national income accounts section is based on the United Nations System of National Accounts, while the data on balance of payments are based on International Monetary Fund accounting standards. Historical data are obtained from official sources, statistical publications, ADB estimates, and databases, as well as from documents of ADB, the International Monetary Fund, and the World Bank. Projections for 2016 and 2017 are generally ADB estimates made on the bases of available quarterly or monthly data, though some projections are from governments.

Most countries report by calendar year. The following record their government finance data by fiscal year: Armenia; Azerbaijan; Brunei Darussalam; the Cook Islands; Fiji; Hong Kong, China; Kazakhstan; the Kyrgyz Republic; the Lao People's Democratic Republic; Samoa; Singapore; Taipei,China; Tajikistan; Thailand; and Uzbekistan. The Federated States of Micronesia, Nauru, the Republic of Marshall Islands, and Palau report government finance and balance-of-payments data by fiscal year. South Asian countries (except for the Maldives and Sri Lanka), Myanmar, Samoa, and Tonga report all variables by fiscal year.

Regional and subregional averages are provided in the three tables. The averages are computed using weights derived from gross national income (GNI) in current US dollars following the World Bank Atlas method. The GNI data for 2013–2014 are obtained from the World Bank's World Development Indicators Online. Weights for 2014 are carried over through 2017. The GNI data for the Brunei Darussalam, the Cook Islands, and Taipei,China were estimated using the Atlas conversion factor. Because Myanmar and Nauru have no GNI data, they are excluded from the computation of all subregional averages and totals.

The following paragraphs discuss the three tables in greater detail.

Table A1: Growth rate of GDP (% per year). The table shows annual growth rates of GDP valued at constant market price, factor cost, or basic price. GDP at market price is the aggregation of value added by all resident producers at producers' prices including taxes less subsidies on imports plus all nondeductible value-added or similar taxes. Constant factor cost measures differ from market price measures in that they exclude taxes on production and include subsidies. Basic price valuation is the factor cost plus some taxes on production, such as those on property and payroll taxes, and less some subsidies, such as those on labor-related subsidies but not product-related subsidies. Most countries use constant market price valuation. Fiji, Pakistan, and Sri Lanka use constant factor cost, while the Maldives and Nepal use basic price. The series for Taipei,China has been changed to accommodate its adoption of the chain-linking method.

Table A2: Inflation (% per year). Data on inflation rates represent period averages. The inflation rates presented are based on consumer price indexes. The consumer price indexes of the following economies are for a given city or group of consumers only: in Cambodia for Phnom Penh, in the Marshall Islands for Majuro, in Solomon Islands for Honiara, and in Nepal for urban consumers.

Table A3: Current account balance (% of GDP). The current account balance is the sum of the balance of trade for merchandise, net trade in services and factor income, and net transfers. The values reported are divided by GDP at current prices in US dollars. In the case of Cambodia, the Lao People's Democratic Republic, and Viet Nam, official transfers are excluded from the current account balance.

Table A1 Growth rate of GDP (% per year)

	2013	2014	2015	2016		2017	
				ADO2016	Update	ADO2016	Update
Central Asia	6.6	5.2	3.0	2.1	1.5	2.8	2.6
Armenia	3.3	3.6	3.0	2.0	2.0	2.3	2.3
Azerbaijan	5.8	2.8	1.1	–1.0	–2.5	1.0	1.0
Georgia	3.3	4.6	2.8	2.5	3.0	3.5	4.0
Kazakhstan	6.0	4.2	1.2	0.7	0.1	1.0	1.0
Kyrgyz Republic	10.9	4.0	3.5	1.0	1.0	2.0	2.0
Tajikistan	7.4	6.7	6.0	3.8	3.8	4.0	4.0
Turkmenistan	10.2	10.3	6.5	6.5	5.5	7.0	5.5
Uzbekistan	8.0	8.1	8.0	6.9	6.9	7.3	7.3
East Asia	6.8	6.6	6.1	5.7	5.8	5.6	5.6
China, People's Rep. of	7.8	7.3	6.9	6.5	6.6	6.3	6.4
Hong Kong, China	3.1	2.7	2.4	2.1	1.5	2.2	2.0
Korea, Rep. of	2.9	3.3	2.6	2.6	2.6	2.8	2.8
Mongolia	11.6	7.9	2.3	0.1	0.3	0.5	1.4
Taipei,China	2.2	3.9	0.6	1.6	0.9	1.8	1.5
South Asia	6.2	6.7	7.0	6.9	6.9	7.3	7.3
Afghanistan	3.9	1.3	0.8	2.0	2.0	3.0	3.0
Bangladesh	6.0	6.1	6.6	6.7	7.1	6.9	6.9
Bhutan	3.6	3.8	5.9	6.4	6.4	6.1	6.1
India	6.6	7.2	7.6	7.4	7.4	7.8	7.8
Maldives	4.7	6.5	2.1	3.5	3.5	3.9	3.9
Nepal	3.8	5.7	2.3	1.5	0.8	4.8	4.8
Pakistan	3.7	4.1	4.0	4.5	4.7	4.8	5.2
Sri Lanka	3.4	4.9	4.8	5.3	5.0	5.8	5.5
Southeast Asia	5.0	4.5	4.4	4.5	4.5	4.8	4.6
Brunei Darussalam	–2.1	–2.3	–0.6	1.0	1.0	2.5	2.5
Cambodia	7.4	7.1	7.0	7.0	7.0	7.1	7.1
Indonesia	5.6	5.0	4.8	5.2	5.0	5.5	5.1
Lao People's Dem. Rep.	7.8	7.5	6.7	6.8	6.8	7.0	7.0
Malaysia	4.7	6.0	5.0	4.2	4.1	4.4	4.4
Myanmar	8.4	8.7	7.2	8.4	8.4	8.3	8.3
Philippines	7.1	6.2	5.9	6.0	6.4	6.1	6.2
Singapore	4.7	3.3	2.0	2.0	1.8	2.2	2.0
Thailand	2.7	0.8	2.8	3.0	3.2	3.5	3.5
Viet Nam	5.4	6.0	6.7	6.7	6.0	6.5	6.3
The Pacific	3.9	9.4	7.2	3.8	2.7	3.1	3.5
Cook Islands	0.5	4.5	4.8	0.0	4.2	0.2	4.0
Fiji	4.7	5.3	4.0	2.7	2.4	4.5	4.5
Kiribati	2.4	3.8	3.0	1.8	1.8	2.0	1.5
Marshall Islands	2.1	–1.0	0.5	1.5	1.5	2.0	2.0
Micronesia, Fed. States of	–3.6	–3.4	1.4	2.5	2.0	3.5	2.5
Nauru	15.4	17.5	–10.0	3.0	3.0	15.0	15.0
Palau	–2.4	4.2	9.4	3.0	2.0	7.0	5.0
Papua New Guinea	5.0	13.3	9.9	4.3	2.2	2.4	3.0
Samoa	–1.9	1.2	1.6	2.0	5.0	0.5	2.0
Solomon Islands	2.8	2.0	2.9	3.0	2.7	2.8	2.5
Timor-Leste	2.9	5.9	4.1	4.5	5.0	5.5	5.5
Tonga	–3.1	2.0	3.4	2.8	3.1	2.7	2.6
Tuvalu	1.3	2.0	3.5	3.5	3.0	3.0	3.0
Vanuatu	2.0	2.3	–1.0	2.5	3.5	3.8	3.8
Average	6.5	6.3	5.9	5.7	5.7	5.7	5.7

Table A2 Inflation (% per year)

	2013	2014	2015	2016 ADO2016	2016 Update	2017 ADO2016	2017 Update
Central Asia	5.9	5.8	6.1	10.8	11.5	5.9	6.4
Armenia	5.8	3.0	3.7	3.8	1.5	4.0	4.0
Azerbaijan	2.4	1.4	4.0	12.0	12.0	5.2	5.2
Georgia	−0.5	3.1	4.0	5.0	3.0	4.0	4.0
Kazakhstan	5.8	6.7	6.6	12.6	14.7	4.6	6.0
Kyrgyz Republic	6.6	7.5	6.5	10.0	5.0	8.0	8.0
Tajikistan	5.0	6.1	5.1	8.5	8.5	7.5	7.5
Turkmenistan	6.8	6.0	5.5	6.6	5.0	6.0	4.4
Uzbekistan	11.7	9.1	8.5	10.0	10.0	11.0	11.0
East Asia	2.4	1.9	1.3	1.6	1.9	2.0	2.2
China, People's Rep. of	2.6	2.0	1.4	1.7	2.0	2.0	2.2
Hong Kong, China	4.4	4.4	3.0	2.5	2.4	2.7	2.5
Korea, Rep. of	1.3	1.3	0.7	1.4	1.1	2.0	2.0
Mongolia	9.9	12.8	6.6	3.0	3.2	7.0	5.4
Taipei,China	0.8	1.2	−0.3	0.7	1.3	1.2	1.5
South Asia	9.3	6.9	4.9	5.2	5.2	5.7	5.7
Afghanistan	7.4	4.7	−1.5	3.0	4.5	3.5	6.0
Bangladesh	6.8	7.3	6.4	6.2	5.9	6.5	6.1
Bhutan	8.8	9.6	6.6	4.0	3.3	5.0	4.6
India	9.8	6.7	4.9	5.4	5.4	5.8	5.8
Maldives	2.3	2.1	1.0	1.2	1.2	1.4	1.4
Nepal	9.9	9.1	7.2	10.5	9.9	8.2	8.5
Pakistan	7.4	8.6	4.5	3.2	2.9	4.5	4.7
Sri Lanka	...	5.5	3.8	4.5	4.5	5.0	5.0
Southeast Asia	4.2	4.1	2.7	2.6	2.0	2.9	2.9
Brunei Darussalam	0.4	−0.2	−0.4	0.2	−0.6	0.4	0.4
Cambodia	3.0	3.9	1.2	2.5	2.8	3.0	3.4
Indonesia	6.4	6.4	6.4	4.5	3.5	4.2	4.0
Lao People's Dem. Rep.	6.4	4.2	1.3	1.8	1.6	2.5	2.3
Malaysia	2.1	3.1	2.1	2.7	2.1	2.5	2.5
Myanmar	5.7	5.9	11.0	9.5	9.5	8.5	8.5
Philippines	2.9	4.1	1.4	2.3	1.8	2.7	2.8
Singapore	2.4	1.0	−0.5	−0.6	−0.8	0.4	0.8
Thailand	2.2	1.9	−0.9	0.6	0.4	2.0	2.0
Viet Nam	6.6	4.1	0.6	3.0	2.5	4.0	4.5
The Pacific	4.9	3.5	3.9	4.5	4.7	4.7	5.5
Cook Islands	2.6	1.6	3.0	1.8	0.7	2.0	2.0
Fiji	2.9	0.6	1.4	3.0	3.5	3.0	3.0
Kiribati	−1.5	2.1	1.4	0.3	0.7	0.8	2.0
Marshall Islands	1.9	1.1	−2.2	2.0	−1.3	2.5	1.0
Micronesia, Fed. States of	2.2	0.7	−1.1	−0.3	−0.3	0.3	1.5
Nauru	0.5	3.0	11.4	6.6	6.6	1.7	1.7
Palau	2.8	4.0	2.2	1.5	1.5	2.5	2.5
Papua New Guinea	5.0	5.2	6.0	6.0	6.5	6.0	7.5
Samoa	−0.2	−1.3	1.9	2.0	0.1	2.0	2.0
Solomon Islands	5.4	5.2	−0.3	4.4	3.3	5.7	4.5
Timor-Leste	9.5	0.7	0.6	2.0	1.2	3.0	3.0
Tonga	0.8	2.1	−0.7	−0.3	2.0	0.5	1.9
Tuvalu	2.0	1.1	3.5	3.5	2.0	2.0	2.0
Vanuatu	1.4	1.0	2.5	1.9	1.9	2.4	2.4
Average	3.8	3.0	2.1	2.5	2.6	2.7	2.9

... = data not available.

Table A3 Current account balance (% of GDP)

	2013	2014	2015	2016		2017	
				ADO2016	Update	ADO2016	Update
Central Asia	1.8	2.0	–3.7	–3.9	–5.0	–3.0	–3.9
Armenia	–7.3	–7.6	–2.7	–5.2	–4.8	–5.0	–5.0
Azerbaijan	16.6	13.9	–0.4	–0.6	–0.6	1.5	1.5
Georgia	–5.7	–10.6	–12.0	–9.5	–12.0	–9.2	–11.5
Kazakhstan	0.5	2.9	–3.2	–3.5	–5.5	–3.1	–4.9
Kyrgyz Republic	–25.1	–25.3	–14.8	–17.0	–17.0	–15.0	–15.0
Tajikistan	–2.9	–9.1	–5.9	–4.8	–4.8	–5.5	–5.5
Turkmenistan	–7.2	–6.7	–12.3	–12.3	–13.3	–10.0	–10.0
Uzbekistan	1.6	1.4	0.3	0.2	0.2	0.8	0.8
East Asia	2.5	3.5	4.0	3.6	3.1	3.3	2.7
China, People's Rep. of	1.5	2.6	3.0	2.7	2.0	2.5	1.7
Hong Kong, China	1.5	1.3	3.1	2.0	2.3	1.8	2.1
Korea, Rep. of	6.2	6.0	7.7	6.5	7.0	5.5	6.0
Mongolia	–25.4	–11.5	–4.8	–8.0	–8.3	–15.0	–16.7
Taipei,China	10.4	15.2	14.5	14.8	14.8	15.3	15.3
South Asia	–1.4	–1.3	–1.0	–1.4	–1.1	–1.6	–1.6
Afghanistan	8.7	2.4	4.7	2.0	4.5	–0.7	1.1
Bangladesh	1.6	0.8	1.5	–0.5	1.7	–1.0	1.0
Bhutan	–25.6	–26.4	–28.7	–28.8	–29.9	–27.0	–27.0
India	–1.7	–1.5	–1.3	–1.6	–1.4	–1.8	–1.8
Maldives	–4.6	–3.9	–8.8	–12.6	–10.1	–10.5	–10.0
Nepal	3.4	4.6	5.1	10.3	6.2	6.4	4.6
Pakistan	–1.1	–1.3	–1.0	–1.0	–0.9	–1.2	–1.6
Sri Lanka	–3.4	–2.5	–2.0	–2.0	–2.0	–1.8	–2.0
Southeast Asia	1.9	3.0	3.7	2.8	3.4	2.7	2.7
Brunei Darussalam	20.9	27.7	7.7	–1.3	–4.5	2.0	–2.0
Cambodia	–14.2	–11.9	–11.2	–11.1	–11.1	–10.0	–10.2
Indonesia	–3.2	–3.1	–2.1	–2.6	–2.3	–2.8	–2.4
Lao People's Dem. Rep.	–30.6	–25.0	–20.3	–17.0	–16.0	–20.0	–19.0
Malaysia	3.5	4.4	3.0	1.2	1.2	2.3	2.3
Myanmar	–4.9	–5.9	–8.9	–8.3	–8.3	–7.7	–7.7
Philippines	4.2	3.8	2.9	2.7	2.0	2.8	1.8
Singapore	17.6	17.4	19.7	18.8	19.5	19.5	19.5
Thailand	–1.2	3.8	8.8	7.5	9.5	4.0	4.0
Viet Nam	4.5	4.9	0.5	–0.2	3.0	0.0	4.0
The Pacific	14.1	5.6	4.6	4.1	7.2	4.8	5.8
Cook Islands	30.1	32.4	26.7	37.3	37.3	41.3	41.3
Fiji	–9.8	–7.2	–4.0	–7.0	–7.0	–4.4	–1.2
Kiribati	15.7	44.7	77.2	15.0	–7.0	–10.0	–2.6
Marshall Islands	–9.9	–4.4	16.2	11.1	10.0	8.9	8.9
Micronesia, Fed. States of	–9.7	6.7	15.1	19.5	3.8	30.1	2.0
Nauru	15.7	–7.3	...	...	...	...	..
Palau	–9.3	–11.8	–0.5	–2.3	–2.3	–1.3	–1.3
Papua New Guinea	–23.8	–5.1	4.6	3.8	7.9	7.2	9.0
Samoa	–2.5	–7.0	–4.6	–4.3	–3.9	–5.1	–5.3
Solomon Islands	–4.3	–5.4	–4.5	–5.9	–4.4	–7.2	–6.1
Timor-Leste	182.1	76.0	16.3	26.1	36.1	11.8	10.2
Tonga	–8.5	–5.0	–8.3	–1.9	–6.0	–3.2	–7.6
Tuvalu	26.4	27.3	–37.4	–21.4	–1.2	–18.7	–18.7
Vanuatu	–0.8	22.7	–10.4	–15.0	–15.0	–11.0	–13.5
Average	1.8	2.7	3.1	2.6	2.4	2.4	2.0

... = data not available.